Blockchain and Deep Learning
for Smart Healthcare

Scrivener Publishing
100 Cummings Center, Suite 541J
Beverly, MA 01915-6106

Publishers at Scrivener
Martin Scrivener (martin@scrivenerpublishing.com)
Phillip Carmical (pcarmical@scrivenerpublishing.com)

Blockchain and Deep Learning for Smart Healthcare

Edited by

Akansha Singh
*School of Computer Science Engineering and Technology,
Bennett University, Greater Noida, India*

Anuradha Dhull
*Department of Computer Science Engineering, The NorthCap University,
Gurugram, India*

and

Krishna Kant Singh
Delhi Technical Campus, Greater Noida, India

Scrivener
Publishing

WILEY

This edition first published 2024 by John Wiley & Sons, Inc., 111 River Street, Hoboken, NJ 07030, USA and Scrivener Publishing LLC, 100 Cummings Center, Suite 541J, Beverly, MA 01915, USA
© 2024 Scrivener Publishing LLC
For more information about Scrivener publications please visit www.scrivenerpublishing.com.

Wiley Global Headquarters

111 River Street, Hoboken, NJ 07030, USA

For details of our global editorial offices, customer services, and more information about Wiley products visit us at www.wiley.com.

Limit of Liability/Disclaimer of Warranty

Library of Congress Cataloging-in-Publication Data

ISBN 978-1-119-79174-4

Cover image: Pixabay.Com
Cover design by Russell Richardson

Set in size of 11pt and Minion Pro by Manila Typesetting Company, Makati, Philippines

Printed in the USA

10 9 8 7 6 5 4 3 2 1

Contents

xii CONTENTS

Preface

The value of blockchain technology in the healthcare market is expected to surpass \$1.6 billion by 2025. Blockchain technology is poised to revolutionize more than just payment and cryptocurrency. Many vertical industries will be reshaped by the new trusted data models enabled and inspired by the blockchain—healthcare is no exception. In fact, healthcare may hold the greatest opportunities for the meaningful use of the technology. Early pioneers have explored some of the first use cases for medical payments, electronic health records, HIPAA/data privacy, drug counterfeiting, and credentialing of healthcare professionals. The research has just begun to scratch the surface in how to automate the complexities of today's healthcare systems and design new systems that focus on trust, transparency, and the alignment of incentives.

Healthcare as an industry has unique requirements associated with security and privacy due to additional legal requirements to protect patients' medical information. In the Internet age where sharing of records and data becomes more prevalent with cloud storage and the adoption of mobile health devices, so too does the risk of malicious attacks and the risk of private information being compromised as it is shared. As health information is becoming more easily obtained through smart devices, and patients are traveling to multiple doctors, the sharing and privacy of this information are a concern. The unique requirements the healthcare industry is facing are in the form of authentication, interoperability, data sharing, the transfer of medical records, and considerations for mobile health. The disruptive integration of blockchain technology with Deep Learning techniques will reveal the answers to the many potential problems associated with the healthcare sector.

This book is based on two of the most emerging fields—blockchain technology and Deep Learning—applied to the healthcare sector. The book will be an essential guide to all academicians, researchers, and industry individuals who are working in their related field. This book will provide insights into the convergence of Deep Learning and blockchain technology in healthcare system and services.

There are a number of books available in Deep Learning and blockchain technology individually. There is no such book available that focuses on the application of Deep Learning and blockchain technology in the healthcare system. Thus, this book is unique in terms of the topics and related content it covers. The readers from a large domain will be interested in the book as it covers three major fields. Moreover, it will be appealing for the readers who tend to do research in this field as the book covers the latest research topics.

The Editors
October 2023

Part 1
BLOCKCHAIN FUNDAMENTALS AND APPLICATIONS

Blockchain Technology: Concepts and Applications

Hermehar Pal Singh Bedi[1]*, Valentina E. Balas[2], Sukhpreet Kaur[1] and Rubal Jeet[1]

1Department of Computer Science and Engineering, Chandigarh Engineering College, Landran, Mohali, Punjab, India
2Department of Automatics and Applied Software, University of Arad, Arad Romania

Abstract

Many new technologies evolve and deplete over time, but the most significant technological innovation in recent years has been blockchain technology, which not only has changed almost all aspects of life but also could incorporate all the existing technologies. In this chapter, we will be elaborating all the concepts of blockchain technology and try to understand its purpose in today's world. We will also look into its use cases especially from a security point of view. As we delve a bit more into the details, we will be looking into the workings of blockchain technology, the different types of blockchains available depending on the network and the consensus mechanism, its structure, and the opportunities for blockchains. Lastly, we will also be exploring some of the challenges that blockchain is facing due to public perception and also the future prospects of blockchain technology.

Keywords: Blockchain, cryptocurrency, smart contracts, decentralized applications

1.1 Introduction

The proposal of a protocol similar to that of blockchain was proposed by cryptographer David Chaum in his dissertation "Computer Systems

---

Corresponding author: hermeharbedi@gmail.com

Akansha Singh, Anuradha Dhull and Krishna Kant Singh (eds.) Blockchain and Deep Learning for Smart Healthcare, (3–34) © 2024 Scrivener Publishing LLC

Established, Maintained, and Trusted by Mutually Suspicious Groups" in 1982 [1]. In 1991, researchers Haber *et al.* and Stornetta *et al.* have illustrated the algorithms on a secured chain of blocks very effectively using cryptography [2, 3]. Nakamoto *et al.* introduced the method of decentralized blockchain in 2008. He used blockchain for all the transactions made on the Bitcoin network using a ledger in a public domain. Originally, Satoshi Nakamoto used the words "block" and "chain" as two different words, but later were combined to make a single word, "blockchain".

Blockchain technology is interpreted by many IT professionals as the biggest innovative technological research in today's digital world in terms of secured assets. Blockchain is the technique of sharing the ledger, which is also one of the best techniques of decentralization of both catalogs and accounts on big data [4]. It is a shared and immutable, i.e., unchangeable and incorruptible, ledger that clears the path for the procedure of documenting the transactions made and tracking the different transactions and assets of any network related to any business. Assets can be of two types: tangible and intangible.

- **Tangible assets:** These are the physical assets that can be touched such as property, money, vehicles, etc.
- **Intangible assets:** These are the assets that do not exist in real life but have real-life monetary value such as the crypto-currency, patents, trademarks, etc.

When the defined network is decentralized, then different nodes are used to write, share, and lock the consistent transactions in a distributed ledger [5]. Blockchain works similarly, with the difference being that the data in blockchain are organized into chronological and cryptographical linked blocks, and it also uses different types of mechanisms based on consensus and smart contracts [6].

1.2   Blockchain Types

Broadly, there are four types of blockchains available, which are shown in Figure 1.1.

- **Public blockchains** are the blockchains that do not require any permissions and are not managed by any company or individual. In public blockchains, anyone can become the node. Public blockchains are purely decentralized and hence

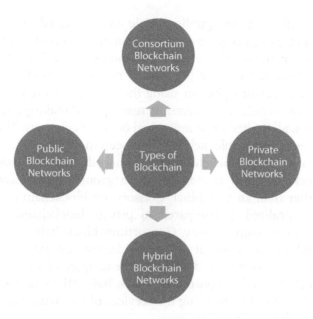

Figure 1.1 Types of blockchains available.

allows equal access of blockchains to each and every node. Moreover, each node has the right to create and validate a block of data. There are different blockchains available in the public domain, including Bitcoin, Ethereum, and Litecoin. Mostly, the public blockchains are used for exchanging and mining cryptocurrencies. Public blockchains are criticized by many because of security reasons as the information in the public domain can be accessed by anyone joining the network [7]. In public blockchains, all the nodes are treated equally and none of the nodes available on the network have any special privileges. We can interchangeably use permissionless and public blockchain [8]. The public blockchain features access in real-life examples [9].

- **Private blockchains** or managed or permissioned blockchains are blockchains that require some permissions, which are managed or controlled by some company or an individual. In managed blockchains, the company or the individual who owns the blockchain grants permissions and makes the decision in creating the nodes. It is not necessary that each node enjoys the same rights similar to public blockchains. They are not purely decentralized as not all the information is available to the public. Ripple and Hyperledger are the examples of permissioned or managed blockchain technologies available. The terms "permissioned" and "private" are used interchangeably [8]. All the nodes in this blockchain have different rights for using the services of the network, which includes data accessing, reading, and making transactions, all limited to an individual or some company. The use cases of private blockchains have been increasing [8].

- **Consortium blockchain** is a managed and permissioned blockchain that is managed by a group of organizations rather than an individual. Consortium blockchain is more decentralized as compared to private blockchain, which results in high security. Consortium blockchain is mostly used in the financial services industry and supply chain sectors. Quorum and Corda are examples of consortium blockchains. In a consortium blockchain, all the nodes have different rights for using the services of the network, and it is all limited to the company.
- **Hybrid blockchain** is a singly managed blockchain, which also requires the oversight of some other public blockchains for the validation of transactions. Transactions made in hybrid blockchains are kept private, which can be verified whenever required by enabling access through a smart contract. A hybrid blockchain allows organizations to establish a private and secured system that requires permissions alongside a public permissionless system, which enables them to administer and decide about the level of rights to be given to each member for accessing the data. Either it can be made private with restricted rights or it can be made public [10]. XinFin is an example of a hybrid blockchain.

Some of the papers also divide the blockchain into only two types, depending on their architecture:

- Permissioned
- Permissionless

Permissioned blockchains include the blockchain networks, in which all the nodes do not have the right to access, read, write, and transact, but all these facilities are limited to some company or individual. Permissioned blockchains include both private and consortium blockchains discussed

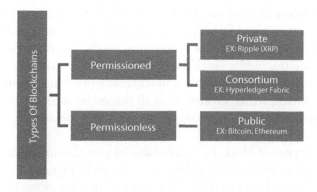

Figure 1.2 Types of blockchains.

above and are also sometimes referred to as private blockchains [8]. They use QuorumChain and majority voting consensus, because of which they are faster than permissionless blockchains [11]. Permissioned blockchains are comparatively more secured than public or permissionless blockchains as not all the nodes can access the data available on the network.

Table 1.1 Comparison of different blockchains [13].

Property	Public blockchain	Private blockchain	Consortium blockchain
Consensus determination	All different nodes in the network	Only limited to one network of company	Only selected nodes
Type: Permissionless/ Permissioned	Permissionless	Permissioned	Permissioned
Security	Secured as it is immutable.	Less secured as it is mutable and can be tempered.	Less secured as it is mutable and can be tempered.
Identity	Anonymous identity [12]	Known identity of users [12]	Known identity of users [12]
Consensus Type	Proof of work	QuorumChain	QuorumChain and majority voting

Permissionless blockchains include the blockchain networks, in which all the nodes are treated equally, have access to all the information on the network, and can broadcast the transaction on the network. Public blockchains include the public blockchain discussed above and are also sometimes referred to as permissionless blockchains [8]. It uses proof-of-work (PoW) consensus, which ensures that all the nodes are only permitted to take any decision if they reach consensus. This also has an adverse effect of slowing down the network [11].

Thus, the types of blockchains available can be classified into two types and then further divided into subtypes as shown in Figure 1.2.

The differences between different types of blockchains are illustrated in Table 1.1.

1.3   Consensus

In blockchain, the consensus is the procedure by which all the shareholders agree on one common thing. These shareholders are known as full nodes; only these full nodes validate each transaction entering the blockchain network. All the blockchains have their own algorithms for the development of consensus; this is because different blockchains are meant for different purposes such as trading, storing data, and security systems [14]. Consensus is also sometimes referred to as the driving force of the blockchains. Depending on the type of blockchain, the consensus is determined as in public blockchains; all the nodes are consensus determinants, whereas in private blockchains, only selected nodes are consensus determinants. There are different types of consensuses like PoW and QuorumChain, developed by JP Morgan. The PoW consensus is used in Bitcoin blockchain.

PoW consensus mechanism: It is a security algorithm and is used to provide a consensus to a new block entering the network. PoW sets some instructions called a protocol for mining. Mining is the process of solving the computational problems, which are in coordination with the PoW protocol. The nodes that want to take part in the mining have to follow the PoW protocol for the affixation. In such cases, nodes have to choose the block that has the largest hash value, and only then can it attach the block [15]. Initial blockchains were implemented using the PoW consensus mechanism. Popular blockchains Bitcoin and Ethereum are both based on the PoW consensus mechanism [16].

Proof-of-stake (PoS) consensus mechanism: It is a security algorithm that is used to provide a consensus to a new block entering the network. PoS also sets some instructions called a protocol for mining. In PoS, the trusted nodes or entities work together to add records into the PoS protocol and to accept the block on the blockchain network; the trusted nodes go through the voting process [15]. Nowadays, in the PoS consensus mechanism, solution hunting has been completely removed and the nodes are now selected based on the stake they have instead of the traditional computational problem solving [16]. Popular blockchains like Cardano and Algorand are based on the PoS consensus mechanism.

Proof-of-concept (PoX) consensus mechanism: This consensus mechanism was basically developed to overcome the problems that were faced by the PoW consensus mechanism. These were (1) to improve the performance in terms of security and incentives and (2) to use computational resources in a better way. Various different consensus mechanisms require the solving of mathematical problems like usage of proof of exercise in evaluating product problems in matrices or finding solutions of various functions in proof of useful work [16].

Hybrid consensus mechanism: These mechanisms use PoW–PoS combinations of consensus mechanisms to form a new kind of consensus mechanisms. One such example of hybrid consensus mechanism is the proof-of-activity (PoA) consensus mechanism as it uses PoW for the creation of a block and PoS for verification of a block and adding the transactions [16]. Blockchains like Casper and Peercoin are based on the hybrid consensus mechanism. Table 1.2 provides the comparison of the two mostly used consensus mechanism i.e., PoW and PoS.

Table 1.2 Differences between PoW and PoS consensus mechanisms.

Property	PoW	PoS
Criterion for selection	Solving computational problems	Stake based
Block generation speed	Slow	Fast
Power consumption	More	Less
Transaction speed	Slow	Fast

1.4   How Does Blockchain Work?

The record list of blockchain is growing very rapidly, and these lists of records are known as blocks. In other words, the blocks can be defined as the database, as in this database, all the transactions made are recorded and cannot be manipulated. Hence, a blockchain can be referred to as a chain of blocks, as it is used to transfer the information or to make transactions from one person to another as illustrated in Figure 1.3. The very first block of this mechanism is called the genesis block. The unique hash codes have been assigned to each block, which helps in the detection of the right block. Hash code acts as the fingerprint of the human hand. Each block in the chain has three parts: Data; Hash, which can be addressed to as the address of the node or block; and Hash of the preceding block. This makes this process an even more secured way of making payments and transferring data. This is because if the hash and data get manipulated, then all the succeeding blocks will become invalid and the transaction will not be executed. The blocks are used as servers and they are stored in the nodes. The data between the nodes are shared continuously as all nodes are connected to each other. Hence, all the data are preserved as the nodes can store and spread the data. Therefore, the nodes can be said to be the fundamental unit of blockchain, without which it cannot be formed.

The following steps are involved in making a particular transaction using blockchain technology:

Step 1: **Input and Authentication:** In this step, the authorized user will input a transaction, and that transaction should be authenticated first.
Step 2: **Formation of a Block:** After successful authentication of the transaction, a block is generated, which represents a specific transaction.
Step 3: **Transferring Data:** Now, once a block has been created, the same information is shared among the nodes of the network.

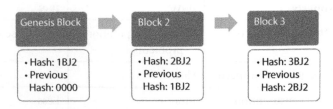

Figure 1.3 Mechanism of a blockchain.

Step 4: **Consensus:** Authorized nodes now verify the transaction and adds it to the existing blockchain.
Step 5: **Distribution.** In this step, all the information is updated across the network, after which the transaction is finalized.

Figure 1.4 represents a sample transaction made on the blockchain network. Firstly, the input for the transaction is declared. After the input, the transaction becomes the node, which is further broadcasted to all other nodes available on the network for consensus. After broadcasting, the consensus step takes place if the block is accepted by all or majority of the nodes (depending on type of consensus), then finally when the transaction is completed through all the steps, that block is added to the network chain.

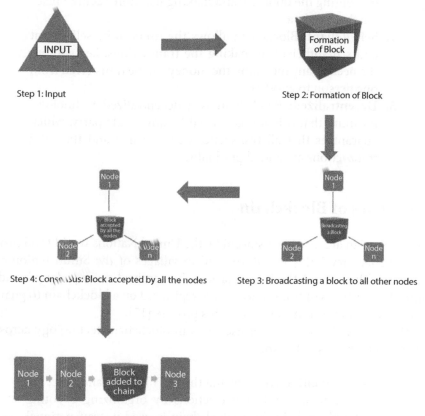

Figure 1.4 All steps included to make a transaction on a blockchain network.

1.5   Need of Blockchain

There are many reasons to use blockchain technology:

1. **Security:** Blockchain is a secured way of doing transactions and storing the data, as it is immutable and it is almost impossible to hack the blockchain network due to the hash code. If a block gets hacked, then also all the succeeding blocks are inaccessible, preventing the loss of all the data available.
2. **Transparency:** All the changes made to the public blockchain are viewable to the public.
3. **Reliability:** Blockchain verifies the identity of all the users, preventing the duplicity and making it a more secured place for sharing data.
4. **Self-Reliant:** Blockchain allows the users to be self-reliant and self-sufficient in making the transactions; i.e., without the need of any mediator, the money can be transferred from one person to another.
5. **Decentralized:** Blockchain is a decentralized technology, meaning that it is not governed by any single party, which guarantees that all transactions are verified and the valid transactions are added gradually.

1.6   Uses of Blockchain

Humanitarian aid, a project started by the United Nations world food program in January 2017, was developed in villages of the Sindh region of Pakistan. The data of the beneficiaries who received money, daily bread, and all other types of transactions were registered on a blockchain to guarantee security and transparency of this process [17].

There are different types of use cases in blockchain technology across the various sectors of the society:

- **Government Sector:** During the COVID-19 pandemic, the governments conducted elections by organizing e-Voting using blockchain. Even blockchain is used in transnational personalized governance services and digitization of documents.

- **Financial Sector:** Cryptocurrency and the digital currency are used in blockchain in almost every financial sector. Other than these, blockchain is also used to make payments and remittance.
- **Health Sector:** Blockchain technology is being utilized as an efficient method to address healthcare concerns. It can be used for observation, pregnancies, risk data management of medical scripts, supply chains, data exchange, and directing an investing pill for medical use. There are different cases such as the practitioner's license, billing insurances, sharing medical records with patients, and clinical trials that can benefit from blockchain technology [18].
- **Market:** In markets, the blockchain is used for making the billing system, for transferring data, and in the supply chain management.
- **Internet of Things:** Blockchain technology is a secured way of transferring data between different parties. Blockchain allows the devices to operate securely and autonomously.
- **Authorship:** Blockchain technology is also used for confirming and preserving the authorships to the artists.
- **Big Data:** The combination of blockchain and big data leads to more efficient analytics. This is because of three main reasons:

  ➤ **Security:** The data cannot be tempered by blockchain; hence, we can ensure the security of data in all terms.
  ➤ **Transparency:** The source or the initial point of the data can be easily traced as it is stored on blockchain.
  ➤ **Flexibility:** Since blockchain can store both structured and unstructured kinds of data, it makes the model more flexible and hence accurate.

- **Information Security:** Since the data available on blockchain are decentralized and integrated, they prevent data breach, identity theft, and cyberattacks, thereby securing the data from any misuse.

1.7   Evolution of Blockchain

There have been advancements in the usage of blockchain, depending on which the blockchain can be divided into three parts, which is demonstrated in Figure 1.5:

Phase 1: Cryptocurrency: The very first phase of blockchain or the phase that gave birth to blockchain was cryptocurrency, which started during 2008–2009 with the origin of the famous Bitcoin by Satoshi Nakamoto.

Phase 2: Smart Contracts: The second phase of the blockchain started with the development of Ethereum, which leads to the development of smart contracts from 2013 to 2015. These are the computer programs or the software stored on the blockchain, which started working when the predefined conditions are met. Smart contracts are used as the alternative for traditional contracts. The government voting system and the supply chain are examples of smart contracts.

Phase 3: Blockchain 3.0: The third or the current phase of the blockchain is the development of the decentralized applications, which started in 2018. In this phase, different applications started to integrate with the blockchain. The codes for these applications are running on a dispersed network that is connected peer-to-peer at their backend. Peepeth, a social media application, and Cryptokitties, a decentralized game, are examples of decentralized applications. Decentralized applications are abbreviated as DApps.

All these phases of blockchain are discussed in detail below.

Phase 1: Blockchain in Cryptocurrencies

Cryptocurrencies are encrypted data strings that denote a unit of currency. They are based on blockchain technology and are digital currencies. Bitcoin is believed to be the first and the largest cryptocurrency in the world, followed by Ethereum. The use of blockchain in cryptocurrencies was part

Figure 1.5 Evolution of blockchain.

of the first or the initial phase of using blockchain. Cryptocurrencies are also believed to be the source of blockchain. Today, there are more than 2000 different cryptocurrencies circulating, with a total market capital of around 900 billion dollars [19]. Some examples of cryptocurrencies are Bitcoin (BTC), Ether (ETH), Dogecoin (DOGE), Binance coin (BNB), Cardano (ADA), Litecoin (LTC), Polkadot (DOT), and Solana (SOL).

Bitcoin: It is a digital currency that is decentralized in nature, developed by Nakamoto *et al.* in 2008. Bitcoin is also sometimes referred to as a programmed coin or a digital coin. Bitcoin is believed to be the first originator of the blockchain technology. Bitcoin uses the digital ledger to keep track and execute the transactions, which works on the principle of blockchain. In total, Bitcoin has a supply capping of 21 million, meaning only 21 million Bitcoins can be mined. Mining is the procedure of finding and updating the transaction to the Bitcoin's public ledger of the already completed transactions. The researcher describes the programmed coin as a technology of digital signatures. To avoid the problem of double spending, a trusted central authority known as mint can be introduced. The main function of mints would be to check all the transactions for double spending, but introducing the mints was similar to banks, and to overcome this, each transaction was made public, and to avoid any conflicts in the future, the participants are required by the network to agree with the history of the transactions [20].

Blockchain in Bitcoin
Transactions in Bitcoin: Transactions are made after the verification of the hash function of the transaction is done in the past and the public key of the next owner. All transactions are done digitally. Digital signatures are the private keys, which are unique to all the users. The first owner's public key and the digital signature of the first owner available on the block of the second owner are verified in order to successfully transfer the Bitcoins. Thus, a single block of Bitcoin contains three sub-blocks that are the current owner's public key, the hash, and the digital signatures of the previous owner.
Timestamp Server: To make participants agree on the order of transactions of the competing transactions, Satoshi Nakamoto proposed a method consisting of three steps.

Step 1: The competent transactions are grouped together.
Step 2: The hash of the transactions made was computed and published to external outlet with a large audience like a newspaper.

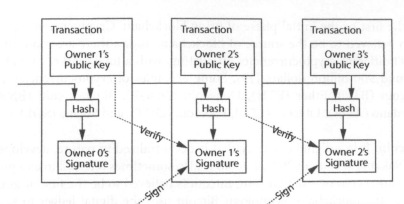

Figure 1.6 Transaction in Bitcoin [20].

Step 3: As more transactions are recorded, and thus more blocks are added, each new hash/digest will be computed from the current block AND the previous hash/digest. Since hashes cannot be reversed, if block B's hash can be computed from block A's hash, it proves that block A came before block B [21].

Figure 1.6 shows the process of how a transaction is made a Bitcoin, as was proposed by Satoshi Nakamoto [20].

PoW: In Bitcoin, a PoW network, which is almost identical to that of Adam Back's Hashcash, has been used instead of the newspaper. The PoW has been implemented by increasing a nonce (number only used once) in the block. Its value is increased until it reaches zero bits, which is the requirement of PoW [20].

Networking: The following steps are involved in the networking of the Bitcoin:

Step 1: Every node on the network of blockchain has the information of all transactions since it is broadcasted to them.

Step 2: Each and every node gathers new transactions within a block.

Step 3: All nodes work on locating a harder PoW for its block.

Step 4: Upon the successful finding of PoW, the information related to the block is broadcasted to the whole network by the concerned node.

Step 5: After the validation of the transactions of the block, the nodes will accept that block into the network.

Step 6: Acceptance of a block by the node is expressed by using the hash function of the accepted block and then generating the following blocks in the chain [20].

Ethereum: Ethereum (ETH) is a blockchain-based decentralized smart contract, which was developed by V. Buterin, G. Wood, and C. Hoskinson in 2013 and was launched in July 2015. ETH cryptocurrency is second in market capitalization after the Bitcoin. All the concepts of the transaction-based machines are built using ETH only [21]. Ethereum's native cryptocurrency is Ether, which a user must spend as a cost of processing a transaction on the ETH network. Ethereum is also an example of public cryptocurrency and hence does not require any permission and is not managed by any company or individual. Ethereum is built using the Solidity and Vyper smart contract languages. ETH is used for Decentralized Finance (DeFi) and the Non-Fungible Tokens (NFTs).

1.8   Blockchain in Ethereum

Ethereum Virtual Machine (EVM): EVMs are basically stack-based architecture having a stack size of 256 bits and do not follow the standard Von Neumann Architecture. Instead of storing the codes in random access memory (RAM) or storage, it stores the data in the virtual read-only memory (ROM) and hence interacts only with specific instructions [22].
Ethereum Accounts: In ETH, the term "Accounts" is described as the state of the objects that have a 20-byte address. Each account has four fields:

1. Number only used once (nonce) counter to make sure that the transactions are not processed repeatedly;
2. The current balance of account in ETH;
3. The contract code of the account, which is the hash function of root; and
4. The account's codehash.

There are two types of accounts in ETH

1. **Externally owned accounts:** The different types of private keys are used to own these accounts; moreover, they do not have any association with any type of code. All the messages can be forwarded by them after creating and signing a transaction [23].

2. **Contract accounts:** They are associated with different codes and these accounts are owned by the contract code as well. In these types of accounts, communication is done using messages and the code is activated after receiving the message, which, in turn, allows the account to read and write transactions in the internal storage. Using this method, messages are sent to different accounts in the network [23].

Gas: Gas is the fee required to conduct any transaction on the ETH network. The only payment method acceptable to pay the gas is in Ether, the native cryptocurrency of the ETH network.

Gas Price: This quantitative parameter gives the value any account will spend on each and every unit of gas. It basically gives the value of Ether. It is measured in gwei, where 1 gwei = 0.000000001 Ether [21, 22].

Gas Limit: It is the capacity that each and every transaction can consume in terms of gas units.

Transaction Fees = Gas Price * Gas Limit [24]

In ETH, all the transactions consist of blocks grouped together and they contain three parts:

1. **Block header:** It contains the following information: parentHash, ommersHash, beneficiary, stateRoot, transactionsRoot, receiptsRoot, difficulty, number, gasLimit, gasUsed, logsBloom, nonce, extradata, timestamp, and mixHash.
2. **Information about set of transactions**
3. **Set of other block headers for the current block ommers:** Ommers are the blocks whose parent is equal to the current block's parent's parent.

Transactions in Ethereum: Transactions are the instructions given by the account holder to the network. When an account holder sends an instruction or makes a transaction, the ETH network is appropriately updated. Each transaction alters the EVM, and then this information is shared with all the nodes in the network. After the broadcast, miners initiate the transaction and pass on the changes made to all other nodes [25].

State Transaction Function: The basic structure behind the workings of the ETH is as follows:

Step1: Check the credibility of transaction

Step 2: Calculate the transaction fee

Step 3: The transaction fee is deducted from the account of the sender and the nonce counter is incremented. If there is insufficient balance, then exit.

Step 4: For each byte in the transaction, some quantity of gas is subtracted.

Step 5: Release the transaction amount into the receiver's account. If no receiver's account is found, then create one. If the receiver has a contract account, then run the code stored in the smart contract account. The code is executed until it is completed or until some type of failure occurs.

Step 6: If the transaction is unsuccessful due to insufficient balance or due to some failure, then all types of updates and changes done so far are returned back and fees are refunded to the sender [23].

Table 1.3 explains the differences between the Bitcoin network and the Ethereum network of blockchain.

Litecoin: Litecoin (LTC) is a cryptocurrency that was developed by Charles Lee in 2011. It is denoted by a silver coin in reference to the Bitcoin, which was earlier named as the gold coin [27]. It used the source code of Bitcoin after making some changes. The main difference between LTC and Bitcoin is the processing time of transaction made, which is about 2.5 min in LTC and 10 min in Bitcoin. Moreover, the mining of Bitcoin requires fast computing and processing along with a high electricity consumption, whereas LTC does not require such high configuration. It only requires an ordinary computer [27].

Table 1.3 Comparison of different blockchain networks [26].

Property	Bitcoin network	Ethereum network
Currency	Bitcoin	Ether
Latency	10 min	12–14 s
Throughput	7 Tx/s	9–10 Tx/s
Application	Bitcoin only has a financial application	Ethereum does not have only financial application, it is also used for smart contracts
Programming language	C++	Solidity

Dogecoin: Dogecoin (DOGE), referred to as the memecoin, was developed by Billy Markus, a programmer by profession in Portland, Oregon. It was officially released in December 2013. DOGE was created as a "fun crypto-currency", which could reach a broader demographic area than the Bitcoin. DOGE was created as a rival coin to Bitcoin. DOGE is based on the already existing structure of Luckycoin, which is the system of rewarding for min-ing a block of coin. This system of rewarding was changed in 2014 to the static block reward. Luckycoin was based on the Litecoin technology of the cryptocurrency discussed above. Earlier, the supply of DOGE was limited to 100 billion, but later it was decided and announced that there will be no capping on the total number of coins; hence, the DOGE network will produce infinite coins. DOGE is even faster than the Litecoin, which has a processing time of around 2.5 min. DOGE reduced the processing time to 1 min [28]. This is the only reason that Tesla CEO Elon Musk said "DOGE is a way better crypto coin than Bitcoin when it comes to the transactions per day" [29].

Ripple: Ripple (XRP) was developed by Open Coin in 2012. XRP is also a payment system and a cryptocurrency similar to Bitcoin. XRP is very fast in comparison to other systems. It is because it is able to transfer money to other users in the network within a couple of seconds using this network [27].

Phase 2: Blockchain in Smart Contracts
Smart contracts lead to the next phase of the blockchain. They are basi-cally the software, as they are intended to execute and document legally relevant events in the terms of a contract automatically. In smart contracts, the buyer's and seller's information is directly inscribed into the code. They are operated using the virtual machines that dedicatedly worked for them. These machines use ledgers that are distributed in nature and are embed-ded in a blockchain [30]. The various components include the program code, storage, and a balance [31]. A smart contract can be made and used by any node available on the blockchain by simply pushing a transaction onto the blockchain. They can be developed and deployed on various blockchain networks such as Bitcoin and Ethereum. Deploying a smart contract on ETH is easy as compared to that on Bitcoin as Bitcoin uses the bytecode scripting language, which is based on stacks, making it less com-patible [32], whereas in ETH, there are two types of accounts as discussed above. All accounts under this category are coordinated by the logic of pro-gram code, state, storage, and balance. EVM supports the smart contracts by interpreting the compiled source code, which is converted into the byte-code. Each node executes the same instruction to run a smart contract [31].

There were some challenges related to the scalability of smart contracts in both of these blockchain networks, which was overcome by the Hyperledger fabric. The major difference between Hyperledger and Bitcoin or ETH is based on permissions only. The former is a permissioned blockchain network whereas the latter is a permissionless blockchain network.

1.9   Advantages of Smart Contracts

They have many advantages, because of which they are gaining popularity. Some of the advantages of smart contracts are listed below:

1. **Security:** Since these are based on blockchain, they use the best data encryption, which is also used in cryptocurrencies, making it one of the most secured ways of transacting.
2. **Speed:** Since smart contracts work on the software codes, they are very fast, which helps prevent the wastage of time and also manual labor.
3. **Accuracy:** Smart contracts omit the need to fill the forms manually, which reduces the risk of errors and hence making it more accurate. Smart contracts store all the terms and conditions, so they can be used later.
4. **Efficiency:** Because of the speed and the accuracy of the smart contracts, they become more efficient. Better efficiency results in creating more transactions per unit time.
5. **Eco-friendly:** As smart contracts are based on software and reduce the use of paper, they are eco-friendly.
6. **Transparency:** All the terms and conditions are clearly mentioned and visible to both parties, which reduces the risk of dispute between the parties.
7. **Backup:** They have the advantage that they are able to record the details of each transaction for backup, so that they can be easily accessible in the future [33].

1.10   Use Cases of Smart Contracts

Smart contracts are being used for several different things such as:

1. **Online Voting System:** Smart contracts are a secured way of conducting a poll as it does not allow the manipulation of

transactions made (votes casted in this case). All the votes that are cast by the nodes are protected by ledgers, so it is difficult to decode and manipulate.

2. **Supply Chain:** In supply chain, the different applications included are management systems related to inventory and the automation of payments and tasks.

3. **Financial Sector:** Different tools are integrated for book-keeping, which, in turn, reduced the possibility of manipulation of any type of records [34].

1.11   Real-Life Example of Smart Contracts

Suppose you are buying any property and you sent the payment to the seller in cryptocurrency. The seller sends you a receipt, which is stored in virtual contract. The seller is supposed to send you the digital key to access the receipt by a certain date. If the seller has not sent you the key on the specified date, then the refund would automatically be initiated by the blockchain. If the seller has sent you the key before the specified date, then the key would be delivered to you and the money you transacted would be deposited into the seller's account.

1.12   Blockchain in Decentralized Applications

Decentralized applications are open-source software, which works on peer-to-peer blockchain networks instead of a single computer [35]. Decentralized applications are abbreviated as DApps. Most of the times, DApps are built on the Ethereum blockchain network, due to which DApps are becoming more popular. The major benefit of using a DApp is that it is easily accessible. Also, it does not have any point of failure [34]. It is not necessary for a DApp to run on a blockchain network. Some of the DApps that do not run on the blockchain network are Tor, BitTorrent, and Popcorn Time [36]. DApps that run on the blockchain technology are Peepeth, a social media application, and Cryptokitties.

Recently, a new concept of metaverse is also gaining popularity. Metaverse is simply the network of three-dimensional (3D) virtual worlds that focuses on connecting the society. Metaverse is also a type of new social media, wherein the public can literally feel like they are present in some other world with some other people around them. Metaverse is also a type of DApp. Metaverse applications are built using the blockchain network.

Most common examples of DApps built using the multi-metaverse inter-planetary scenario are Fortnite and Solana. Solana is also a blockchain, which, like many other blockchain networks, has its own money known as SOL [37]. Recently, Facebook has also been renamed to Meta. Meta comes from the same term metaverse.

1.12.1   Advantages of DApps

- **Security:** If any of the node is working on the network, then the network will be available, because of which it is very difficult for hackers to hack the node and hence making the network one of the most secured technologies [35].
- **Data Integrity:** As DApps are based on blockchains, the data available on DApps are also immutable; therefore, the data are protected [35].
- **User Privacy:** No personal data are required to use any of the inapp functions of DApps [35].

1.12.2   Role of Blockchain in Metaverse

- **Ensuring Data Security:** DApps collect a wide range of sensitive data to provide users with the best possible experiences. This type of network always has security issues in terms of data breach. Since it has sensitive information, it is required that it should not be leaked to unauthorized people. To prevent this data breach, blockchain is used as blockchain with its consensus mechanisms. It is helpful as the users will have full control over the data, which, in turn, will ensure the security of the data on the network [38].
- **Ensuring the Quality of Data:** The metaverse is dependent on the data from multiple sources and from various fields, to make key decisions for the stakeholders. Hence, the data must be accurate and of good quality. Blockchain provides an audit of transactions, which allows users to authenticate all the transactions. Through authentication and validation, the quality of data can be improved, which will lead to the enhanced quality of the metaverse.
- **Enabling Data Sharing:** One of the major principles on which metaverse is dependent is augmented reality (AR) and virtual reality (VR) technologies. Data have to be shared between the AR and VR, and to make the metaverse

experience seamless, we need to provide a seamless data sharing between both of these. To provide a seamless data sharing, blockchain's advanced encoding information system is used, which makes data sharing seamless and secured.

- **Ensuring Data Integrity:** The data of the metaverse must be preserved regularly and accurately so that stakeholders do not lose their faith in the metaverse. The data of the metaverse is stored in the shape of a block as in blockchain so that it cannot be amended without the consent of the majority of stakeholders [38].

1.12.3   Uses of Blockchain in Metaverse Applications

- **NFTs:** Non-fungible tokens or NFTs are unique tokens that act as certificates to virtual assets that indicate the ownership. Since NFTs are unique, they can also be used as the identification proof to freely trade the assets [39].
- **Financial System:** Since, in the metaverse, millions of transactions happen, such as exchange of goods in a short period of time, these transactions must be secured and efficient and should take less time to execute. All these conditions are fulfilled by blockchain technology as blockchains are secured, efficient, and fast; hence, blockchain technology has applications in both large-scale and small-scale systems in the metaverse [38].

1.12.4   Some Popular Examples of Metaverse Applications

1. **Decentraland:** It is a distributed platform, built using the blockchain network, which allows the developers to build and monetize their applications. Decentraland is based on the Ethereum's blockchain network and has its own financial tokens as is the case with Ethereum. Money that is used to buy land on the decentraland is known as MANA. The virtual land is owned and governed by the users [36, 40].

2. **SuperWorld:** It is also a real estate-focused metaverse application, which is based on the blockchain network. In SuperWorld, the user can buy and sell the property available in the metaverse. There are many popular real-life properties available on the SuperWorld such as the Taj Mahal and Eiffel

Tower [41]. Properties available on the SuperWorld can be purchased using the Ethereum's token ETH.

3. **Cryptovoxels:** It is a metaverse DApp, based on Ethereum's blockchain network, that allows the user to build, enjoy, and also monetize virtual reality environments [37].

1.13   Decentraland

Decentraland is a virtual world wherein the users can buy a parcel of land in exchange for money. Non-fungible digital assets in Decentraland are known as Land. When the development of Decentraland started in 2016, there was only an infinite 2D graph consisting of pixels of different colors, which stored the metadata of the owner of the land. This stage of Decentraland is termed "Stone Age". Further in late 2016, the team of decentraland decided to develop the 3D virtual world, which was termed the "Bronze Age". Decentraland uses the topology of peer-to-peer network while interacting with its different users. There are mainly three parts of Decentraland, the decentralized ledger, a protocol, and a P2P network. Land ownership in Decentraland is acquired by an ERC 20 token known as MANA. Prices of land in decentraland depends on its adjacencies and the traffic load. All the unclaimed land was originally sold at the rate of 1000 MANA, but are now sold based on the secondary market [41].

Decentraland consists of a three-layered architecture:

Layer 1: Consensus Layer: This layer's main function is to track land ownership and to maintain the content ledger of the land. All the details were fetched by the Ethereum network using land smart contracts. Land contracts burn MANA to create a new entry in the registry [40].

Layer 2: Land Content Layer: This layer basically downloads the assets using a decentralized distribution system. A system that is decentralized in nature is used in this for storing and distributing the information required by the nodes of the network. This decentralized mechanism allows the decentraland to work without the need of any centralized authority, allowing the existence of the world as long as there are users distributing the content. The parcel contains different files, which are required for parcel rendering. This document has three files in it [40]:

- **Content files:** This file contains the reference to 3D meshes, audio files, textures, and other content related to the rendering of the land.

- **Scripting entry point:** This file controls the behavior and appearance of the content placed in the parcel.
- **P2P interactions:** This allows the client and user interaction by connecting the client to the server, which bootstraps the user–user connection.

Layer 3: Real-Time Layer: This layer allows the users from around the world to connect to each other. Users can communicate with each other using the servers hosted by the landowners or the third-party servers [40].

Opportunities in Blockchain
There are a lot of opportunities related to blockchain technology as there are a lot of use cases for blockchain in all fields, which deals with the data and specifically the transactions of the data. This does not mean that the use of blockchain is only limited to the FinTech industry, but as mentioned earlier, blockchain is also used for the following purposes as well:

- Healthcare
- Information Security
- E-commerce
- Banks
- Cloud Computing
- Government Sector
- Financial Sector/Investments/Cryptocurrencies
- Data Analytics
- Internet of Things

In addition, Blockchain also generates industry-oriented employment in the following fields:

- **Blockchain Developer:** The main responsibilities of a blockchain developer are to design, implement, and support a network that is developed using blockchain [42]. Basically, blockchain developers are the programmers who develop and deploy the blockchain network. These people have a lot of experience working with C++, Python, and JavaScript [43].
- **Blockchain Engineer:** Blockchain engineers work on the development of the blockchain infrastructure and building the blockchain-based user-oriented applications on it [42].

- **Blockchain Solution Architect:** The individuals in this category help in developing, designing, assigning, and connecting various components of blockchain that help the teams of experts [43].
- **Blockchain UX Designer:** These individuals have to work at the front end of the blockchain so as to make the blockchain user experience much better and convenient. Blockchain UX designers have to design the user interface, which is more alluring to regular consumers [43].
- **Blockchain Quality Engineer:** These individuals conduct the tests and automation of the frameworks for the blockchain. A blockchain quality engineer plays an important role in securing the transactions made through the blockchain network [43].
- **Blockchain Platform Engineer:** These individuals provide their expert opinions and development support to the blockchain initiative throughout the company and provide subject matter opinions on the blockchain architecture and administrative requirements [42].

1.14   Challenges Faced by Blockchain

The following are some of the challenges faced by blockchain technology:

- **Selfish Mining:** Selfish mining forbids the sharing of information related to mined node with all other nodes in the network. It is one of the major challenges faced by blockchain as it can lead to network vulnerability.
- **Initial Cost:** The initial cost of developing a blockchain network is very high; this is due to the fact that there are comparatively less experts available in this new technology. Moreover, the cost of specialized software also contributes to the high initial cost. This cost can be reduced by generating more blockchain specialists and by generating mass awareness about blockchain.
- **Integration with Legacy Systems:** Another major challenge faced by blockchain is shifting the already existing systems to the blockchain. Now, to shift, there are only two possible ways, one is by destroying the already existing legacy systems and then reconstructing them on a blockchain network, and

the other one is by making a combination of blockchain and the already existing legacy systems, by incorporating the blockchain network on the already existing systems. The latter solution is comparatively a feasible and effective way of transforming the legacy systems to the blockchain networks [44].

- **Scalability:** Scalability is the major challenge faced by blockchain technology. It is because, daily, a large number of transactions are taking place, which, in turn, leads to the generation and addition of new blocks to the chain. The current transaction rate of blockchain network varies from 7 transactions per second (tps) to 3500 tps, depending on the number of nodes in the network, platform of the network, its architecture, consensus approach, and many other factors [45].

- **Public Perception and Awareness:** Due to very low public awareness, blockchain faces a lot of challenges. Because blockchain is a new technology, the public is not yet familiar with it and hence creates rumors about it, which has a negative impact on the public.

- **Signature Verification:** Signature verification is a very big challenge in the blockchain technology as all the transactions have to be signed with a cryptographic scheme, which requires very high-power consumption for the calculations to sign the transaction [15].

- **Security:** Cybersecurity has always been the key focus of all the nations. There have been cases where cyberattacks have been done using blockchain or, to be more specific, cryptocurrencies. This is because cryptocurrencies are also decentralized, because of which the person buying and selling the cryptocurrency is not visible to anyone and hence can steal money from someone's account even while maintaining anonymity. One such example is a Singapore-based crypto exchange, which lost around 443.93 Bitcoins, which was equivalent to approximately 19 million dollars [46].

Blockchains face these challenges because it is comparatively a new technology; hence, people are not familiar with it and, thus, do not believe in it.

1.15   Weaknesses of Blockchain

- **Interoperability:** Interoperability is the ability to exchange information between two systems or software and then use that information. There are mainly three situations in which interoperability is required by blockchain:

  - When the entity is moved to a new blockchain network, then it should support the old legacy systems.
  - When two different entities use two different blockchain networks, then both the entities need to interoperate with each other.
  - When the blockchain network uses all its storage capacity, then the new network, which would be set up, must interoperate with the earlier network [45].

- **High Power Consumption:** This technology consumes a lot of power to complete a transaction. One of the reasons for high power consumption is the signature verification and the other is the real-time ledger.
- **Disposal of records:** Since blockchain is immutable, the records stored in blockchain cannot be disposed or deleted after use. This can lead to data breach, which is a security flaw.
- **Attacks:** There are some flaws in some blockchains, because of which they can be attacked by different threats such as the following:

  - **Attack of 51%:** This is the attack when the same results are evaluated while calculating the hash function by the two different miners, because of which the blockchain breaks and, hence, now there are two chains and both of them are considered to be true. Attack of 51% can also be understood as if more than 50% of the systems that are used for the service tells a lie, then the lie is considered to be true [15, 44].

o **Double Spending:** The double spending attack is very much similar to the "Attack of 51%", but in this attack, the money is sent again by splitting the chain. To prevent double spending in Bitcoin, Satoshi Nakamoto introduced the concept of mints, which was discussed earlier [15].

o **DDos's Attack:** In this attack, there are several similar kinds of requests.

o **Sybil's Attack:** It is the attack that takes place when one node accepts many essences. As the network is not able to differentiate between authorized and unauthorized physical machines, this attack happens. Sybil's attack leads to the Attack of 51% and double spending [15].

1.16   Future of Blockchain

Blockchain is the technology of the future. Most of the services have started shifting to blockchain, and in the coming years, almost all the services will be available on the blockchain. The most beneficial sector would be the banking sector as the infrastructure cost, the cross-border payments, and other day-to-day trading will be replaced by the blockchain in the coming years, which will indeed reduce the risk of cyberattacks. The following sectors will be affected by the blockchain in the future:

- **Big Data Analytics:** If Big Data Analytics and blockchain are combined together, then this combination may lead to secured and hassle-free data management and data analysis [44].
- **Combating Crime:** Blockchain can be used for tracking criminals in the near future [44].
- **Industries:** Industries will incorporate blockchain that will abolish the already existing systems; this is because the transactions made using the blockchain network are faster and also secure [44].
- **National Currency:** El Salvador in 2021 declared Bitcoin as the legal tender to trade or, in simple words, the national currency. Similarly, in the coming years, it is possible that more countries will declare cryptocurrency as their national currency.

- **Communication:** It might be possible in the near future that people start communicating with each other using blockchain, one of the starting points of which has been established using the metaverse applications. The messages transferred using blockchain would be highly secured.

1.17   Conclusion

In this chapter, we have introduced one of the hottest topics in the field of Computer Science, i.e., the blockchain. Blockchain technology has different use cases spread among different fields. We have discussed what blockchain is, what is its need, and what are the future applications of blockchain. Moreover, we have also tried to talk over the challenges faced by blockchain technology because, today, not many people know much about an emerging technology. Further, different kinds of blockchains available depending on the network and the consensus mechanisms have also been elaborated. One of the most important use of blockchain, or the point from which blockchain is supposed to have originated, "the Bitcoin", is also presented in this chapter.

References

1. Sherman, A.T., Javani, F., Zhang, H., Golaszewski, E., On the origins and variations of blockchain technologies. *IEEE Secur. Priv.*, 17, 1, 72–77, January 2019. arXiv:1810.06130.
2. Narayanan, A., Bonneau, J., Felten, E., Miller, A., Goldfeder, S., *Bitcoin and cryptocurrency technologies: A comprehensive introduction*, Princeton University Press, Princeton, 2016.
3. Haber, S. and Stornetta, W.S., How to time-stamp a digital document. *J. Cryptol.*, 3, 2, 99–111, January 1991.
4. Ghosh, J., The blockchain: Opportunities for research in information systems and information technology. *J. Global Inf. Technol. Manag.*, 22, 4, 235–242, 2019.
5. Kakavand, H., Kost De Sevres, N., Chilton, B., *The blockchain revolution: An analysis of regulation and technology related to distributed ledger technologies*, Social Science Research Network (SSRN), Rochester, NY, 2017.
6. Anwar, H., *Blockchain vs. distributed ledger technology*, 2019, Available online at: https://bit.ly/2SFTRZ0.

7. Ali Syed, T., Alzahrani, A., Jan, S., Siddiqui, M.S., Nadeem, A., Alghamdi, T., A comparative analysis of blockchain architecture and its applications: Problems and recommendations. *IEEE Access*, 7, 176838–176869, 2019.

8. Aras, T.S. and Kulkarni, V., Blockchain and its applications – A detailed survey. *Int. J. Comput. Appl.*,180, 3, 29–35, 2017.

9. Peters, G. and Panayi, E., *Understanding modern banking ledgers through blockchain technologies: Future of transaction processing and smart contracts on the internet of money*, Social Science Research Network, Rochester, NY, 2015.

10. Mohapatra, D., Bhoi, S.K., Jena, K.K., Nayak, S.R., Singh, A., A blockchain security scheme to support fog-based internet of things. *Microprocess. Microsyst.*, 89, 104455, 2022.

11. Rawat, D.B., Chaudhary, V., Doku, R., Blockchain technology: Emerging applications and use cases for secure and trustworthy smart systems. *J. Cybersecur. Priv.*, 1, 1, 4–18, 2020.

12. Baiod, W., Light, J., Mahanti, A., Blockchain technology and its applications across multiple domains: A survey. *JITIM*, 29, 4, Article 4, 2021.

13. Zheng, Z., Xie, S., Dai, H.N., Chen, X., Wang, H., An overview of blockchain technology: Architecture, consensus, and future trends. *2017 IEEE 6th International Congress on Big Data*, Honolulu, HI, *USA*, 2017.

14. Babu, E.S., Dadi, A.K., Singh, K.K., Nayak, S.R., Bhoi, A.K., Singh, A., A distributed identity-based authentication scheme for Internet of Things devices using permissioned blockchain system. *Int. J. Knowl.-Based Intell. Eng. Syst.*. 39, 10, e12941, 2022.

15. Strebko, J. and Romanovs, A., The advantages and disadvantages of the blockchain technology. *2018 IEEE 6th Workshop on Advances in Information, Electronic and Electrical Engineering (AIEEE)*, pp. 1–6, Vilnius, Lithuania, 2018.

16. Nguyen, C., Hoang, D.T., Nguyen, D., Niyato, D., Nguyen, H., Dutkiewicz, E., Proof-of-stake consensus mechanisms for future blockchain networks: Fundamentals, applications and opportunities. *IEEE Access*, 7, 85727–85745, 2019.

17. Rakhra, A., Gupta, R., Singh, A., Blockchain and internet of things across industries, in: *Machine Learning Approaches for Convergence of IoT and Blockchain*, pp. 1–34, 2021.

18. Jeet, R. and Singh Kang, S., Investigating the progress of human e-healthcare systems with understanding the necessity of using emerging blockchain technology. *Mater. Today: Proc.*

19. Gupta, R., Rakhra, A., Singh, A., Internet of things security using AI and blockchain, in: *Machine Learning Approaches for Convergence of IoT and Blockchain*, pp. 57–91, 2021.

20. Nakamoto, S., *Bitcoin: A peer-to-peer electronic cash system*, Technical report, Manubot, 2019, https://bitcoin.org/bitcoin.pdf.

21. Singh, K.K., Balamurugan, B., Smieee, N.C., Kshatriya, B.S.R., Machine learning approaches for convergence of IoT and blockchain. *Open Comput. Sci.*, 10, 1, 459–460, 2020.
22. Wood, G., *Ethereum: A secure decentralised generalised transaction ledger.* Ethereum project yellow paper, vol. 151, pp. 1–32, 2014.
23. https://ethereum.org/en/whitepaper/
24. Kasireddy, P., *How does ethereum work, anyway?* 2017, Available at http://www.easygoing.pflog.eu/32_blockchain_P2P/ethereum_blockchain.pdf.
25. https://www.sofi.com/learn/content/how-do-ethereum-transactions-work/
26. Sabry, S.S., Kaittan, N.M., Ali, I.M., The road to the blockchain technology: Concept and types. *Period. Eng. Nat. Sci.*, 7, 4, 1821–1832, 2019.
27. Jumaili, M.L.F. and Karim, S.M., Comparison of tow two cryptocurrencies: Bitcoin and litecoin. *J. Phys.: Conf. Ser.*, 1963, 012143, 2021.
28. Chohan, U.W., *A history of dogecoin,* Discussion series: Notes on the 21st century, 2021, Available at: https://papers.ssrn.com/sol3/papers.cfm?abstract_id=3091219.
29. Kumar, P., Yadav, P., Agrawal, R., Singh, K.K., Amalgamation of IoT, ML, and blockchain in the healthcare regime, in: *Machine Learning Approaches for Convergence of IoT and Blockchain*, pp. 93–108, 2021.
30. https://www.simplilearn.com/tutorials/blockchain-tutorial/what-is-smart-contract
31. Alharby, M., Aldweesh, A., van Moorsel, A., *Blockchain-based smart contracts: A systematic mapping study of academic research (2018), 2018 International Conference on Cloud Computing, Big Data and Blockchain (ICCBB)*, pp. 1–6, Fuzhou, China, 2018.
32. Lewis, A., *A gentle introduction to smart contracts*, Available online at: https://bitsonblocks.net/2016/02/01/a-gentle-introductionto-smart-contracts/.
33. https://medium.com/@ChainTrade/10-advantages-of-using-smart-contracts-bc29c508691a
34. https://corporatefinanceinstitute.com/resources/knowledge/deals/smart-contracts/
35. https://www.techtarget.com/iotagenda/definition/blockchain-dApp#:~:text=A%20decentralized%20application%20(dApp)%20is,device%20but%20are%20P2P%20supported.
36. https://blockchainhub.net/decentralized-applications-dapps/#:~:text=Tor%2C%20BitTorrent%2C%20Popcorn%20Time%2C,Origins%20of%20Bitcoin%20and%20Web3).
37. https://thedapplist.com/learn/what-is-metaverse/
38. Gadekallu, T., Huynh-The, T., Wang, W., Yenduri, G., Ranaweera, P., Pham, Q.V., Costa, D.B., Liyanage, M., Blockchain for the metaverse: A review. *Future Gener. Comput. Syst.*, 143, 401–419 2023.
39. Nadini, M., Alessandretti, L., Di Giacinto, F., Martino, M., Aiello, L.M., Baronchelli, A., Mapping the NFT revolution: Market trends, tradenetworks, and visual features. *Sci. Rep.*, 11, 1, 1–11, 2021.

40. https://decentraland.org/whitepaper.pdf
41. https://101blockchains.com/top-metaverse-examples/
42. Miah, M., Rahman, M., Hossain, S., Rupai, A., Introduction to blockchain, in: *Blockchain for Data Analytics*, 2019.
43. https://www.cloudcredential.org/blog/career-opportunities-in-blockchain/
44. Priyadarshini, I., Introduction to blockchain technology, in: *Cybersecurity in Parallel and Distributed Computing*, 2019.
45. *National strategy on blockchain*, Ministry of Electronics and Information Technology, Government of India, India, December 2021.
46. https://www.techtarget.com/searchsecurity/news/252512281/Cryptocom-confirms-35M-lost-in-cyber-attack#:~:text=Additionally%2C%20Crypto.com%20confirmed%20that,it%20serves%2010%20million%20customers.-

Blockchain with Federated Learning for Secure Healthcare Applications

Akansha Singh[1]* and Krishna Kant Singh[2]

[1]School of CSET, Bennett University, Greater Noida, India
[2]Delhi Technical Campus, Greater Noida, India

Abstract

As big data and artificial intelligence develop, the public's demand for privacy continues to grow. Consequently, the topic of federated learning is raised. It is a fresh approach to cross-platform privacy defense. A workable paradigm for federated learning has been developed. Acknowledged by an increasing number of scholars and businesses today, it places a strong emphasis on data security and privacy. For instance, if users are unable to train appropriate models due to a lack of data, federated learning may combine multiple models without disclosure, and users may upgrade the integrated model. Conversely, when consumers do not have enough federated learning, they may not only supply data labels for learners to learn from but also migrate models, via a safe model sharing method. The fundamental concept and associated technologies are introduced in this work. Then, the general categories of federated learning and the real-world examples of federated learning are addressed, and the present problems and potential research prospects of federated learning are sorted. Federated states are anticipated to exist in the near future. Learning can provide shared security services that are safe for many applications and encourage the steady development of artificial intelligence.

Keywords: Blockchain, federated learning, healthcare, big data, artificial intelligence, deep learning

Corresponding author: akanshasing@gmail.com

Akansha Singh, Anuradha Dhull and Krishna Kant Singh (eds.) Blockchain and Deep Learning for Smart Healthcare, (35–44) © 2024 Scrivener Publishing LLC

2.1   Introduction

With the fast growth of smart environments and the complexity of relationships between individuals and intelligent devices, federated learning (FL) is a new development to enhance the precision and accuracy of data mining by protecting information privacy and security [1]. Very confidential material, such as patient medical records, safety industrial information, and banking personal information, should be collected and gathered to train and test with a high potential for security and confidentiality in the Internet of Things (IoT) domains of smart city, smart healthcare, and smart industry [2]. The use of blockchain technology for the adaptation of intelligent learning has the potential to affect the maintenance and upkeep of information security and privacy. Finally, blockchain-based FL mechanisms are a highly popular issue and a scientific breakthrough in data science and AI [3]. This chapter provides a thorough analysis of the privacy and security topic in the field of blockchain-based FL methods on scientific datasets in order to present an impartial road map of the current state of this problem. Based on the findings of this study, blockchain-based FL has risen significantly in the last five years, and blockchain technology has been increasingly used to resolve issues involving patient healthcare records, image retrieval, cancer datasets, industrial equipment, and economic data in IoT applications and smart environments.

2.2   Federated Learning

By separating the capacity to do machine learning from the need to put the training data in the cloud, federated learning allows mobile devices to cooperatively develop a shared prediction model while maintaining all the training data on the device [4]. By extending model training to the device as well, this extends beyond the usage of local models that generate predictions on mobile devices (such as the Mobile Vision API and On-Device Smart Reply).

The process goes as follows: your device gets the most recent model, refines it using data from your phone, and then compiles the modifications into a brief, targeted update. Only this model update is sent through encrypted connection to the cloud, where it is quickly averaged with updates from other users to enhance the shared model [5]. No specific updates are saved in the cloud; all training data are kept on your device. Federated learning ensures privacy while enabling better models, reduced latency, and less power use. Additionally, this strategy has another immediate advantage: in addition to updating the shared model, the enhanced model on your phone may also be utilized right away, enabling experiences that are tailored to your phone's use [6].

Researchers are very interested in exploring the potential and usefulness of federated learning (FL), a recently developed technology. FL just tries to respond to the fundamental query: Can we train the model without transferring data to a central location?

The FL framework puts a heavy emphasis on cooperation, which is not always possible with conventional machine learning techniques. Additionally, FL enables algorithm(s) to learn from experience, which is another thing that is not always possible with typical machine learning techniques [7]. FL has been used in many different areas, including mobile apps, IoT, transportation, and the military. Because of its applicability and the many trials that have previously been done, FL is quite trustworthy. Despite FL's tremendous potential, several of its technological components, including as platforms, hardware, software, and other related data protection and data access, are still not well understood. It is often thought to be impractical to collect and distribute customer data in a single place due to rigorous restrictions governing data protection [8]. Traditional machine learning algorithms are additionally hampered by the fact that they need a significant amount of training data.

Google originally advocated for federated learning in 2016. Its design objective is to allow effective learning across several users or computing nodes while preserving data privacy, information security, and regulatory compliance. Federated learning has been employed in numerous fields, such as mobile next-word prediction issues, and has shown strong performance and resilience as a solution to the issue of data silos [9].

2.3   Motivation

The massive data needed to fuel AI applications is often rather enormous. However, people have discovered that huge data are difficult to find in many application sectors. Most of the time, we are dealing with "small data", which are either limited in size or are lacking crucial details like values or labels. Experts in the relevant fields often expend a lot of effort to give adequate labels for data. For instance, physicians are often used in medical image analysis to make time-consuming and laborious diagnoses based on scan pictures of patient organs. Therefore, it is often impossible to gather high-quality and substantial training data. Instead, we deal with data silos that are difficult to connect.

The ownership of data is a topic that is becoming more and more prevalent in contemporary society. Who has the right to utilize the data to develop AI technologies? The proprietor of an AI-driven product recommendation business asserts ownership over data pertaining to the items and buy transactions; however, it is unclear who is in charge of the data pertaining to user purchasing and payment habits. A conventional and naïve strategy is to gather and transmit the data to one central place where powerful computers can train and create ML models since data are created and held by many people and organizations. This approach is outdated now.

As AI penetrates ever-widening application fields, worries about user privacy and data confidentiality grow. Users worry more and more that their personal data may be misused for political and commercial objectives without their knowledge. Owing to their recent actions, numerous big Internet businesses have received significant fines.

2.4   Federated Machine Learning

Federated learning also permits learning at the periphery, which allows model training to be applied to data that are dispersed among millions of devices [10]. At the same time, it enables you to improve outcomes attained in the center from peripheral locations.

- You choose a model that is either not trained at all or has been pre-trained on the main server.
- The dissemination of the first model to the customers would be the following phase (devices or local servers).
- It continues to be trained locally by each client using local data. The fact that these training data, which may include private images, emails, health measurements, or chat logs, may be secret is crucial. In cloud-based contexts, gathering these data may be difficult or perhaps impossible.
- The revised models are sent to the central server through encrypted communication channels after being locally trained. It is important to note that the server only receives trained model parameters in this case rather than actual data (e.g., weights in neural networks). The correctness of the shared model is increased by averaging and aggregating the updates from all clients [11].
- This model is then returned to all computers and servers.

2.5   Federated Learning Frameworks

The federated learning paradigm needs frameworks and libraries, much as other ML initiatives need, in order to enable the functioning data flow between a server and clients to train algorithms.

TensorFlow Federated (TFF): It is a Python-based, open-source framework for training machine learning models on dispersed data, and was created by Google [12]. This framework has been at the forefront of federated learning exploration. TFF functions primarily in two API layers: Developers may connect pre-existing machine learning models to TFF using the federated learning (FL) API without having to get too technical with the federated learning architecture. The Federated Core (FC) API provides low-level APIs that provide developers the chance to create cutting-edge federated algorithms.

OpenFL: OpenFL (Open Federated Learning), a platform created by Intel, uses the data-private federated learning paradigm to train machine learning algorithms. A Python API and a command-line interface are included with the framework [13]. While it can also operate with other frameworks, Open FL can work with training pipelines created using PyTorch and TensorFlow.

Federated Learning by IBM: Data scientists and machine learning engineers may easily integrate federated learning processes into the business context thanks to the IBM Federated Learning framework. Numerous algorithms, topologies, and protocols are supported by this federated learning platform out of the box.

2.6   FL Perspective for Blockchain and IoT

The disruptive nature of blockchain means that it may be used in every industry. It ensures the seclusion and safety of the disk space. Among its many advantageous aspects are the ideas of absoluteness, a digital ledger, and decentralization. Blockchain relies on a consensus algorithm and smart contract. Data and records of completed transactions can be stored on the blockchain, which is organized into blocks. Simply said, the blockchain serves as a trustworthy decentralized database [14]. Each trade is recorded in its own data block, which includes the specifics of the time, date, price, and people involved. Blockchain and other distributed ledger technologies enable nearly all nodes to validate transactions without needing to communicate with one another. Each block in the network contains two hash codes, the one from the past and the one from the present [15]. The hash code of a preceding block is equivalent to the hash code of the present block. Since the blockchain protects the confidentiality and integrity of the data, if a block's content is changed, all of the data sources should be updated within a reasonable amount of time. The network ensures the integrity of all blocks by hashing transaction data and encrypting data at rest. Because they are being validated by miner nodes, these blocks are added to the blockchain using a process that uses a technique to ensure that no data have been altered [16]. Therefore, blockchain guarantees both safety and openness. The blockchain is a distributed ledger that stores data in chronological blocks, each of which must comply with a predetermined set of criteria. Each node operates autonomously but under the same system, and a process is generated when a new block is added to the chain of blocks. Each and every one of the blockchain network's activities is recorded and may be accessed by any member in the network at any time. It is possible to categorize blockchain networks as private, public, or consortium chains according to the tasks they perform. In permissionless or public blockchain networks, all miner nodes can verify and validate transactions without the need for a centralized administration node [17]. In addition to taking part in consensus procedures, miner nodes rely on mutual validation to keep themselves trustworthy. Cryptocurrencies like Ethereum are a good illustration of this. Organizational data and trades are managed by a central node on the consortium's blockchain network. Both public and private users may access the data. Data may be made public or accessible only to certain categories of private users based on the nature of the business relationship. These networks contain both public and private information. They are not completely centralized. The Hyperledger Fabric infrastructure is a good example. The private blockchain network ensures complete confidentiality for all data and transactions. The information is hidden from anyone who is not a part of the network [18]. Admin nodes are somewhat analogous to consortium networks in that only the admin may invite new members to the network, e.g., Hyperledger, multichain networks, etc. Blockchain is the most secure and private option for storing sensitive medical information. The patient's medical records are encrypted using blockchain technology and the Hyperledger Fabric in this article. Hyperledger can keep tabs on the EMR and trace changes over time. The proposed work's primary objective is to provide a foundation for a recommendation system while also securing the data. Lastly, it presents the suggestion module, which analyzes the patient's medical records and suggests a course of therapy [19]. Also, the information is used to train machine learning models that will be used to give patients the most accurate and personalized treatment suggestions possible.

2.7 Federated Learning Applications

In principle, federated learning appears to be a fantastic strategy that helps alleviate the primary challenges that are typically encountered when adopting standard ML models with data stored in one central place. This is because federated learning distributes data across several locations. Research on federated learning is still going strong despite the fact that it is relatively new to the field of artificial intelligence. However, there are already several applications of FL that are put into practice.

- Healthcare
Considering that sensitive health information cannot be freely shared owing to HIPAA and other regulations, the healthcare industry is one of those that stands to profit the most from federated learning. In this approach, vast amounts of data from a variety of healthcare databases and devices may contribute to the creation of AI models while still maintaining compliance with applicable rules. The use of federated learning for the purpose of prognosticating clinical outcomes in COVID-19 patients is one of the real-life instances. In order to protect their identities when training an FL model, the scientists used data from 20 different sources located all over the world. This model, which was referred to as EXAM (electronic medical record chest X-ray AI model), was developed with the intention of predicting the future oxygen needs of patients who were experiencing signs of COVID-19 [20]. The model was educated using data from vital signs, laboratory results, and chest X-rays as inputs.

- Advertising
It should come as no surprise that personalization places a significant emphasis on the data associated with each unique user. On the other hand, an increasing number of individuals are becoming worried about how much of the information that they would rather not disclose with anybody is brought up in contexts such as social networking sites, eCommerce platforms, and other locations. Advertising, which is dependent on the personal data of users, may use federated learning in order to remain

afloat and keep people's anxieties at bay. Facebook is now in the process of overhauling the way its advertisements function in order to place a greater emphasis on user privacy. The business is experimenting with on-device learning by locally running algorithms on users' phones in order to determine which advertisements the user finds most intriguing. After that, the findings are consolidated and encrypted before being transmitted back to the cloud server. After that, the marketing teams may evaluate the data.

• Autonomous vehicles

Because it is able to make accurate predictions in real time, federated learning is a technique that is used in the production of autonomous vehicles. It is possible that the data may contain real-time updates on the state of the roads and traffic, which would make it possible for more rapid decision-making and ongoing education. The experience of riding in a vehicle that drives itself might be improved and made safer as a result of this. The field of automobile manufacturing is a potentially fruitful application area for the federated use of machine learning. On the other hand, the sole activity taking place in this field at present is research. One of the research studies has shown that federated learning may shorten the amount of time required for training in the prediction of the wheel steering angle in autonomous cars.

2.8　Limitations

There are several applications of machine learning where federated learning is not applicable. If the model is too huge to run on the user's device, the developer will need to find alternative ways to circumvent the user's privacy settings in order to protect personal data.

On the other hand, it is the responsibility of the developers to ensure that the information stored on user devices is relevant to the program. Intensive data cleaning methods are an essential part of the conventional machine learning development cycle. These practices require data engineers to eliminate potentially misleading data points and fill in the blanks wherever data are absent. It is not a good idea to train machine learning models on data that do not apply to the problem at hand.

There is no way for the data engineers to evaluate the training data and determine whether or not it will be useful to the program while the data are stored on the user's device. Because of this, federated learning should be restricted to applications in which the data collected from users do not need any preparation.

The tagging of data is another limitation of federated machine learning. The vast majority of machine learning models are supervised, which indicates that they call for training examples that are annotated by human annotators and are labeled by hand. For instance, the ImageNet dataset is a repository that was compiled with the help of crowdsourcing and includes millions of photographs along with the categories that best describe them.

In federated learning, the developers cannot expect users to go out of their way to label training data for the machine learning model unless outcomes can be inferred from user interactions (for example, predicting the next word the user is typing). This is because the developers cannot expect outcomes to be inferred from user interactions. Applications of unsupervised learning, such as language modeling, are more suited for federated learning than supervised learning applications.

References

1. Zhang, C., Hu, X., Xie, Y., Gong, M., Yu, B., A privacy-preserving multitask learning framework for face detection, landmark localization, pose estimation, and gender recognition. *Front. Neurorob.*, 13, 112, 2020.
2. Gong, M., Feng, J., Xie, Y., Privacy-enhanced multi-party deep learning. *Neural Netw.*, 121, 484–496, 2020.
3. Xie, Y., Wang, H., Yu, B., Zhang, C., Secure collaborative few-shot learning. *Knowl. Based Syst.*, 203, 106157, 2020.
4. Albrecht, J.P., How the GDPR will change the world. *Eur. Data Prot. Law Rev.*, 2, 287, 2016.
5. Parasol, M., The impact of China's 2016 cyber security law on foreign technology firms, and on China's big data and smart city dreams. *Comput. Law Secur. Rev.*, 34, 1, 67–98, 2018.
6. Gray, W. and Zheng, H.R., General principles of civil law of the people's Republic of China. *Am. J. Comp. Law*, 34, 4, 715–743, 1986.
7. Gong, M., Xie, Y., Pan, K., Feng, K., Qin, A.K., A survey on differentially private machine learning. *IEEE Comput. Intell. Mag.*, 15, 2, 49–64, 2020.
8. Mehta, S., Singh, A., Singh, K.K., Resource management and allocation in fog computing, in: *Recent Trends in Communication and Electronics*, pp. 600–603, CRC Press, 2021.
9. Liu, Y., Kang, Y., Xing, C., Chen, T., Yang, Q., A secure federated transfer learning framework. *IEEE Intell. Syst.*, 35, 4, 70–82, 2020.
10. McMahan, H.B., Moore, E., Ramage, D., Arcas, B.A.Y., *Federated learning of deep networks using model averaging*, CoRR, 2016, abs/1602.05629.
11. Konečny, J., McMahan, H.B., Ramage, D., Richtárik, P., *Federated optimization: Distributed machine learning for on-device intelligence*, 2016, arXiv preprint arXiv:1610.02527.

12. Yang, Q., Liu, Y., Chen, T., Tong, Y., Federated machine learning: Concept and applications. *ACM Trans. Intell. Syst. Technol.*, 10, 2, 1–19, 2019.
13. Aono, Y., Hayashi, T., Wang, L., Moriai, S. *et al.*, Privacy-preserving deep learning via additively homomorphic encryption. *IEEE Trans. Inf. Forensics Secur.*, 13, 5, 1333–1345, 2017.
14. Padikkapparambil, J., Ncube, C., Singh, K.K., Singh, A., Internet of Things technologies for elderly healthcare applications, in: *Emergence of Pharmaceutical Industry Growth with Industrial IoT Approach*, pp. 217–243, Academic Press, 2020.
15. Chen, Y.-R., Rezapour, A., Tzeng, W.-G., Privacy-preserving ridge regression on distributed data. *Inform. Sci.*, 451, 34–49, 2018
16. Kim, H., Park, J., Bennis, M., Kim, S.-L., *On-device federated learning via blockchain and its latency analysis*, 2018, arXiv preprint arXiv:1808.03949.
17. Sharma, D. K., Mishra, J., Singh, A., Govil, R., Singh, K. K., Singh, A., Optimized resource allocation in IoT using fuzzy logic and bio-inspired algorithms. *Wirel. Pers. Commun.*, 1–21, 2023.
18. Mohapatra, D., Bhoi, S.K., Jena, K.K., Nayak, S.R., Singh, A., A blockchain security scheme to support fog-based internet of things. *Microprocess. Microsyst.*, 89, 104455, 2022.
19. Ahmed, S.T., Kumar, V.V., Singh, K.K., Singh, A., Muthukumaran, V., Gupta, D., 6G enabled federated learning for secure IoMT resource recommendation and propagation analysis. *Comput. Electr. Eng.*, 102, 108210, 2022.
20. Singh, K.K. and Singh, A., Diagnosis of COVID-19 from chest X-ray images using wavelets-based depthwise convolution network. *Big Data Min. Anal.*, 4, 2, 84–93, 2021.

Futuristic Challenges in Blockchain Technologies

Arun Kumar Singh[1*]**, Sandeep Saxena**[1]**, Ashish Tripathi**[2]**, Arjun Singh**[3]
and Shrikant Tiwari[2]

[1]*Department of Computer Science and Engineering, Greater Noida Institute of
Technology, Greater Noida, India*
[2]*School of Computing Science and Engineering, Galgotias University,
Greater Noida, India*
[3]*Department of Information Technology, G. L. Bajaj Institute of Technology
and Management, Greater Noida, India*

Abstract

Internet of Things (IoT)-based services have grown rapidly worldwide, and IoT
is evolving at a very fast pace in industry and research, yet it is still not able to
address privacy and security vulnerabilities, although traditional security and
secrecy approaches are inappropriate due to lack of decentralized and resource
limitation for most of their devices. Blockchain technology has recently come into
focus to support the infrastructure for Bitcoin transactions. It also offers security
and privacy in peer-to-peer networks, including an inventory along with a
decentralized ledger, connected blocks of transactions, and additional transactions,
as contrasted with addresses to operational data in the network that are
distributed in a blockchain-like way. For documents enabling micro-payments or
agreeing devices, decentralized blockchain renders it more secure and resistant to
a single point failure than a conventional process. IoT devices have become a big
part of our daily lives, such as smart home devices, smartphones, and internet-
enabled gadgets for humans. Now, the security of the latest trending IoT devices
has become one of the major concerns of the IT industry. In this chapter, we will
discuss the latest challenges in blockchain and IoT technology. New IoT technology
is being employed in a wide range of industries, from the home to healthcare,
telecommunications, and energy to the environment, manufacturing, and construction.
Security is becoming more important for IoT systems because of the

*Corresponding author: arun.k.singh.iiit

Akansha Singh, Anuradha Dhull and Krishna Kant Singh (eds.) Blockchain and Deep Learning
for Smart Healthcare, (45–72) © 2024 Scrivener Publishing LLC

exchange of personal data produced by sensors and the ability to combine real and virtual worlds. It is also necessary to use strategies that are not too heavy to protect IoT devices. This paper's purpose, thus, is to highlight the security difficulties and critical concerns that are anticipated to develop in the IoT environment in order to guide authentication procedures to provide a safe IoT service.

Keywords: Blockchain, IoT, decentralized, public ledger, consensus protocol, proof of work (PoW), soft fork

3.1   Introduction

Decentralized digital ledgers or transaction data of all events are the primary functions of the blockchain, which is dispersed across all participants. In order for such a transaction to be authenticated, a majority of responders in the ecosystem must approve. As a consequence, once information is inserted, it cannot be removed.

All online transactions are processed on a blockchain, which may be a transparent and secure examination of every single transaction ever made. The digital currency Bitcoin, which is decentralized and peer-to-peer, is a well-known example of how blockchain technology is being put to use.

Bitcoin may be controversial, but the blockchain consensus mechanism has proven to be flawless in a variety of applications, both financial and operational. Most people assume that blockchain technology provides a mechanism for obtaining consensus on digital protocols; however, this hypothesis is not emphasized by the fact.

Entities of the establishment can be confident that a technical event occurred by creating an irrefutable record in a shared ledger. An open, democratic, and ecological future economy can be developed as an alternative to a centralized one. Its transformation in this industry is only getting started with this new technology, and there is much room for growth.

Blockchain has grown in prominence over the last several years since it is the new standard of Bitcoin. Its applications are expanding in various domains, including cybersecurity for the Internet of Things (IoT), the financial sector, businesses, and health clinics.

Additionally, IoT has gained widespread acceptability due to its implementation in home automation systems and urban projects worldwide. Regrettably, Internet of Things (IoT) network devices have limited computing power, storage capacity, and communication bandwidth. As a result, they are more vulnerable to assaults than other end-point devices such as mobile phones, tablets, or personal computers. This article focuses on significant IoT [1] security challenges and contrasts them with current solutions available in the literature. Additionally, concerns that remain unresolved after the installation of blockchain are emphasized.

3.2   Blockchain

Technology has revolutionized our lifestyles in the digital age, and it will always be an improvement in innovation and has made it easier to offer security with the authorization to interact and control these devices. Over the years, we discovered that technology has made it feasible to provide access control with the express consent to interact and control these devices. Business, intelligent transportation, smart cities, and many industries are providing incredibly effective facilities in many areas around the world, which is facilitated by interacting devices to the internet; in general, electrical equipment interacts with the internet, which are non-homogenous electronic devices with various functions and can meet the requirements of the network [2].

Blockchain technology is a steadily growing ledger that maintains secure, sequential, and unchangeable records of all previous transactions. Each block contains a ledger (shown in Figures 3.1 and 3.2) of most transaction records and, once finished, is added to the blockchain [3, 4].

Numerous industries, including manufacturing, banking, education, and medical, employ blockchain technology to take advantage of its distinct set of features. Blockchain technology (BT) promises improvements in dependability, cooperation, organization, identification, and transparency [5–7].

Bitcoin was first proposed in 2009 by an author using the alias Satoshi Nakamoto, who suggested that cryptography and an effective and efficient system ledger might be combined to create a digital currency application [8]. The development of blockchain technology has been a slow and steady process. Blockchain technology is currently divided into three categories: Blockchain version 1.0 to 3.0, depending on its intended use. Blockchain technology has steadily expanded into market monitoring, healthcare system, intelligent energy, copyright protection, and supply chain management [9].

When a transaction occurs inside a blockchain network, it is recorded in a series of blocks known as a blockchain. Figure 3.1 shows that each block

Block-1
Hash   1A23D@#
Previous Hash 000000000

Block-2
Hash   @123AW7
Previous H 1A23D@#

Block-3
Hash $tyuA12
Previous Hash @123AW7

Figure 3.1 Connectivity of blocks in blockchain.

has a previous block header and a counter for transactions. The following parameters can get in each of the block headers:

1. A block version identifies the program and its validation criteria.
2. The hash value of the Root of the "Merkle Tree" contains the hash value of all the transactions and a summary of all transactions.
3. Current universal time as of January 1970 is used as a calculation of time stamp.
4. "M-Bits" refers to the amount of data necessary for verification of the transaction.
5. Nonce is any four-byte value that begins at 0 and increases with each transaction hash.
6. The parent block's hash value is stored in their hash block.

Each executed record/transaction is processed in a chain of blocks in the blockchain shown in Figure 3.2, which is recognized by a public ledger. As even more blocks are added to the chain, the existing number of blocks can increase as the respective chain expands exponentially. Cryptosystem and consensus mechanism procedures are used to protect user privacy. Decentralization, persistence, anonymity, and auditability are fundamental features of blockchain technology.

It is possible to save money and boost efficiency by using blockchain because of these attributes [10]. The blockchain life cycle describes in Figure 3.3 how users request the transition for adding a new block to validate through proof of work (PoW).

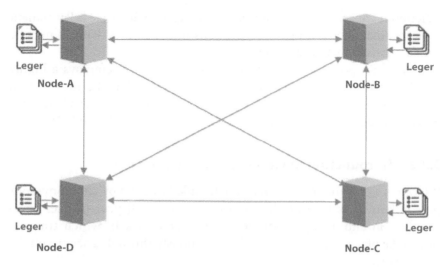

Figure 3.2 Distributed ledgers of blockchain.

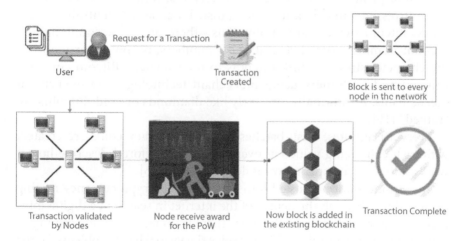

Figure 3.3 Blockchain transaction life cycle.

3.2.1   Background of Blockchain

In 1991, research scientist Stuart Haber and computer scientist W. Scott Stornetta characterized the blockchain technique. Researchers design a method to capture time-stamped information based on the notion of a cryptographically protected sequence of blocks. Moreover, Satoshi

Nakamoto conceived decentralized blockchains in 2008 [11]. Permanent indicates that after a transaction happens inside a blockchain, it may be added consistently to the ledger.

Blockchain positioned the data in a safe manner. It employs a highly sophisticated cryptographic mechanism to ensure that the information within the blockchain is secure. Immutable means that once all transactions are added to the blockchain, the ledger cannot be altered [12].

3.2.2 Introduction to Cryptocurrencies: Bitcoin

Bitcoin is a cryptocurrency that was founded in 2008 by an anonymous person known as Satoshi Nakamoto. It follows [59] peer-to-peer communication and an open-source crypto framework in which transactions take place and are managed anonymously through a secure public ledger [13].

Because Bitcoin is a digital currency, there are no coins or banknotes to mint or print. No government, financial institution, or other authority controls Bitcoins, making them a distributed and decentralized currency. Bitcoin owners are anonymous—there are no account names, account numbers, social security [14] numbers, or any other identifying characteristics that link Bitcoins to their owners. Bitcoin connects vendors and customers using blockchain technology and encryption mechanisms. Additionally, precisely like diamonds or gold, Bitcoins are "mined" [15].

Every 10 minutes, fresh batches of cryptocurrency coins are created, with each coin being valued at over $8000 [64]. Before I describe how it works, allow me to explain how it does not work [16].

To begin, do not be misled into believing that cryptocurrency mining entails sifting through the depths of the internet in search of a digital mineral that can be turned into Bitcoins. There is no real metal for mining or extracting imaginary mines. Miners solve the virtual hard problems for the validation of the transaction [17].

It is termed mining because those who obtain new Bitcoins do so in limited and finite quantities, analogous to gold. As a result, the procedure has been dubbed mining. To understand how Bitcoin mining works, you should first understand that everything Bitcoin miners perform is complete bookkeeping. A massive public ledger stores all records of Bitcoin transactions up to the current day [18].

Any Bitcoin transaction between two parties must be recorded and authenticated in the ledger by the miners. The miner should ensure that the sender is sending money for mining Bitcoin. Once the money transfer is allowed, it is validated in the virtual ledger by the miners. Additionally, it is highly encrypted using extremely sophisticated computations that are nearly hard to hack or break to prevent prospective attackers from hacking this ledger. This mining service provides them with Bitcoins [19].

There is a perpetual rivalry between miners, who eagerly await the approval of their set of tasks in order to do the calculations required to encode the transactions inside the shared ledger. Each new batch creates profitable opportunities for the miners who completed the transaction. The computing procedure, on the other hand, is extremely frightening. Computing and cryptography challenges are solved with specialized equipment equipped with high-tech processing units [20].

3.2.3   Different Cryptocurrencies

Numerous alternative currencies have gained popularity since the notion was established. The following are other examples of cryptocurrencies:

1. Ether: Ethereum is the second most well-known virtual money [58]. It is related to the notion of Bitcoins but has some different characteristics. It is a blockchain-only platform. The Ethereum Virtual Machine is what makes it unique. In Ethereum, the blockchain is not used to store transaction data but to ensure a decentralized application [21].
2. Ripple: Ripple is more of a payment system designed and developed by a firm called Ripple. It is built on the notion of real-time gross settlement. It was released for the first time in 2012 [22].
3. Litecoin (LTC): Litecoin, which was launched in 2011, is almost identical to Bitcoin. The usage of Segregated Witness and the Lightning Network distinguishes it [23].

Features of Cryptocurrencies:

a. Portability: Unlike fiat currency, cryptocurrencies may simply be moved between accounts using online devices such as computers, tablets, or even cell phones. With fiat currency, this must be accomplished physically or by identical bank transactions [24].

b. Minimal risk for interruption: David John Grundy, world-wide head of blockchain at one of the world's major banks, Danske Bank, claims that the only way to halt blockchains is to control the internet itself; this is the opinion of Grundy. Everyone should know by now that achieving that level of success is quite unlikely. It is the equivalent of asserting that someone can prevent the sun from shining or the wind from blowing.

c. As with authentic gold, cryptocurrencies such as Bitcoin often have a finite number of units that are defined or fixed in their own blockchain proprieties. Bitcoin has a maximum supply of only 21 million items. On the other hand, Litecoin has a cap of 84 million units, which is likewise limited by its operational protocols.

d. Cryptocurrencies, like gold, are inherently decentralized and independent. This means that, similar to gold, government actions or policy changes have a negligible direct influence on their long-term values, if at all.

e. Impossible to forge: Blockchain technology is a game changer when it comes to online transactions and data or record keeping. As such, it is nearly hard to manufacture counterfeit versions of it, and as blockchains evolve, this becomes increasingly difficult [17].

3.2.4   Proof of Work (POW)

A consensus technique name "proof of work (POW)" is employed by some of the most prominent cryptocurrency infrastructures, including Litecoin and Bitcoin. This method (POW) is used to validate the transaction when adding a new block to the chain [25]. Minors (a group of individuals) compete against one another to complete the network transaction in this method. Miners receive payouts as soon as they successfully construct a legitimate block or block. Bitcoin is the most well-known use of proof of work (PoW) [26].

Furthermore, the whole cryptocurrency mining process is very energy-intensive and time-consuming. The following points have been observed in the mining of cryptocurrency.

- By mining, we may earn Bitcoin without having to invest our own money.
- Bitcoin miners are compensated with Bitcoins for completing the work of adding "blocks" of validated transactions to the blockchain.
- Bitcoin is a binary executable file that may be stored in an application known as a "virtual wallet" on a computer, smartphone, or any other digital device.
- Mining rewards are awarded to the miner who solves a complicated hashing riddle or challenges first, and the likelihood of a miner solving it is related to their contribution to the system's total mining power [27].

3.3 Issues and Challenges with Blockchain

a. **Scalability**

The first difficulty in blockchain technology is scalability. For example, Bitcoin grows at a rate of 1 MB each block every 10 minutes and presently measures 241 GB in size, but Ethereum currently consumes over 3 TB of data. Nodes wishing to validate transactions must first download the full Bitcoin blockchain, which may be problematic in the long term [28].

b. **Transactional velocity**

The second difficulty is connected to the transaction speed of a blockchain. In 2019, Bitcoin can handle just seven transactions per second, but other blockchains such as Ethereum can process 20. On the other hand, on China's 2018 Singles' Day, Alibaba handled 325,000 transactions per second (generating $30.8 billion in revenue in 24 hours). It will take time for blockchain to reach these levels [29].

Consider the most centralized payment system, Visa, and the largest decentralized payment system, Bitcoin. In contrast, Visa can handle 65,000 transactions per second, whereas only 7 transactions per second can be processed by Bitcoin. Visa has a centralized design, which means that the controlling authority determines the flow of the transaction; it does not alert other peers about transactions in an unnecessary manner, which saves time and money.

In the case of blockchain, validation takes many minutes since the transaction must be approved by a majority (big number) of nodes. The primary reason behind Bitcoin's transaction speed is that it operates on a proof-of-work (POW) mechanism, which is both safe and sluggish. There is a workaround for this in the form of proof of stake (POS), which is faster for entry validation but is not optimal for distributed consensus protocols [30].

c. **Privacy leaking**

The primary risk of blockchain technology is transaction privacy leakage, as the data and balances of public keys are exposed to everyone on the network. Owing to the virtuosity of its architecture, blockchain presents several fundamental [55] privacy issues. Specifically, a blockchain's distributed design requires that each node on the blockchain has visibility of the transaction records since each node is fully functional. Because of the shared ledger of blockchain, significant concerns regarding secrecy and the safety of data stored and accessible on the shared ledger arise. Nowadays, many businesses adhere to regulatory-mandated privacy policies. Their customers place their faith in them with regard to private or sensitive information. However, if all information is maintained in a public ledger, it ceases to be private [31]. Security is the other critical issue. However, only a few circumstances have robust procedures that can handle this. Blockchains are more secure than cyberattacks on blockchain-based applications and networks are still feasible, just as they are on conventional computing infrastructure.

d. **The 51% attack**

Satoshi Nakamoto, Bitcoin's creator, characterized the cryptocurrency from the perspective of the largest CPU mining network existing at publication. From the perspective of a blockchain platform, a 51% attack (shown in Figure 3.4) happens whenever a malicious member or group of peers gets control of even more than 50% of the show's miners or hash rate. When a miner (or group of miners) possesses over 50% of the program's hash, the history generated by the other network members may be disabled, and a separate transaction history can be established [32].

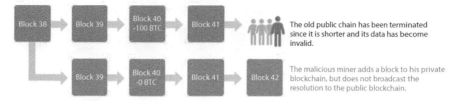

Figure 3.4 The 51% attack.

e. **Self-interested mining**

It is a significant issue in blockchains. Selfish mining is a type of assault, also known as a block withholding attack, that is defined as a malevolent effort to undermine the blockchain network's integrity as we anticipate that the miner will declare a block as soon as it is discovered. If the block is confirmed, the miner gets rewarded for it. However, by failing to broadcast their blocks, the miner effectively creates their private blockchain.

While the rest of the network continues to add blocks to the blockchain, the effect is that both chains will appear entirely different. The selfish miner's primary goal is to constantly be one or two blocks ahead of the rest of the block chain network. The miner gets all of the rewards from these blocks, resulting in resource waste on the side of the opposing party [33, 34]. Selfish mining is sometimes influenced by luck, but it is primarily influenced by the hashing power or hash rate available to the miner, or we may argue that the block is subject to cheating even if it only consumes a small portion of the hashing power. It is feasible for numerous participants in a blockchain mining process to participate in selfish mining.

f. **Fork issues**

It has to do with the version of the decentralized node, as well as agreements for software updates. The program must be updated regularly to address bugs or improve performance. These upgrades are referred to as "forks" in the context of cryptocurrency, shown in Figure 3.5. Given the decentralized nature of cryptocurrencies, all participants in the network are referred to as nodes and must adhere to the same rules and regulations in order to function properly.

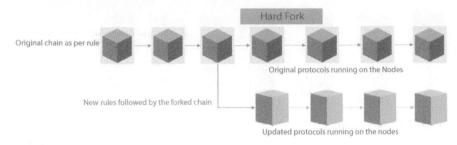

Figure 3.5 Hard fork in the blockchain.

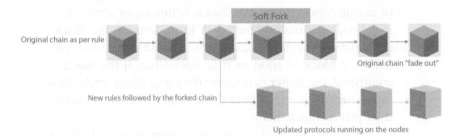

Figure 3.6 Soft fork in the blockchain.

In the crypto-blockchain world, there are two sorts of forks: soft forks and hard forks [35].

g. Flexible forks

When a system releases a new version, and if the new version is incompatible with the previous version, the new nodes cannot mine alongside the older nodes, but the older nodes and new nodes can continue to function on the same network. This is referred to as a soft fork. Soft forks keep older nodes in the dark about changes to the consensus rules. For instance, if a soft fork introduces a new rule that reduces the block size from 3 MB to 2 MB, the network's older nodes will still be able to execute transactions with a block size of 2 MB or less [36, 37]. This is referred to as a soft fork shown in Figure 3.6.

h. Sturdy forks

When a new version of the system is released, and if it is incompatible with the previous version, the older nodes cannot be agreed upon with the mining of new nodes, thereby splitting the chain in two. This is referred to as a hard fork [38].

i. **A lack of awareness and comprehension**

The third barrier to the adoption of blockchain technology in the corporate sector, particularly for small and medium-sized businesses, is a lack of knowledge of the technology and a lack of understanding of how it works. Numerous businesses and organizations are unaware of what blockchain technology is or how it might be used. This impedes significant investment and concept exploration. Organizations must acquaint themselves with this growing technology. They should improve their comprehension on all levels. The more effective the educational initiatives are, the more accessible all of this knowledge will be.

j. **Consumption of energy**

Bitcoin is the first and most popular application of the blockchain. Blockchain technology utilizes a proof-of-work (PoW) technique to validate transactions. To validate transactions using PoW, a mathematical processing capability is required. This computing capability necessitates a significant quantity of energy. Bitcoin requires around 200 GB of storage capacity on each node in the blockchain network.

According to researchers at the University of Cambridge, Bitcoin consumes more energy than the whole country of Switzerland. The energy is mostly utilized to maintain the entire network operational at all times. That is only one application of blockchain technology; consider what would happen if we had many more similar networks.

k. **Issues with regulation**

Another issue in the case of blockchain is that various nations have different rules and regulations. Blockchain has a reputation problem due to the fact that it is surrounded by hackers and fraudsters who are alleged to be utilizing the technology for unlawful or criminal operations. This negative perception of blockchain reflects poorly on the blockchain technology system as a whole and is causing people to think twice about embracing it. The decentralized structure approach will erode the central bank's power over economic policies and money transactions. Concerned authorities should be required to focus on this issue and develop new strategies and policies.

l.   **The total cost of ownership**
The next significant difficulty is the extremely high cost of replacing the old system with a new blockchain-based one. This has a variety of costs in terms of time and money. By adopting the blockchain's new infrastructure.

3.4   Internet of Things (IoT)

The IoT is a quickly growing field with significant technological, social, and economic implications.

Consumer goods, durable goods, automobiles and vehicles, industry and utility components, sensors, and other ordinary objects are being connected to the internet and equipped with strong data analytics capabilities to alter how we work, live, and play, as shown in Figure 3.7 [39]. The IoT

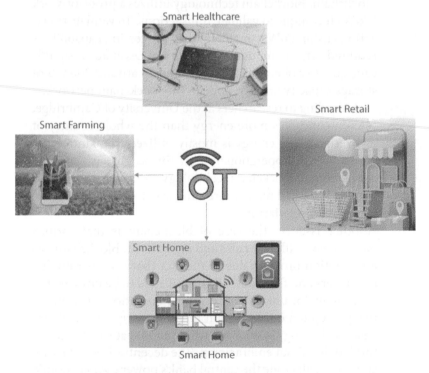

Figure 3.7 Internet of Things (IoT).

is one of the most exciting technologies of the digital revolution age, as it connects everything else to the i-net (internet). It is the underlying technology that powers self-driving cars, smart air conditioners, smart homes, smart utility metering, and smart cities, among others. However, there are several security concerns regarding the Internet of Things' future [40].

3.5   Background of IoT

The first piece of equipment to be linked to the internet was a personalized Coca-Cola vending machine located at Carnegie Mellon University. This equipment was willing to report its inventory as well as whether or not newly loaded drinks were cold. The current perspective on the Internet of Things was influenced by the work that Mark Weiser did in 1991 on ubiquitous computing called "The Computer of the Twenty-First Century." This work was also presented at educational venues like UbiComp and PerCom.

The term [57] "Internet of Things" refers to circumstances in which internet access, as well as computing functionality, are enhanced to things, sensor systems, and some other everyday things which were not generally considered to be computers. This enables such gadgets to start producing, sharing, and studying information with minimal engagement from a human being.

In summary, the Internet of Things (IoT) is a network of interconnected things and equipment that are equipped with embedded sensors, applications, network connectivity, and the requisite components to collect and exchange information, consequently keeping things responsive [41].

The Internet of Things Applications

1. The Smart Home
2. Wearable Technology
3. Connected Automobiles
4. The Industrial Internet of Things
5. Smart Cities
6. IoT in Agriculture
7. Smart Retail
8. Energy Engagement
9. Internet of Things in Healthcare
10. Internet of Things in Poultry and Agriculture

3.5.1   Issues and Challenges Faced by IoT

Various security issues exist in IoT; some of them are described below in detail.

a) Denial of service (DOS)
Attacks such as denial of service (DOS) aim to prevent legitimate individuals and organizations from accessing network services. It is the most prevalent attack, and it has the greatest impact. As a general principle, adversaries may use flooding techniques to drain network memory resources, CPU and bandwidth. There is a range of tactics that cybercriminals might use in this attack, including delivering erroneous packets of data or overwhelming the network with information. Authorized users are unable to access services as a consequence of this policy.

b) Security holes
This may expose a firm to a community of numerous, ever-increasing security weaknesses. Over 10,000 new malware risks are detected every hour, according to studies. If companies do not keep their technologies up to date, they are escalating the vulnerability exponentially. If their machine is still Windows-based XP, they are way more likely to get contaminated than someone using Windows 10. As of July 14, 2015, Microsoft no longer provides security updates or support for Windows Server 2003, putting users at significant risk of cyberattacks and victimization.

In April 2014, Microsoft Office 2003 attained end-of-support status, which means that security patches would no longer be provided. In spite of the fact that Office is merely a simple productivity tool suite such as Word, Excel, PowerPoint, Outlook, etc., it may nonetheless expose your network to security risks [56]. Documenting everything they want and how frequently it needs to be updated is the greatest approach to help ensure you are constantly up to date.

With headquarters in Amsterdam, the Netherlands, Gemalto is an information security company that has conducted a study on the IoT's growth and its influence on security. Ninety-one percent of consumers lack faith in the security of IoT devices, according to a recent study. This is despite the fact that more than two-thirds of customers and over 80% of businesses favor government involvement in establishing IoT security standards. Indeed, its current State of IoT Security study report, which was issued in late October, revealed the following statistics:

a) Ninety-six percent of enterprises and 90% of consumers feel that IoT security laws should be implemented.
b) While 54% of customers possess an average of four Internet of Things devices, only 14% say they are informed about the security of IoT devices.
c) Sixty-five percent of customers are worried about a hacker gaining control of their Internet of Things device, while 60% are concerned about data leakage.
d) It is evident that both consumers and companies are concerned about IoT security and have low faith in IoT internet providers and equipment vendors to secure IoT devices and, more crucially, the authenticity of the data produced, stored, and sent by these devices.

c) IoT malware and ransomware
Accordingly, as the number of Internet of Things (IoT)-connected devices continues to grow in the following years, so will the quantity of malware and ransomware that are utilized to exploit these devices.

Instead of using encryption to lock people out of their devices and platforms in the classic sense, there is a continuing hybridization of malicious programs that tries to bring the two types of attacks together. In addition to obtaining user data, ransomware attacks might possibly target device functioning by restricting or disabling it while also taking user data [42].

For example, a basic IP camera is great for gathering sensitive information from a variety of places, such as your house, business, or even the neighborhood gas station, without the need for additional equipment. The camera may then be locked, and the film can be sent to an affected web address, from which sensitive data can be extracted via the malware access point, perhaps causing an issue with your information. Attacks on IoT devices will proliferate as the number of connected devices grows and as new permutations are discovered.

d) Artificial intelligence (AI) and robotics
Even though [61] IoT systems have become more prevalent in our daily lives, industries will soon have to manage thousands upon thousands, if not millions, of IoT devices. This volume of user information might be difficult to control and analyze; it would not possibly be cost-effective [1, 65]. AI techniques and digitization are currently used to filter enormous amounts of data, but they may assist IoT administration and network

security personnel in enforcing data-specific regulations and detecting predicted information and traffic trends.

Nevertheless, utilizing autonomous systems and making fully independent decisions that impact millions of activities throughout infrastructures like the healthcare system, power, and transportation may be too risky, given that a single program's inaccuracy or disobedient technique proposed is sufficient to destroy an entire facility.

e) Unreliable communication

In the Internet of Things, a large number of devices transmit data in an unencrypted format. The above is one of the most significant IoT security issues now facing the industry. It is time for all firms to guarantee that their cloud services and equipment have the highest degree of security possible. Transport security and protocols like TLS are the strongest defense against such security attacks; another option is to create separate networks for each device. The data communicated may also be secured by using private communication.

f) Home invasions

Home invasion is one of the most frightening hazards that IoT may provide. The proliferation of the Internet of Things (IoT) devices in private residences and workplaces has spawned the home automation industry. These IoT gadgets offer a serious security risk since they disclose your IP address, which may be used to determine your location. In what way do you feel about the fact that your home's location has been made public? It is bad enough! Hackers might recoup their costs by reselling these sensitive data on dark web markets frequented by organized crime. Additionally, if you integrate IoT devices into home surveillance systems, there is a risk that they might be hacked and put your home at risk. Home invasions have become one of the greatest hazards to IoT [43].

g) Access to a car through the internet

One of the threats posed by the Internet of Things (IoT) is the hijacking of your automobile. IoT-enabled smart automobiles are on the approach to becoming a reality. As a result, it has a larger chance of being hijacked by criminals because of its IoT connection. The intelligent car's access control might even be hacked by a competent intruder, allowing anyone to take control of your vehicle. Anyone may take control of your automobile at any time, which puts you at risk of committing heinous crimes such as killing or violating traffic rules. An intruder might threaten you in exchange of your so-called "smart" automobile. As a result, IoT faces a further significant threat.

h) Devices connected to the Internet of Things (IoT) are hunting for digital money

There remains stiff competition among [63] cryptocurrencies in the modern period. Even though most consider blockchain to be robust to hacking, the frequency of breaches in blockchain-based industries appears to be on the rise. The most susceptible component is not the blockchain itself but the blockchain application development that runs on it. Social engineering is now employed to retrieve identities, credentials, and secret keys; in the future, technology will be utilized more frequently to attack blockchain-based applications [44]. In December 2018, crypto-mining had the greatest increase in internet security issues. With just a few lines of code, intruders were able to install crypto-mining malware on unknowing machines and mine for digital currency in the background. IoT has led to a significant increase in the number of assaults against cryptocurrencies.

i) On-demand updates

Now, civilization has become the norm. People who we interact with, as well as the clients we serve, do not just want constant, on-demand access to information, documents, production, and customer support; they expect it. If system problems and accompanying downtime prevent customers from obtaining the services they need, most will not hesitate to relocate their business elsewhere. In order to stay abreast of what their customers desire, manufacturers get frequent information on the problems and concerns they are encountering. Even more frequently than not, you can guarantee that your competitors are thereby those with the appropriate, functional technology that can meet their customers' needs for now. Because of this, your rival will have an opportunity to sell his goods before you do, lowering the value of your own product and your firm's position in the market.

j) Cost increases with the use of intelligent services

Maintaining a system that is more than a decade old might be prohibitively costly. Aside from the fact that technology ages quicker, it is not much different from keeping an old house or car. In fact, manufacturers estimate that repairing a system 4 years or older would cost roughly twice as much. Windows XP might cost Microsoft $31 million a year to maintain, as CNN Money revealed earlier this year. If a new serious defect or security hole is identified in the system, Microsoft will no longer actively create security updates or fixes for the system. However, since the Navy wanted the

Table 3.1 Comparison of features of different blockchain platforms and IoT.

Features	IOTA	Hyperledger fabric	Ethereum	Bitcoin
Consensus protocols	At the moment, a coordinator is responsible for giving final approval to the transaction using an algorithm called the Tip Selection Algorithm.	Practical Byzantine Fault Tolerance (PBFT)	Proof of Work (PoW), Proof of Stack (PoS)	Proof of Work (PoW)
The validity of consensus protocol	NO	YES	NO	NO
Participation of miners	Public	Private	Private–Public Hybrid	Public
Trustless implementation and operation	YES	Authorized consensus mechanism nodes	YES	YES
Scalable?	YES	NO	NO	NO
Completely operational platform	In the process of transitioning	YES	YES	YES

(Continued)

Table 3.1 Comparison of features of different blockchain platforms and IoT. (*Continued*)

Features	IOTA	Hyperledger fabric	Ethereum	Bitcoin
Throughput of transaction	Presently, the throughput ranges between 7 and 12 transactions per second, with the Facilitator being just the constraint.	Can accomplish thousands of transactions every second (it depends on the number of committers, orders, and endorsers)	Eight to nine transactions per second	Seven transactions per second
Blockchain forks	The validity of consensus; thus, not really forks, but a tangle may be eliminated with time.	NO	YES	YES
Transaction fee	YES	Optional	NO	NO
Execution of smart contracts	YES	NO	NO	NO
Authentication and integrity of transaction	YES	YES	YES	YES
Data confidentiality	NO	YES	NO	NO
Key management	NO	Yes, through certificate authority (CA)	NO	NO

(Continued)

Table 3.1 Comparison of features of different blockchain platforms and IoT. (*Continued*)

Features	IOTA	Hyperledger fabric	Ethereum	Bitcoin
Authentication of user	It was validated using Digital Signatures.	Yes, through a certificate authority	It was validated using Digital Signatures.	It was validated using Digital Signatures.
Authentication of a device	NO	NO	NO	NO
Vulnerability to attacks	34% attack	Greater than one-third faulty nodes	51% attack	51%, linking attacks
Selection of different techniques	Monetary only	YES	YES	Financial only
References	[45, 46]	[47]	[48, 49]	[8]
References	[50, 62]	[51]	[52]	[53]

option of maintaining its legacy systems, Microsoft provided the US Navy with the expense of maintaining and updating them.

k) IoT Authentication Techniques
Although IoT may access all users' data, the user's personal privacy must be secured from dangerous intrusions [1]. Malicious users should not have access to the system. As a result, before granting authorization, it is important to confirm the digital credentials. As a result, there are several methods for verifying a user's identity. Nonetheless, the most common is the authentication technique, which is based on the previous exchange of secret keys and sensitive information. As a consequence, in this part, researchers will look at the strategies used to enforce authenticity in the IoT context. Some important features of [60] blockchain platforms and IoT are compared and given in Table 3.1.

3.6   Conclusion

The two most important technologies in this era are blockchain and the Internet of Things (IoT); after the union of these two, it will provide much-needed and necessary services in our society. As regards security, this is handled by blockchain and the transparent and decentralized features of IoT. In the future, we can use the performance of these technologies in an efficient way in health, smart cities, transportation, energy, and agriculture. This technology is the future frame for the upcoming digital society, and it can control electronic devices anywhere in the world; it also supports the economic sector like cryptocurrency.

The Internet of Things has played a crucial role in the fast growth of current technologies. These technologies have simplified data sharing. However, user data security should not be overlooked. As a result, the research conducted in this work is primarily concerned with the security of the Internet of Things. As a consequence, as previously stated, IoT is vulnerable to a variety of threats [54], including DOS, password predicting, replay, and insider attacks. Because authentication is the very first security service that IoT must provide, we have discussed the authentication methodologies used for IoT. One of the most common strategies for enforcing authentication includes the one-time password, ECC-based mutual authentication, ID-based authentication, and the certificate-based authentication, which is used by blockchain for authentication.

References

1. Singh, A.K., Tripathi, A., Choudhary, P. and Vashist, P.C., A review on open challenges in intrusion detection system, in: *Cyber Security in Intelligent Computing and Communications*, pp. 49–58, 2022.
2. Hoy, M.B., An introduction to the blockchain and its implications for libraries and medicine. *Med. Ref. Serv. Q.*, 36, 3, 273–279, 2017.
3. Garzik, J. and Donnelly, J.C., Blockchain 101: An introduction to the future, in: *Handbook of Blockchain, Digital Finance, and Inclusion*, vol. 2, pp. 179–186, Academic Press, 2018.
4. Crosby, M., Pattanayak, P., Verma, S. and Kalyanaraman, V., Blockchain technology: Beyond bitcoin. *Appl. Innov.*, 2, 6-10, 71, 2016.
5. Cachin, C., Architecture of the hyperledger blockchain fabric, in: *Workshop on Distributed Cryptocurrencies and Consensus Ledgers*, vol. 310, pp. 1–4, 2016, July.
6. Seebacher, S. and Schüritz, R., Blockchain technology as an enabler of service systems: A structured literature review, in: *International Conference on Exploring Services Science*, pp. 12–23, Springer, Cham, 2017, May.
7. Zheng, Z., Xie, S., Dai, H.N., Chen, X., Wang, H., Blockchain challenges and opportunities: A survey. *Int. J. Web Grid Serv.*, 14, 4, 352–375, 2018.
8. Nakamoto, S., *Bitcoin: A peer-to-peer electronic cash system Bitcoin: A peer-to-peer electronic cash system*, Bitcoin.org, 2009, Disponible en https://bitcoin.org/en/bitcoin-paper.
9. Zhao, J.L., Fan, S., Yan, J., Overview of business innovations and research opportunities in blockchain and introduction to the special issue. *Financ. Innov.*, 2, 1, 1–7, 2016.
10. Pattanayak, P. and Kumar, P., SINR based limited feedback scheduling for MIMO-OFDM heterogeneous broadcast networks. In *2016 Twenty Second National Conference on Communication (NCC)*, pp. 1–6, IEEE, 2016, March.
11. Kishigami, J., Fujimura, S., Watanabe, H., Nakadaira, A., Akutsu, A., The blockchain-based digital content distribution system, in: *2015 IEEE Fifth International Conference on Big Data and Cloud Computing*, IEEE, pp. 187–190, 2015, August.
12. Vo, H.T., Mehedy, L., Mohania, M., Abebe, E., Blockchain-based data management and analytics for micro-insurance applications. In *Proceedings of the 2017 ACM on Conference on Information and Knowledge Management*, pp. 2539–2542, 2017, November.
13. Brown, S.D., Cryptocurrency and criminality: The Bitcoin opportunity. *Police J.*, 89, 4, 327–339, 2016.
14. Singh, A.K., Samaddar, S.G., Misra, A.K., Enhancing VPN security through security policy management. In *2012 1st International Conference on Recent Advances in Information Technology (RAIT)*, pp. 137–142, IEEE, 2012, March.
15. Grinberg, R., Bitcoin: An innovative alternative digital currency. *Hastings Sci. Tech. LJ*, 4, 159, 2012.

16. Segendorf, B., Eklööf, H., Gustafsson, P., Landelius, A., Cicović, S., What is libra, in: *Economic Commentaries*, vol. 9, pp. 1–13, 2019.
17. Li, S., Qin, T., Min, G., Blockchain-based digital forensics investigation framework in the internet of things and social systems. *IEEE Trans. Comput. Soc. Syst.*, 6, 6, 1433–1441, 2019.
18. Garay, J., Kiayias, A., Leonardos, N., The bitcoin backbone protocol: Analysis and applications, in: *Annual International Conference on The Theory and Applications of Cryptographic Techniques*, Springer, Berlin, Heidelberg, pp. 281–310, 2015, April.
19. Narayana, V.L., Gopi, A.P., Chaitanya, K., Avoiding interoperability and delay in healthcare monitoring system using block chain technology. *Rev. d'Intelligence Artif.*, 33, 1, 45–48, 2019.
20. Ali, S.T., March. Bitcoin: Perils of an unregulated global P2P currency (Transcript of discussion), in: *Cambridge International Workshop on Security Protocols*, pp. 294–306, Springer, Cham, 2015.
21. Extance, A., The future of cryptocurrencies: Bitcoin and beyond. *Nature News*, 526, 7571, 21, 2015.
22. de Souza, M.C., de Souza, E.T.D.C., Pereira, H.C.I., Cryptocurrencies bubbles: New evidences. *The Empirical Economics Letters*, 16, 7, pp.739–746. 2017.
23. Gkillas, K. and Katsiampa, P., An application of extreme value theory to cryptocurrencies. *Econ. Lett.*, 164, 109–111, 2018.
24. Clayton, J., *Statement on cryptocurrencies and initial coin offerings*, world, 2017.
25. Bentov, I., Gabizon, A., Mizrahi, A., Cryptocurrencies without proof of work, in: *International Conference on Financial Cryptography and Data Security*, Springer, Berlin, Heidelberg, pp. 142–157, 2016, February.
26. King, S., *Primecoin: Cryptocurrency with prime number proof-of-work*, vol. 1, 6, 2013 July 7th.
27. Liu, D. and Camp, L.J., Proof of work can work. In *WEIS*, 2006, June.
28. Chauhan, A., Malviya, O.P., Verma, M., Mor, T.S., Blockchain and scalability, in: *2018 IEEE International Conference on Software Quality, Reliability and Security Companion (QRS-C)*, IEEE, pp. 122–128, 2018, July.
29. Kiayias, A. and Panagiotakos, G., *Speed-security tradeoffs in blockchain protocols*, Cryptology ePrint Archive, 2015.
30. Nofer, M., Gomber, P., Hinz, O., Schiereck, D., Blockchain. *Bus. Inf. Syst. Eng.*, 59, 3, 183–187, 2017.
31. Gai, K., Wu, Y., Zhu, L., Qiu, M., Shen, M., Privacy-preserving energy trading using consortium blockchain in smart grid. *IEEE Trans. Ind. Inf.*, 15, 6, 3548–3558, 2019.
32. Ye, C., Li, G., Cai, H., Gu, Y., Fukuda, A., Analysis of security in blockchain: Case study in 51%-attack detecting. In *2018 5th International Conference on Dependable Systems and Their Applications (DSA)*, pp. 15–24, IEEE, 2018, September.

33. Nayak, K., Kumar, S., Miller, A., Shi, E., Stubborn mining: Generalizing selfish mining and combining with an eclipse attack, in: *2016 IEEE European Symposium on Security and Privacy (EuroS&P)*, IEEE, pp. 305–320, 2016, March.

34. Khan, M.A. and Salah, K., IoT security: Review, blockchain solutions, and open challenges. *Future Gener. Comput. Syst.*, 82, 395–411, 2018.

35. Lin, I.C. and Liao, T.C., A survey of blockchain security issues and challenges. *Int. J. Netw. Secur.*, 19, 5, 653–659, 2017.

36. Back, A., Corallo, M., Dashjr, L., Friedenbach, M., Maxwell, G., Miller, A., Poelstra, A., Timón, J., Wuille, P., *Enabling blockchain innovations with pegged sidechains*, vol. 72, pp. 201–224, 2014, http://www. opensciencereview. com/papers/123/enablingblockchain-innovations-with-pegged-sidechains.

37. Samaniego, M., Jamsrandorj, U., Deters, R., Blockchain as a service for IoT, in: *2016 IEEE International Conference on Internet of things (iThings) and IEEE Green Computing and Communications (GreenCom) and IEEE Cyber, Physical and Social Computing (CPSCom) and IEEE Smart Data (SmartData)*, IEEE, pp. 433–436, 2016, December.

38. Puddu, I., Dmitrienko, A., Capkun, S., µchain: How to forget without hard forks, Cryptology ePrint Archive, 2017.

39. Singh, A.K., Firoz, N., Tripathi, A., Singh, K.K., Choudhary, P., Vashist, P.C., Internet of things: From hype to reality, in: *An Industrial IoT Approach for Pharmaceutical Industry Growth*, pp. 191–230, Academic Press, 2020.

40. Wortmann, F. and Flüchter, K., Internet of things. *Bus. Inf. Syst. Eng.*, 57, 3, 221–224, 2015.

41. Li, S., Da Xu, L., Zhao, S., The internet of things: A survey. *Inf. Syst. Front.*, 17, 2, 243–259, 2015.

42. Wani, A. and Revathi, S., Ransomware protection in IoT using software defined networking. *Int. J. Electr. Comput. Eng.*, 2088–8708, 10, 2020.

43. Francis, A. and Pingle, Y.P., Automation in baking using AI and IoT, in: *2020 7th International Conference on Computing for Sustainable Global Development (INDIACom)*, IEEE, pp. 52–57, 2020, March.

44. Hamza, W.S., Ibrahim, H.M., Shyaa, M.A., Stephan, J.J., IoT botnet detection: Challenges and issues. *Test Eng. Manag.*, 83, 15092–15097, 2020.

45. IOTA Foundation. *IOTA data marketplace*. IOTA, 2017, December 1, https://www.iota.org/.

46. Bull, P., Austin, R., Popov, E., Sharma, M., Watson, R., Flow based security for IoT devices using an SDN gateway, in: *2016 IEEE 4th International Conference on Future Internet of Things and Cloud (FiCloud)*, IEEE, pp. 157–163, 2016, August.

47. Androulaki, E., Barger, A., Bortnikov, V., Cachin, C., Christidis, K., De Caro, A., Enyeart, D., Ferris, C., Laventman, G., Manevich, Y., Muralidharan, S., Hyperledger fabric: A distributed operating system for permissioned block-chains, in: *Proceedings of The Thirteenth Eurosys Conference*, pp. 1–15, 2018, April.

48. James, Decentralized Justice in the Era of Blockchain, 2018, https://heinonline.org/HOL/LandingPage?handle=hein.journals/ijodr5&div=11&id=&page=.

49. Etherscan. https://etherscan.io, 2018.

50. Rahman, Z., Yi, X., Mehedi, S., Islam, R., Kelarev, A., Blockchain applicability for the internet of things: Performance and scalability challenges and solutions. *Electronics*, 11, 9, 1416, 2022.

51. Zhao, Z., Comparison of hyperledger fabric and ethereum blockchain. In *2022 IEEE Asia-Pacific Conference on Image Processing, Electronics and Computers (IPEC)*, pp. 584–587, IEEE, 2022, April.

52. Lin, D., Wu, J., Yuan, Q., Zheng, Z., Modeling and understanding ethereum transaction records via a complex network approach. *IEEE Trans. Circuits Syst. II: Express Br.*, 67, 11, 2737–2741, 2020.

53. Wu, J., Liu, J., Chen, W., Huang, H., Zheng, Z., Zhang, Y., Detecting mixing services via mining bitcoin transaction network with hybrid motifs. *IEEE Trans. Syst. Man Cybern.: Syst.*, 52, 4, 2237–2249, 2021.

54. Singh, A.K., Tewari, P., Samaddar, S.G., Misra, A.K., Communication based vulnerabilities and script based solvabilities. In *Proceedings of the 2011 International Conference on Communication, Computing & Security*, pp. 477–482, 2011, February.

55. Alferidah, D.K. and Jhanjhi, N.Z., A review on security and privacy issues and challenges in internet of things. *International Journal of Computer Science and Network Security (IJCSNS)*, 20, 4, 263–286, 2020.

56. Camp, J., Asgharpour, F., Liu, D., Bloomington, I.N., Experimental evaluations of expert and non-expert computer users' mental models of security risks. *Proceedings of WEIS 2007*, pp. 1–24, 2007.

57. Chaudhary, S., Johari, R., Bhatia, R., Gupta, K., Bhatnagar, A., CRAIoT: Concept, review and application (s) of IoT, in: *2019 4th International Conference on Internet of Things: Smart Innovation and Usages (IoT-SIU)*, IEEE, pp. 1–4, 2019, April.

58. Cuffe, P., The role of the erc-20 token standard in a financial revolution: The case of initial coin offerings, in: *IEC-IEEE-KATS Academic Challenge*, IEC-IEEE-KATS, Busan, Korea, 22-23 October 2018.

59. Dong, Z. and Camp, L.J., PeerSec: Towards peer production and crowdsourcing for enhanced security, in: HotSec, 2012, August.

60. Hamledari, H., *Impact assessment of blockchain-enabled smart contracts on the visibility of construction payments*, Stanford University, 2021.

61. Hassan, M.U., Rehmani, M.H., Chen, J., Privacy preservation in blockchain based IoT systems: Integration issues, prospects, challenges, and future research directions. *Future Gener. Comput. Syst.*, 97, 512–529, 2019.

62. Khrais, L.T., Comparison study of blockchain technology and IOTA technology, in: *2020 Fourth International Conference on I-SMAC (IoT in Social, Mobile, Analytics and Cloud)(I-SMAC)*, IEEE, pp. 42–47, 2020, October.

63. Makhdoom, I., Abolhasan, M., Ni, W., January. Blockchain for IoT: The challenges and a way forward, in: *ICETE 2018-Proceedings of the 15th International Joint Conference on e-Business and Telecommunications*, 2018.

64. Shakya, V., Kumar, P.P., Tewari, L., Blockchain based cryptocurrency scope in India, in: *2021 5th International Conference on Intelligent Computing and Control Systems (ICICCS)*, IEEE, pp. 361–368, 2021, May.
65. Singh, A.K., Tripathi, A., Singh, K.K., Choudhary, P., Vashist, P.C., Artificial intelligence in medicine, in: *Machine Learning and the Internet of Medical Things in Healthcare*, pp. 67–87, Academic Press, 2021.

4

AIML-Based Blockchain Solutions for IoMT

Rishita Khurana[1], Manika Choudhary[1], Akansha Singh[2]*
and Krishna Kant Singh[3]

*¹Department of Computer Science and Engineering, Amity School of Engineering
and Technology Amity University, Noida, Uttar Pradesh, India*
*²School of Computer Science Engineering and Technology, Bennett University,
Greater Noida, India*
³Delhi Technical Campus, Greater Noida, India

Abstract

The ongoing increase in urbanization has required the social, ecological, and monetary advancement of urban areas in order to fundamentally upgrade living conditions. The Internet of Things (IoT), information and communication tools, and different advancements have been synchronized to determine the difficulties faced in smart cities. The key objective is to make the most adequate utilization of accessible assets and innovations to foster quality of life, which include support and efficiency in different fields such as healthcare, agriculture, communication, transport, and smart grid. The integration of emerging and evolving technologies can prove to be an important asset in dealing with the security issues that are prevalent in smart cities. For example, an IoT-enabled application can play a vital part here; however, it also presents different security, protection, dormancy, and dependability issues. To address these challenges, another evolving technology, i.e., blockchain integrated with artificial intelligence (AI) and machine learning (ML), can be employed to efficiently deal with the aforementioned data security and protection issues and can offer excellent assistance due to various services available, which include immutability, trust-free, and decentralization, among other features. In this work, a thorough review of AI–ML blockchain solutions for IoT communication is presented along with examination of the challenges observed and identified with blockchain use in the sixth-generation (6G) technology. Potential directions for surpassing these difficulties are mapped out.

Corresponding author: akanahasing@gmail.com

Akansha Singh, Anuradha Dhull and Krishna Kant Singh (eds.) Blockchain and Deep Learning
for Smart Healthcare, (73–94) © 2024 Scrivener Publishing LLC

Keywords: Artificial intelligence, blockchain, IoT, machine learning, communication, 6G networks

4.1 Introduction

The evolving technology Internet of Things (IoT) comprises smart devices that facilitate communication between one another. These devices are enabled to gather and trade information. In addition, IoT has a huge scope of life applications, including industry, transportation, coordination, medical care, brilliant climate, just as close to home, social gaming robots, and city data nowadays. These smart IoT devices can have a wired or a remote association. In this regard, the remote IoT is the primary concern. Different advancements and protocols in remote correspondence can be utilized to associate smart devices such as ZigBee, Internet Protocol Version 6 (IPv6), Bluetooth Low Energy (BLE), Near Field Communication (NFC), and Z-Wave.

The integration of IoT devices in building smart cities comes with a ton of difficulties and challenges. Some of these challenges refer to data storage, data processing, integrity, security, confidentiality, privacy, and communication.

In the field of communication, the sixth-generation (6G) network is gaining a lot of attention despite that a full coverage of the fifth-generation (5G) technology is not yet available and that its specifications are still in development. The main thrust in the 6G jump is the intrinsic associated knowledge in the telecommunication networks with advanced networking and artificial intelligence (AI) and machine learning (ML). However, the integration of AI and 6G does not yield better security and privacy. Therefore, the combination of novel technologies such as blockchain, AI, and ML with IoT can prove to be fruitful in terms of managing and dealing with the security and privacy issues in 6G network communication. The evolution from 1G to the 6G network in terms of security is displayed in Figure 4.1.

The standard capacity and the details of the 6G technology are yet to be characterized. Therefore, the literature is still extremely restricted, providing only scarce information on the security and protection provided by 6G networks. In this paper, we attempt to reveal insights into what security might mean for the imagined 6G network and to present a concise discussion of the related difficulties and relevant possible solutions.

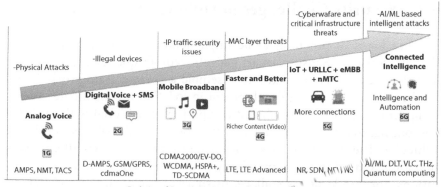

Evolution of Communication network security landscapes.

Figure 4.1 Evolution from 1G to 6G communication network in terms of security.

Specifically, the security and protection challenges that might emerge with the expected 6G necessities, new architecture design, new applications, and empowering advancements in technologies are studied. In addition, the possible security AI and ML blockchain solutions for 6G are examined.

4.2 Objective and Contribution

The primary aim of this review paper was to determine all the issues and challenges with IoT applications. The authors also discovered AI and ML blockchain solutions to overcome these challenges. The fundamental objective was to determine the research difficulties and the solutions for handling the security issues.

The contributions of this paper are as follows:

1. The paper discusses the challenges and security issues encountered while integrating IoT applications and identifies the corresponding solutions to these problems.
2. An overview of the evolution of the 6G network is presented.
3. Problems in various key domains such as healthcare, agriculture, communication, transport, and smart grid are also discussed.
4. A broad overview of comparable advancements such as AI-, ML-, and blockchain-integrated IoT solutions is presented and highlighted.

4.3   Security Challenges in Different Domains

IoT has loads of potential to be implemented in various applications that are constant. Sensors, smart gadgets, radiofrequency identification, and the Web are coordinated to assemble a shrewd framework. There has been so much recent development in IoT that it consolidates everything from sensors to distributed computing transitional with fog/edge computing. IoT has various types of networks, i.e., distributed, grid, and vehicular. The use of IoT has a massive effect on everyday life: sensors that are deployed in the human body to observe patients in critical conditions, for checking gas spillage, in smart kitchens, in the agriculture domain, and for smart transportation, among many others. Sensors are valuable devices that are associated through wired or wireless heterogeneous networks. However, the IoT networks also present various security and privacy issues. The issues encountered in various domains are discussed in this section. Figure 4.2 shows the prevalence of IoT in various domains.

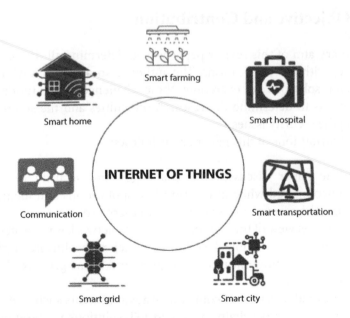

Figure 4.2 Internet of Things used in different domains.

4.4   Healthcare

Wearable IoT smart devices are an incredible innovation for patients as they can monitor the well-being of users and caution medical services even in critical situations. These are especially valuable for remote patients and senior patients who live on their own. Patients can now effectively monitor their pulse, blood pressure, calorie count, and significantly more. These data assist medical specialists with examining patients' clinical history, the information from which will similarly help with decision-making regarding changes in the administered medicines and the treatment plan. Since improvements in the continuous monitoring of patients using IoT are conceivable with the utilization of sensors and fog or edge computing, in Jaiswal *et al.* [1], an IoT-based cloud framework was proposed for information assortment in the medical care framework. In addition, in Moosavi *et al.* [2], the authentication and authorization of smart devices in the framework of medical services was performed. In the medical services framework, legitimate security and protection conventions should be created to guarantee information security.

4.5   Agriculture

One of the most promising and attractive application domains in IoT is agriculture. The sensors are deployed to screen the soil quality, manage the water supply, and develop conditions for growing crops, among others, which work on cultivating proficiency by decreasing the time and cost spent in a smart agriculture framework. A client can remotely screen all distinct features from far-off areas in real time. In studies [3, 4], the authors proposed a smart irrigation system by utilizing AI and IoT to improve farming. In addition, in Kamienski *et al.* [5], smart water management and the climate conditions in the farming framework were comprehensively discussed. A lot of studies have been performed in the agriculture domain by integrating technologies such as IoT, but data are still lacking in terms of a number of specific issues, including infrastructure, secure processing of the important information collected, and mobility.

4.6   Transportation

Smart transportation is changing how metropolitan regions approach versatility and crisis response while decreasing the clogging in city roads with the help of sensors, high-speed networks, and advanced communication technologies.

Development has made an extensive headway from using horses to get from one place to another. With the launch of smart transportation structures and IoT, the world is entering the accompanying period of advancements in transportation. The production and growth of IoT devices and 6G communication technologies will primarily facilitate more opportunities such as smart management, smart transportation, and smart monitoring. Smart transportation essentially makes a city more convenient and cost-effective. IoT-enabled vehicles can gather data from roadside to obtain information regarding routes, traffic, and travel time. In Neto *et al.* [6], the issues in smart transportation using IoT were addressed. In another study [7], an IoT-based intelligent transportation system (IoT-ITS) for smart transportation was proposed by the authors.

4.7   Smart Grid

Another application of IoT is smart grid, where a grid framework can be mechanized by utilizing IoT. IoT can perform real-time monitoring of the electric power generation and distribution among consumers. The network protection arrangement approach was extensively discussed in Yin *et al.* [8]. In Meloni *et al.* [9], an IoT cloud-based framework was proposed. The smart grid system can also be improved using IoT technology.

4.8   Smart City

IoT allows enabling the initiatives of smart cities worldwide. Smart cities provide the ability to perform necessary tasks remotely, such as managing and controlling devices, monitoring, and smart parking systems, among others. A developing city has a host of issues, including traffic and water, waste, and environmental management. A solution is necessary to screen, control, and resolve existing issues. In Gharaibeh *et al.* [10], the challenges and issues faced during the implementation of smart cities were determined and explained. A survey focusing on the solutions to the problems using IoT was also conducted. A smart city can develop more and more if security and privacy are maintained using AI, ML, and blockchain.

4.9   Smart Home

The smart home framework has now been changed to an intelligent one using IoT. Appliances including the fridge, TV, surveillance camera, gas and temperature sensor, and light can detect the home climate, communicate, and associate with the Web through a wired or remote network. Indeed, even the fridge can make a request to the enrolled retail shop and offer warnings to the client. Because of the improvements in smart appliances, the expectation for everyday comfort has become more agreeable. Singh *et al.* [11] presented a smart home framework that is dependent on IoT innovation.

4.10   Communication

The emerging and evolving 6G network will bring with it a lot of applications that will further need the extended capabilities of networks in comparison to the presently developed 5G network. There are a lot of implications on the implementation of security in 6G networks. With additional upgraded versatile broadband, extreme information rates will hinder difficulties with regard to traffic handling for security, e.g., attack detection, pipelines based on AI and ML, traffic investigation, and unavoidable encryption. The issue can be raised in a disseminated security system since traffic ought to be arranged regionally and in various sections of the organization, going from the edge to the center of the support cloud.

Specifically, IoT with extremely assorted capacities will challenge the safety arrangement and activity, e.g., AI/ML and security concerns. A significant viewpoint is the manner by which to incorporate novel security-enabled influences in data-heavy devices. In any case, the security requirement will be more complicated since the network elements will be significantly more versatile, changing the edge network every now and again and getting administration in various authoritative spaces. In the 6G network, AI/ML will be pushed perceptually closer to the source of information of interest for super low detectability while conducting ML capacities over the network in order to accomplish the execution gains due to streamlined models and dynamic gathering. Notwithstanding, defeating the pragmatic requirements of some network components such as IoT, for

Table 4.1 Related surveys on 6G utilizing blockchain, artificial intelligence, and Internet of Things.

Reference	Year of publication	Contribution
[12]	2021	The security issues and impediments of the IoT-enabled smart cities are examined and a blockchain-based design is presented for IoT-enabled smart city implementation.
[13]	2021	The impact of the tip determination strategy for DAG blockchain on range allocation utility is investigated. A unique tip determination strategy for worldwide utility, based on the range supply–demand, is also presented.
[14]	2020	An original design of intelligent 6G-based QoE and QoS enhancement in modern NIB and a 6G-based NIB system is presented in relation to the drawn-out development.
[15]	2020	This paper presents and studies some best-in-class procedures dependent on AI and ML and their applications in 6G to help ultra broadband, ultra massive access, and ultra reliable and low-latency administration.
[16]	2020	The rapidly expanding RoF market and related technologies from the merging of IoT–RoF with discussion on the current innovations in different dimensions are presented. Moreover, the challenges for RoF-supported 6G–IoT framework and emerging technology solutions are discussed.
[17]	2020	The survey gauges fundamental difficulties in the incorporation of blockchain and IoT to accomplish significant levels of arrangements by addressing the inadequacies and limitations of both technologies.

DAG, directed acyclic graph; *QoE*, quality of experience; *QoS*, quality of service; *NIB*, network in box; *RoF*, radio over fiber; *AI*, artificial intelligence; *ML*, machine learning; *IoT*, Internet of Things.

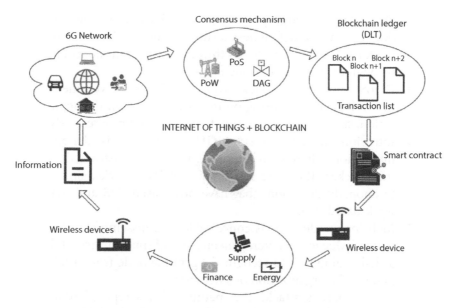

Figure 4.3 Blockchain in the sixth-generation (6G) system.

example, computational inadequacies and intermittent networks are difficult tasks. Some relevant work has also been done in the field of communication utilizing blockchain, AI, and IoT, which is detailed in Table 4.1.

The 6G system confers numerous benefits, and one of them is endogenous security. To adjust to the current remote network, the plan for the 6G security framework will take on a disseminated and decentralized design. With comparable qualities of minimization and appropriated structure to 6G, blockchain innovation is a fundamental apparatus for improving the execution of 6G endogenous security. The process of the integration of IoT with blockchain in 6G is depicted in Figure 4.3.

4.11   Security Attacks in IoT

The most common IoT attacks are outlined below.

1. Jamming attack: This is a subpart of the denial of service (DoS) attack in which the assailant attempts to influence and disturb the channel of communication. In López *et al.* [18], insights regarding jamming attack were further clarified by the authors.

2. DoS attack: A large portion of IoT devices are low-end devices that are defenseless against assailants. In this type of attack, the attacker floods the server with Internet traffic through the framework/machine.

3. DDoS: This type of attack involves an immense volume of network packets focusing on the node present in the application, causing administration to be hindered progressively.

4. Intrusion detection system (IDS) attack: This denotes interaction wherein the network traffic is constrained by the attacker. There are a few types of IDS attacks, similar to anomaly detection, that have host-based IDS and network-based IDS.

5. Malicious node: This is conceivable in a disseminated IoT network due to the heterogeneous idea of smart devices. It is a challenging task to recognize a genuine node from a fake node in the organization of a network.

6. Power analysis attack: The method of this type of attack has been clarified in studies. This is primarily performed to acquire the computational force of the nodes so that the fundamental cryptographic calculation cannot be executed in IoT network protection, which should likewise be maintained to establish trust among nodes.

7. Internal attack: Internal attack was discussed in Tariq et al. [19], while access control attack was examined in detail in Yan et al. [20].

8. Wormhole attack: This attack occurs at the IPv6 over low-power wireless personal area network (6LoWPAN) layer where the attacker attempts a passage between two nodes that are associated.

9. Side-channel security attack: Cloud-based IoT applications alongside the security challenges are clarified in Yi et al. [21].

10. Man-in-the-middle attack: In this type of attack, the message or the change in message is relayed by the attacker at the time of transmission in the insecure channel, which is explained in Li et al. [22].

4.12   Solutions for Addressing Security Using Machine Learning

ML is a strategy used to perform computations intelligently. The model necessitates planning and testing the utilization of distinct learning strategies. As previously discussed, there are numerous applications of IoT. Part of the application prerequisites is that choice ought to be taken before the actual condition happens. For instance, foreseeing the fire in a kitchen or any modern region and alerting the sound to forestall the fire. This could be conceivable if ML innovations are utilized in applications of IoT. Similarly, the security issue present in the IoT framework needs to be addressed in order to make the framework more secure. In Kotenko et al. [23], a proficient system was required to measure and register the massive information assortment utilizing the ML strategy. In Hossain et al. [24], a survey was conducted to address the security issue faced when utilizing ML in an application of smart networks. In Deng et al. [25], interruption recognition in IoT applications was addressed.

4.13   Solutions for Addressing Security Using Artificial Intelligence

The development of smart devices with a detection and operation capacity makes the IoT framework more convenient. The number of devices associated with the network is huge, creating an enormous volume of information. Measuring and performing calculations are difficult tasks in IoT. Therefore, AI proves to be fruitful technology, along with other emerging technologies that address the security issues in IoT. As displayed in Figure 4.5, IoT and AI can be combined for the investigation of the framework, to work on functional productivity, and to further develop the precision rate. Wang et al. [26] provided proof that AI could assist with the immense volume, unstructured information, and heterogeneous information to be registered continuously, which makes the framework reasonable. Zolotukhin et al. [27] proposed a large margin cosine estimation (LMCE) technique to distinguish the attacker in IoT-enabled applications. In Falco et al. [28], malware detection work in the IoT system was addressed utilizing AI.

Essentially, in Gia *et al.* [29], a model utilizing blockchain and AI in the IoT framework was proposed in order to make the framework design tamper-proof. Figure 4.4 displays the integration of IoT and AI, with some fundamental advantages shown. Researchers have indicated that AI can be the main thrust for IoT applications through their integration. Table 4.2 discusses the contributions to IoT security through the utilization of AI and ML.

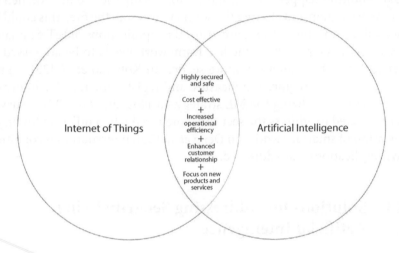

Internet of Things

Highly secured
and safe
+
Cost effective
+
Increased
operational
efficiency
+
Enhanced
customer
relationship
+
Focus on new
products and
services

Artificial Intelligence

Figure 4.4 Diagram of the integration of Internet of Things and artificial intelligence.

Table 4.2 Related survey work on 6G utilizing artificial intelligence and machine learning.

Reference	Year of publication	Contribution
[30]	2021	The proposed model handles the security issues concerning the dangers from bots. Distinctive AI calculations, e.g., k-nearest neighbor (KNN), naive Bayes model, and multilayer perceptron artificial neural network (MLP-ANN), were utilized to create a model where information is prepared by the BoT-IoT dataset.

(Continued)

Table 4.2 Related survey work on 6G utilizing artificial intelligence and machine learning. (*Continued*)

Reference	Year of publication	Contribution
[31]	2021	The authors distinguish AI as an answer to address a part of the current computational and security challenges. The execution stage accessible for the integration of IoT with AI is also clarified in the paper.
[32]	2020	A survey of the prerequisites of security and current security solutions for IoT domains is efficiently discussed. The authors also shed light on the gaps in the security framework that call for AI and ML solutions.
[33]	2020	The framework of IoT is examined following a comprehensive examination of ML approaches regarding the significance of the safety of IoT in terms of various types of potential attacks.
[34]	2019	The emphasis in this paper is primarily on IoT NIDS through ML as the learning calculations showed decent rates in terms of security and protection. The study provides a thorough investigation of various NIDS proposals for IoT, which is different from other reviews that focused on conventional frameworks.
[35]	2019	The proposed model is exhibited to be able to naturally recognize IoT devices in the system, regardless of whether network action is malicious or harmless, and to effectively identify which attack was sent on which device associated with the system.
[36]	2019	The most popular rule-based AI arrangement method, i.e., decision tree, is applied on the noise-free quality dataset to fabricate the prediction model.

(*Continued*)

Table 4.2 Related survey work on 6G utilizing artificial intelligence and machine learning. (*Continued*)

Reference	Year of publication	Contribution
[37]	2021	A secure structure for IoT dependent on SDN is proposed. The structure is a theory for the incorporation of SDN and IoT. The primary focus is on IoT developments, e.g., brilliant smart city applications, where security is basic and network traffic is colossal.

ML, machine learning; *IoT*, Internet of Things; *NIDS*, network-based intrusion detection system; *SDN*, software-defined networking.

4.14 Solutions for Addressing Security Using Blockchain

The blockchain technology is a decentralized system where each block is associated with one another. The message is communicated in the blockchain organization. In Figure 4.5, the distributed framework dependent on blockchain technology in IoT applications is displayed. A block basically comprises heaps of legitimate exchange and its related qualities. The smart contracts in Mohanta *et al.* [38] are self-executable programs used to complete the business transactions in the system. Diverse consensus algorithms are utilized by the blockchain network, as in Panda *et al.* [39], to reach agreement among nodes. The details of the blockchain design and

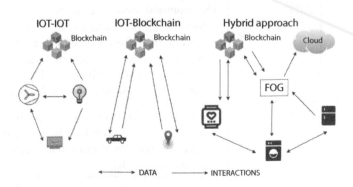

Figure 4.5 Integration of Internet of Things and blockchain.

application regions are described in Hakak *et al.* [40]. In Ahmed *et al.* [41], the authors portrayed the system and the related work on IoT security alongside blockchain as an organization approach. The utilization of blockchain technology in IoT is briefly discussed in Minoli [42]. Several of the security challenges in IoT and a comparison of blockchain solutions, alongside the execution challenges, are examined in Sharma *et al.* [43]. In Table 4.3, details of the surveys with regard to blockchain and IoT security issues are portrayed.

Table 4.3 Related surveys on Internet of Things security utilizing blockchain.

Reference	Year of publication	Contribution
[44]	2021	This paper discusses the concept of blockchain and the relevant factors that provide a detailed analysis of potential security attacks and present existing solutions that can be deployed as countermeasures to such attacks.
[45]	2021	This article deliberately breaks down the best in class of IoT security dependent on blockchain, giving extraordinary consideration to the security highlights, issues, innovations, approaches, and related situations in blockchain-imbedded IoT. The integration of blockchain and IoT is a significant and expected advance in the computational correspondence framework.
[46]	2020	A conceptual framework for securing smart city utilizing blockchain technology is proposed and explained through a possible use case investigation. An overview of a realistic three-blockchain-based smart city is also introduced.
[47]	2020	An assessment of the security issues resolved using ML, AI, and blockchain with research challenges is presented.

(Continued)

Table 4.3 Related surveys on Internet of Things security utilizing blockchain. (*Continued*)

Reference	Year of publication	Contribution
[48]	2020	Contextual analysis is performed utilizing the Ethereum-based blockchain framework in a brilliant IoT framework and the outcomes are examined.
[49]	2019	This paper focuses on addressing important security issues in IoT and outlines these issues against existing solutions found in the literature.
[50]	2018	This paper proposes a system of high-level security dependent on blockchain for various IoT devices in the full life cycle. In addition, it recommends issues for further research and future work.
[51]	2018	This paper expounds on the possible security and privacy issues considering the communication of the components of IoT and focuses on how the distributed ledger-based blockchain (DL-BC) technology adds to it.

IoT, Internet of Things; *ML*, machine learning; *AI*, artificial intelligence.

4.15 Summary

The authors have investigated the security and privacy issues encountered while executing the IoT technology in various domains on the conversion of cities into smart cities. Different databases including IEEE Xplore, ScienceDirect, and Google Scholar, among others, were searched in order to determine the work done in solving these challenges. The articles were thoroughly read and examined before making the decision to include them in the tables provided. The aim of this survey was to highlight and identify the solutions for addressing the aforementioned issues and challenges. Privacy and security concerns have been proven to be the most difficult tasks that need addressing in order to ensure the success of the implementation and use of IoT applications.

4.16   Critical Analysis

1. Machine learning and artificial intelligence
There are two types of ML: supervised and unsupervised learning. IoT applications create a massive amount of data. Information is required throughout the confirmation cycle in order to avoid any malicious or repetitive information before the calculation is done. A total of 15 research papers addressing security issues in IoT applications were considered for the survey; eight of these studies were finally included in the analysis. The IoT technology tends to be accompanied with various security issues such as an intrusion identification framework, malware detection, distributed DoS, jamming attack, authentication, and anomaly detection, among others.

2. Blockchain
In the review, the characteristics of blockchain technology and a comparison of research studies are referenced in Table 4.2. It was found that blockchain is the most promising innovation recently developed by analysts to address the security issues in IoT applications. Identity verification, secure communication, authentication, authorization, and access control are just some of the security issues that are addressed by blockchain technology.

4.17   Conclusion

In this chapter, the authors have thoroughly explored the different security challenges that exist in IoT applications. Furthermore, an overview of how to address the prevailing security challenges was provided. From the review, it was discovered that a number of studies have already been performed on different innovations including ML, AI, and blockchain technology, which were found to be able to address the current security issues. Hence, an exhaustive study was conducted on these technologies--AI, ML, and blockchain—and their combination with IoT. Security is a significant issue that requires addressing. In this paper, the authors highlighted the emerging innovations ML, Al, and blockchain incorporated into IoT in order to make the IoT framework safer for use in different domains.

References

1. Jaiswal, K. *et al.*, An IoT-cloud based smart healthcare monitoring system using container based virtual environment in edge device. *2018 International Conference on Emerging Trends and Innovations in Engineering and Technological Research (ICETIETR)*, IEEE, 2018.
2. Moosavi, S.R. *et al.*, SEA: A secure and efficient authentication and authorization architecture for IoT-based healthcare using smart gateways. *Proc. Comput. Sci.*, 52, 452–4595, 2015.
3. Mehra, M., *et al.*, IoT based hydroponics system using deep neural networks. *Comput. Electron. Agric.*, 155, 473–4865, 2018.
4. Goap, A. *et al.*, An IoT based smart irrigation management system using machine learning and open source technologies. *Comput. Electron. Agric.*, 155, 41–495, 2018.
5. Kamienski, C. *et al.*, Smart water management platform: IoT-based precision irrigation for agriculture. *Sensors*, 19, 2, 276, 2019.
6. Neto, A.J.V. *et al.*, Fog-based crime-assistance in smart iot transportation system. *IEEE Access*, 6, 11101–111115, 2018.
7. Muthuramalingam, S. *et al.*, IoT based intelligent transportation system (IoT-ITS) for global perspective: A case study, in: *Internet of Things and Big Data Analytics for Smart Generation*, pp. 279–300, Springer, Cham, 2019.
8. Yin, X.C. *et al.*, Toward an applied cyber security solution in IoT-based smart grids: An intrusion detection system approach. *Sensors*, 19, 22, 4952, 2019.
9. Meloni, A. *et al.*, Cloud-based IoT solution for state estimation in smart grids: Exploiting virtualization and edge-intelligence technologies. *Comput. Netw.*, 130, 156–165, 2018.
10. Gharaibeh, A. *et al.*, Smart cities: A survey on data management, security, and enabling technologies. *IEEE Commun. Surv. Tutor.*, 19, 4, 2456–2501, 2017.
11. Singh, K.K., Elhoseny, M., Singh, A., Elngar, A.A. (Eds.), *Machine Learning and the Internet of Medical Things in Healthcare*, Academic Press, 2021.
12. Kumari, A., Gupta, R., Tanwar, S., Amalgamation of blockchain and IoT for smart cities underlying 6G communication: A comprehensive review. *Comput. Commun.*, 172, 2021, 102–108, 2021.
13. Zhang, H. *et al.*, A DAG blockchain enhanced user-autonomy spectrum sharing framework for 6G-enabled IoT. *IEEE Internet Things J.*, 9.11, 2021, 8012–8023, 2021.
14. Du, J. *et al.*, Machine learning for 6G wireless networks: Carrying forward enhanced bandwidth, massive access, and ultra reliable/low-latency service. *IEEE Veh. Technol. Mag.*, 15, 4, 122–134, 2020.
15. Chen, N. and Okada, M., Toward 6G Internet of Things and the convergence with RoF system. *IEEE Internet Things J.*, 8, 11, 8719–8733, 2020.
16. Sekaran, R. *et al.*, Survival study on blockchain based 6G-enabled mobile edge computing for IoT automation. *IEEE Access*, 8, 143453–143463, 2020.

17. Sodhro, A.H. *et al.*, Towards ML-based energy-efficient mechanism for 6G enabled industrial network in box systems. *IEEE Trans. Industr. Inform.*, 17.10, 2020, 7185–7192, 2020.
18. López, M., Peinado, A., Ortiz, A., An extensive validation of a SIR epidemic model to study the propagation of jamming attacks against IoT wireless networks. *Comput. Netw.*, 165, 106945, 2019.
19. Tariq, N. *et al.*, A blockchain-based multi-mobile code-driven trust mechanism for detecting internal attacks in the internet of things. *Sensors*, 21, 1, 23, 2021.
20. Yan, H. *et al.*, IoT-FBAC: Function-based access control scheme using identity-based encryption in IoT. *Future Gener. Comput. Syst.*, 95, 344–353, 2019.
21. Yi, H. and Nie, Z., Side-channel security analysis of UOV signatures for cloud-based Internet of Things. *Future Gener. Comput. Syst.*, 86, 704–708, 2018.
22. Li, C. *et al.*, Securing SDN infrastructure of IoT–fog networks from MitM attacks. *IEEE Internet Things J.*, 4, 5, 1156–1164, 2017.
23. Kotenko, I., Saenko, I., Branitsky, A., Framework for mobile Internet of Things security monitoring based on big data processing and machine learning. *IEEE Access*, 6, 72714–72723, 2018.
24. Hossain, E. *et al.*, Application of big data and machine learning in smart grid, and associated security concerns: A review. *IEEE Access*, 7, 13960–13988, 2019.
25. Deng, L. *et al.*, Mobile network intrusion detection for IoT systems based on transfer learning algorithm. *Cluster Comput.*, 22, 4, 9889–9904, 2019.
26. Wang, S. and Qiao, Z., Robust pervasive detection for adversarial samples of artificial intelligence in IoT environments. *IEEE Access*, 7, 88693–88704, 2019.
27. Zolotukhin, M. and Hämäläinen., T., On artificial intelligent malware tolerant networking for IoT. *2018 IEEE Conference on Network Function Virtualization and Software Defined Networks (NFV-SDN)*, IEEE, 2018.
28. Falco, G. *et al.*, A master attack methodology for an AI-based automated attack planner for smart cities. *IEEE Access*, 6, 48360–48373, 2018.
29. Gia, T.N. *et al.*, Edge AI in smart farming IoT: CNNs at the edge and fog computing with LoRa. *2019 IEEE AFRICON*, IEEE, 2019.
30. Pokhrel, S., Abbas, R., Aryal, B., *IoT security: Botnet detection in IoT using machine learning*, 2021, arXiv preprint arXiv:2104.02231.
31. Mohanta, B.K., Satapathy, U., Jena, D., Addressing security and computation challenges in IoT using machine learning, in: *Advances in Distributed Computing and Machine Learning*, pp. 67–74, Springer, Singapore, 2021.
32. Hussain, F. *et al.*, Machine learning in IoT security: Current solutions and future challenges. *IEEE Commun. Surv. Tutor.*, 22, 3, 1686–1721, 2020.

33. Tahsien, S.M., Karimipour, H., Spachos, P., Machine learning based solutions for security of Internet of Things (IoT): A survey. *J. Netw. Comput. Appl.*, 161, 102630, 2020.

34. Chaabouni, N. *et al.*, Network intrusion detection for IoT security based on learning techniques. *IEEE Commun. Surv. Tutor.*, 21, 3, 2671–2701, 2019.

35. Anthi, E. *et al.*, A supervised intrusion detection system for smart home IoT devices. *IEEE Internet Things J.*, 6, 5, 9042–9053, 2019.

36. Sarker, I.H., A machine learning based robust prediction model for real-life mobile phone data. *Internet Things*, 5, 180–193, 2019.

37. Singh, P., Singh, N., Singh, K.K., Singh, A., Diagnosing of disease using machine learning, in: *Machine Learning and the Internet of Medical Things in Healthcare*, pp. 89–111, Academic Press, 2021.

38. Mohanta, B.K., Panda, S.S., Jena., D., An overview of smart contract and use cases in blockchain technology. *2018 9th International Conference on Computing, Communication and Networking Technologies (ICCCNT)*, IEEE, 2018.

39. Panda, S.S. *et al.*, Study of blockchain based decentralized consensus algorithms. *TENCON 2019-2019 IEEE Region 10 Conference (TENCON)*, IEEE, 2019.

40. Hakak, S. *et al.*, *Recent advances in blockchain technology: A survey on applications and challenges*, 2020, arXiv preprint arXiv:2009.05718.

41. Ahmed, S.T., Kumar, V.V., Singh, K.K., Singh, A., Muthukumaran, V., Gupta, D., 6G enabled federated learning for secure IoMT resource recommendation and propagation analysis. *Comput. Electr. Eng.*, 102, 108210, 2022.

42. Minoli, D., Positioning of blockchain mechanisms in IoT-powered smart home systems: A gateway-based approach. *Internet Things*, 10, 100147, 2020.

43. Sharma, D. K., *et al.*, Optimized resource allocation in IoT using fuzzy logic and bio-inspired algorithms. *Wirel. Pers. Commun.*, 1–21, 2023.

44. Gupta, R., Rakhra, A., Singh, A., Internet of Things security using AI and blockchain, in: *Machine Learning Approaches for Convergence of IoT and Blockchain*, pp. 57–91, 2021.

45. Da X., Li, Y. L., Ling L., Embedding blockchain technology into IoT for security: A survey. *IEEE Internet Things J.*, 8.13, 2021, 10452–10473, 2023.

46. Hakak, S. *et al.*, Securing smart cities through blockchain technology: Architecture, requirements, and challenges. *IEEE Netw.*, 34, 1, 8–14, 2020.

47. Mohanta, B.K. *et al.*, Survey on IoT security: Challenges and solutions using machine learning, artificial intelligence and blockchain technology. *Internet Things*, 11, 100227, 2020.

48. Mohanta, B.K. *et al.*, Addressing security and privacy issues of IoT using blockchain technology. *IEEE Internet Things J.*, 8, 2, 881–888, 2020.

49. Sultan, A., Mushtaq, M.A., Abubakar, M., IoT security issues via blockchain: A review paper. *Proceedings of the 2019 International Conference on Blockchain Technology*, 2019.
50. Qian, Y. *et al.*, Towards decentralized IoT security enhancement: A blockchain approach. *Comput. Electr. Eng.*, 72, 266–273, 2018.
51. Kumar, N.M. and Mallick, P.K., Blockchain technology for security issues and challenges in IoT. *Proc. Comput. Sci.*, 132, 1815–1823, 2018.

5

A Blockchain-Based Solution for Enhancing Security and Privacy in the Internet of Medical Things (IoMT) Used in e-Healthcare

Meenakshi[1]* and Preeti Sharma[2]

[1]Computer Science and Engineering Department, SOET, BML Munjal University,
Gurgaon, Haryana, India
[2]Computer Science and Engineering, CUIET, Chitkara University, Rajpura,
Punjab, India

Abstract

This paper proposes a novel architecture in the domain of the Internet of Medical Things (IoMT) in e-healthcare addressing security and privacy challenges. It also provides an analysis of the safety and confidentiality challenges, along with necessities, threats, and upcoming scope of research. With outstanding development IoMT has a massive impact on people's normal lifestyle. For instance, instead of a physical visit to the clinic, a patient's medical history data are remotely handled and processed in a real-time framework and thereafter moved to a third party for later use, i.e., data stored in a cloud. With the increasing requirements on quality medical care and the constantly rising care expenses, system- and web-oriented medical care is considered as an innovative solution to address medical challenges worldwide. Specifically, the new advances in the Internet of Things (IoT) have prompted the development of IoMT. Albeit such cost-effective and web-based systems and devices might actually change the current responsive care to preventive care, concerns regarding the privacy and security of patient data in such web-based frameworks are frequently ignored. As medical devices obtain and cycle individual health-related sensitive information, these gadgets and their related correspondence must therefore be exceptionally secure in order to ensure the privacy of patients. Miniature IoMT devices have a limited calculation power, and genuinely restricted security features can be executed in these gadgets. Moreover, with their wide utilization, managing these devices and guaranteeing the safety of

*Corresponding author: preetisharma@ncuindia.edu

Akansha Singh, Anuradha Dhull and Krishna Kant Singh (eds.) Blockchain and Deep Learning for Smart Healthcare, (95–112) © 2024 Scrivener Publishing LLC

the IoMT framework are becoming a challenge, which are proving as significant issues that hinder the implementation of IoMT in medical applications. This paper recommends a novel design in the area of IoMT in e-medical care addressing the security and protection challenges. In addition, it explores the security and protection challenges, prerequisites, dangers, and future research directions.

Keywords: IoMT, security, privacy, blockchain, health, IoT

5.1   Introduction: E-Health and Medical Services

Blockchain is a universal distributed ledger technology that simplifies the process of recording transactions and tracking assets throughout the corporate network. These can either be houses, cars, money, and land or intangible assets such as intellectual property rights, i.e., patents and author's rights, or other valuables [1] that can be sold and tracked on the blockchain network, reducing the risks and costs for each participant. This is the perfect move for blockchain. By considering an efficient and affordable blockchain development environment, one can gain a deeper understanding of the system [2]. A reliable and secure system is needed to execute and record financial transactions.

To overcome these and other challenges, there is a need for fast payment networks, trust-building mechanisms that do not require special hardware and monthly refunds or fees, and transparent and reliable scrapbooking solutions. Industrialized countries spend a large portion of their gross domestic product (GDP) on healthcare; however, hospital costs continue to rise due to ineffective practices and the loss of health data [3].

This is where blockchain generation can provide improvements. Blockchain enables a lot of processes, e.g., from securely encrypting an affected individual's statistics to handling outbreaks [4]. Estonia is a pioneer on this subject, commencing the application of the advantages of blockchain in the healthcare domain in 2012 [5]. Currently, blockchain is used to manage the healthcare billing system, 94% of clinical data, and 98% of prescription data [6].

5.1.1   What is Blockchain?

The term "blockchain" refers to common immutable transaction chains where every transaction chain is a block, and these blocks are saved collectively with an encryption key ("hash"). These keys or signatures are saved in shared registers with the help of node grids or the manner linking them [7]. Each node has a duplicate of the complete chain that is continuously synchronized and updated. According to the National Institute of Standards and Technology (NIST), the advantages of blockchain standards and technology encompass protection from unauthorized access. The decentralized nature of the virtual ledger and the lack of ability to adjust transactions published later with the aid of using the network of customers at the shared ledger [8]. This generation is likewise referred to as distributed ledger technology (DLT) [9].

5.1.2   What are the Advantages and Challenges of Blockchain in Healthcare?

The most important challenges for blockchain applications in the healthcare sector include the following:

- Security of the network infrastructure at all levels;
- Identity verification of all participants; and
- Unified authorization template for accessing electronic health information.

DLT could be used in a lot fitness care areas; however, not all of fitness care activities are transactional. Due to the information on the general public chain being broadly distributed, these data cannot be used to select personal statistics along with fitness information identification. Providers need to consider privacy issues in order to assist in securing fitness statistics (protected health information, PHI) [10]. Secondly, blockchain presents risks of various attacks, even though it provides integrated safety from different digital attacks. Therefore, significant consideration must be given to data security, especially within the subject of scientific care [11].

Blockchain generation should no longer be used indiscriminately in healthcare due to blockchain data being immutable. This might not be viable for obtaining massive amounts of data or information that can be regularly changed [44]. All identity data need to be stored off-chain [12]. DLT expert comment: With the upward push of the General Data Protection Regulation (GDPR) coupled with the Health Insurance Portability and Accountability (HIPAA), as well as the different policies that have been implemented for more than a decade, an individual's privacy has now emerged as shaping the management of PHI [13]. Compared with conventional healthcare methods, the use of blockchain entails decentralized control, immutable databases, data sources, traceable data, and reliable data, as well as the supply of data to any legal consumer through encryption of an individual's non-public key. Therefore, prevention of unauthorized access to the database control system [14] is necessary.

5.2   Literature Review

Huang and his team [15] outlined the benefits of blockchain. In addition, they looked at the challenges and potential outcomes and how these may be applied to more healthcare sectors. The current state of blockchain application development in the healthcare industry, as well as its limitations and potential study areas, is covered in the article. This study attempted to show how blockchain technology may be applied in healthcare, what issues this technology might encounter in the future, and what the future holds for blockchain.

In Mukherjee *et al.* [16], the authors focused on how blockchain technology can be used in the agricultural sector and offered a comparative review of the current approaches aimed at enhancing the security, efficacy, and the dependability of blockchain-based food supply chains. An innovative approach that combines blockchain with Internet of Things (IoT)-based sensor modules was also presented in this study, which is applicable in real-world situations. The suggested approach essentially uses a multi-tier design with blockchain technology present in each layer. Environmental conditions that might affect crop quality feed each layer.

Benchoufi and Ravaud [17] presented the fundamental idea behind blockchain, which is that any service dependent on reliable third parties can be developed at the top of the blockchain in a transparent, decentralized, secure, and "trustless" manner (in fact, there is trust, but it is hardcoded in the blockchain protocol *via* a complex cryptographic algorithm). Users therefore have a great deal of autonomy, control, and faith in the accuracy and reliability of the data. Blockchain enables a clinical trial's entire document flow to reach a significant level of historicity and data inviolability. As a result, it guarantees traceability, precludes *a posteriori* reconstruction, and enables safely automating the clinical study using so-called smart contracts.

The study by Zhang *et al.* [18] offered assessment measures to evaluate blockchain-based distributed applications (dApps) for compliance of the healthcare industry, their expected capability, and feasibility.

Blockchain technology has the potential to contribute to personalized, authentic, and secure healthcare in the future by combining all real-time clinical data related to a patient's health and presenting these in a modern secure healthcare environment. By using blockchain as a model, both the recent and current changes in the healthcare industry were examined in Siyal *et al.* [1], along with the difficulties encountered and the prospects for the future. The uses of blockchain were also discussed.

The analysis of blockchain data is useful for both academic and commercial purposes. In Kalodner *et al.* [4], BlockSci, an open-source blockchain analysis software platform, was introduced. BlockSci is flexible in terms of supporting various blockchains and analysis tasks. It is orders of magnitude faster than when utilizing general-purpose graph databases as it uses an analytical (as opposed to transactional) in-memory database. The architecture of BlockSci was described in this paper; moreover, four analyses that demonstrated its functionality, shedding light on the economic, security, and privacy aspects of cryptocurrencies, were provided.

In the study by Fröwis *et al.* [5], the authors concentrated on clustering algorithms and attribution tags, which are essential components of contemporary Bitcoin analytics methodologies. Generally accepted guidelines and standards for supporting claims and presenting evidence in court were then established, and these were extrapolated to contemporary Bitcoin forensic procedures. Potential sources of erroneous interpretations in algorithmic clustering techniques were also demonstrated by giving an empirical examination of CoinJoin transactions. In order to promote compliance with current legal and technical standards in the field of cryptocurrency forensics, a set of legal key requirements was constructed and translated into a technical data sharing framework. Modern Bitcoin analytics tools could be integrated with the suggested framework to enable more effective and efficient investigations while protecting the analytical evidence and the fundamental rights of individuals who may be impacted.

An intangible good that is not physically transmitted from the seller to the buyer is called service. However, due to dishonest buyers and brokers, traditional trading platforms have set several limits in terms of trading services. In Liu *et al.* [10], STEB, a blockchain-based service trading ecosystem that combines blockchain technology with smart contracts, encryption, and digital authentication methods, was proposed. In order to guarantee the integrity of the transaction data and provide precise user privacy protection, a dual-chain design that combines two different blockchains—TraChain and SerChain—and a hierarchical encryption scheme of the data on the chain were also proposed.

The study of Schniederjans *et al.* [12] aimed to understand future research questions so that scholars can widen their views and use knowledge mangement to advance the supply chain digitization research paradigm. This accomplished through both an extensive review of the literature and textual analysis and predictions on the digitization-related industry and field applications, technologies, and subjects. This paper applied the field of knowledge management to supply chain management using a theoretical framework for knowledge management and offered future research questions about how scholars can use the largely untapped areas of supply chain digitization and the emerging areas to explain how the human dimension of supply chain management can be further explored in order to optimize supply chain digital performance.

There are numerous approaches for technological developments to increase the effectiveness of electronic health record (EHR) and personal health record (PHR) system implementation. The clinical narratives and other unstructured data contained in EHRs and PHRs can be mined for information using natural language processing techniques that are rule-based or machine learning- and deep learning-based. This enables secondary research (i.e., phenotyping). Furthermore, it is anticipated that the application of blockchain technology on health information systems will primarily benefit EHRs and PHRs. The biggest obstacles to using these technologies are governance restrictions, a lack of trust, insufficient scalability, security, privacy, poor performance, and exorbitant costs [14].

Because of its characteristics including decentralization, immutability, transparency, and traceability, blockchain is a practical technology that can enhance the healthcare data sharing and storing system. However, due to security and authorization concerns, interoperability issues, and a lack of technical expertise in blockchain technology, many healthcare organizations are still unwilling to implement this technology [19].

The goal of Bumblauskas and his team [20] was to illustrate how a corporation situated in the Midwest of the United States is implementing blockchain technology in the manufacturing and supply chain delivery system for eggs from farm to consumer. How blockchain might be used and deployed to transport commodities across global supply chains more precisely and transparently was one of the main research concerns addressed. Blockchain and IoT-enabled technology were adopted to monitor products from farm to fork. By establishing traceable and transparent food supply chains, consumers could also obtain the information they need to make informed decisions about the food they buy and the companies they support.

Blockchain technology makes it possible to have a distributed, decentralized environment without the need for centralized power. Transactions are secure and reliable due to the application of cryptographic principles. Blockchain technology has dominated several industries in recent years, largely due to the popularity and the positive interest generated b cryptocurrencies. Healthcare is one industry where the blockchain technology has enormous potential as it can help integrate fragmented systems and improve the management of electronic medical data, taking a more patient-centered approach to healthcare systems (EHRs). The most recent blockchain research in the healthcare industry was analyzed in this systematic review. The objective was to highlight the obstacles and potential directions of blockchain research in healthcare, as well as to showcase the potential uses of this technology [21].

The inherent transparency of blockchain allowed enabling user- and group-based secret sharing by integrating custom software that makes use of a number of well-known cryptographic techniques. Cyran [22] created a containerized solution to speed up deployment, which ensures portability, makes the installation simple, and lowers the administrative overhead maintenance expenses. This blockchain solution was created using a distributed microservice architecture to ensure simplicity of implementation in a hospital system. This architecture enables separating the system's essential functions into independent services that can be scaled as needed to meet the needs of a particular hospital system deployment.

If systems are modified to resolve shortcomings by developing more standardized systems that are simpler to use, are truly interoperable, and offer patients better access to and control over their health data, Kellermann and Jones [3] believed that the original promises of health information technology (IT) can be realized. However, providers must play their share by redesigning care procedures to fully benefit from the efficiencies provided by health IT, within the framework of revised payment schemes that are value-based, i.e., prioritize patient care.

5.3   Architecture of Blockchain-Enabled IoMT

The use of blockchain in conjunction with IoMT has the ability to overcome concerns regarding security and privacy. This is referred to as blockchain-enabled IoMT. The architecture of blockchain-enabled IoMT is shown in Figure 5.1.

5.3.1   Opportunities of Blockchain-Enabled IoMT

IoMT is affected by concerns of safety and confidentiality. Incorporating blockchain into IoMT has opened up possibilities for addressing such concerns. The study by Chanson *et al.* [23] shed light on the benefits of blockchain-enabled IoMT in the aforementioned areas.

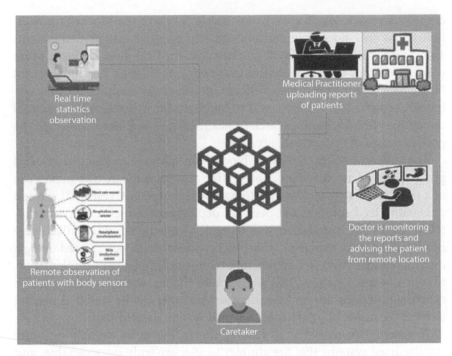

Figure 5.1 Blockchain-enabled Internet of Medical Things (IoMT) architecture.

5.3.2   Security Improvement of IoMT

The decentralization of blockchain could lower the risk of failure of the system caused by single-point failures or further malicious activities, such as distributed denial-of-service (DDoS) attacks, hence improving the security and reliability of the system [24].

The incorporation of blockchain into IoMT can possibly enhance the security in IoMT fundamentally [43]. Firstly, the implicit security features of blockchain, including asymmetric encryption/decryption schemes and computerized signature, could support the protection of IoMT data. Secondly, combining blockchain with an extra security mechanism, e.g., authentication and access controls, could additionally upgrade the security of the framework [25]. Thirdly, brilliant contracts included in IoT devices can consequently initiate auto-upgrade algorithms for firmware update of these devices, similarly improving the security of the system [42]. Furthermore, the decentralization of blockchain may lessen the risk of framework failure caused by single-point failure or additional malicious activities, such as DDoS attacks. Hence, the reliability and security of the system are improved [26].

5.3.3   Privacy Preservation of IoMT Data

Blockchain could offer privacy protection *via* masking the blockchain account addresses and encrypting blockchain transaction data [41]. By integrating blockchain-enabled IoMT with other security safeguarding methods such as homomorphic obfuscations and other cryptographic algorithms, users can have better privacy protection. This permits protection-sensitive IoMT information to be deposited and handled locally prior to being moved to cloud storage [27].

5.3.4   Traceability of IoMT Data

In blockchain-enabled IoMT, the use of digital signs and accessibility control mechanisms may improve the traceability of "off-chain IoMT data." For example, including off-chain IoMT data hash values in blockchain helps to ensure the traceability of IoMT data while lowering the costs of blockchain storage [40]. The distribution chain is used for tracing the sequence and determining the starting point of an item. Traceability is a block layout in the blockchain framework where every block uses the hash key for connection to the two blocks next to each other [28].

Furthermore, in blockchain-enabled IoMT, information may be classified as either "on-chain" or "off-chain" data, contingent upon whether the information is stored in blockchain or not. Data deposited in the blockchain are virtually traceable across the framework. The traceability and non-repudiation of on-chain data may be guaranteed through employing blockchain's decentralized consensus algorithms and asymmetric cryptographic methods (e.g., computerized signs). Nonetheless, considering the massive size of IoMT data, predominantly clinical photographs and video recordings, the storage of all these data in blockchain is therefore unrealistic [22]. Thus, IoMT information such as photographs and motion pictures should be stored off chain, with blockchain simply holding the metadata or hash values of these "off-chain" IoMT data. In addition, in blockchain-enabled IoMT, the utilization of computerized signs and access control instruments may enhance the traceability of off-chain IoMT data [39]. For instance, assigning off-chain IoMT data hash values in blockchain supports guaranteeing IoMT information tracking while reducing blockchain storage expenses [3].

5.4   Proposed Methodology

The majority of IoMT devices are built to send and store data in the cloud, where these can be processed and analyzed. This innovation in healthcare systems allows medical professionals to attend to patients who are being monitored using medical and healthcare devices in a faster and more accurate manner. However, it raises the possibility of the users' data being misused or stolen while stored in cloud servers. The privacy of users' data, particularly personal data, must be safeguarded. However, numerous examples of large-scale security breaches of cloud systems, such as those of Facebook and Yahoo, raised the question whether patients' sensitive health information can truly be protected.

Indeed, malicious attackers have been increasingly targeting medical servers and e-health systems, as personal health data are quite valuable on the black market. As a result, medical service providers must implement even more stringent security measures, which increases the costs of developing, operating, and maintaining these services.

In addition to devising assault countermeasures, post-attack procedures must also be thoroughly examined. Financial data, such as credit card security codes, may be rapidly rendered invalid and useless, while personal health information might expose an individual's present health status. When such data are stolen as a result of a security breach, retrieving and eradicating the stolen information are crucial, but difficult to accomplish. Strong restrictions must be put in place and serious punishments must be imposed by governments and healthcare organizations to ensure patient data protection.

5.4.1   Overview of the Proposed Architecture

Blockchain was created to securely store financial ledger entries in a decentralized manner, with each block in the blockchain being interconnected. This system could also be applied to medical data distributed across medical servers, providing IoMT-based healthcare systems with enhanced protection regarding security and privacy. However, the construction of blocks in blockchain demands a substantial amount of processing resources on the devices used, which is not practical for resource-constrained IoMT devices. Blockchain, on the other hand, can be used to protect EHRs deposited on medical servers. MedRec, for example, is a pioneering study on the use of blockchain for medical data access and permission management.

Blockchain technology has a number of indisputable qualities that make it ideal for IoMT applications. Blockchains, for instance, can enhance the data storage, security, and privacy protection in IoMT due to their immutability and traceability characteristics. This improves the efficiency of medical case tracing and tracking while also preventing data loss and tampering.

5.4.2 Blockchain-Enabled IoMT Architecture

In this section, we outline a proposed architecture for integrating blockchain into IoMT systems. Its advantages and disadvantages are also discussed.

The combination of blockchain and IoMT can enhance the interoperability of the IoMT system, significantly increasing the security and enhancing privacy protection in IoMT. Figure 5.2 displays the architecture of the proposed system. In this design, the perception/actuation layer, data administration layer, and medical services layer are all effectively supported by the blockchain layer.

In this architecture, blockchain acts as a crucial infrastructure connecting various IoMT tiers. To assist medical professionals (e.g., doctors) in

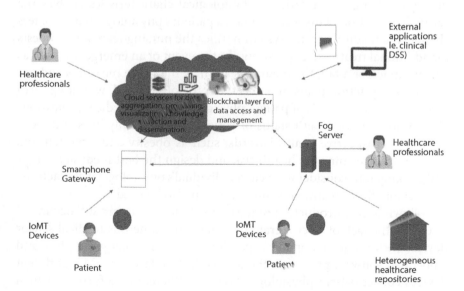

Figure 5.2 System architecture of the proposed blockchain–Internet of Medical Things (B-IoMT) system.

providing better medical care, cloud servers identify and extract certain properties from the collected physiological data. In this way, medical teams can obtain processed data in a manner that is simple to observe and that allows them to offer better diagnosis and treatment advice. This data management system can be used to run the algorithms and programs in order to evaluate the diagnostic and rehabilitative progress of a patient, with the patient's consent. This layer employs identity authentication or access control techniques to ensure that only authorized parties can access a patient's physiological data, protecting the confidentiality and privacy of that data. Furthermore, patient data and associated profiles will be anonymized before being shared with other parties, such as research centers.

The results of basic visual data analysis are delivered to users through the medical service layer. The exhibited data are then used to create reports, which are distributed to the healthcare professionals involved in the diagnostic, clinical observation, and intervention processes (including doctors, patients, and nursing staff).

With the proper authentication and authorization credentials, medical professionals (e.g., doctors) can read reports on patients' physiological data and offer them prompt medical advice.

Depending on their daily activity, medical professionals can monitor individual patients and view reports. On the one hand, real-time monitoring of changes in a patient's physiological characteristics enables the early identification of disorders. When a patient's physiological parameters change, the medical service system notifies the nursing team and requests for additional treatment suggestions. In the event of an emergency, such as a heart attack or a fall, the medical team may then take measures and put the necessary action plans into effect. On the other hand, with long-term monitoring and analysis of patient physiological data, medical professionals can observe the health status of patients in their daily lives and identify some prospective health hazards, such as obesity and hypertension. In order to determine the health risk and design the best medical strategy while taking into consideration each individual's physiological characteristics, personalized treatment simulations can also be used.

Following the introduction of IoMT, the following issues still occur.

One is the lack of interoperability. There are numerous medical sensor devices with unique computer capabilities, memory, energy supplies, and embedded software present in the data collection layer of IoMT. Different devices collect patient physiological data in different data formats, which complicates data handling at the data management layer.

Another element that hinders interoperability is the diversity of wireless and wired protocols. After gathering patients' physiological data, the medical sensor devices send these data to edge servers.

The transmission mechanism makes use of a number of wireless protocols. Some powerful wearable medical sensor systems use WiFi, narrowband IoT (NB-IoT), and Bluetooth low energy (BLE) protocols. Near-field communication (NFC) and radiofrequency identification (RFID) are protocols employed by medical sensor devices that are implanted in patients. It is difficult for medical facilities to exchange medical information with one another due to the lack of interoperability between IoMT systems.

The privacy and security of patients are seriously at stake when private physiological data are exposed. On the other hand, the bulk of medical sensor devices in the data collection layer have limited resources. Because of the processor, memory, and battery constraints of medical sensor systems, the use of conventionally complex encryption techniques is also impractical.

Integration of distributed ledger technology with IoMT
In this section, we propose an architecture for integrating blockchain into IoMT systems, along with its advantages and disadvantages [29]. The convergence of blockchain and IoMT can improve the interoperability of the IoMT system and significantly enhance its security and privacy protection. This is shown in the system architecture of the proposed design. In this model, the perception/actuation layer, the data administration layer, and the medical services layer are all effectively supported by the blockchain layer [30]. Blockchain is a crucial infrastructure that connects the various IoMT levels in this architecture [31].

Blockchain consists of a chain of blocks, distributed consensus, peer-to-peer (P2P) networks, smart contracts, and cryptographic methods (such as digital signatures and public encryption). It can therefore provide IoMT a certain amount of security. Data privacy in IoMT can be further protected using authentication, homomorphic obfuscation, and group signatures on blockchains. Furthermore, the P2P networks in blockchain systems can link various IoMT sectors to improve the overall interoperability of the system [33].

Data privacy protection for IoMT
Due to the limited storage capacity of IoMT, lightweight cryptographic algorithms in the proposed architecture are studied. For IoMT applications, a

private blockchain-based access control system is particularly developed. The anonymity of this approach is maintained by elliptic curve cryptography (ECC)-enabled signature technology [32]. To ensure that patients have control over the accessibility of their medical data, a study [33] also presented a blockchain-based data access method. In this system, simple public key cryptographic algorithms are performed using the ECC cryptographic function. Another article put forth a system for storing private data on the blockchain in order to protect the privacy of patient EHR [34]. For patients' pseudonymity, a platform employs the ECC cryptographic mechanism [35].

In addition to access restriction systems [36], attribute-based signing techniques can safeguard patients' privacy. For a blockchain-based EHR system, the authors developed an attribute-based signature method. Numerous authorities are involved in this method to guarantee patient privacy and the immutability of the data in EHRs. The properties in this system are revocable, thanks to the KUNodes approach that safeguards the confidentiality of users' identities (both patients and doctors).

Problems with the proposed architecture
Despite its several advantages, there are still a few challenges that need to be overcome before the proposed architecture can be widely implemented.

Limitations on resources
The implementation of the suggested architecture may be constrained by the limitations in its storage and computing capabilities. One issue is that the IoMT network might produce a massive amount of physiological data, which would call for high-capacity computing and storage. The chains of the blockchain network have also been expanded, and each node now stores a copy of the entire chain. Consequently, the computing power of each node in the blockchain network is constrained.

One solution to this issue might be to incorporate cloud services into this architecture. Storing sensitive data (such as patients' sensitive private information) on the blockchain in this manner enables uploading a sizable amount of less privacy-sensitive data to distant clouds. The processing of most medical data will take place on the cloud, which will lighten the burden on the blockchain nodes.

5.5   Conclusion and Future Work

In the modern era, the IoT technology is being used in almost every industry, including farming, medical care, and smart city concept programs.

In the healthcare domain, IoT has multiple functions, such as regular health monitoring of patients and drug traceability, among others. The advances of the IoT technology has prompted the development of IoMT.

However, there are a number of safety concerns in IoMT, which may be addressed by assimilating this technology with blockchain. Through this merging, hospitals and health providers are able to keep and share a patient's medical record by blockchain easily and efficiently. Blockchain is a decentralized technology that could be utilized to improve the security of the system. Blockchain technology, in conjunction with healthcare, is beneficial to ensuring that confidential patient EHRs are protected from tampering and leak [45].

In this paper, a secure and blockchain-enabled framework for e-healthcare data for the Internet of Medical Things (IoMT) was presented. Furthermore, blockchain, which has found application in e-healthcare in such a short period of time, was also discussed. How blockchain could be used in the field of the Internet of Things (IoT), as well as the opportunities and challenges it brings, was examined. The proposed scheme depicts the area of IoMT in e-healthcare while addressing protection and security concerns. This paper also looked at the protection and security challenges, requirements, risks, and future research directions.

References

1. Siyal, A.A., Junejo, A.Z., Zawish, M., Ahmed, K., Khalil, A., Soursou, G., Applications of blockchain technology in medicine and healthcare: Challenges and future perspectives. *Cryptography*, 3, 1, 1–16, Mar. 2019, doi: 10.3390/cryptography3010003.
2. Cresswell, K.M., Bates, D.W., Sheikh, A., Ten key considerations for the successful implementation and adoption of large-scale health information technology. *J. Am. Med. Inf. Assoc.*, 20, E1, 2013, doi: 10.1136/amiajnl-2013-001684.
3. Kellermann, A.L. and Jones, S.S., What it will take to achieve the as-yet-unfulfilled promises of health information technology. *Health Aff.*, 32, 63–68, 2013, doi: 10.1377/hlthaff.2012.0693.
4. Kalodner, H. *et al.*, BlockSci: Design and applications of a blockchain analysis platform. *Proc. 29th USENIX Secur. Symp.*, pp. 2721–2738, 2020.
5. Fröwis, M., Gottschalk, T., Haslhofer, B., Rückert, C., Pesch, P., Safeguarding the evidential value of forensic cryptocurrency investigations. *Forensic Sci. Int. Digit. Investig.*, 33, 200902, Jun. 2020, doi: 10.1016/j.fsidi.2019.200902.

6. Rožman, N., Diaci, J., Corn, M., Scalable framework for blockchain-based shared manufacturing. *Robot. Comput. Integr. Manuf.*, 71, 102139, Oct. 2021, doi: 10.1016/j.rcim.2021.102139.

7. Mackey, T.K. and Nayyar, G., A review of existing and emerging digital technologies to combat the global trade in fake medicines. *Expert Opin. Drug Saf.*, 16, 5, 587–602, May 2017, doi: 10.1080/14740338.2017.1313227.

8. Ozdagoglu, G., Damar, M., Ozdagoglu, A., The state of the art in blockchain research (2013–2018): Scientometrics of the related papers in web of science and scopus, in: *Contrib. to Manag. Sci*, pp. 569–599, 2020, doi: 10.1007/978-3-030-29739-8_27.

9. Noh, S.-W., Park, Y., Sur, C., Shin, S.-U., Rhee, K.-H., Blockchain-based user-centric records management system. *Int. J. Control Autom.*, 10, 11, 133–144, Nov. 2017, doi: 10.14257/ijca.2017.10.11.12.

10. Liu, W., Feng, W., Huang, M., Xu, Y., Zheng, X., STEB: A secure service trading ecosystem based on blockchain. *PLoS One*, 17, 6, e0267914, Jun. 2022, doi: 10.1371/journal.pone.0267914.

11. Li, G., Sheng, X., Wu, J., Yu, H., Securing transmissions by friendly jamming scheme in wireless networks. *J. Parallel Distrib. Comput.*, 144, 260–267, Oct. 2020, doi: 10.1016/j.jpdc.2020.04.013.

12. Schniederjans, D.G., Curado, C., Khalajhedayati, M., Supply chain digitisation trends: An integration of knowledge management. *Int. J. Prod. Econ.*, 220, 107439, Feb. 2020, doi: 10.1016/j.ijpe.2019.07.012.

13. Jaquet-Chiffelle, D.O., Casey, E., Bourquenoud, J., Tamperproof time-stamped provenance ledger using blockchain technology. *Forensic Sci. Int. Digit. Investig.*, 33, Jun. 2020, doi: 10.1016/j.fsidi.2020.300977.

14. Negro-Calduch, E., Azzopardi-Muscat, N., Krishnamurthy, R.S., Novillo-Ortiz, D., Technological progress in electronic health record system optimization: Systematic review of systematic literature reviews. *Int. J. Med. Inform.*, 152, 104507–104507, May 2021, doi: 10.1016/j.ijmedinf.2021.104507.

15. Huang, G., Al Foysal, A., Huang, G., Al Foysal, A., Blockchain in healthcare. *Technol. Invest.*, 12, 3, 168–181, Jul. 2021, doi: 10.4236/ti.2021.123010.

16. Mukherjee, U., Dutta, S., Bandyopadhyay, S.K., Assembling blockchain and IoT for smart food-supply chain. *Asian J. Adv. Agric. Res.*, 49–58, Sep. 2021, doi: 10.9734/ajaar/2021/v16i330177.

17. Benchoufi, M. and Ravaud, P., Blockchain technology for improving clinical research quality. *Trials*, 18, 1, Jul. 2017, doi: 10.1186/S13063-017-2035-Z.

18. Zhang, P., Walker, M.A., White, J., Schmidt, D.C., Lenz, G., Metrics for assessing blockchain-based healthcare decentralized apps. *2017 IEEE 19th Int. Conf. e-Health Networking, Appl. Serv. Heal. 2017*, vol. 2017–December, pp. 1–4, Dec. 2017, doi: 10.1109/healthcom.2017.8210842.

19. Abu-elezz, I., Hassan, A., Nazeemudeen, A., Househ, M., Abd-alrazaq, A., The benefits and threats of blockchain technology in healthcare: A scoping review. *Int. J. Med. Inform.*, 142, Oct. 2020, doi: 10.1016/j.ijmedinf.2020.104246.

20. Bumblauskas, D., Mann, A., Dugan, B., Rittmer, J., A blockchain use case in food distribution: Do you know where your food has been? *Int. J. Inf. Manag.*, 52, Jun. 2020, doi: 10.1016/j.ijinfomgt.2019.09.004.
21. Hölbl, M., Kompara, M., Kamišalić, A., Zlatolas, L.N., A systematic review of the use of blockchain in healthcare. *Symmetry (Basel)*, 10, 10, 2018, doi: 10.3390/sym10100470.
22. Cyran, M.A., Blockchain as a foundation for sharing healthcare data. *Blockchain Healthc. Today*, Mar. vol. 1, 2018, doi: 10.30953/bhty.v1.13.
23. Chanson, M., Bogner, A., Bilgeri, D., Fleisch, E., Wortmann, F., Blockchain for the IoT: Privacy-preserving protection of sensor data. *J. Assoc. Inf. Syst.*, 20, 9, 1271–1307, 2019, doi: 10.17705/1JAIS.00567.
24. Cheung, A.W.K., Roca, E., Su, J.J., Crypto-currency bubbles: An application of the Phillips–Shi–Yu (2013) methodology on Mt. Gox bitcoin prices. *Appl. Econ.*, 47, 23, 2348–2358, May 2015, doi: 10.1080/00036846.2015.1005827.
25. Treiblmaier, H. and Sillaber, C., The impact of blockchain on e-commerce: A framework for salient research topics. *Electron. Commer. Res. Appl.*, 48, Jul. 2021, doi: 10.1016/j.elerap.2021.101054.
26. Garaus, M. and Treiblmaier, H., The influence of blockchain-based food traceability on retailer choice: The mediating role of trust. *Food Control*, 129, Nov. 2021, doi: 10.1016/j.foodcont.2021.108082.
27. Jones, S.S., Rudin, R.S., Perry, T., Shekelle, P.G., Health information technology: An updated systematic review with a focus on meaningful use. *Ann. Intern. Med.*, 160, 1, 48–54, Jan. 2014, doi: 10.7326/m13-1531.
28. *Blockchain in healthcare*, Scientific Research, China, 2021, https://www.scirp.org/journal/paperinformation.aspx?paperid=110991 (accessed Feb. 15, 2023).
29. Thakur, S. and Breslin, J.G., Scalable and secure product serialization for multi-party perishable good supply chains using blockchain. *Internet Things*, 11, 100253, 2020, doi: 10.1016/j.iot.2020.100253.
30. Fröwis, M., Gottschalk, T., Haslhofer, B., Rückert, C., Pesch, P., Safeguarding the evidential value of forensic cryptocurrency investigations. *Forensic Sci. Int. Digit. Investig.*, 33, 200902, 2020, doi: 10.1016/j.fsidi.2019.200902.
31. Akyildirim, E., Corbet, S., Cumming, D., Lucey, B., Sensoy, A., Riding the wave of crypto-exuberance: The potential misusage of corporate blockchain announcements. *Technol. Forecast. Soc. Change*, 159, 120191, February, 2020, doi: 10.1016/j.techfore.2020.120191.
32. Lisi, A., De Salve, A., Mori, P., Ricci, L., Fabrizi, S., Rewarding reviews with tokens: An Ethereum-based approach. *Future Gener. Comput. Syst.*, 120, 36–54, 2021, doi: 10.1016/j.future.2021.02.003.
33. Benedetti, H. and Nikbakht, E., Returns and network growth of digital tokens after cross-listings. *J. Corp. Financ.*, 66, 101853, July 2019, 2021, doi: 10.1016/j.jcorpfin.2020.101853.
34. Huang, C. *et al.*, RepChain: A reputation-based secure, fast, and high incentive blockchain system via sharding. *IEEE Internet Things J.*, 8, 6, 4291–4304, 2021, doi: 10.1109/JIOT.2020.3028449.

35. Shrestha, R. and Nam, S.Y., Regional blockchain for vehicular networks to prevent 51% attacks. *IEEE Access*, 7, 95033–95045, 2019, doi: 10.1109/ACCESS.2019.2928753.

36. Manzoor, A., Braeken, A., Kanhere, S.S., Ylianttila, M., Liyanage, M., Proxy re-encryption enabled secure and anonymous IoT data sharing platform based on blockchain. *J. Netw. Comput. Appl.*, 176, 102917, 2021, doi: 10.1016/j.jnca.2020.102917.

37. Belhadi, A., Djenouri, Y., Srivastava, G., Jolfaei, A., Lin, J.C.-W., Privacy reinforcement learning for faults detection in the smart grid. *Ad Hoc Netw.*, 119, 102541, April, 2021, doi: 10.1016/j.adhoc.2021.102541.

38. Li, G., Dong, M., Yang, L.T., Ota, K., Wu, J., Li, J., Preserving edge knowledge sharing among IoT services: A blockchain-based approach. *IEEE Trans. Emerg. Top. Comput. Intell.*, 4, 5, 653–665, 2020, doi: 10.1109/TETCI.2019.2952587.

39. Baniata, H., Anaqreh, A., Kertesz, A., PF-BTS: A privacy-aware fog-enhanced blockchain-assisted task scheduling. *Inf. Process. Manag.*, 58, 1, 102393, 2021, doi: 10.1016/j.ipm.2020.102393.

40. Reyna, A., Martín, C., Chen, J., Soler, E., Díaz, M., On blockchain and its integration with IoT. Challenges and opportunities. *Future. Gener. Comput. Syst.*, 88, 2018, 173–190, 2018, doi: 10.1016/j.future.2018.05.046.

41. Roehrs, A., da Costa, C.A., da Rosa Righi, R., OmniPHR: A distributed architecture model to integrate personal health records. *J. Biomed. Inform.*, 71, 70–81, 2017, doi: 10.1016/j.jbi.2017.05.012.

42. Zheng, W., Zheng, Z., Li, P., Chen, R., NutBaaS: A blockchain-as-a-service platform. *IEEE*, p. 99, 7, 2019.

43. Shala, B., Trick, U., Lehmann, A., Ghita, B., Shiaeles, S., Novel trust consensus protocol and blockchain-based trust evaluation system for M2M application services. *Internet Things*, 7, 100058, 2019, doi: 10.1016/j.iot.2019.100058.

44. Hafid, A., Hafid, A.S., Samih, M., New mathematical model to analyze security of sharding-based blockchain protocols. *IEEE Access*, 7, 185447–185457, 2019, doi: 10.1109/ACCESS.2019.2961065.

45. Guo, Z., Shi, L., Xu, M., Yin, H., MRCC: A practical covert channel over monero with provable security. *IEEE Access*, 9, 31816–31825, 2021, doi: 10.1109/ACCESS.2021.3060285.

6

A Review on the Role of Blockchain Technology in the Healthcare Domain

Aryan Dahiya, Anuradha*, Shilpa Mahajan and Swati Gupta

Computer Science Engineering (CSE), The NorthCap University, Gurugram, Haryana, India

Abstract

Blockchain technology has gained a lot of attention due to the growing interest in a variety of applications, including data management, financial services, cyber security, IoT, food science, the healthcare sector, and brain research. The use of blockchain technology for the provision of safe and secure healthcare data management has attracted considerable interest. By aggregating all real-time clinical data relevant to a patient's health and presenting it in a cutting-edge, secure healthcare environment, blockchain technology has the potential to support personalized, genuine, and secure healthcare in the future. In this chapter, both the recent and present trends in the healthcare sector using blockchain as a paradigm have been evaluated, and the uses of the blockchain in addition to the issues experienced and the future outlook have been discussed.

Keywords: Blockchain, healthcare, application, challenges, medical management

6.1 Introduction

Healthcare is a clinical field that generates, accesses, and disseminates vast amounts of data on a daily basis. Owing to the sensitive nature of the data and other restrictions, such as security and privacy, storing and sharing this much data is essential but also very difficult. Safe, secure, and scalable (SSS) data sharing is essential for diagnosis and collaborative clinical decision-making in the healthcare industry and clinical settings [1].

---

*Corresponding author: anuradha@ncuindia.edu

Akansha Singh, Anuradha Dhull and Krishna Kant Singh (eds.) Blockchain and Deep Learning for Smart Healthcare, (113–146) © 2024 Scrivener Publishing LLC

To allow clinical practitioners to send the clinical data of their patients to the appropriate authority for a prompt follow-up, the data-sharing practice is very important.

In contrast, telemedicine and e-health are two widely used fields where clinical data are electronically communicated to a professional (at a remote location) for an expert opinion. The patient's data are transferred in these two online clinical settings either via "store-and-forward technology" or by using online real-time clinical monitoring (e.g., telemonitoring, telemetry, and the like). By exchanging clinical data, clinical specialists can diagnose and treat patients remotely using these online clinical settings. Because of the case-sensitive nature of patient data, security, sensitivity, and privacy of the clinical data present some of the biggest issues in all such clinical setups. Therefore, it is crucial to be able to share data securely, safely, and at scale in order to allow relevant clinical communications regarding remote patient cases. A group of clinical specialists can gather recommendations or confirmations through the safe and effective interchange of data, thus improving diagnostic precision and facilitating effective treatment [2]. In addition, there are several interoperability problems that continue to exist in this industry. Such clinical data exchanges require a wide-ranging, trustworthy, and healthy level of participation from all parties. There are several possible barriers to this process, including the sensitive nature of clinical data, data-sharing agreements, procedures, challenging patient matching algorithms, ethical guidelines, and governing laws. Both parties must be able to agree on these fundamentals before ever conducting any clinical data exchange [3].

Blockchain makes it possible for numerous parties to collaborate on a single ledger that everyone can accept as accurate. Each new piece of information (transaction) is put into a "block," which is a chain of blocks known as a "blockchain" because each block links to the one before it by using the hash of the previous block. The network timestamps transactions by hashing them into a continuous chain of proof-of-work using hashes, producing a record that cannot be changed without doing new proof-of-work. Currency and payment support, as well as safety data, may be supported by these recorded transactions. Each new transaction must be verified by a node in this network to ensure that it is complete.

Every block that is added to a blockchain increases the immutability of each transaction since every node in the network verifies each transaction before it is included. The procedure for creating a blockchain is depicted in Figure 6.1. Verification of ledgers occurs at many stages. A public blockchain has ledgers that are open for everyone to examine, and anybody can verify and add a block of transactions to the blockchain. Depending on

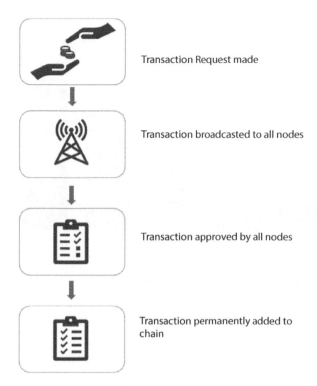

Figure 6.1 Generalized workflow of the blockchain process.

the type of blockchain, everyone on the internet is typically allowed to observe transaction blocks on a private blockchain, but only certain personnel in the organizations are authorized to verify and contribute blocks of transactions.

During the past few years, researchers have been experimenting with ways to employ applications of the Internet of Things, artificial intelligence, machine learning, and computer vision to help doctors and clinical practitioners diagnose and treat a variety of chronic conditions. As shown in Figures 6.2 and 6.3; there has been a lot of interest in using blockchain applications for safe and secure healthcare data delivery, sharing biomedical and e-health data, brain simulation, and thinking [4].

By combining the benefits of blockchain (as shown in Table 6.1)—all of the clinical data that are available in real time about a patient's health—and presenting them as a modern, secure healthcare system, blockchain technology has the ability to support personalized, dependable, and secure healthcare in the future. This article contains recent advancements in the healthcare industry by using blockchain as a model; applications like

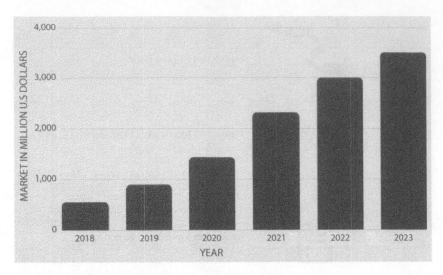

Figure 6.2 Blockchain market trend in healthcare.

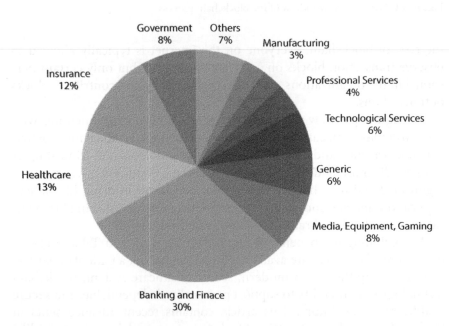

Figure 6.3 Industry-wise blockchain usage sector (2018–2023).

Table 6.1 Key benefits of using blockchain technology.

Key elements	Functionality description
Decentralized	A decentralized management structure is necessary for healthcare because of the spread of stakeholders, without anybody acting as the central authority over the world's health data [5].
Improved data security and privacy	Since the data once recorded to the blockchain cannot be damaged, edited, or recovered, this characteristic of blockchain significantly enhances the security of the health data kept on it. Each and every piece of health data is put to the blockchain in chronological order, is time-stamped, and is encrypted [6].
Health data ownership	Patients must be the owners of their data and in charge of how the data are utilized. Patients should have the ability to notice instances of data misuse and require the assurance that their health information will not be used improperly by third parties [7].
Availability/ robustness	Owing to records' duplication over several nodes, which makes the system resistant to data loss, data corruption, and different security assaults on data availability, the availability of the health data stored on the blockchain is ensured [8].
Transparency and trust	Blockchain fosters confidence in distributed healthcare apps because of its openness and transparency. This makes it easier for healthcare stakeholders to approve such applications [9].
Data verifiability	It is possible to confirm the veracity and integrity of documents stored on blockchains without having access to their plaintext. This capability is quite helpful when it comes to healthcare scenarios where record verification is necessary [10].
Transparent	Potential users may simply update the data that have been captured and saved on a blockchain since it is transparent. Data theft or alteration might be avoided thanks to blockchains' transparency [11].

(Continued)

Table 6.1 Key benefits of using blockchain technology. (*Continued*)

Key elements	Functionality description
Immutable	Once records are stored, they are permanently reserved and are difficult to change without concurrent control of more than 51% of the node [12].
Autonomy	As a result of the blockchain system's independence and autonomy, each node may safely access, transfer, store, and update data, ensuring its dependability and freedom from outside interference [13].
Open source	Blockchain technology is designed in a way that gives everyone connected to the network open-source access. Anyone has the right to not only openly review the information but also create numerous upcoming apps thanks to this unparalleled adaptability [14].
Anonymity	It is a more secure and dependable system since nodes communicate data while maintaining anonymity regarding the identity of the individual [15].

electronic health records (EHRs), clinical research, medical fraud detection, neuroscience, and pharmaceutical industry and research, among others; challenges associated with blockchain; future aspects; and scope.

Research Questions:
The study intended to answer the following research questions:

1. **RQ1**: What is the role of blockchain in healthcare and to what extent is blockchain established in healthcare and how did this change over time?
2. **RQ2**: What are the applications of blockchain in healthcare?
3. **RQ3**: What are the challenges of blockchain technology used in the healthcare domain?

The rest of the paper is organized as follows:

- **Section 2** contains the systematic literature methodology, findings of the data, and sources.
- **Section 3** describes applications of the emerging blockchain technology in healthcare.

- **Section 4** presents the challenges faced in healthcare when utilizing blockchains.
- **Section 5** highlights the future perspectives of blockchain technology in healthcare.
- **Section 6** presents the conclusion and implications.

6.2   Systematic Literature Methodology

6.2.1   Data Sources

Two main fields of interest in this work for gathering the fundamental data were blockchain and healthcare. The focus of this study was more on the analysis of publications published on top databases such as Google Scholar, Springer Link, and PubMed. The systematic review included the nine top and well-known electronic databases shown in Table 6.2:

The study has done a systematic literature assessment of academic and industry publications between 2018 and 2023 in order to comprehend the potential of the blockchain in healthcare, evaluate its applicability, and identify implementation challenges. Table 6.3 shows the types of databases selected and the number of results. Because of the unique features of the blockchain and the longer wait times for reviews and publication of academic works, the focus of this study was more on the analysis of

Table 6.2 Electronic databases used for the review.

Google Scholar
Web of Science (WoS)
IEEE Xplore
PubMed
Medline EBSCO
Springer Link
Elsevier Science Direct
MDPI
ACM Digital Library

Table 6.3 Summary of search results.

Database	Number of results	Papers selected
Google Scholar	15,000	16
Web of Science (WoS)	236	4
IEEE Xplore	3,026	5
PubMed	4,021	10
Medline EBSCO	2,256	1
Springer Link	8,592	9
Elsevier Science Direct	3,548	2
MDPI	220	10
ACM Digital Library	177	3
Total		60

Note: The keywords used for the searches were as follows:
• "blockchain", "healthcare"
• "blockchain", "healthcare", "applications"
• "blockchain", "healthcare", "applications", "challenges"
• "Blockchain", "medical management", etc.

publications published on databases such as Google Scholar, Springer Link, and PubMed. Table 6.3 shows a summary of search results.

6.2.2   Selection of Studies

A number of publications were obtained from online digital libraries as the initial step in the selection process. Figure 6.4 shows the flow diagram of the search. The papers either were included in the systematic review or were not depending on the criteria. The following stages made up the selection process:

• The inclusion and exclusion criteria were used to filter the search results.

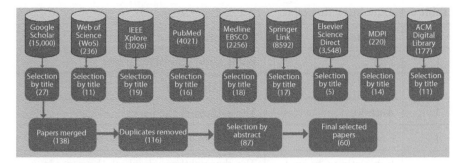

Figure 6.4 Selection process for relevant papers.

- By focusing simply on the title and abstract, we evaluated and chose the results depending on how well they answered the study questions. We disregarded (the number of) findings.
- Nine distinct databases' redundant entries were eliminated. After eliminating the duplicates from the 138 publications that were discovered, 116 publications were left for the following stage.
- A thorough reading was used to further examine the remaining data. The reviewed article ought to be closely related to the stated research topics. The remaining outcomes also needed to provide a unique and significant blockchain-based contribution to the healthcare industry. Owing to the introduced idea's generality and the lack of additional information regarding its design or implementation, several findings were excluded. Twenty-nine more results were disregarded. Sixty publications were ultimately included in the systematic review. The procedure itself was rigid to make sure that only pertinent and excellent studies were taken into consideration.

6.2.3   Data Extraction and Mapping Process

Information from those 60 papers after compiling the pertinent publications was obtained. The publications' title, authors, publication type (conference proceedings, journal papers, etc.), publication year, and the number of citations based on Google Scholar citations served as our starting point as shown in Table 6.4. Two main fields of interest in this work for gathering the fundamental data were blockchain and healthcare.

Table 6.4 Data extraction table.

S. no.	Data items	Description
1	Year	Publication year of the paper
2	Title	Title of the paper
3	Authors	The authors of the paper
4	Country	Country of affiliation of the authors
5	Publication Channel	The channel through which the paper is published
6	Publication Type	Journal/Conference/Workshop/etc.
7	Publication Source	Academia/Industry/Both
8	Paper Type	Type based on classification scheme
9	Paper Contribution	Main contributions of the paper
10	Summary	Our own summary or abstract of the paper

6.2.4   Results

The findings of the systematic review are reported in this section. As shown in Figure 6.3, finally, 60 papers were retrieved from the scientific databases using our search procedure. A number of papers were eliminated after the initial screening, which is based on the titles of the papers, leaving 138 merged papers for additional screening. The papers that were rejected are those that are unrelated to healthcare; yet, our search protocol retrieved them since healthcare may have been referenced in their abstracts as one of the non-financial use cases of blockchain. Further, the number of selected papers were reduced to 116 by eliminating duplicates. Finally, 60 papers were chosen for inclusion in the study at the conclusion of the final screening process.

6.3   Applications of Blockchain in the Healthcare Domain

The blockchain technology (BCT) was initially intended for its most well-known applications in the economics and cryptocurrency domains, but today, its utility is growing in a number of other sectors, including the

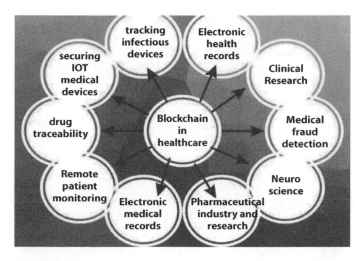

Figure 6.5 Applications of blockchain in the healthcare domain.

healthcare sector. The blockchain applications used (as shown in Figure 6.5) in the healthcare sector discussed in this paper are as follows:

1. Electronic health records (EHRs)
2. Clinical research
3. Medical fraud detection
4. Neuroscience
5. Pharmaceutical industry and research
6. Electronic medical records management
7. Remote patient monitoring
8. Drug traceability
9. Securing IoT medical devices
10. Tracking infectious diseases

6.3.1 Blockchains in Electronic Health Records (EHRs)

Since it makes the data easier to access, share, and use as a foundation for more effective and efficient decision-making, medical professionals, hospitals, and healthcare equipment have all contributed to the need for a significant increase in the digitization of medical records over the past 10 years. Electronic health records (EHRs) were not intended to manage lifetime records across several institutions, and as life events cause patients to switch from one provider to another, they disperse their data among numerous institutions, losing easy access to past data. To control data

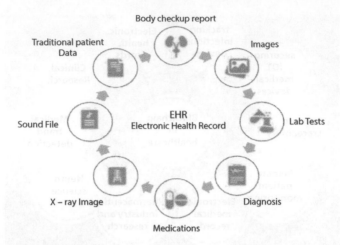

Figure 6.6 EHR process flow.

exchange, secrecy, and authentication, a "MedRec" prototype makes use of unique blockchain capabilities [16].

It operates on a decentralized records management system, claims to give patients a thorough, unchangeable history, and enables simple access to their individual medical records across several physicians and treatment facilities [17].

MeDShare offers improved data provenance, individualized audit control, and fewer potential risks to data security and privacy, making it an ideal solution for sharing medical data and maintaining electronic health records among cloud service providers, hospitals, and healthcare research groups. Figure 6.6 shows the EHR process flow. Doctors, radiologists, healthcare professionals, pharmacists, and researchers routinely share very sensitive and crucial patient data discovered in EHR for proper diagnosis and treatment [18]. Because of the substantial threats to the patient's health and the need to maintain the most recent medical records, the storage, transfer, and dissemination of this extremely sensitive patient information among numerous organizations may put the patient's treatment in danger [19].

6.3.2   Blockchains in Clinical Research

Clinical trials may encounter a variety of problems, such as patient enrollment, record-keeping, data privacy, data integrity, and data sharing. Blockchain, the upcoming internet technology, can offer workable solutions to these issues like evaluation, testing, monitoring, and reporting as shown in Figure 6.7 [20]. These problems are being addressed by healthcare researchers using blockchain technology as presented in Figure 6.8, showing the flow diagram of blockchain technology in clinical research. Blockchain applications, together with artificial intelligence (AI) and machine learning, will soon revolutionize the healthcare sector. In the research plan put forth by Timothy *et al.*, clinic-based data management systems are used side by side with permissioned Ethereum, a blockchain platform that offers smart contract capability [21]. The main objective of the study was to help patients who were having trouble enrolling. The study's

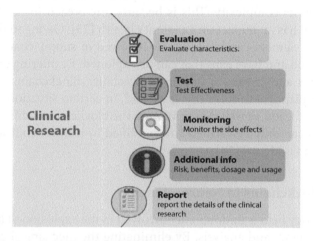

Figure 6.7 Blockchain in clinical research features.

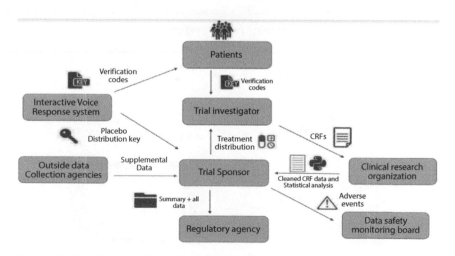

Figure 6.8 Flow diagram of blockchain in clinical research.

findings showed that Ethereum made transactions more quickly than bitcoin, and the conclusion that followed recommended adopting Ethereum smart contracts to improve the transparency of data management systems in clinical trials [22].

6.3.3   Blockchains in Medical Fraud Detection

In the medical industry, one key application of blockchain technology is medical fraud detection. Supply management is an essential concern to safeguard in every industry, but it is especially crucial in the healthcare sector given its complexity. This is because any breach in the healthcare supply chain has an impact on a patient's health [23]. Owing to the numerous moving elements and individuals involved in supply chains, they are prone to fraud and have gaps that can be exploited. By offering greater data transparency and increased product traceability, blockchains offer a safe and secure platform to solve this issue and, in certain situations, avoid the possibility of fraud as well. Manipulating the blockchain is difficult since a record in it can only be verified and modified by a smart contract process as shown in Figure 6.9 [24].

6.3.4   Blockchains in Neuroscience

The neurology field is undoubtedly involved in the explosion of blockchain application news and analysis. By eliminating the mechanical connection

Figure 6.9 Process of fraud detection method using blockchain.

with the environment's infrastructure and enabling the control of devices and data by mental commands, modern neural technologies aim to create a new paradigm of the modes of neuroscience shown in Figure 6.10; such neural devices have the ability to interpret patterns of brain activity and transform those patterns into commands for operating external equipment. They can also use brain activity data to determine a person's present mental state [25]. Neural interface devices with multiple sensitive sensors, computation chips, and wireless connection are able to read and analyze brain impulses. They interpret the brain's electrical activity, which is then communicated to the controlled equipment for further decoding. The person wears a single device on their head that houses all of this technology. Blockchain philosophy will be applied by complex algorithms and big data to store those brain impulses on the neural interface. Neurogress is one of the businesses to affirm that they will be utilizing blockchain technology. The company, which was established in 2017 and is registered in Geneva, specializes in developing neural-control systems that allow users to command robotic arms, drones, smart appliances, and AR/VR gadgets with their thoughts. The brain-reading accuracy of Neurogress' control system is improved by machine learning, which necessitates preserving 90% of the brain's data in order to train the system's artificial intelligence (AI) [26]. The solution will "guarantee security and confidentiality of personal data" because any anomalous activity would be simple to track. Therefore, it is

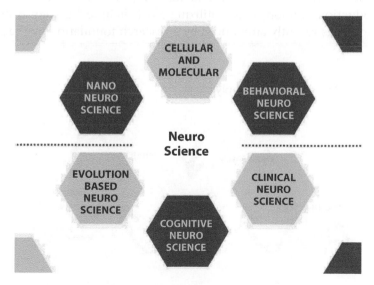

Figure 6.10 Blockchain in neuroscience features.

clear that blockchains are a type of information technology with several significant potential applications, including brain augmentation, brain simulation, and brain thinking. The need for a storage medium arises when digitizing the complete human brain, and this is where blockchain technology once again makes an appearance [27].

6.3.5 Blockchains in Pharmaceutical Industry and Research

The pharmaceutical industry is one of the areas of healthcare delivery with the quickest growth. The pharmaceutical business aims to assure the legitimacy and safety of medical supplies and medications that are directly marketed to the general public in addition to assisting with the introduction of new and promising pharmaceuticals onto the market. Figure 6.11 depicts a pharmaceutical supply chain using blockchain. A speedier rate of patient recovery is ultimately promoted by the pharmaceutical industry's funding for the development and testing of safe drugs [28]. When fake medications are introduced into the supply chain or production is compromised by counterfeiters, drug companies frequently struggle to keep track of their products in a timely manner, which can pose major risks. As a result, making and distributing bogus pharmaceuticals now rank among the world's worst health concerns, particularly in developing countries. Blockchain may be the most appropriate technology for evaluating, monitoring, and assuring the manufacturing procedures of potential medications both throughout their research and production [29]. An idea to detect and halt the production of phony drugs utilizing blockchain technology as its primary tool was recently announced by a research foundation by the name

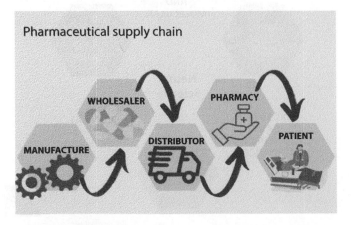

Figure 6.11 Pharmaceutical supply chain.

of Hyperledger. If patients are to receive effective and genuine medicine delivery, it is urgently necessary to monitor, evaluate, and ensure the overall process of generating and supplying pharmaceutical drugs through the use of digital technologies worldwide, and particularly in developing nations. In this situation, a digital drug control system (DDCS) may be a dependable means of preventing the sale of counterfeit drugs. For the inspection and evaluation of innovative pharmaceuticals utilizing a blockchain-based DDCS, the major pharmaceutical companies Sanofi, Pfizer, and Amgen started a cooperation pilot study [30].

6.3.6   Electronic Medical Records Management

Medical data about patients are gathered and digitally recorded in the EMR. By asking access from patients, the authors suggested using a blockchain implementation to safeguard EMR and manage access to these data. The technology ensures authentication, confidentiality, and other features as shown in Figure 6.12 and is built on a permissionless blockchain. Additionally, it is made to deal with the single point of failure issue. Despite being one of the pioneering efforts in EMR management apps, this solution still has some scalability and data encryption issues [31]. A smartphone application for gathering and exchanging health data between patients, healthcare professionals, and insurance companies was also demonstrated by Liang *et al.* For access control and privacy purposes, their system made use of a blockchain with permissions. The system provided evidence of the data process' scalability and effectiveness [32]. Data encryption, however, was not taken into account. Furthermore, Dagher *et al.* presented their work. For access management and interoperability utilizing a permissioned Ethereum blockchain, they suggested the Ancile architecture. To maintain

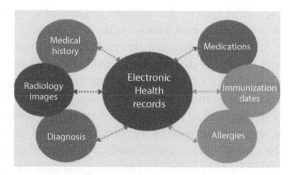

Figure 6.12 Medical record management features.

many capabilities, including the consensus procedure, the records' tracking, permissions, re-encryption, node classification, and their relationship histories, their framework is made up of a number of smart contracts. The authors presented a data-sharing system based on a peer-to-peer network for storing the data description and a consortium blockchain for keeping the data fingerprint. Super peers and edge peers are two different sorts of nodes that make up this solution. The first category, which is associated with large healthcare providers with strong processing and storage capacity, offers the primary infrastructure for data sharing. The second kind, which belongs to small providers, is where the real patient data are kept. It offers privacy protection, security, integrity, and auditability. The system still requires some work, though, as it relies on manual processes for uploading data and authorizing access to it, which could result in higher operation costs and access latency [33].

6.3.7   Remote Patient Monitoring

For Telecare medical information systems, Ji *et al.* suggested a blockchain-based location sharing strategy that protects anonymity. Decentralization, unforgeability, confidentiality, and layered privacy protection are all provided by the system; however, scalability and interoperability issues are not addressed. Uddin *et al.* introduced yet another piece. It offered a patient software agent with decentralized control to manage a remote patient monitoring system that had three layers, consisting of hospital, doctors, and users as shown in Figure 6.13. They used a blockchain network to integrate three layers of devices into their solution: the body area sensor network, the fog level, and the cloud level. The process of remote patient monitoring system manager is depicted in Figure 6.14. Despite the system's ability to provide private, secure, and reliable communication, the interoperability problem was not addressed [34]. To increase the security of an RPM system, the authors suggested a healthcare architecture built on a permissioned blockchain. Additionally, they provided some thoughts on how to safeguard the exchange of huge data through the usage of blockchain and decentralized artificial intelligence while also enhancing patient quality of life. In order to assure the early detection of diseases, AI can apply machine learning algorithms for analytics and diagnosis. They demonstrated a platform for tracking patients' vital signs that is built on the Hyperledger Fabric blockchain and smart contracts. Additionally, the system makes use of medical sensors that clinicians can regulate remotely [35]. They collected physiological data for the trial using the Libelium e-health biometric sensor platform toolbox, including ECG,

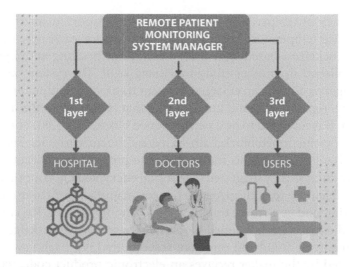

Figure 6.13 Remote patient monitoring system manager.

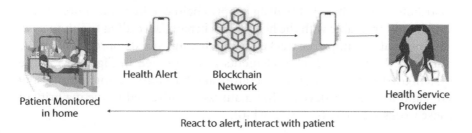

Figure 6.14 Process of remote patient monitoring system manager.

electromyogram (EMG), blood pressure, and body temperature. The platform guarantees data integrity, privacy, and access management. Scalability is also considered, although interoperability is not [36].

6.3.8 Drug Traceability

It has been proposed in numerous publications to combine blockchain technology with medicine supply chains for traceability and data monitoring of medicinal supplies during transportation. Bocek *et al.* employed Ethereum blockchain, for instance, in the pharmaceutical supply chain to store data and maintain their immutability while making them publicly available. They suggested using thermal sensitive devices to send temperature data during the transit of pharmaceuticals as their answer. To guarantee the accuracy of temperature data during the transport, a smart contract with precise temperature requirements is set up for each new shipment [37]. A blockchain-based system for medication tracking and regulation was established in another study by Huang *et al.* The system, known as Drug ledger, is built on an enlarged unspent transaction output process for packaging, repackaging, and unpackaging that is specific to the drug supply chain. It is intended to be a permissioned blockchain [38]. The authors created a permissioned blockchain-based architecture to track fake medications. The purpose of this framework is to protect pharmaceuticals and verify producers. They suggested creating an encrypted QR code that would be accessible only to authorized parties for manufacturers to use to store information and contribute transactions to the Blockchain. Raj *et al.* have suggested using a permissioned blockchain based on Hyperledger Fabric to stop medicine fraud and carry out traceability [39]. Each new medication created by the maker receives an electronic product code, which he registers in the blockchain as his own digital asset. This allows the maker to use a smart contract to transfer ownership of the drug to the entities (like distributors) who buy it. The drug supply chain can be made more secure, visible, and traceable with the help of blockchain, according to Sahoo *et al.* The medications might be tracked using this suggested approach from the maker to the user and other elements as mentioned in Figure 6.15. The system tracks and monitors temperature and humidity during transit using GPS and IoT sensor devices. The main issue addressed in the majority of these works was data traceability [40].

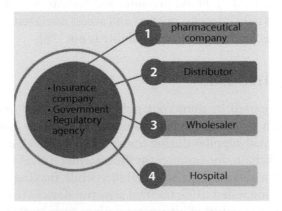

Figure 6.15 Elements in drug traceability process.

6.3.9   Securing IoT Medical Devices

Medical device sales have increased significantly over the past few years, in large part due to recent IoT advances. There are many different IoT medical gadgets and wearables on the market right now. They are employed to gather, manage, and exchange health information with the medical staff. However, using such devices exposes sensitive data to manipulation by outside parties because they rely on a centralized paradigm with a client-server architecture. The alteration of the patient's data poses security and privacy concerns and may result in a single point of failure. Many researchers suggested using an IoT decentralized system to address these problems as a fix. Blockchain technology has been presented in numerous recent works as a way to safeguard data that are altered by IoT medical devices in healthcare systems [41]. The first use case of IoT and blockchain in the medical sector was presented by Dey *et al.* They proposed using biosensors for data collection and measurement, and smart contracts for insurance coverage and hospital bill calculation. They suggested using the Interplanetary File System (IPFS) to store medical records in order to lessen the strain on the blockchain. Additionally, Azbeg *et al.* proposed a framework for diabetic self-management in which they secured IoT medical devices and addressed privacy issues with a permissioned blockchain as shown in Figure 6.16. The authors suggested using blockchain-based smart contracts to control and safeguard medical equipment like blood pressure monitors and insulin pumps. Data are kept in a specific EHR database, and the data that link it are kept as transactions in a permissioned blockchain using smart contracts in real time. A membership service provider, peer nodes, an orderer that places transaction orders, an HTTP-based API

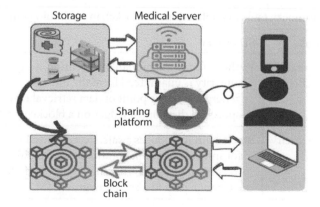

Figure 6.16 Process of IoT blockchain used in healthcare domain.

gateway serving as a device-to-blockchain interface, and other components make up the proposed system. Additionally, Srivastava *et al.* presented a brand-new Blockchain model suitable for IoT devices that does away with the PoW algorithm. The majority of these efforts addressed the access control issue that IoT systems have. In the interim, only two efforts addressed scalability, but none of them addressed interoperability [42].

6.3.10   Tracking Infectious Disease

Numerous technology firms from around the world have embraced blockchain to create platforms and applications that aid in the fight against the COVID-19 epidemic. To safeguard the transfer of data connected to COVID-19, blockchain technology was incorporated into a variety of solutions. For instance, the World Health Organization established the Hyperledger Fabric-based MiPasa platform to assist the gathering of COVID-19 data. It makes it easier for scientists, technicians, authorities, and public health professionals to share data. This would facilitate the development of remedies to support pandemic management efforts and contain the outbreak. Civitas is an additional implementation of a COVID-19 traceability solution. The COVID-19 passport application was developed by the company Emerge to monitor COVID-19 transmission among the community. A verifiable digital record of the COVID-19 testing results and transmission tracking is created using Blockchain technology [43].

The various uses of blockchain technology in the healthcare industry are summarised in Table 6.5. The table demonstrates its important contribution to data security and cooperation, demonstrating how it transforms the administration of electronic health records, pharmaceutical supply chain

Table 6.5 Summary table of applications of blockchain technology in healthcare.

Applications	Summary
Electronic Health Records (EHR)	Without requiring human intervention, a digital EHR's integrity is guaranteed from the moment of data generation to the point of data retrieval through an approved distributed ledger on a blockchain [44].
Clinical Research	Blockchain introduces a safe, decentralized foundation for information collaborations that can take place in clinical research. This enables the study team to exchange data in a secure manner [45].

(Continued)

Table 6.5 Summary table of applications of blockchain technology in healthcare. (*Continued*)

Applications	Summary
Medical Fraud Detection	By preventing any duplication or change of the transaction, blockchain, which has the property of being immutable, aids in fraud detection and ultimately enables a transparent and safe transaction [46].
Neuroscience Research	Several cutting-edge applications of blockchain technology involve improving, simulating, and reasoning with the brain. To store the full digitalized human brain, a medium must be employed; here is where blockchain innovation comes into play [47].
Pharmaceutical Industry and Research	In order to prevent the forging or theft of goods, blockchain uses its power of thorough tracking to monitor every step of the pharmaceutical supply chain. The origin of the medication, its components, and ownership are regularly discovered at each stage [48].
Electronic Medical Records Management System	An electronic (digital) database powered by computers that holds a person's medical information. An electronic medical record contains information on a patient's medical history, including diagnosis, treatments, tests, medications, allergies, and vaccinations [49].
Remote Patient Monitoring	Remote patient monitoring, also known as remote physiologic monitoring, is the process of remotely tracking patients' medical and other health data and electronically transferring those data to healthcare professionals for evaluation and, if necessary, suggestions and instructions [50].
Drug Traceability	The impact a medicine has on a patient is documented after use in a database for statistical purposes. Only dependable parties will be permitted to join the network and push data to the blockchain, which will be used to store transactions [51].

(Continued)

Table 6.5 Summary table of applications of blockchain technology in healthcare. (*Continued*)

Applications	Summary
Securing IoT Medical Devices	Medical devices are used to gather, manage, and exchange health information with the medical staff. It works as a way to safeguard data that are altered by IoT medical devices in healthcare systems. They can be used as biosensors for data collection and measurement, and smart contracts for insurance coverage and hospital bill calculation [52].
Tracking Infectious Diseases	Utilizing blockchain technology, information storage for infectious diseases will enable information recoding and storage throughout an epidemic. Each entity in such a disease direct reporting system is able to upload disease-related data or information on an independent node basis [53].

integrity, and research data sharing. Blockchain ensures secure and timely data flow between stakeholders while protecting against unauthorised changes and data breaches due to its decentralised and immutable nature. The use of regulated access to data for medical research is made possible by smart contracts, which also streamline operations and lower administrative expenses. Table 6.5 demonstrates how blockchain can revolutionise healthcare data management and provide a safer and more effective healthcare ecosystem.

6.4   Blockchain Challenges

Blockchain is a totally new technology and has not been fully effective yet. Because blockchain is a new technology, there are many challenges obstructing the adoption of blockchain in healthcare; under this section, primary challenges (as shown in Figure 6.17) of blockchain technology in the healthcare sector are discussed.

6.4.1   Resource Limitations and Bandwidth

The computing and storage capabilities of IoT devices are constrained. However, blockchain uses a significant amount of computational power. Additionally, as time passes, the size of the blockchain database continues to expand. The bandwidth is another factor to take into account. Although

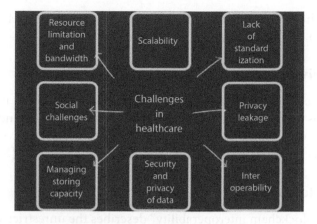

Figure 6.17 Blockchain challenges in the healthcare sector.

the majority of Internet of Things (IoT) devices use very little bandwidth, blockchain needs and the sheer number of connected devices may necessitate a substantial bandwidth consumption. These issues are addressed using a number of ways. The usage of permissioned blockchains for IoT systems is one of these solutions. Blockchain networks powered by energy-efficient consensus algorithms like proof of stake or similar algorithms provide a further answer [54].

6.4.2 Scalability

According to Croman *et al.*'s analysis, the maximum throughput, latency, bootstrap time, and cost per confirmed transaction are all connected to the scalability of Bitcoin. It also refers to a consensus algorithm's capacity to grow to a high number of nodes in order to scale the size of the network. Throughput and latency are the measurements that, in general, are given more attention. Throughput counts the number of successful transactions handled per second whereas latency refers to the time required to validate and process a transaction. The blockchain network's consensus method determines both parameters.

6.4.3 Lack of Standardization

Any health infrastructure must embrace universal standards for data collection, interchange, and storage. Although Blockchain has been used in a number of healthcare applications, there are still no guidelines in place to control its adoption. Because of this, standardization has become a serious problem that needs to be addressed soon. A number of organizations, including the International Standards Organization and the IEEE Standards Association, are developing blockchain standards.

6.4.4   Privacy Leakage

Since the healthcare industry demands high levels of privacy, using open blockchains to store and distribute private data is not recommended. Every transaction on a public blockchain is viewable by everyone. Even with an anonymous identity, that may be dangerous for sensitive data [55].

6.4.5   Interoperability

The term "blockchain interoperability" describes the unrestricted connection between various blockchain networks. The fact that the blockchain-based healthcare systems use several blockchain networks and platforms makes this difficulty crucial. Therefore, a way to make the many block-chains work together is required. Cross-blockchains based on framework is one of the techniques used to enable interoperability in blockchain technology.

6.4.6   Security and Privacy of Data

With the use of applications built on blockchain technology, a third party's involvement in a transaction is no longer necessary. Since the blockchain technique allows the entire community to validate the records in a block-chain architecture rather than a single trustworthy third party, the data are vulnerable to potential privacy and security issues. Because each node has access to the data transmitted by a single node, data privacy will be compromised. The patient must choose one or more representatives who, in the event of an emergency, will be able to access their information and/ or medical history on their behalf in the absence of a third party to grant permission [56].

6.4.7   Managing Storage Capacity

Another challenge on this front is managing storage capacity. Because it was designed to store and process transaction data, which is a certain type of data, blockchain does not need a lot of storage. As it grew into the healthcare sector, storage issues became obvious. In the healthcare sector, a sizable amount of data must be processed every day. In a blockchain sce-nario, all of the data, including patient information, health information, test results, MRI scans, X-rays, and other medical images, will be accessible to all nodes in the chain, requiring a sizable amount of storage space. The databases used to support this technology also tend to grow quickly because blockchain applications are transaction-based. As databases get larger, the speed at which records can be found and accessed slows down, rendering them completely unsuitable for the kinds of transactions where speed is essential. A blockchain system must therefore be reliable and scalable.

6.4.8   Standardization Challenges

Since blockchain technology is still in its infancy, there will surely be challenges with standardization on the way to its actual use in healthcare and medicine. International standardization organizations would have to offer several thoroughly authenticated and accepted standards. The amount, data type, and organizational structure of the information shared in blockchain applications should be evaluated following these predetermined standards. Together with scrutinizing the shared data, these rules must serve as precautionary safety measures [57].

6.4.9   Social Challenges

Although blockchain technology is still in its infancy, it faces not only the aforementioned technological challenges but also social challenges such as cultural transformations. Accepting and using technology that is fundamentally different from the way things have always been done is never an easy process.

6.5   Future Research Directions and Perspectives

Blockchain technology has many benefits to offer the medical business (as shown in Figure 6.18), and its use in healthcare applications has the potential to revolutionize that sector. The article contained some potential future research avenues for the blockchain in healthcare applications by referring to the various issues listed above. Research should focus on reworking blockchain models to make them better suited for IoT devices. This can be done by creating new blockchain topologies and new consensus algorithms that are intended specifically for IoT devices. Additionally, efforts should be undertaken to develop the legal and regulatory frameworks that will guarantee the adoption of blockchain technology in the healthcare industry. It is also recommended to conduct more research into the potential fusion of numerous technologies that could have a favorable impact on

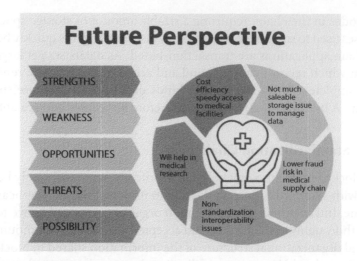

Figure 6.18 Future perspectives of blockchain in the healthcare domain.

the healthcare industry [58]. Systems that utilize blockchain, IoT, big data, cloud computing, fog, and artificial intelligence in addition to these other technologies such as a healthcare system that gathers medical data using IoT devices can be designed. Before being processed in the cloud, the gathered data could be filtered through fog computing. Artificial intelligence would then be used to analyze the enormous amount of acquired data, and of course, blockchain technology would be used to maintain communication and access control. This will make it possible for us to create a whole healthcare system that makes use of cutting-edge technologies. Blockchain technology is expected to promote medical science in the future, much to how the internet revolutionized healthcare and led to telemedicine, by reducing the costs of monitoring, configuration, and maintaining a central server for data and for the administration handling the medical data. Because of the distributed ledger's accessibility, the amount of time that must be spent processing data will be greatly reduced as soon as a patient enrolls in a study [59].

6.6   Implications and Conclusion

A review on the role of blockchain technology in healthcare applications was done in this report. IoT gadgets and wearables developed for healthcare and medical purposes are multiplying quickly every day. These gadgets have an internet connection and can gather and analyze health information before sharing it with the medical staff. Another advanced technique for securely storing and sending data is blockchain. It makes it possible to share private information in a trustworthy and safe way. By citing examples of current applications, such as remote patient monitoring and tracking, disease prediction, medical records management, drug traceability, and combating infectious diseases like COVID 19, a brief discussion on the integration of these two technologies in the healthcare industry was done in this paper. The study also discussed several current solutions as well as the various difficulties that arise when integrating blockchain-based healthcare systems. In addition, a few potential study directions are presented. Finally, our goal with this work is to present a condensed state of the art for further investigations.

Healthcare sometimes falls behind other sectors in implementing new technology, but the potential integrity of the data may provide a reason for blockchain adoption in the near future. Managing electronic health records in the blockchain might concentrate on a few essential topics. People are motivated to employ smart contracts and manage all minor and big transactions in the healthcare sector because of the suggested usage for them. The unbreakable chain of blocks provided by smart contracts would allow for the consideration of personalized care without violating clinical frameworks. A blockchain smart contract across convergent clinical systems would prevent any copies from being made in the parent centralized system. Blockchain technology may help researchers by providing verifiable and time-stamped versions of academic works. Similar to how smart contracts give patients control over their data, a blockchain record of the paperwork would give researchers a permanent record of their discoveries. Blockchain technology is essential for the vast pharmaceutical business.

People will become more involved in their healthcare as a result of this blockchain-based healthcare framework, which will ultimately improve their quality of life in a more appropriate way [60].

References

1. Nofer, M., Gomber, P., Hinz, O., Schiereck, D., Blockchain. *Bus. Inf. Syst. Eng.*, 59, 183–187, 2017.
2. Meunier, S., Blockchain 101: What is blockchain and how does this revolutionary technology work? in: *Transforming Climate Finance and Green Investment with Blockchains*, pp. 23–34, Academic Press, 2018.
3. Ammous, S., *Blockchain technology: What is it good for?* 2016, Saifedean Ammous, Available at SSRN 2832751.

4. Risius, M. and Spohrer, K., A blockchain research framework: What we (don't) know, where we go from here, and how we will get there. *Bus. Inf. Syst. Eng.*, *59*, 385–409, 2017.

5. Zarrin, J., Wen Phang, H., Babu Saheer, L., Zarrin, B., Blockchain for decentralization of internet: Prospects, trends, and challenges. *Cluster Comput.*, *24*, 4, 2841–2866, 2021.

6. Patil, P., Sangeetha, M., Bhaskar, V., Blockchain for IoT access control, security and privacy: A review. *Wirel. Pers. Commun.*, *117*, 1815–1834, 2021.

7. Dimitrov, D.V., Blockchain applications for healthcare data management. *Healthc. Inform. Res.*, *25*, 1, 51–56, 2019.

8. Assiri, B., Leader election and blockchain algorithm in cloud environment for e-health, in: *2019 2nd International Conference on New Trends in Computing Sciences (ICTCS)*, IEEE, pp. 1–6, 2019, October.

9. Schmitz, J. and Leoni, G., Accounting and auditing at the time of blockchain technology: A research agenda. *Aust. Account. Rev.*, *29*, 2, 331–342, 2019.

10. Zhang, Y., Deng, R.H., Shu, J., Yang, K., Zheng, D., TKSE: Trustworthy keyword search over encrypted data with two-side verifiability via blockchain. *IEEE Access*, *6*, 31077–31087, 2018.

11. Rizal Batubara, F., Ubacht, J., Janssen, M., Unraveling transparency and accountability in blockchain, in: *Proceedings of The 20th Annual International Conference on Digital Government Research*, pp. 204–213, 2019, June.

12. Hofmann, F., Wurster, S., Ron, E., Böhmecke-Schwafert, M., The immutability concept of blockchains and benefits of early standardization, in: *2017 ITU Kaleidoscope: Challenges for a Data-Driven Society (ITU K)*, pp. 1–8, IEEE, 2017, November.

13. Queralta, J.P., Qingqing, L., Zou, Z., Westerlund, T., Enhancing autonomy with blockchain and multi-access edge computing in distributed robotic systems, in: *2020 Fifth International Conference on Fog and Mobile Edge Computing (FMEC)*, IEEE, pp. 180–187, 2020, April.

14. Muzammal, M., Qu, Q., Nasrulin, B., Renovating blockchain with distributed databases: An open source system. *Future Gener. Comput. Syst.*, *90*, 105–117, 2019.

15. Dorri, A., Kanhere, S.S., Jurdak, R., Gauravaram, P., LSB: A lightweight scalable blockchain for IoT security and anonymity. *J. Parallel Distrib. Comput.*, *134*, 180–197, 2019.

16. Ekblaw, A., Azaria, A., Halamka, J.D., Lippman, A., A case study for blockchain in healthcare:"MedRec" prototype for electronic health records and medical research data, in: *Proceedings of IEEE Open & Big Data Conference*, vol. 13, p. 13, 2016, August.

17. Ekblaw, A., Azaria, A., Vieira, T., Lippman, A., *MedRrec: Medical data management on the blockchain*, Viral Communications, 2016.

18. Azaria, A., Ekblaw, A., Vieira, T., Lippman, A., MedRec: Using blockchain for medical data access and permission management, in: *2016 2nd International Conference on Open and Big Data (OBD)*, pp. 25–30, IEEE, 2016, August.

19. Blockchain for medical data access, permission management and trend analysis, pp. 93-97, Massachusetts Institute of Technology, Program in Media Arts and Sciences (Massachusetts Institute of Technology), 2017.
20. Benchoufi, M. and Ravaud, P., Blockchain technology for improving clinical research quality. *Trials*, *18*, 1, 1–5, 2017.
21. Charles, W., Marler, N., Long, L., Manion, S., Blockchain compliance by design: Regulatory considerations for blockchain in clinical research. *Front. Blockchain*, *2*, 18, 2019.
22. Maslove, D.M., Klein, J., Brohman, K., Martin, P., Using blockchain technology to manage clinical trials data: A proof-of-concept study. *JMIR Med. Inform.*, *6*, 4, e11949, 2018.
23. Saldamli, G., Reddy, V., Bojja, K.S., Gururaja, M.K., Doddaveerappa, Y., Tawalbeh, L., Healthcare insurance fraud detection using blockchain, in: *2020 Seventh International Conference on Software Defined Systems (SDS)*, IEEE, pp. 145–152, 2020, April.
24. Kapadiya, K., Patel, U., Gupta, R., Alshehri, M.D., Tanwar, S., Sharma, G., Bokoro, P.N., Blockchain and AI-empowered healthcare insurance fraud detection: An analysis, architecture, and future prospects. *IEEE Access*, *10*, 79606–79627, 1–2, 2022.
25. Taherdoost, H., Neuroscience and blockchain. *Hamed Taherdoost. Neuroscience Blockchain. Arch. Neurol. Neurosci.*, *12*, 4, 2022.
26. Cho, S.H., Cushing, C.A., Patel, K., Kothari, A., Lan, R., Michel, M., Cherkaoui, M., Lau, H., *Blockchain and human episodic memory*, 2018, arXiv preprint arXiv:1811.02881.
27. Soltanisehat, L., Alizadeh, R., Hao, H., Choo, K.K.R., Technical, temporal, and spatial research challenges and opportunities in blockchain-based healthcare: A systematic literature review. *IEEE Trans. Eng. Manag.*, 1, 1–16, 2020.
28. Schöner, M.M., Kourouklis, D., Sandner, P., Gonzalez, E., Förster, J., *Blockchain technology in the pharmaceutical industry*, Frankfurt School Blockchain Center, Frankfurt, Germany, 2017.
29. Fernando, E., Success factor of implementation blockchain technology in pharmaceutical industry: A literature review, in: *2019 6th International Conference on Information Technology, Computer and Electrical Engineering (ICITACEE)*, pp. 1–5, IEEE, 2019, September.
30. Haq, I. and Esuka, O.M., Blockchain technology in pharmaceutical industry to prevent counterfeit drugs. *Int. J. Comput. Appl.*, *180*, 25, 8–12, 2018.
31. McDonald, C.J., The barriers to electronic medical record systems and how to overcome them. *J. Am. Med. Inform. Assoc.*, *4*, 3, 213–221, 1997.
32. Ludwick, D.A. and Doucette, J., Adopting electronic medical records in primary care: Lessons learned from health information systems implementation experience in seven countries. *Int. J. Med. Inform.*, *78*, 1, 22–31, 2009.
33. Hillestad, R., Bigelow, J., Bower, A., Girosi, F., Meili, R., Scoville, R., Taylor, R., Can electronic medical record systems transform healthcare? Potential health benefits, savings, and costs. *Health Aff.*, *24*, 5, 1103–1117, 2005.

34. Hathaliya, J., Sharma, P., Tanwar, S., Gupta, R., Blockchain-based remote patient monitoring in healthcare 4.0, in: *2019 IEEE 9th International Conference on Advanced Computing (IACC)*, pp. 87–91, IEEE, 2019, December.

35. Griggs, K.N., Ossipova, O., Kohlios, C.P., Baccarini, A.N., Howson, E.A., Hayajneh, T., Healthcare blockchain system using smart contracts for secure automated remote patient monitoring. *J. Med. Syst., 42*, 1–7, 2018.

36. Uddin, M.A., Stranieri, A., Gondal, I., Balasubramanian, V., A decentralized patient agent controlled blockchain for remote patient monitoring, in: *2019 International Conference on Wireless and Mobile Computing, Networking and Communications (WiMob)*, pp. 2–8, IEEE, 2019, October.

37. Uddin, M., Salah, K., Jayaraman, R., Pesic, S., Ellahham, S., Blockchain for drug traceability: Architectures and open challenges. *Health Inf. J., 27*, 2, 2–8, 14604582211011228, 2021.

38. Huang, Y., Wu, J., Long, C., Drugledger: A practical blockchain system for drug traceability and regulation, in: *2018 IEEE International Conference on Internet of Things (iThings) and IEEE Green Computing and Communications (GreenCom) and IEEE Cyber, Physical and Social Computing (CPSCom) and IEEE Smart Data (SmartData)*, pp. 1137–1144, IEEE, 2018, July.

39. Musamih, A., Salah, K., Jayaraman, R., Arshad, J., Debe, M., Al-Hammadi, Y., Ellahham, S., A blockchain-based approach for drug traceability in health-care supply chain. *IEEE Access, 9*, 9728–9743, 2021.

40. Kumar, R. and Tripathi, R., Traceability of counterfeit medicine supply chain through blockchain, in: *2019 11th International Conference on Communication Systems & Networks (COMSNETS*, pp. 568–570, IEEE, 2019, January.

41. Srivastava, G., Crichigno, J., Dhar, S., A light and secure healthcare blockchain for iot medical devices, in: *2019 IEEE Canadian conference of Electrical and Computer Engineering (CCECE)*, pp. 1–5, IEEE, 2019, May.

42. Malamas, V., Dasaklis, T., Kotzanikolaou, P., Burmester, M., Katsikas, S., A forensics-by-design management framework for medical devices based on blockchain, in: *2019 IEEE World Congress on Services (SERVICES)*, vol. 2642, pp. 35–40, IEEE, 2019, July.

43. Zhu, P., Hu, J., Zhang, Y., Li, X., Enhancing traceability of infectious diseases: A blockchain-based approach. *Inf. Process. Manag., 58*, 4, 102570, 2021.

44. Dubovitskaya, A., Baig, F., Xu, Z., Shukla, R., Zambani, P.S., Swaminathan, A., Wang, F., ACTION-EHR: Patient-centric blockchain-based electronic health record data management for cancer care. *J. Med. Internet Res., 22*, 8, e13598, 2020.

45. Zhang, P., White, J., Schmidt, D.C., Lenz, G., Rosenbloom, S.T., FHIRChain: Applying blockchain to securely and scalably share clinical data. *Comput. Struct. Biotechnol. J., 16*, 267–278, 2018.

46. Mohan, T. and Praveen, K., Fraud detection in medical insurance claim with privacy preserving data publishing in TLS-N using blockchain, in: *Advances*

in Computing and Data Sciences: Third International Conference, ICACDS 2019, Springer Singapore, Ghaziabad, India, April 12–13, 2019, pp. 211–220, 2019, Revised Selected Papers, Part I 3.

47. Taherdoost, H., Neuroscience and blockchain. *Hamed Taherdoost. Neuroscience and Blockchain. Arch. Neurol. Neurosci., 12*, 4, 1–2, 2022.

48. Alshahrani, W. and Alshahrani, R., Assessment of blockchain technology application in the improvement of pharmaceutical industry, in: *2021 International Conference of Women in Data Science at Taif University (WiDSTaif)*, pp. 1–5, IEEE, 2021, March.

49. Vora, J., Nayyar, A., Tanwar, S., Tyagi, S., Kumar, N., Obaidat, M.S., Rodrigues, J.J., BHEEM: A blockchain-based framework for securing electronic health records, in: *2018 IEEE Globecom Workshops (GC Wkshps)*, pp. 1–6, IEEE, 2018, December.

50. Srivastava, G., Dwivedi, A.D., Singh, R., *Automated remote patient monitoring: Data sharing and privacy using blockchain*, 2018, arXiv preprint arXiv:1811.03417. https://doi.org/10.48550/arXiv.1811.03417

51. Panda, S.K. and Satapathy, S.C., Drug traceability and transparency in medical supply chain using blockchain for easing the process and creating trust between stakeholders and consumers. *Pers. Ubiquitous Comput.*, 1–17, 2021.

52. Seliem, M. and Elgazzar, K., BIoMT: Blockchain for the internet of medical things, in: *2019 IEEE International Black Sea Conference on Communications and Networking (BlackSeaCom)*, pp. 1–4, IEEE, 2019, June.

53. Zhu, P., Hu, J., Zhang, Y., Li, X., Enhancing traceability of infectious diseases: A blockchain-based approach. *Inf. Process. Manag., 58*, 4, 102570, 2021.

54. Salimitari, M. and Chatterjee, M., *An overview of blockchain and consensus protocols for IoT networks*, pp. 1–12, 2018, arXiv preprint arXiv:1809.05613.

55. Henry, R., Herzberg, A., Kate, A., Blockchain access privacy: Challenges and directions. *IEEE Secur. Priv., 16*, 4, 38–45, 2018.

56. Joshi, A.P., Han, M., Wang, Y., A survey on security and privacy issues of blockchain technology. *Math. Found. Comput., 1*, 2, 121, 2018.

57. Deshpande, A., Stewart, K., Lepetit, L., Gunashekar, S., *Distributed ledger technologies/blockchain: Challenges, opportunities and the prospects for standards. Overview report*, vol. 40, p. 40, The British Standards Institution (BSI), 2017.

58. Zhao, G., Liu, S., Lopez, C., Lu, H., Elgueta, S., Chen, H., Boshkoska, B.M., Blockchain technology in agri-food value chain management: A synthesis of applications, challenges and future research directions. *Comput. Ind., 109*, 83–99, 2019.

59. Hassan, M.U., Rehmani, M.H., Chen, J., Privacy preservation in blockchain based IoT systems: Integration issues, prospects, challenges, and future research directions. *Future Gener. Comput. Syst., 97*, 512–529, 2019.

60. Abu-Elezz, I., Hassan, A., Nazeemudeen, A., Househ, M., Abd-Alrazaq, A., The benefits and threats of blockchain technology in healthcare: A scoping review. *Int. J. Med. Inf., 142*, 104246, 2020.

in Computing and Data Science. Third International Conference, ICCIDS 2019 Springer Singapore (Database Ltd.), April 12–13, 2019, pp. 311–320, 2019. Revised selected Papers, Part I.

47. Bhardwaj, H., Nanoscience and Blockchain. Human Interaction Neuroscience and Biochemistry. Technion in Neuroscience 1, 4, 1–5, 2022.

48. Abraham, W. and Abbasi-Fri, R., Assessment of blockchain technology application in the improvement of pharmaceutical industry in 2021. International Conference on Blockchain and Applications of Life University (ICBC 2021), pp. 1–7, IEEE, 2021, March.

49. Nora, J., Nelson, A., Estwerea, Ivey, S., Rymar, N.C., Bardai, M.S., Rodriguez, A.B., HEAL, A blockchain based framework for securing electronic health records. In 2018 IEEE Cybersecurity Workshop (DC Washer) pp. 1–6, IEEE, 2018, December.

50. Srivastava, G., Dwivedi, A.D., Singh, R., Automated remote patient monitoring: Data sharing and privacy using blockchain, 2018. arXiv preprint arXiv:1811.03417, https://doi.org/10.48550/arXiv.1811.03417.

51. Benfa, Z.K. and Adepetun, S.C., Drug traceability and transparency in medical supply chain using blockchain for easing the process and creating trust between stakeholder and consumers. Peer Ubiquitous Comput, 1–15, 2021.

52. Schaub, M. and Pascoal, K., BlOMT blockchain for the internet of medical things since 2017, IEEE International ANDSec conference on Computing sharing and networking (blockchain Chain), pp. 1–4, IEEE, 2019, June.

53. Zhu, P., Liu, J., Abass, I., Li, X., Tobacco up based utility of infectious diseases: A blockchain based approach. Inf., Process. Manage. 58, 4, 102576, 2021.

54. Silmukami, M. and Chatterjee, M., An overview of blockchain and consensus protocol for IoT network. pp. 1–16, 2018. arXiv preprint arXiv:1809.05613.

55. Herm, B., Hierbele, A., Kale, A., Blockchain access privacy: Challenges and directions. IEEE Secur. Priv., 16, 4, 38–45, 2018.

56. Haber, A.F., Zhou, M., Wang, Y., A survey on security and privacy issues of blockchain technology. Math Found. Comput., 1, 2, 121, 2019.

57. Gordande, A., Stephens, R., Espitil, E., Grunberg, S., Distributed ledger technologies and their relevance to the health sector and the future of care. A Governance report and their guide to blockchain healthcare (IEEE, 2017.

58. Zhao, G., Liu, S., Lopez, C., Liu, H., Elgueta, S., Chen, H., Boshkoska, B.M., Blockchain technology in agri-food value chain management: A synthesis of applications, challenges and future research directions. Comput. Ind., 109, 83–99, 2019.

59. Dagan, M.D., Reiner, M.H., Chen, L., Privacy preservation in blockchain based IoT systems: Integration issues, prospects, challenges, and future research directions. Future Gener. Comput. Syst., 97, 512–529, 2019.

60. Abu-elezz, I., Hassan, A., Nazeemudeen, A.A., Househ, M., Abd-Alrazaq, A., The benefits and threats of blockchain technology in healthcare: A scoping review. Int. J. Med. Inf., 142, 104246, 2020.

7

Blockchain in Healthcare: Use Cases

Utsav Sharma[1], Aditi Ganapathi[1], Akansha Singh[2*] and Krishna Kant Singh[3]

[1]ASET, Amity University, Noida, India
[2]SCSET, Bennett University, Greater Noida, India
[3]Delhi Technical Campus, Greater Noida, India

Abstract

The creation of state-of-the-art trusted frameworks for healthcare services that are centered around patients is necessitated by the increasing life expectancy, ease of access to healthcare, and better standards of living over the years. While conditions in the healthcare sector have been constantly improving, there are still various unresolved issues that need to be addressed. Moreover, with the evolution of technology, the existing methods of keeping records, tracking credentials, and ensuring the security of data can be made more efficient at a lower cost. One of the proposed systems is blockchain. This is an emerging field, with more and more companies using this technology to benefit practitioners in the healthcare sector, as well as patients. The application of blockchain can have a revolutionary positive impact in the field of medicine.

Keywords: Blockchain, decentralization, interoperability, medicare

7.1 Introduction

Blockchains have varied definitions. According to Hileman and Rauchs [1], a distributed database is one where data are stored in multiple computers, while a distributed ledger is a distributed data type that assumes the possibility of the presence of malicious users or nodes. From these two definitions, the authors have defined blockchain as a distributed ledger that consists of blocks containing data, which are linked together to form chains. All of the data in a blockchain are visible to all the devices connected to the network. A report by the Institution of Engineering and

---

*Corresponding author: akanshasing@gmail.com

Akansha Singh, Anuradha Dhull and Krishna Kant Singh (eds.) Blockchain and Deep Learning for Smart Healthcare, (147–170) © 2024 Scrivener Publishing LLC

Technology (IET) defined blockchain as a decentralized ledger that, using strong encryption algorithms, ensures that the data are recorded and managed in a secure and truthful manner. It is common practice to define blockchain technology merely on the basis of its security, data privacy, and transparency features. Several research works, such as that of Ali *et al.* [2], have shown that blockchain can minimize transactional ambiguity, unstable states, and uncertainty by providing full transaction transparency and the supplementation of uniform and validated data across all network participants.

7.1.1   Features of Blockchains

I. Decentralization
Decentralization in blockchain allows all computing devices in the network to access all blocks in the chain. Each transaction is done by only two nodes at a time, without a need for third-party validation. This has been termed resistance to censorship, according to Ali *et al.* [2].

II. Trustless
Blockchain enables the Internet to establish a distributed network status, by assuming that no node is trustworthy, to be exchanged across connecting networks. This forms a network solely based on trust, or the lack thereof [3]. This is made possible by the peer-to-peer feature of blockchain, along with its strong encryption and data storage capabilities.

III. Immutability
Immutability is a core blockchain attribute arising from the fact that transactions cannot be modified or deleted after they have been successfully checked and registered into the blockchain [4]. This is achieved because all the data and transactions are stored in blocks with two hash keys, one pointing to the previous block and the other to the next block. Any compromise on the information would generate hash values that do not match. This is easily identified by all the other nodes [5].

IV. Security
The use of cryptographic algorithms, such as SHA-256, on the hash functions stored in the blocks ensures maximum privacy and data security [6].

7.2   Challenges Faced in the Healthcare Sector

Table 7.1 displays a few issues faced in the medical sector and the stakeholders impacted by such issues. A number of problems faced in the healthcare sector are also discussed in detail in this section.

I.   **Interoperability**

Interoperability denotes the coordination of various entities. It can be challenging in two ways. As Bogoeva *et al.* [8] suggest, the smooth integration of blockchain, an emerging technology, with the already existing technologies can be problematic to give full utilization. Similarly, according to Shahnaz *et al.* [6], there might be an issue in integrating various sources of data, or health information exchange (HIE), as there is a lack of uniformity in the terminologies used in various hospitals and clinics, in addition to having varying functional and technical capabilities. This will cause a problem in the data exchange being uninterpretable and, therefore, unusable by all stakeholders.

II.   **Data breach**

Data breaches have become an increasing concern in the modern world, where information is equivalent to power.

Table 7.1 Issues faced in the healthcare sector and their relationship with stakeholders [7].

| Issues | Healthcare stakeholders | | | | |
	Provider	Patient	Player	Research organizations	Supply chain
Record Management	Yes	Yes	Yes	Yes	Yes
Data Exchange	Yes	Yes	Yes	Yes	Yes
Security	Yes	Yes	Yes	No	Yes
Lack of Data Provenance	No	Yes	Yes	Yes	Yes
Privacy	No	Yes	No	No	No
Monetization	No	Yes	No	No	No

Studies have shown that, since October 2009, approximately 173 million data records have been breached in electronic health record (EHR) systems. Trends suggest that more and more hospitals are being marked as targets for cybercrime attacks [6].

III. **No remote access**

People from many small towns and villages, as well as from many lesser developed countries, travel to big cities for the examination and treatment of their illnesses. However, follow-up checkups can be tedious due to the return travel arrangements after surgery. Regular multiple trips to the city and back are expensive for patients, not to mention the inconvenience these cause. Similarly, during the coronavirus outbreak, people were confined within the four walls of their homes, resulting in the inability to visit any hospitals, more so in the fear of catching the virus from hospitals during treatment.

IV. **Disconnect among medical workers**

Medical providers around the world do not seem to operate in a well-organized and unified fashion. There is a gap in the market for a forum that will unify healthcare communities and enable them to be on the same page, allowing them to exchange knowledge, share information, and ask questions. A lot of things could change if there is a single channel devoted solely to the healthcare industry. Everyone can benefit from each other's knowledge, which results in a more inclusive, collaborative, and a motivated healthcare industry.

7.3   Use Cases of Blockchains in the Healthcare Sector

7.3.1   Blockchains for Maintaining Electronic Health Records

Because blockchain are able to store decentralized information, they have vital benefits in the management of EHRs. Blockchain is a fast-growing field, with skills being gained at an exponential rate, therefore giving rise to various new frameworks and applications. These considerations have been presented through the EHR and electronic medical record (EMR) frameworks. The crucial advantages of blockchain (paired with artificial intelligence, AI) include, firstly, *client confidence*: ability of the consumer

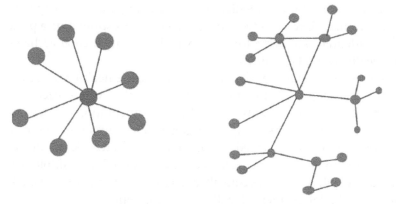

Figure 7.1 Comparison between a centralized and a decentralized network.

to see the trajectory of every task's end-to-end, alongside cooperation with creators, retailers, and conveyance, among others. Secondly, *amenability*: medical practitioners go through massive amounts of medical records that help with the management of patients' well-being. Therefore, the storage of these data into a single decentralized system assists in the smooth operation of their management. As an example, FarmaTrust's blockchain-based system gives online alert/warning if any malfunction occurs in stock sequence optimization: When information is entirely at a single domain, organizations apply AI to intricately predict mandates and correspondingly elevate supply.

The digital adaptation of patients' medical records is called electronic health records (EHRs). An EHR collects, manages, and assembles robust data electronically. The EHR system is quite slow when it is utilized by Medicare benefactors. Hospital-based authentication, lagging of mobile applications, invoicing, and the condensing of information must be refined; thus, medical registers are deemed handy. Organizational utilities, automatic medical practitioner mandatory access, laboratory plans, fluoroscopy specimens, pharmaceutical arrangements, and substantiated medical certification comprise the fundamental mechanisms of an electronic medical documentation. EHRs utilize HL7 (Health Level Seven International), which is a set of standards and guidelines for communication in healthcare. The realization of shareware, drug, and information technology grids is imperative for the successful implementation of an EHR system.

The age-old method of maintaining written or physical records has its own drawbacks, vis-à-vis the safekeeping of health registers, client ownership of files, and the integrity of information, among others. By introducing blockchain technology to medical record-keeping, data security risks can be greatly minimized. This technology propositions stipulating a protected and confidential manifesto for the stockpiling of medicinal archives and other health-related documents.

Prior to the emergence of modern methods, the healthcare sector used a table-based approach to store medical histories, where each individual patient record was handwritten. This documentation framework was unproductive, time-consuming, disorganized, and was not secure, as the data could be easily accessed. Another major drawback of this system was data redundancy, as medical records were stored in multiple registers across all hospitals or clinics consulted in cases where a patient visited multiple medical establishments for different treatments.

The healthcare industry has experienced increasing changes in EHR systems, a digital representation of a patient's medical data. These networks were employed to store hospital-based records and medical results in multiple layers. They were generated to enhance the security aspect of their users by preventing failures and improving secure access. The aims of the EHR system are to interpret the complications encountered by the address-based medical registers and to deliver a capable, speedy, well-secured, and tamper-proof system that would modernize the interface of the medical community.

The Gates Foundation has sponsored a procedure in South Africa to merge the HIV clinic documents of the country, backing the 90/90/90 domestic strategy—90% of all HIV-prone individuals should be aware of their status with regard to HIV, 90% of the population must be cured with Lithogogue prescriptions, and 90% of infected individuals must have proof that their HIV has been suppressed, which should be supported by two continuous epidemiological load checks, 6 months apart. To engineer this scheme, The Gates Foundation selected a variation of biometrics, a mobile application accessible using the most basic mobile phones, and blockchain. At the moment, South Africa has substructural challenges including erratic electricity and pricey bandwidth. Therefore, a distributed, decentralized class of information, which is independent of changes due to failure of a single isolated module, makes sense. Nevertheless, it is vital to ensure the reliability of the disseminated information. Thus, a combination of interactive networks on a decentralized record-keeping system alongside blockchain that authenticates the integrity of information through a hash of each of 10,000 accounts should work well.

The advantages of the digitization of EMRs include a profit in medical efficiencies, massive improvements in record-keeping, security, and reduced hospital-based expenditures for patrons. On the contrary, the challenges of EHRs include costly software packages, issues in system security and patient confidentiality, and unclear future government regulations. Future technologies for EHRs include bar cataloging, radiofrequency identification, and speech recognition.

a) Hospital-centred and administrative need for an EHR

There are many hospital-based and administrative prerequisites that a hospital, or the clinic of a general practitioner, must meet for the EHR to be a success. EHR serves as the main database that stores and manages patients' records of clinical symptoms, invoicing, frequency of hospital visits and maintenance of hospital assessments.

Patient documentation

An EHR must have a record of the consultant's notes, patient's age, medications, doctor's prescriptions, clinical results, neurological and roentgenogram images, any other medical interventions, and all other comprehensive face-to-face consultations with the physician. These system requirements need to be complete and updated as time is an issue and doctors will be seeing a lot of patients on a given day.

Quality assertion

Blockchain-enabled EHR stores a huge amount of data including patients' test results, radiography images, and other medical procedures. As such, it allows keeping track of any and all data as and when needed by physicians or hospitals, especially in relation to, e.g., insurance claims and other civic protocols. In addition, these data can be used by surgeons to determine appropriate tests for patients or to perform any more tests if necessary. Blockchain-enabled EHR also features the medical sector to present facts with quality sources to state authorities.

Tracking patients' use and Medicare overheads

Medicare invests a lot of time monitoring the data and the usage of patients, including the duration of services availed, tests, number of visits, and an approximation of all the hospital services offered to them. These figures are used to follow employment developments and reporting bills, as well as for accounting and reserve allocations. An EHR can modernize these processes and save precise and instantaneous concurrent data. These indicators, when matched with financial data, can be used to track Medicare expenses and recover costs.

Health record transparency and maneuverability

At present, patients' health records are in tabular form in registers, which makes the transfer of a patient's medical data a tedious task. When a patient visits another clinic or sees an alternative medical practitioner, his/her register also needs to be transferred to the new clinic. This is a big responsibility as all data have to be duplicated and redirected to the new doctor, which frequently results in information deficiency. Old records belong to and are stored by hospitals, which is a tedious documentation process. An EHR is a solution to this issue, allowing data to be retrieved as and when needed.

Invoicing and cataloging

Accurate invoicing and cataloging are imperative in healthcare. Medicare and other health insurance companies require exact certification of a patient's medical condition. Relevant medical inventories precisely portray this, and new documentation automatically initiates payment gateway for patients to pay. Therefore, errors in the data processing are associated with charging errors. The EHR system assists with appropriate certification and has records of prognosis that could help authorities design appropriate Medicare claims.

Confidentiality

In healthcare, patient confidentiality is a priority. The Health Insurance Portability and Accountability Act (HIPAA) stipulates Medicare benefactors to safeguard patients' privacy and confidentiality of their medical data, failure of which can incur serious fines. EHRs, therefore, must have high cyber security measures incorporated into the system in order to prevent malicious access to any medical data. The rules, biometrics, and complex firewall systems in EHRs are employed for this purpose. However, the subject of whether automated registers or hardcopy accounts are safer is an ongoing debate. With automated documentation, accountants can determine an unauthorized access to the records as most EHRs record each instance a documentation is retrieved. This is not possible with tabular data registers.

7.3.2   Electronic Health Record Applications

Accounting applications

EHRs, to a certain degree, are highly useful for bookkeeping and accounting, the feature of EHR that records patient's registration, documenting the patient number on the proof that incorporates personal credentials, medical protection particulars, administrator, and patient's primary illness. This generates a distinctive patient ID number that is solely for use by a specific Medicare supplier.

Automated doctor order admittance
A requirement for all EHRs is the application called Automated Doctor Order Admittance, which is a handy mechanism used by doctors to procure laboratory, pharmaceutical, and fluoroscopy (X-rays, among others) facilities and supplementary medical orders. This confers benefits to Medicare benefactors by permitting doctors to order test equipment online without the use of forms, which guarantees accuracy in the transmission and reports the appropriate region to which the patient will be attended. It also allows Medicare specialists to identify relevant analyses that need to be accomplished.

Laboratory procedures
Most testing laboratories in Medicare set hitherto practice Laboratory Intelligence Systems (LIS), which are generally incorporated into the EHR for patient information and for dispute of test outcomes. Currently, nearly every laboratory doctor and laboratory analysis equipment contact use the LIS. This computerized e-technique also encompasses clinic briefings, its outcomes, calendars, and additional responsibilities.

Ultrasound and radiology techniques
Radiology Intelligence Organizations (RIS/RIO) are other divisions with intelligent systems affiliated with EHRs. These systems, similar to other testing techniques, store patient reports, the tests required, their outcomes, and rotas and perform identity tracing. Furthermore, these methods are used with a picture archiving and communication system (PACS). This system administers and stores primary fluoroscopy results, which are pooled and can be observed in the EHR.

Hospital-based certification
Hospital-based certification is a huge part of an EHR, as medics, attendants, and previous Medicare experts record a massive volume of data on each patient. This information ranges from hospital-based notes to reports, assessments, and the Medication Administration Record (MAR). Other components of this documentation include vital signs, discharge summaries, transcription documents, and utilization management.

Dispensary framework
Pharmacies in big hospitals are highly computerized, which use machines to collect medications and prepare automatically incorporated prescription orders. These arrangements are an added structure in EHR. Hospital pharmacies additionally employ block classification on suppositories and

information of patients to confirm accurate dosage, the identity of the recipient, correct duration, and medication supervision. It is critical that pharmacies align with the EHR system due to the issues of counterfeit drugs. Here, blockchain technology is again advantageous and is used to improve the transactions of pharmaceutical drugs. In Medicare, inaccuracies in prescriptions comprise the prominent issue in miscalculations that cause injury in patients. An essential constituent of EHR's dispensary framework is e-prescribing. One cause of prescription error is a doctor's incomprehensible handwriting. E-prescribing resolves this issue by directing the medication order online to the relevant pharmacy or the clinic's pharmacy. EHR is a useful system that could help reduce the errors in medication prescription and delivery.

Other applications

EHRs realize further applications that help in a more widespread and thorough documentation. A primary application is infirmary-centred judgment maintenance. This assists doctors and caregivers to elect the accurate progression of work on a certain patient and his/her condition. Another important application is assessment of quality. These frameworks assist in tracking patients' results and equip Medicare suppliers the necessary data to provide figures to relevant national organizations.

7.3.3   Blockchains in Clinical Trials

Clinical trials are clinical experiments in humans used to assess the effectiveness of a medical, surgical, or a psychological procedure. They are the most common method for researchers to determine whether a new medication, such as a synthetic medicine, diet, or a medical product, is safe and efficient for use in humans.

The participation of patients is the most important factor in clinical trials. According to Benchoufi *et al.* [9], the US Food and Drug Administration (FDA) has published a study on the prevalence of clinical investigator-related limitations, revealing that nearly 10% of the trials they examined showed discrepancies in consent processing, including the inability to re-consent as new information comes to light. An incapability to provide copies of the documentation to participants was also shown. Moreover, the utilization of inaccurate, obsolete, non-validated, and unauthorized consent forms was noted. Cases have been noted [9] where the consent documents have been found to be backdated.

One of the major problems in modern biomedical research is the resolution of methodology concerns. Basically, the lack of reproducibility, which can be linked to issues of scientific negligence ranging from defects to frauds, jeopardizes the results of the clinical study and lessens the efficiency of the research.

As blockchain allows data monitoring, sharing, and management, it has the potential to have a global effect on clinical research. It represents a decentralized, secure monitoring system for any information exchange that may result from clinical trials, as well as a peer-to-peer integrated network that allows data sharing on the operations side while also providing all the requisite transparency and privacy protection for the patient population. At the practical level, "the data level," data inviolability and historicity are two major features. In terms of data inviolability and historicity, blockchain guarantees that facts are documented in the proper chronological order, largely eliminating the need for *a posteriori* reconstruction evaluation.

Firstly, the encrypted verification of each transaction ensures data integrity. This is critical for maintaining the trustworthiness of the data—preventing forgery, "beautification," and, in certain ways, data invention. Secondly, the main features of blockchain technology include data transparency and historicity: with blockchain, each transaction is timestamped. This information is open to the public, and any user may obtain a copy of the timestamped data evidence. In a clinical trial, complicated streams of heterogeneous data and metadata circulate, meaning a large number of medical stakeholders and all records whose presence can be verified using blockchain. As a result, the presence of data may be proven, although the data remains private.

Diverse medical trial phases can be chained together, such that each stage relies on its precursor, in addition to archiving clinical study metadata on the blockchain. Smart contracts, which use blockchain technology to accomplish these "slicing" and "chaining" procedures, will ensure a high degree of accountability, tracking, and control over clinical trial samples.

We defined a timeline of events in the conduct of clinical trials using blockchain technology [10], as follows.

I.   Prior to the start of the clinical trial, a data-sharing strategy, including the calendar, database documents, and, when applicable, a data-sharing contract, must be published so that these metadata can be timestamped in chronological sequence in the unverifiable blockchain.

II. Permissions and the clinical trial procedure, which involves the method of testing, primary and secondary results, and approval and rejection requirements, can be incorporated into the data structures recorded on the blockchain before the trial starts. Consents, the protocol, and its modifications are then in one-to-one communication with the data structures, providing robust evidence of their existence. This function can help avoid common issues associated with non-traceable clinical trial procedures, such as incomplete reporting of outcomes, under-reporting of non-significant outcomes, and discrepancies between the protocol and final report results. These problems are a well-known cause of prejudice. Details such as the method of data collection, identification process, dates of transactions to differentiate between early and late events, and dates of repeated events in the blockchain metadata set can also be stored.

III. Before the conclusion of the research, in the case of a blinded analysis, the statistical analysis plan is time-stamped before unblinding of the results. The statistical methods, description of harm incidents, and multiple variable changes, if any, are all included in this plan. For example, sample size is an important factor to consider when determining the power of a study. Since research teams seldom know exactly what will happen, predicting the necessary power in advance is difficult, resulting in an *a posteriori* calculation bias. The dataset size, category I and II errors, the approximate event rate, and the diagnostic impact of interest are all timestamping a collection of metadata on the blockchain. Timestamping would be a turning point in the blockchain, showing the *a priori* calculated sample size.

IV. To avoid analytical errors, the analytical code should be distributed and made open. Since scripts change over time and a defined version of the code is then used to interpret data, this exact status of the script should be fixed and timestamped to guarantee that the circumstances in which information was reviewed and evaluated are repeatable. Given today's scientific developments, the blockchain timestamp script is the only reliable, unchangeable time-stamping process.

Benchoufi and Ravaud [10] conducted a proof-of-concept experiment in which, for a clinical trial, they used a blockchain system to collect participant consent. They timestamped each patient's consent on the blockchain in a hypothetical experimental study and asked for consent renewal for each procedure update. They created a unique master document containing all of the compiled consent data in a single file system, a code called ChainScript, each linked to a version of the updated protocols. Because of the strict one-to-one relationship between the encrypted data and the usable consent data, this master document reflected a stable, comprehensive proof of existence of the entire consent collection process. This evidence could also be confirmed on any publicly accessible website.

7.3.4   Blockchains in Improving Patient–Doctor Interactions

The most significant issue confronting healthcare systems worldwide is determining how to exchange medical information with known and unknown parties for different purposes while maintaining data confidentiality and protecting patient confidentiality. Despite the quality of data being higher than they had ever been, each EHR stores information differently, leaving it unclear who reported what and when.

The healthcare system needs efficient patient data management. Each individual is unique, which means that their health status is as well. Furthermore, patients often conceal information, making it challenging for a doctor to diagnose the condition and prescribe a medication. As a result, it is a common occurrence that doctors lack a comprehensive and accurate medical history that would enable them to provide high-quality patient care.

Because health records contain sensitive data and due to the continuing challenges of compatibility, patient record matching, and health information sharing, blockchain can be a viable solution. Without physical human interference, the data provided by EHRs on an authorized blockchain shared database will be perfectly consolidated community-wide, with guaranteed credibility from the stage of data creation to the point of use. Blockchain solution for the healthcare sector radically reduces the time spent acquiring patient data and improves data exchange.

A case study of Medicalchain has been conducted to examine the scope of blockchains in improving patient–doctor interactions [11, 12].

7.4   What is Medicalchain?

Medicalchain is a blockchain solution for EHRs. It is led by Dr. Abdullah Albeyatti, Mo Tayeb, Jay Povey, and Robert Miller Jr. and is based in

Figure 7.2 The Medicalchain logo [12].

London, UK. Various healthcare officials and related bodies, such as physicians, clinics, laboratories, pharmacists, and insurance providers, are able to seek permission to view and communicate with health records using Medicalchain. Each activity is reported as a transaction on Medicalchain's distributed ledger, which will be auditable, transparent, and stable.

Users must sign up to use the Hyperledger blockchain network, which is permission-based. Hyperledger simulation and access control languages are used to control network permissions. Hyperledger Fabric is a modular architecture-based framework for distributed ledger solutions that offers high levels of privacy, stability, versatility, and extensibility. It gives patients power over who can see their data, how much they can see, and for how long they can see it. This blockchain project is still in progress.

7.4.1   Features of Medicalchain

The Medicalchain platform brings to the table various features that make it highly useful in enhancing the interaction between patients and their physicians. These characteristics are listed below.

I.   *Enhanced privacy and access control*: Users can configure access permissions and grant specific organizations the consent to input information to their blockchain through enhanced confidentiality and access regulation.

II.   *Robust licensing of health records*: Patients can opt to authorize foreign entities, such as pharmaceutical firms, use of their EMRs for research purposes.

III.   *Real-time and secure doctor-to-patient communication*: Patients can share their information, get multiple opinions, and connect with medical practitioners online in real time and on a secure channel.

IV. *Unified app development platform*: Third-party program-mers can create distributed apps on the Medicalchain framework using the Unified Application Development Platform built on top of Medicalchain. Prescription evalu-ations, wearable device interactive elements, calorie mea-suring apps, diet and dietary recommendations, and other fitness apps are all possible. These apps may be personal-ized based on the details provided by the user.

7.4.2   Flow of the Processes in Medicalchain

Figure 7.3 details the blockchain operation implemented in Medicalchain. The steps involved in a typical Medicalchain transaction are given below.

I.   Information of the patient that is to be added to the block-chain is collected from a vast variety of sources: Any data generated by wearable health tracking devices owned by the patient can be added to the blockchain. Moreover, the physician is also able to input data into the patient's block; even the pharmacist who dispenses the medications can feed in data.

II. The data collected from all the aforementioned sources are then encrypted and given an identity. These are then stored

Figure 7.3 Operation of Medicalchain blockchain [12].

as part of the patient's personal blockchain. Thereafter, they are submitted to cloud storage.

III. When certain patient information needed accessing, the identity given to that particular data is entered, and the corresponding encrypted data are then easily retrieved.

IV. Encrypted data cannot be displayed directly on screens. These are first decrypted before being visible on the relevant interface.

7.4.3   The Medicalchain Currency

All payment transactions on Medicalchain are done using Medicalchain tokens, shortened as MedTokens. For patients to have access to a personal blockchain that can host their data and store their records, they must purchase it using MedTokens. As an incentive to spread the use of Medicalchain among workers in the healthcare industry, Medicalchain also rewards doctors, pharmacists, and other healthcare professionals with MedTokens for reviewing medical data. Moreover, pharmaceutical companies can also exchange data using MedTokens—patients can grant the companies access to their health data *via* apps—and they can, in this manner, earn more MedTokens for future use.

1.   Blockchains and Pharmaceutical Drug Supply and Counterfeiting

Pharmacological exploration and advancement is an intricate and time-consuming procedure, from medicine discovery to its development

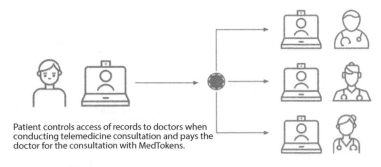

Patient controls access of records to doctors when conducting telemedicine consultation and pays the doctor for the consultation with MedTokens.

Figure 7.4 The patient controls access to the records and can exchange them for MedTokens [13].

to, lastly, authoritarian sanction. After the drug development and commercialization processes, the subsequent hurdle for manufacturers is the distribution of these prescribed products to the clients in an unadulterated state and to warrant that they are getting authentic merchandise produced by legal and authentic manufacturers and not by fraudsters.

However, the contemporary supply chain management (SCM) coordination of the pharmacological industry is outdated and does not stipulate transparency and the necessary improvements for manufacturing companies and administrative firms regarding pharmaceutical drug distribution; particularly, it cannot meet the network security demands of the 21st century. This state of SCM leads to the fabrication, circulation, and utilization of counterfeit drugs. Counterfeit medicines pose serious risks to the well-being of the community and cause massive problems particularly in emerging economies. Undoubtedly, fake drugs pose public health hazards.

Secondly, these medications do not contain the required dose of the active ingredient to fully treat the ailment, in turn causing drug resistance; furthermore, the use of counterfeit drugs results in the intake of genuine drugs being ineffective. As a matter of fact, fake medicines are made containing the wrong dose, in either high or low volumes, or with no dose of medicine, or they contain toxic ingredients, causing serious health complications. In addition, the manufacturers of these drugs sometimes use the labels of genuine manufacturers and produce counterfeit products used in daily life, which are less harmful.

Furthermore, in numerous instances, they damage the pills for medicating tumors, sedatives, cardiac conditions, antibodies, contraception drugs, and previous medications, which may have incredibly grave consequences. Research revealed that 10% to 15% of the world's total pharmaceutical production are fake medicines. Approximately 30% of the pharmaceuticals sold in emerging economies are fake. The World Health Organization approximates that, of the 1 million yearly casualties caused by malaria, 0.2 million are the consequence of forged malarial medications. Fake medicines for tuberculosis and malaria treatment kill 0.7 million human lives annually.

Counterfeiting is conceivably one of the most popular thriving businesses. However, the evolution in technology has hugely aided this industry, enabling the increase of the manufacture and circulation of fabricated goods due to the possibility of producing large amounts of products in such a short time, the reason authorities have declared counterfeiting as the crime of the 21st century. The International Anti-Counterfeiting Coalition (IACC) concurs that counterfeiting is proving to be one of the world's prevalent and steadily increasing illegal industries, with an anticipated value over USD 600 billion annually, as projected by studies.

Exploiting the credibility of blockchain technology, reliability and safekeeping can be assimilated into the pharmaceutical supply chain. With USD 10 billion spent annually to combat counterfeit drugs, made worse by security concerns, a chain-of-custody document that blockchain can hypothetically realize seems ideal.

To impede counterfeit pharmaceuticals, the drug manufacturing industry needs a proficient, well-organized SCM, and an indisputable answer to making improvements to this system is blockchain technology. Supply chain safekeeping is one aspect that has recently received consideration. The advantages of blockchain can be applied to simplifying complex manufacturing processes and resolving concerns regarding forgery. Blockchain is primarily utilized to enhance confidentiality and information security, which are of utmost significance. The relevance of blockchain has been recommended in many domains, and place which keeps data smartly/efficiently (Smart decentralized database), blockchain has been proven effective. With the versatility of blockchain applications, a lot of ideas imperative to encompassing its qualities in the drug and Medicare domains have been propositioned. Benchoufi and Ravaud [10] shed light on the use of blockchain for enhancing hospital-based biomedical research. They reviewed the inclusive use of blockchain in Medicare, but did not provide any explanation on the use of blockchain in the pharmaceutical supply chain. Medical records are incredibly valuable and are susceptible to various forms of attacks. MedShare is another service organization that incorporates blockchain in the healthcare sector to decentralize the system of storing and transferring medical records from one unit to another in an ethical environment. MedRec presents a framework for the collection of health information and to stipulate it for research work as a prospect for academics. It represents a system for patient data collection and storage and for effortless access to these data by integrating blockchain security. Mettler [13] also cited the use of blockchain in the pharmaceutical sector; however, the study lacked the implementation element. Numerous studies have been carried out on this topic.

While on the subject, it can be stated that the drug manufacturing industry needs a restructuring of its supply chain framework. The core of this novel scheme is the integration of the features of blockchain in order to ensure accountability and safekeeping of the drug supply chain and to offer transparency to the manufacturers and supervisory administration of the SCM system. In cases where both information confidentiality and accessibility are consistently required, then blockchain technology is the best solution. Each time drug and fabrication to production is ordered, the deal can be recognized to form a perpetual memoire of that upshot, from fabrication to retailing. This will noticeably reduce delays, expenditures, and external errors, which are currently prevalent.

7.5   Implementing Blockchain in SCM

To integrate blockchain technology into the pharmaceutical SCM framework, we ought to first understand how blockchain register functions operate. Blockchain has an inherent unique setup comprising two types of cryptographic codes. These codes are used to dispense a list of transactions to all participants. A participant can either be a gadget, human, or a unit. The individual characteristics of the participants are concealed, and they are recognized using respective codes. These cryptic key provides no hint with reference to the participant, but supplementary information such as forename and personal or qualification identification can be used for association.

However, this method maintains such supplementary information offline and merges them with on-chain statistics (code pair) by means of certain proof only. In the setting of pharmaceutical SCM, the members will be the manufacturer, packager, surgeon, and patient, among others. All these participants will be identified by their distinctive code pair on the system. Prescriptions will be considered as capital, with each assigned an inimitable code (or hash). The authentication will be ascribed with prescription in the form of a QR code. With knowledge of this basic design, the proposed scheme can be realized in diverse situations depending on personal preferences. A larger percentage of middle-man server handling data between patients and doctors application programming interfaces are also accessible, which can be used to move the data and transactions to the blockchain setup grid; however, the number of such is limited. Each of these application programming interfaces offers various types of assistance. Regardless of the instruction setup, any environment encountered, the fundamental framework of our organization will be the same.

The specific blockchain network for warehousing businesses and transactions is correspondingly a critical piece; however, before making a decision, it is important to understand the different forms and modes of blockchain. Blockchain has two core forms: unrestricted blockchain and permissioned or cloistered blockchain. In permissioned blockchain, not everybody has autonomy to the script in the blockchain; only verified individual contributors with prearranged access can participate in the respective blockchain. With regard to prescription delivery, a cloistered blockchain is more appropriate. The subsequent step is to utilize a specific blockchain framework to secure information on the contracts; however, this is absolutely dependent on the discretion of the creator. Some of the currently existing categories of blockchain systems include, Bitcoin, which is the pioneer, BigchainDB, Hyperledger, and Ethereum.

7.5.1　Working of this Technique

In this section, we discuss how a blockchain-enabled pharmaceutical SCM system works. Imagine an arrangement of a tenable and reliable system where only verified individuals are granted permission to join the network. On the background is a cloistered blockchain to accumulate every part of the mandatory businesses, and immediately when information is input into the system, on no account can it be corrupted. Moreover, we used a comprehensible and user-friendly application participants can familiarize themselves with in order to exchange connections and transactions toward the blockchain.

When a factory manufactures a new product, a distinct inimitable code/key/hash is crafted and ascribed to the merchandise. The outcome will then be enumerated on the blockchain using this hash (exclusive identification). The merchandise will be reflected as an ordinal virtue on the blockchain system, and its unique code will be used to track it in whatever instance required as and when on the system. Any supplementary evidence of the outcome can be kept offline or online in the chain dependent on the manufacturer. Offline information is when offline inferences to off-chain will be fused with the information on-chain by applying a certain form of attribute. Predictably, in almost all blockchain-grounded functions, an ID-digest of each of the information off-chain is duplicated and affiliated to the numbers on-chain. Nevertheless, the chief task is to store bulky collections off-chain besides text figures, which should be on-chain.

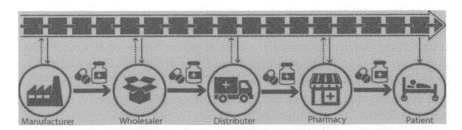

Figure 7.5 Use of blockchains to prevent drug counterfeiting.

Subsequently, when the outcome is documented in the blockchain through the producer, its ownership can effortlessly be relocated to an alternative member *via* a user-friendly application. For instance, the vendor wants to access the prescriptions from the manufacturer, and it will tangibly hand over the medicines to the vendor and a transferral contract will be enumerated to the blockchain instantaneously. The broker will repeat this uniform progression of transfer of the medications to a local merchant, and the local merchant will conduct the same trade with a middleman.

7.6 Why Use Blockchain in SCM

Listed below are the primary reasons for blockchain being a good fit for improving and digitizing pharmaceutical supply chains.

I. The most important reason for using blockchain in the pharmaceutical SCM system is the smart contract. A smart contract is a piece of code that contains the actual rights and obligations that include the terms and conditions for the payment and delivery of goods and services agreed upon by all the signees and can be automatically executed. Smart contracts can add greater intelligence and more power to blockchain. They can be used to make state-of-the-art and cutting-edge customized blockchain-based systems.

II. It the best option to record the journey of a product across the supply chain. Every time the product changes ownership, a new transaction will be pushed to the blockchain. Storing the history of a product makes it easy to reveal its actual origin and milestones. This approach will bring more transparency to transactions in the pharmaceutical supply chain.

III. When suppliers can rapidly and conveniently identify damaged goods, recalls will be less costly and more effective. As a result of the ability of blockchain technology to create a more open and traceable supply chain, quicker and more reliable recalls are possible.

IV. Anything from consumer-managed products to product recalls are supported by global supply chains. To avoid injuries or disease, it is often necessary to recall consumer goods or raw materials. Recalls on consumer goods have a detrimental effect on millions of lives around the globe due to lost revenue, repair costs, and disputes. By reducing the number of transactions, blockchain technology will improve product traceability [14].

References

1. Hileman, G. and Rauchs, M., *Global blockchain benchmarking study*, Cambridge Centre of Alternative Finance, Cambridge, United Kingdom, Sept. 2017, URL: https://ssrn.com/abstract=3040224.
2. Ali, Jaradat, A., Kulakli, A., Abuhalimeh, A., A comparative study: Blockchain technology utilization benefits, challenges and functionalities. *IEEE Access*, 9, 12730–12749, 2021. URL: https://ieeexplore.ieee.org/document/9317729.
3. Zarrin, J., Wen, P.H., Babu-Saheer, L., Zarrin, B., Blockchain for decentralization of internet: Prospects, trends and challenges, arXiv:2011.01096v1 [cs. NI], *Cluster Computing*, 24, 4, 2841–2866, November 2020. URL: https://arxiv.org/pdf/2011.01096.pdf.
4. Politou, E., Casino, F., Alepis, E., Patsakis, C., Blockchain mutability: Challenges and proposed solutions, *IEEE Transactions on Emerging Topics in Computing*, 9, 4, 1972–1986. arXiv:1907.07099v1 [cs.CR], July 2019. URL: https://arxiv.org/pdf/1907.07099.pdf.
5. Chen, G., Xu, B., Lu, M. *et al.*, Exploring blockchain technology and its potential applications for education. *Smart Learn. Environ.*, 5, 1, 2018. URL: https://rdcu.be/cf5y2.
6. Shahnaz, A., Qamar, U., Khalid, A., Using blockchain for electronic health records. *IEEE Access*, 7, 147782–147795, 2019. URL: https://ieeexplore.ieee.org/document/8863359.
7. Yaqoob, S., Khan, M.M., Talib, R., Butt, A.D., Saleem, S., Arif, F., Nadeem, A., Use of blockchain in healthcare: A systematic literature review. *Int. J. Adv. Comput. Sci. Appl. (IJACSA)*, 10, 5, 147, 2019, URL: https://thesai.org/Downloads/Volume10No5/Paper_81-Use_of_Blockchain_in_Healthcare.pdf.
8. Bogoeva, A. and Armknecht, F., Blockchain technology in healthcare: Opportunities and challenges, Master Thesis, University of Mannheim, September 2018, URL: https://www.researchgate.net/publication/333145193_Blockchain_in_Healthcare_Opportunities_and_Challenges.
9. Benchoufi, M., Ravaud, P., Porcher, R., Blockchain protocols in clinical trials: Transparency and traceability of consent. *F1000Res.*, 6, 66, 2018. URL: https://www.researchgate.net/profile/Albena-Bogoeva/publication/333145193_Blockchain_in_Healthcare_Opportunities_and_Challenges/links/ 5d3eca36a6fdcc370a6962ad

10. Benchoufi, M. and Ravaud, P., Blockchain technology for improving clinical research quality. *Trials*, 18, 335, 19 July 2017. URL: https://trialsjournal. biomedcentral.com/articles/10.1186/s13063-017-2035-z.

11. *Whitepaper on medicalchain*, 157, Medicalchain, 2018, URL: https://medical-chain.com/Medicalchain-Whitepaper-EN.pdf.

12. URL: https://medium.com/crypt-bytes-tech/medicalchain-a-blockchain-for-electronic-health-records-eef181ed14c2

13. Mettler, M. Blockchain technology in healthcare: The revolution starts here, in: *Proceedings of the 2016 IEEE 18th International Conference on e-Health Networking, Applications and Services (Healthcom)*, 14–16, pp. 1–3, Munich, Germany, September 2016.

14. URL: https://consensys.net/blockchain-use-cases/supply-chain-management/ #traceability

Part 2

SMART HEALTHCARE

Part 2

SMART HEALTHCARE

8

Potential of Blockchain Technology in Healthcare, Finance, and IoT: Past, Present, and Future

Chetna Tiwari* and Anuradha

Department of Computer Science & Engineering, The Northcap University, Haryana, India

Abstract

The focus of this chapter is to explore the potential applications of blockchain technology across different industry sectors. As a decentralized digital ledger, blockchain enables the recording of transactions through a network of computers. Blockchain technology was initially developed for the financial industry, but it has since been found to have potential applications beyond finance. This chapter will explore the evolution of blockchain technology, as well as its various uses and benefits in industries such as healthcare and the Internet of Things. It also discusses the impact it could have on the future of these industries. The research draws on case studies, industry reports, and academic literature to comprehensively analyze blockchain technology's current state and future potential. It also shows the share of blockchain in different industries and explains how finance is the field that uses blockchain the most with 39% as compared to the other fields.

Keywords: Blockchain, supply chain, industrial IoT (IIoT), IoT, decentralized systems, healthcare, finance

8.1 Introduction

We cannot talk about blockchain without talking about Bitcoin. Blockchain technology was first introduced publicly in 2008 when Satoshi Nakamoto released the Bitcoin [1]. People still consider Bitcoin and blockchain as the

---

Corresponding author: chetna20csu029@ncuindia.edu

Akansha Singh, Anuradha Dhull and Krishna Kant Singh (eds.) Blockchain and Deep Learning for Smart Healthcare, (173–204) © 2024 Scrivener Publishing LLC

same thing, but Bitcoin is a part of the blockchain [1]. Blockchain technology is a contemporary and robust database that facilitates transparent information sharing within a company's network. The technology works by storing information in blocks, which are then linked together to form a chain and stored in a database. Blockchain does not allow you to delete or alter the chain without the agreement from the network; because of this, the data stored in the database are consistently ordered [2]. At its core, blockchain technology is a decentralized ledger that enables secure transaction capture between two parties without requiring third-party verification. This brings down the transaction costs to under 1% [1]. Conversely, Bitcoin refers specifically to a digital currency that is created using blockchain technology. Nowadays, blockchain can be applied in other fields other than cryptocurrency. Bitcoin is virtual money and blockchain is used for transmitting virtual money and assets from one user to another in the network [3]. Blockchain is based on a 90s algorithm that was used to protect documents from getting tempered known as the timestamp ordering algorithm. The same method is now extended to ledger and transactions for providing a secure payment facility [3].

The three principles of blockchain are (1) Open ledger, (2) Distributed ledger, and (3) Synchronized ledger [3]. Blockchain refers to a series of connected blocks that are publicly accessible. These blocks are distributed across multiple nodes in the network. A crucial aspect of blockchain technology is that any data that has been added to the ledger cannot be altered or deleted [3]. In a blockchain, each block contains a set of data as well as a hash of the preceding block. The specific type of data stored in the blockchain depends on the blockchain implementation being used [3].

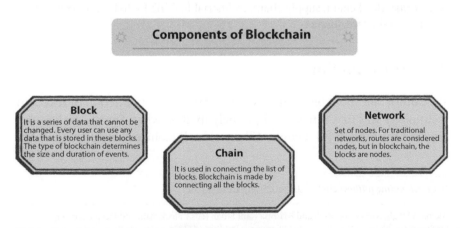

Figure 8.1 Components of blockchain.

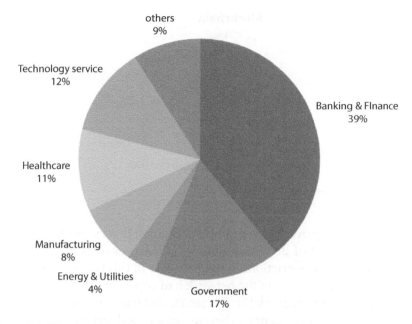

Figure 8.2 The percentage share of different sectors using blockchain.

According to Figure 8.1, blockchain is composed of three main compo-nents: blocks, chains, and networks [1].

Blockchain is reputed to be a particularly secure technology, so demand across various industries is skyrocketing. Blockchain is being used in other industries besides virtual money, but it is still in the early stages of deploy-ment. Figure 8.2 shows the information on the distribution of blockchain across various manufacturing market segments, with 2017 serving as the base year and 2016–2026 serving as the research period. This graph demonstrates how blockchain is mostly employed in the banking and financial sector.

8.2   Types of Blockchain

Blockchain technology can be classified into four main types, which are Public, Private, Hybrid, and Consortium, as shown in Figure 8.3 [2].

1. *Public Blockchain*: This particular form of blockchain is decentralized and accessible to all individuals who possess an internet connection. No one entity or individual possesses

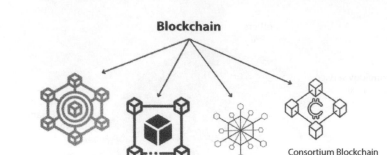

Figure 8.3 Types of blockchain.

ownership over this type of blockchain. It is very much open to the idea of decentralization [2]. The user does not need to face any restrictions in the network. In this type of block-chain, all devices in the network had copies of other devices in the same network [2]. It is secure and trustable and can be used for smart contracts because of its good features. Public blockchains, such as Bitcoin and Ethereum, are well-known examples of this technology in action [2].

2. *Private Blockchain*: This type of blockchain is controlled by one authority and only selected devices can participate in transactions, making it more secure than others [2]. It is not as open as the public blockchain, but only to some autho-rized users [2]. It is only operated in a closed network and only a few people in the company are allowed to participate in the transaction. Private blockchains, such as Hyperledger and Corda, are examples of blockchains that are designed for use by specific organizations or groups of individuals [2].

3. *Hybrid Blockchain*: A hybrid blockchain is a type of block-chain that combines elements of both public and private blockchains. In this, some nodes are controlled by the orga-nization and other nodes are available to the public [2]. In this type of blockchain, information is accessed through smart contracts. An example of this blockchain is the Ripple network and the XRP token [2].

4. *Consortium Blockchain*: The federated blockchain, also referred to as the consortium blockchain, is designed to val-idate transactions and facilitate the initiation and receipt of transactions [2]. In this type, some parts were public, some

were private, and more than one organization manages the blockchain. Consortium blockchains, which are blockchains that are jointly managed by multiple organizations, include examples such as Tendermint and Multichain [2].

8.3   Literature Review

Blockchain is officially introduced in 2008, and since then, many evolutions have occurred in this field, and many other sectors have also started using this technology. Smart contracts, which are self-executing agreements that are programmed directly into the blockchain, were first introduced to the public in 2010. Different organizations use smart contracts for business collaborations within the company or with other companies for business processes. Organizations can automatically make smart contract transactions on blockchains without manual confirmations. In mid-2010, private and consortium blockchains are also introduced to the public, which allows organizations to use blockchain in a controlled manner. It was a very important development for this technology as it ensures that organizations can use this technology without giving out their sensitive information to the public. Many sectors other than finance are now using this technology because of its high security and many other advantages that it has over other technologies. Although this technology has many benefits, it also confronts many challenges in the present.

8.3.1   Challenges of Blockchain

As this is a new technology and still developing at a very rapid speed, it is very popular because of its many advantages, but as with any other technology, it has its own challenges as shown in Figure 8.4. Some of the main challenges blockchain includes are the following:

Scalability: With the growing adoption of blockchain technology, it has become increasingly challenging to validate transactions efficiently, leading to longer processing times and higher fees [4].
Security: While blockchain technology offers enhanced security measures, it is not entirely immune to cyber-attacks. Unfortunately, there have been instances where blockchain-based systems were targeted, resulting in significant financial losses running into millions of dollars [4].
Regulation: As it is a new technology, it is still not regulated according to the government of many countries. This makes it difficult for businesses

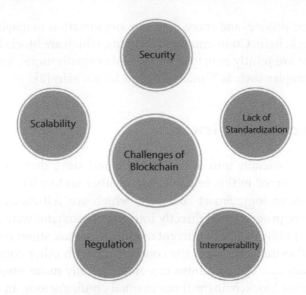

Figure 8.4 Challenges of blockchain.

and individuals to use blockchain and many people will try to make their own guidelines for this technology [4].

Interoperability: There are different types of blockchains, and every kind of blockchain has its own protocol and standards; it is difficult to communicate between two different types of blockchains and work without any problems [4].

Lack of Standardization: The lack of standardization in the blockchain industry can be attributed to its relative novelty and the fact that it is still rapidly evolving [5].

Following an examination of the challenges that blockchain technology faces, the subsequent section of this chapter will delve into how blockchain works.

8.3.2   Working of Blockchain

As noted previously in this chapter, the nature of the data that is stored in a blockchain is dependent on the specific type of blockchain being utilized. The blockchain that underpins Bitcoin contains a wealth of data related to the management of the cryptocurrency. This includes information on transactions, as well as details about the parties involved in each transaction, and the total number of Bitcoins in circulation [3]. As depicted in Figure 8.5 [3], every block within a blockchain consists of data, along with both the current block's hash and the hash of the preceding block. This previous hash value is integral to the process of chaining the blocks together, as it links each block to its immediate predecessor. Hash is a very important factor in the making of blockchain. Every block has its own hash, and it changes if there is any modification in the block, and when a block is created in the chain, it generates its own hash [3]. These are some of the few features of the block that makes it secure.

Whenever a transaction occurs on the network, it must be validated and added to the blockchain. The process of adding a block involves generating a new hash value for that block, as well as carrying over the hash value of the previous block in the chain [6]. As a result of this process, a distinct hexadecimal value of fixed length is produced, which is known as a hash. The difficulty of the blockchain's standards must be met by the generated hash value for a block to be legitimate, which can only be done by performing numerous calculations. Subsequently, the block is appended to the publicly accessible network and linked to the preceding block [6].

Blockchain is a young technology, and various types of studies are being done on it. These studies discuss the various advantages it has in various areas. This chapter lists the top 10 research papers from the previous 5 years and explains which blockchain advantages were discussed in those papers. The types of benefits stated in each referenced research paper from various writers are listed in Table 8.1 along with the papers' respective sources.

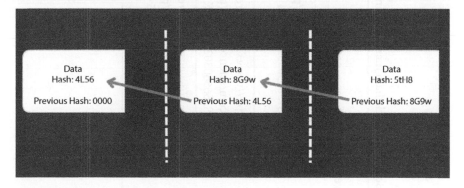

Figure 8.5 Contents of block in blockchain.

Table 8.1 Benefits of blockchain mentioned in different research papers.

Healthcare	Reference paper	Author	Date of publication	1	2	3	4
	https://www.sciencedirect.com/science/article/pii/S1386505620301544 [7]	Israa Abu-elezz, Asma Hassan, Anjanarani Nazeemudeen, Mowafa Househ, Alaa Abd-alrazaq	14 August 2020	✓	✗	✗	✗
	https://www.sciencedirect.com/science/article/pii/S266660302100021X [8]	Abid Haleem, Mohd Javaid, Ravi Pratap Singh, Rajiv Suman, Shanay Rab	15 September 2021	✓	✗	✓	✗
	https://www.sciencedirect.com/science/article/pii/S1877050922005075 [9]	Tiago Guimarães, Ricardo Duarte, Bruno Pinheiro, Daniel Faria, Paulo Gomes, Manuel Filipe Santos	27 April 2022	✓	✓	✗	✗

(Continued)

Table 8.1 Benefits of blockchain mentioned in different research papers. (*Continued*)

Healthcare	Reference paper	Author	Date of publication	1	2	3	4
	https://www.sciencedirect.com/science/article/pii/S1877050920317890 [10]	Noshina Tariq, Ayesha Qamar, Muhammad Asim, Farrukh Aslam Khan	6 August 2020	✓	✗	✗	✓
	https://www.sciencedirect.com/science/article/pii/S1877050922005087 [11]	João Cunha, Ricardo Duarte, Tiago Guimarães, César Quintas, Manuel Filipe Santos	27 April 2022	✓	✗	✓	✗
	https://www.sciencedirect.com/science/article/pii/S2590291122000821 [12]	Jayendra S. Jadhav, Jyoti Deshmukh	23 August 2022	✓	✗	✓	✓

(*Continued*)

Table 8.1 Benefits of blockchain mentioned in different research papers. (*Continued*)

Healthcare	Reference paper	Author	Date of publication	1	2	3	4
	https://www.sciencedirect.com/science/article/pii/S0148296323000048 [13]	Arash Kordestani, Pejvak Oghazi, Rana Mostaghel	12 January 2023	✗	✗	✓	✗
	https://www.sciencedirect.com/science/article/pii/S2590005622000108 [14]	Endale Mitiku Adere	12 March 2022	✗	✓		✓
	https://www.sciencedirect.com/science/article/pii/S138650561930526X [15]	Anton Hasselgren Katina Kralevska, Danilo Gligoroski, Sindre A. Pedersen, Arild Faxvaag	11 December 2019	✓	✗	✗	✓
	https://www.sciencedirect.com/science/article/abs/pii/S2213076419302532 [16]	Gautami Tripathi, Mohd Abdul Ahad, Sara Paiva	19 November 2019	✓	✗	✗	✗

(*Continued*)

Table 8.1 Benefits of blockchain mentioned in different research papers. (*Continued*)

Finance	Reference paper	Author	Date of publication	1	2	3	4
	https://www.sciencedirect.com/science/article/pii/S0040162520309926 [17]	Victor Chang, Patricia Baudier, Hui Zhang, Qianwen Xu, Jingqi Zhang, Mitra Arami	21 June 2020	✓	✗	✗	✗
	https://www.sciencedirect.com/science/article/abs/pii/S2352673419300824 [18]	Yan Chen, Cristiano Bellavitis	20 November 2019	✗	✓	✓	✗
	https://www.sciencedirect.com/science/article/pii/S1319157821000207X [19]	Bela Shrimali, Hiren B. Patel	12 August 2021	✓	✗	✗	✗
	https://journals.sagepub.com/doi/pdf/10.1177/0256090919839897 [20]	Jayanth Rama Varma	2019	✗	✗	✗	✓

(*Continued*)

Table 8.1 Benefits of blockchain mentioned in different research papers. (*Continued*)

Finance	Reference paper	Author	Date of publication	1	2	3	4
	https://link.springer.com/article/10.1007/s42524-020-0140-2 [21]	Yifeng Tian, Zheng Lu, Peter Adriaens, R. Edward Minchin, Alastair Caithness & Junghoon Woo	9 September 2020	✗	✗	✓	✗
	https://www.sciencedirect.com/science/article/pii/S2772485922000606 [22]	Mohd Javaid, Abid Haleem, Ravi Pratap Singh, Rajiv Suman, Shahbaz Khan	22 October 2022	✓	✗	✗	✗
	https://www.sciencedirect.com/science/article/abs/pii/S1062976920301162 [23]	Cameron Harwick, James Caton	5 October 2020	✗	✓	✓	✗
	https://www.worldscientific.com/doi/full/10.1142/S2424862221500024X [24]	Anjee Gorkhali, Rajib Chowdhury	2022	✓	✓	✗	✗

(*Continued*)

Table 8.1 Benefits of blockchain mentioned in different research papers. (Continued)

	Reference paper	Author	Date of publication	1	2	3	4
Finance	https://www.scielo.cl/scielo.php?pid=S0718-27242021000300089&script=sci_arttext&tlng=en [25]	Sonal Trivedi Kiran Mehta Renuka Sharma	2021	✓	✓	✗	✗
	https://www.hct.edu.om/pdf/business/published-papers/students/4Al%20Kemyani.pdf [26]	Mustafa Khalfan Al Kemyani JaifarYaqoob Al Raisi Abdul Rahman Tariq Al Kindi Ibrahim Yahya Al Mughairi Chandan Kumar Tiwari	8 April 2022	✗	✓	✗	✗
IoT	https://www.sciencedirect.com/science/article/abs/pii/S254266051930085X [1]	Qin Wang, Xinqi Zhu, Yiyang Ni, Li Gu, Hongbo Zhu	12 July 2019	✓	✗	✗	✗
	https://www.sciencedirect.com/science/article/pii/S2666281722001512 [27]	Alex Akinbi, Aine MacDermott, Aras M. Ismael	1 October 2022	✓	✗	✗	✓

(Continued)

Table 8.1 Benefits of blockchain mentioned in different research papers. (*Continued*)

IoT	Reference paper	Author	Date of publication	1	2	3	4
	https://www.sciencedirect.com/science/article/pii/S2590005622000108 [14]	Endale Mitiku Adere	12 March 2022	✗	✗	✗	✓
	https://www.sciencedirect.com/science/article/pii/S1110866522000172 [28]	Mahmoud Tayseer Al Ahmed, Fazirulhisyam Hashim, Shaiful Jahari Hashim, Azizol Abdullah	19 February 2022	✗	✓	✗	✗
	https://www.sciencedirect.com/science/article/abs/pii/S0167739X18326542 [29]	Muneeb Ul Hassan, Mubashir Husain Rehmani, Jinjun Chen	1 March 2019	✓	✗	✗	✗
	https://link.springer.com/article/10.1007/s10586-020-03059-5 [30]	Deepa Pavithran, Khaled Shaalan, Jamal N. Al-Karaki, Amjad Gawanmeh	05 February 2020	✓	✗	✗	✗
	https://expert.taylors.edu.my/file/rems/publication/109566_6018_1.pdf [31]	Malak Alamri, NZ Jhanjhi, Mamoona Humayun	May 2019	✓	✗	✗	✗

(Continued)

Table 8.1 Benefits of blockchain mentioned in different research papers. (*Continued*)

IoT	Reference paper	Author	Date of publication	1	2	3	4
	https://www.tandfonline.com/doi/abs/10.1080/10919392.2020.1831870 [32]	Suparna Dhar & Indranil Bose	17 November 2020	✗	✗	✗	✓
	https://www.sciencedirect.com/science/article/abs/pii/S1084804520303076 [33]	Fei Chen, Zhe Xiao, Laizhong Cui, Qiuzhen Lin, Jianqiang Li, Shui Yu	17 September 2020	✓	✗	✗	✓
	https://link.springer.com/chapter/10.1007/978-(981-13-8775-3_3 [34]	V. Dedeoglu, R. Jurdak, A. Dorri, R. C. Lunardi, R. A. Michelin, A. F. Zorzo & S. Kanhere	25 September 2019	✓	✓	✓	✗

(1) Privacy; (2) Decentralization; (3) Transparency; (4) Integrity.

8.4   Methodology and Data Sources

8.4.1   Eligibility Criteria

This chapter investigates the applications of blockchain technology in three diverse fields: finance, healthcare, and the Internet of Things (IoT). This chapter talks about the usage of blockchain in huge sectors like finance, healthcare, and the IoT. This chapter also discusses how blockchain technology can be applied in the aforementioned sectors. This chapter incorporates a comprehensive analysis of primary studies on blockchain technology in various sectors, including finance, healthcare, and IoT, from the year 2019 onward. However, conference abstracts, newspaper and magazine articles, and webzines were excluded from this study. The time for the selection of these information was related to the recent development of technology in this sector since 2019. Any studies that were not written in English were excluded from the analysis.

8.4.2   Search Strategy

To write this chapter, the reference of many different research papers or review papers was used. These references were from the last 5 years' timeline. To make Table 8.1 in the literature review, the top 10 research papers of each field were used, and these papers were from the last 5 years, and these 30 papers were selected because these papers explain the benefits of blockchain like privacy, decentralization, transparency, and integrity in

Table 8.2 Sources of information.

ScienceDirect
IEEE
Springer
SAGE journals
World Scientific
SciELO
Hct.edu.om
Google Scholar

the three sectors that were mentioned in this chapter. The source of all the information for this chapter is included in Table 8.2.

The above mentioned sources were searched using and combining the following keywords: blockchain* AND (Finance*) AND (health-care* OR medicine*) AND (IoT*) AND (benefit* OR advantages*) AND (application*).

8.4.3   Study Selection Process

The filtration process involved three distinct stages. In the identification phase, various databases were searched using specific queries, and any duplicate articles were eliminated. Next, in the screening phase, titles and abstracts were examined to identify relevant articles, and irrelevant ones were eliminated. Finally, in the eligibility phase, the full text of each article was assessed to determine its relevance to the present study. Having covered the definition of blockchain and its associated challenges, the subsequent section of this chapter will explore the various applications of blockchain technology in different domains, including finance, healthcare, and the Internet of Things.

8.5   The Application of Blockchain Technology Across Various Industries

Blockchain technology has the capacity to be employed across multiple domains, such as finance, supply chain management, healthcare, and digital identity. This chapter provides examples of several such applications.

8.5.1   Finance

E- finance
E-finance is the type of finance that is done through an online medium like the internet. E-finance uses ITC (information and communication technology) to provide users with financial services [25]. E-finance usage has grown as e-commerce usage expands across all industries. The financial industry has moved from the real to the virtual world as internet and mobile phone use has grown [25]. Presently, a wide range of financial services, including banking, stock trading, insurance, and more, are available online [25].

Blockchain in Finance

The application of blockchain technology in finance is commonly referred to as blockchain in finance. One of the outcomes of using blockchain in finance has been the creation of decentralized finance, or DeFi [25]. The use of blockchain in business has many advantages.

Blockchain was first introduced to the world in the form of Bitcoin. At first, it was used for cryptocurrency transactions. However, the popularity of blockchain has increased in other industries in the past few years [25]. Because of the many features that blockchain offers—transparency, privacy, digital transactions, etc.—the global market for blockchain technology has experienced a significant surge in recent years, and analysts predict that this trend will continue. It is projected that the market will reach a valuation of $39 billion by the year 2025 [25]. Extensive research has been conducted to explore the various applications of blockchain technology. The following section will focus specifically on the use of blockchain in e-finance. E-finance is the combination of e-banking, e-insurance, and other finance-related things. Because of e-banking, the users can use various services anytime and anywhere, but security is the biggest challenge in its adoption [25]. The security of private data has become crucial due to the abundance of known and unknown dangers in the cyber world. Blockchain technology employs a hash algorithm and timestamps to store data in a chain of blocks, which is more secure than traditional banking due to the absence of third-party interference [25]. Because of

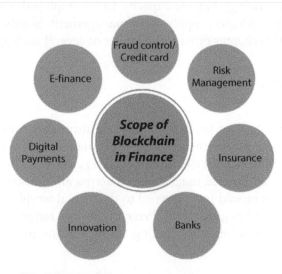

Figure 8.6 Scope of blockchain in finance.

the use of a one-way hash technique, data alteration is impossible, which makes it more secure. Another crucial aspect of blockchain technology is the concept of smart contracts, which are automated contracts that execute themselves based on predetermined terms and conditions [25]. Figure 8.6 outlines the numerous ways in which blockchain technology can be applied to the finance sector. The following section will explore some of these applications in greater detail.

Application of Blockchain in the Finance Sector

In the following section, we will examine how blockchain technology has impacted the financial sector. Blockchain in the banking sector provides transparency, fast transaction, high traceability, and less cost; safely tracks payment history; and reduces the number of frauds [35]. The implementation of blockchain technology in the insurance industry has led to the use of smart contracts, which can help prevent fraudulent claims and remove intermediaries such as agents and brokers. Blockchain brings a huge change in the finance sector by eliminating the role of a third party and by increasing the efficiency of financial work for users [35]. There are many influences of blockchain technology in the finance sector, including an increase in transparency, high transaction speed, high traceability, less cost, safe tracking of payment history, and less fraud threat. The application of blockchain in banking services and operations will eliminate the need for KYC, speed up transactions, cut costs, boost security for both clients and banks, and introduce smart contracts.

Uses of Blockchain in Finance

There are many uses of blockchain in the finance industry, some of which are listed below and are shown in Figure 8.7:

1. Digital Assets: Blockchain is used in the creation and tracking of digital assets such as cryptocurrency, which is used by the users to make transactions or investments. This helps in eliminating the role of a third party for the transaction and makes it easy for consumers to use financial services [36].
2. Smart Contracts: Smart contracts refer to contracts that are programmed to execute automatically based on the terms and conditions specified in the blockchain. By leveraging blockchain technology, these contracts can be created and executed seamlessly. This can lead to increased automation of financial contracts and a reduction in the potential for fraud, as it eliminates the need for third-party intermediaries [37].

Digital Assets

Smart Contracts

Trade Finance

Blockchain in Finance

Supply chain finance

Identity Verification

Banking and Lending

Figure 8.7 Use of blockchain in finance.

3. Supply Chain Finance: A supply chain can monitor the flow of products and services using blockchain, which offers real-time insight into the progress of payments and deliveries. This can lower the risk of deception while increasing the effectiveness and security of supply chain finance [38].

4. Banking and Lending: The lending and banking sectors can utilize blockchain technology to create more secure and efficient systems for managing client identities, credit issuance, and maintaining records. Peer-to-peer financing is also made possible, which lessens reliance on conventional institutions [39].

5. Identity Verification: The implementation of blockchain technology has the potential to facilitate the development of a secure and decentralized identification verification system for individuals and organizations. Such a system could help mitigate fraudulent activity and enable compliance with KYC/AML regulations [40].

6. Trade Finance: Through digitization and management of trade finance tools such as letters of credit, blockchain has the potential to streamline the trade finance process. This may lessen the need for middlemen like banks and facilitate company access to trade funding [41].

8.5.2   Healthcare

Smart Healthcare Industry

Healthcare is a large industry and is spread across the world. With the rapid pace of global development and the increasing prevalence of internet usage, the healthcare industry has similarly expanded its reliance on internet-based technologies to support its growth [16]. Healthcare is an industry with special requirements related to privacy and security because of its legal requirements to protect the patient's privacy [42]. In this modern age, as the use of internet is increasing for sharing data and many other things, the attack to steal sensitive information is also increasing [42].

Blockchain in Smart Healthcare

The healthcare sector is developing at a rapid pace and good-quality health facilities with advanced technology are needed. To realize these critical changes, blockchain is required [8]. In recent times, the health system landscape is becoming more patient-centered with two major aspects: the provision of continuously available services and the availability of high-quality healthcare resources are essential factors in promoting good health outcomes [8]. Blockchain technology has the potential to address issues related to the exchange of healthcare information, which is a time-consuming and repetitive process that can lead to high industry costs [8]. There are numerous benefits associated with blockchain technology, which can be categorized into patient-related and organizational-related benefits, as depicted in Figure 8.8 [7].

Patient-related benefits: One of the advantages that blockchain technology offers in the context of healthcare is enhanced privacy and authorization

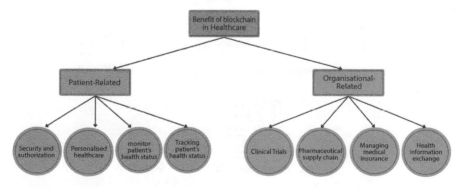

Figure 8.8 Benefit of blockchain in healthcare.

mechanisms for patients [7]. Blockchain technology has the potential to minimize instances of data breaches, as the network is not vulnerable to a single point of failure. It also provides authentication to users that access the health-related data. With the aid of this technology, healthcare professionals can also develop and communicate personalized patient care plans [7]. By using timestamps, blockchain can help physicians to track patient information easily as it stores the records of each transaction [7].

Organizational-related benefits: Apart from patient-based benefits, blockchain also provides organizational-related benefits. It secures the data/patient information that is shared in a healthcare organization [7]. It also provides seamless healthcare data exchange within the organization. It provides the facility for clinical trials for necessary drug testing. Blockchain technology can also be leveraged in pharmaceutical supply chain management, as it has been shown to effectively prevent the circulation of counterfeit drugs [7]. It also manages medical insurance because of its immutability feature. It also helps organizations store and back up medical insurance [7].

Application of Blockchain in Healthcare

In Figure 8.9, we can see an example of how blockchain technology is being utilized in the healthcare industry to enhance various processes.

1. Electronic Health Record (EHR): Data cannot be kept by any intruder thanks to the decentralized database in the

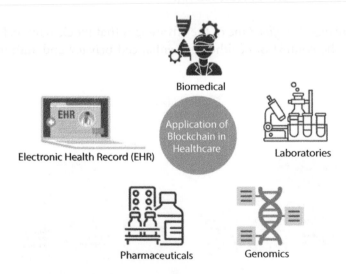

Figure 8.9 Application of blockchain in healthcare.

EHR [43]. Each node in a blockchain has a current duplicate of the ledger, and each node has verified the copy, making it impossible for an outsider to take complete control of the ledger [44]. With the patient's authorization, healthcare providers such as physicians, hospitals, and laboratories may access a patient's data via a permissioned blockchain network [43].

2. Biomedical: Alteration and duplication were prohibited in a transaction in a blockchain-based medicinal application [43]. Blockchain only permits transactions that are safe and open.

3. Laboratories: Only blockchain can establish a secure, decentralized structure for lab-related data, allowing for the safe sharing of those data with other study teams [43].

4. Pharmaceuticals: The pharmaceutical supply chain is meticulously tracked by blockchain, which also keeps a watch on every stage of the process. This prevents any products from needing to be replaced by routine component detection at each stage [43].

5. Genomics: By lowering the expense of each individual genome's sequencing, democratizing possession of genomic data, and facilitating open sharing of genomic data, blockchain technology can contribute to a change in genomics data [43].

Use of Blockchain in Healthcare
Figure 8.10 provides an illustration of how blockchain technology can be applied in the healthcare industry.

1. Electronic Medical Records (EMRs): It can be shared and stored securely and decentralized using blockchain technology, which can increase patient data accessibility and precision while preserving anonymity [45].

2. Clinical Trials: A tamper-proof log of the data gathered during clinical studies can be created using blockchain, which can improve findings' transparency and credibility [45].

3. Identity Verification: The implementation of blockchain technology can be leveraged to create a secure and

Electronic Medical Record

Blockchain in Healthcare

Clinical Trials

Supply Chain Management

Medical Billing and Claims

Identity Verification

Figure 8.10 Use of blockchain in healthcare.

self-governing system that can be used to verify the identity of patients. Such a system could help fulfill legal requirements and decrease instances of deception [40].

4. Medical Billing and Claims: The use of blockchain technology in the medical industry has the potential to simplify the process of invoicing and claims, eliminating the need for intermediaries and reducing the risk of fraudulent activity.

5. Supply Chain Management: Through the use of blockchain, it is possible to monitor the distribution of medical supplies and pharmaceuticals within the supply chain with greater accuracy and transparency. This can help prevent the spread of counterfeit products and provide real-time updates on the status of deliveries [46].

8.5.3   Internet of Things (IoT)

IoT
The Internet of Things (IoT) refers to a system of interconnected physical devices and objects that utilize sensors, software, and other technologies to exchange data with one another over the internet [47]. IoT is a combination of data from different technologies in a network that helps in

the communication between the cloud and device as well as between the devices present in the network [47].

Blockchain in IoT

Internet of Things is a very popular technology as it makes work easier for people. IoT collects data of people's daily activities. As it brings many services to users, it also brings challenge in terms of securing the privacy of customer's data. Currently, IoT uses the centralized approach for privacy and security. The Internet of Things (IoT) currently operates using a centralized model, where a third-party central authority collects and processes data from various devices without any limitations on the usage of those data. To solve this problem and provide a trustable and confidential device to users, blockchain is being used in IoT as it is decentralized, autonomous, and distributed [48]. Blockchain uses decentralization for better efficiency and to avoid single point failure, and it also provides good security and data integrity. IoT security issues are classified into three levels: 1, low level; 2, intermediate level; and 3, high level. Figure 8.11 shows the classification of IoT security issues [48].

As the IoT sector is advancing at a very rapid pace and because it has a very vast global market, many people are using this technology and the number of users continues to grow, which means that IoT generates an enormous amount of data and needs real-time computing power; however, the interface of IoT has low computing power or capacity and it has to pre-process the raw data received from the user to filter out the useful information from the raw data [48]. These raw data then are passed to blockchain for processing or uploading. In blockchain, the minor node will be used to validate the block with the raw data; if it is valid, then the block will be

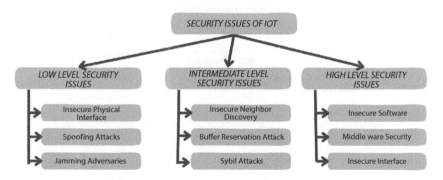

Figure 8.11 Security issues of IoT.

updated in blockchain network for consumers to access the data by using analytics device or software [48].

Application of Blockchain in IoT

Blockchain is a useful technology in the IoT sector, and it has a very high demand in IoT because blockchain can provide service management, device management, and data management [49]. The utilization of blockchain technology extends to various fields, including the Internet of Things (IoT), where it can facilitate data storage, identity management, timestamping, sensor management, and supply chain management. Additionally, blockchain has practical applications in everyday life, such as in the realms of smart healthcare and smart homes, as illustrated in Figure 8.12 [49].

Because of the many advantages of blockchain's application in IoT, many industries and the academia aim to further explore blockchain in future research. Blockchain has many uses in IoT, some of which are listed in the next section.

Use of Blockchain in IoT

Figure 8.13 depicts the utilization of blockchain technology in the context of the Internet of Things.

1. Secure Device Authentication: IoT systems can be protected from malevolent players by using blockchain to validate the identification of IoT devices [50].

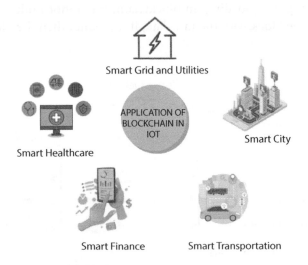

Figure 8.12 Application of blockchain in IoT.

Decentralized Data Sharing

Secure device authentication

**USE OF BLOCKCHAIN
IN IoT AND IIoT**

Supply Chain Tracking

Automated micropayments

Tamper-proof record-keeping

Figure 8.13 Use of blockchain in IoT and IIoT.

2. Decentralized Data Sharing: Without a single middleman, IoT devices can safely exchange data with one another using blockchain [51].

3. Supply Chain Tracking: By tracking the movement of products through supply networks, blockchain can increase accountability and transparency [52].

4. Tamper-Proof Record-Keeping: Data from IoT devices can be securely stored using blockchain, making it difficult for anyone to change the data without being noticed [54].

5. Automated Micropayments: Bitcoin can be used to manage micropayments between IoT devices, enabling them to conduct business with one another without the need for a human intermediary [53].

8.6 Conclusion

Blockchain is a new technology, but because of the many advantages this technology offers, many industries are transitioning from using traditional technologies to using blockchain for the safety of the sensitive information and development of their industry. The technology is extensively used in a wide range of industries, including finance, healthcare, and the Internet of

Things. Finance is the industry that uses blockchain the most. Blockchain secures the data stored because of its decentralized nature and the absence of a third party. Because it is a new and developing technology, there are still many challenges that need to be addressed. Despite these challenges, there are many uses and applications of blockchain in the abovementioned industries. Blockchain will continue to grow and expand globally, and many industries will benefit from this development.

References

1. Wang, Q., Zhu, X., Ni, Y., Gu, L., Zhu, H., Blockchain for the IoT and industrial IoT: A review. *Internet Things*, 10, 100081, 2020.
2. Tolentino-Zondervan, F., Ngoc, P.T.A., Roskam, J.L., Use cases and future prospects of blockchain applications in global fishery and aquaculture value chains. *Aquaculture*, 565, 739158, 2022.
3. Rathee, P., Introduction to blockchain and IoT, in: *Advanced Applications of Blockchain Technology*, pp. 1–14, 2020.
4. Meva, D., Issues and challenges with blockchain: A survey. *Int. J. Comput. Sci. Eng.*, 6, 12, 488–491, 2018.
5. König, L., Korobeinikova, Y., Tjoa, S., Kieseberg, P., Comparing blockchain standards and recommendations. *Future Internet*, 12, 12, 222, 2020.
6. Soni, S. and Bhushan, B., A comprehensive survey on blockchain: Working, security analysis, privacy threats and potential applications, in: *2019 2nd International Conference on Intelligent Computing, Instrumentation and Control Technologies (ICICICT)*, vol. 1, IEEE, pp. 922–926, 2019, July.
7. Abu-Elezz, I., Hassan, A., Nazeemudeen, A., Househ, M., Abd-Alrazaq, A., The benefits and threats of blockchain technology in healthcare: A scoping review. *Int. J. Med. Inform.*, 142, 104246, 2020.
8. Haleem, A., Javaid, M., Singh, R.P., Suman, R., Rab, S., Blockchain technology applications in healthcare: An overview. *Int. J. Intell. Netw.*, 2, 130–139, 2021.
9. Guimarães, T., Duarte, R., Pinheiro, B., Faria, D., Gomes, P., Santos, M.F., Blockchain analytics-real-time log management in healthcare. *Procedia Comput. Sci.*, 201, 702–707, 2022.
10. Tariq, N., Qamar, A., Asim, M., Khan, F.A., Blockchain and smart healthcare security: A survey. *Procedia Comput. Sci.*, 175, 615–620, 2020.
11. Cunha, J., Duarte, R., Guimarães, T., Quintas, C., Santos, M.F., Blockchain analytics in healthcare: An overview. *Procedia Comput. Sci.*, 201, 708–713, 2022.
12. Jadhav, J.S. and Deshmukh, J., A review study of the blockchain-based healthcare supply chain. *Soc. Sci. Humanit. Open*, 6, 1, 100328, 2022.

13. Kordestani, A., Oghazi, P., Mostaghel, R., Smart contract diffusion in the pharmaceutical blockchain: the battle of counterfeit drugs. *J. Bus. Res.*, 158, 113646, 2023.
14. Adere, E.M., Blockchain in healthcare and IoT: A systematic literature review. *Array*, 14, 100139, 2022.
15. Hasselgren, A., Kralevska, K., Gligoroski, D., Pedersen, S.A., Faxvaag, A., Blockchain in healthcare and health sciences—A scoping review. *Int. J. Med. Inform.*, 134, 104040, 2020. https://doi.org/10.1016/j.hjdsi.2019.100391
16. Tripathi, G., Ahad, M.A., Paiva, S., S2HS-a blockchain based approach for smart healthcare system, in: *Healthcare*, vol. 8, 1, p. 100391, Elsevier, 2020, March. https://doi.org/10.1016/j.hjdsi.2019.100391.
17. Chang, V., Baudier, P., Zhang, H., Xu, Q., Zhang, J., Arami, M., How blockchain can impact financial services–the overview, challenges and recommendations from expert interviewees. *Technol. Forecast. Soc. Change*, 158, 120166, 2020.
18. Chen, Y. and Bellavitis, C., Blockchain disruption and decentralized finance: The rise of decentralized business models. *J. Bus. Ventur. Insights*, 13, e00151, 2020.
19. Shrimali, B. and Patel, H.B., Blockchain state-of-the-art: architecture, use cases, consensus, challenges and opportunities. *J. King Saud Univ.-Comp. Inf. Sci.*, 34, 9, 6793–6807, 2022.
20. Varma, J.R., Blockchain in finance. *Vikalpa*, 44, 1, 1–11, 2019.
21. Tian, Y., Lu, Z., Adriaens, P., Minchin, R.E., Caithness, A., Woo, J., Finance infrastructure through blockchain-based tokenization. *Front. Eng. Manag.*, 2, 7, 485–499, 2020.
22. Javaid, M., Haleem, A., Singh, R.P., Suman, R., Khan, S., A review of blockchain technology applications for financial services. *BenchCouncil Transactions on Benchmarks, Standards and Evaluation (TBench).*, 2, 100073, 2022.
23. Harwick, C. and Caton, J., What's holding back blockchain finance? On the possibility of decentralized autonomous finance. *Q. Rev. Econ. Finance*, 84, 420–429, 2022.
24. Gorkhali, A. and Chowdhury, R., Blockchain and the evolving financial market: A literature review. *J. Ind. Integr. Manag.*, 7, 01, 47–81, 2022.
25. Trivedi, S., Mehta, K., Sharma, R., Systematic literature review on application of blockchain technology in e-finance and financial services. *J. Technol. Manag. Innov.*, 16, 3, 89–102, 2021.
26. Al Kemyani, M.K., Al Raisi, J., Al Kindi, A.R.T., Al Mughairi, I.Y., Tiwari, C.K., Blockchain applications in accounting and finance: Qualitative evidence from the banking sector. *J. Res. Bus. Manag.*, 10, 4, 28–39, 2022.
27. Akinbi, A., MacDermott, Á., Ismael, A.M., A systematic literature review of blockchain-based Internet of Things (IoT) forensic investigation process models. *Forensic Sci. Int.: Digit. Investig.*, 42, 301470, 2022.

28. Al Ahmed, M.T., Hashim, F., Hashim, S.J., Abdullah, A., Hierarchical block-chain structure for node authentication in IoT networks. *Egypt. Inform. J.*, 23, 2, 345–361, 2022.
29. Hassan, M.U., Rehmani, M.H., Chen, J., Privacy preservation in blockchain based IoT systems: Integration issues, prospects, challenges, and future research directions. *Future Gener. Comput. Syst.*, 97, 512–529, 2019.
30. Pavithran, D., Shaalan, K., Al-Karaki, J.N., Gawanmeh, A., Towards building a blockchain framework for IoT. *Clust. Comput.*, 23, 3, 2089–2103, 2020.
31. Alamri, M., Jhanjhi, N.Z., Humayun, M., Blockchain for Internet of Things (IoT) research issues challenges & future directions: A review. *Int. J. Comput. Sci. Netw. Secur*, 19, 1, 244–258, 2019.
32. Dhar, S. and Bose, I., Securing IoT devices using zero trust and blockchain. *J. Organ. Comput. Electron. Commer.*, 31, 1, 18–34, 2021.
33. Chen, F., Xiao, Z., Cui, L., Lin, Q., Li, J., Yu, S., Blockchain for Internet of Things applications: A review and open issues. *J. Netw. Comput. Appl.*, 172, 102839, 2020.
34. Dedeoglu, V., Jurdak, R., Dorri, A., Lunardi, R.C., Michelin, R.A., Zorzo, A.F., Kanhere, S.S., Blockchain technologies for IoT, in: *Advanced Applications of Blockchain Technology*, pp. 55–89, 2020.
35. Ali, O., Ally, M., Dwivedi, Y., The state of play of blockchain technology in the financial services sector: A systematic literature review. *Int. J. Inf. Manag.*, 54, 102199, 2020.
36. Harish, A.R., Liu, X.L., Zhong, R.Y., Huang, G.Q., Log-flock: A blockchain-enabled platform for digital asset valuation and risk assessment in e-commerce logistics financing. *Comput. Ind. Eng.*, 151, 107001, 2021.
37. Treleaven, P., Brown, R.G., Yang, D., Blockchain technology in finance. *Computer*, 50, 9, 14–17, 2017.
38. Zhang, T., Li, J., Jiang, X., Analysis of supply chain finance based on block-chain. *Procedia Comput. Sci.*, 187, 1–6, 2021.
39. Garg, P., Gupta, B., Chauhan, A.K., Sivarajah, U., Gupta, S., Modgil, S., Measuring the perceived benefits of implementing blockchain technology in the banking sector. *Technol. Forecast. Soc. Change*, 163, 120407, 2021.
40. Malhotra, D., Saini, P., Singh, A.K., How blockchain can automate KYC: Systematic review. *Wirel. Pers. Commun.*, 122, 2, 1987–2021, 2022.
41. Kowalski, M., Lee, Z.W., Chan, T.K., Blockchain technology and trust rela-tionships in trade finance. *Technol. Forecast. Soc. Change*, 166, 120641, 2021.
42. McGhin, T., Choo, K.K.R., Liu, C.Z., He, D., Blockchain in healthcare appli-cations: Research challenges and opportunities. *J. Netw. Comput. Appl.*, 135, 62–75, 2019.
43. Hathaliya, J., Sharma, P., Tanwar, S., Gupta, R., Blockchain-based remote patient monitoring in healthcare 4.0, in: *2019 IEEE 9th International Conference on Advanced Computing (IACC)*, IEEE, pp. 87–91, 2019, December.

44. Tanwar, S., Parekh, K., Evans, R., Blockchain-based electronic healthcare record system for healthcare 4.0 applications. *J. Inf. Secur. Appl.*, 50, 102407, 2020.

45. Stafford, T.F. and Treiblmaier, H., Characteristics of a blockchain ecosystem for secure and sharable electronic medical records. *IEEE Trans. Eng. Manag.*, 67, 4, 1340–1362, 2020.

46. Reda, M., Kanga, D.B., Fatima, T., Azouazi, M., Blockchain in health supply chain management: State of art challenges and opportunities. *Procedia Comput. Sci.*, 175, 706–709, 2020.

47. Atlam, H.F., Azad, M.A., Alzahrani, A.G., Wills, G., A review of blockchain in internet of things and AI. *Big Data Cogn. Comput.*, 4, 4, 28, 2020.

48. Karthikeyyan, P. and Velliangiri, S., Review of blockchain based IoT application and its security issues, in: *2019 2nd International Conference on Intelligent Computing, Instrumentation and Control Technologies (ICICICT)*, vol. 1, IEEE, pp. 6–11, 2019, July.

49. Abdelmaboud, A., Ahmed, A.I.A., Abaker, M., Eisa, T.A.E., Albasheer, H., Ghorashi, S.A., Karim, F.K., Blockchain for IoT applications: taxonomy, platforms, recent advances, challenges and future research directions. *Electronics*, 11, 4, 630, 2022.

50. Shen, M., Liu, H., Zhu, L., Xu, K., Yu, H., Du, X., Guizani, M., Blockchain-assisted secure device authentication for cross-domain industrial IoT. *IEEE J. Sel. Areas Commun.*, 38, 5, 942–954, 2020.

51. Lin, W., Yin, X., Wang, S., Khosravi, M.R., A blockchain-enabled decentralized settlement model for IoT data exchange services. *Wirel. Netw.*, 29, 1–15, 2020.

52. Zhang, H. and Sakurai, K., Blockchain for iot-based digital supply chain: A survey, in: *Advances in Internet, Data and Web Technologies: The 8th International Conference on Emerging Internet, Data and Web Technologies (EIDWT-2020)*, Springer International Publishing, pp. 564–573, 2020.

53. Robert, J., Kubler, S., Ghatpande, S., Enhanced Lightning Network (off-chain)-based micropayment in IoT ecosystems. *Future Gener. Comput. Syst.*, 112, 283–296, 2020.

54. Somayaji, S.R.K., Alazab, M., Manoj, M.K., Bucchiarone, A., Chowdhary, C.L., Gadekallu, T.R., A framework for prediction and storage of battery life in IoT devices using DNN and blockchain, in: *2020 IEEE Globecom Workshops (GC Wkshps)*, pp. 1–6, IEEE, 2020, December. https://doi.org/10.1109/GCWkshps50303.2020.

9

AI-Enabled Techniques for Intelligent Transportation System for Smarter Use of the Transport Network for Healthcare Services

Meenakshi[1] and Preeti Sharma[2]*

*[1]Computer Science and Engineering Department, SOET, BML Munjal University,
Gurgaon, Haryana, India*
*[2]Computer Science and Engineering, CUIET, Chitkara University, Rajpura,
Punjab, India*

Abstract

Although intelligent transportation systems (ITS) and e-healthcare are two different fields, they can be integrated to offer a seamless and efficient experience to patients, attendants, relatives, and other relevant individuals. ITS can play a crucial role in supporting healthcare services by optimizing the use of transportation networks for treatment and e-healthcare logistic purposes. The combination of ITS and e-healthcare can provide patients with better and more efficient healthcare while also improving the overall transport experience. The biggest challenge in this integration is addressing the existing issues of a complex transportation system. Traffic administration organizations worldwide face the challenge of managing road traffic and networks. ITS, being an excellent mix of data and correspondence systems, seems the best solution that could contribute toward an effective and safe logistic environment alongside the long-term feasibility of transportation systems. For quicker implementation of ITS, electronic media, hardware, programming tools, and automation are necessary. The support of specific specializations such as civil, electrical, mechanical, and industrial engineering might additionally contribute to ensuring that these technologies prove productive and supportive. The rapid advancement of artificial intelligence (AI) offers immense opportunities for enhancing the effectiveness of various areas and ventures,

*Corresponding author: preetisharma@ncuindia.edu

Akansha Singh, Anuradha Dhull and Krishna Kant Singh (eds.) *Blockchain and Deep Learning
for Smart Healthcare*, (205–234) © 2024 Scrivener Publishing LLC

including the transportation sector. Recently, an advanced computational algorithm that imitates the human brain has been introduced by AI. The information, communications, and control (ICT) technology could also be utilized to make the transportation system more effective, smooth, and safety oriented. These steps will act as the base for the fusion of ITS and e-healthcare, which will assist in reducing the medical support response time to routine and critical patients and in further developing public interest in ITS-based healthcare support. A detailed perspective of AI-based ITS merging with e-healthcare is covered in this chapter.

Keywords: ITS, machine learning, artificial intelligence, healthcare, transportation system, genetic algorithms, supervised ML, unsupervised ML, IoT

9.1   Introduction

Artificial intelligence (AI) is the potential of a computer-controlled robot to carry out activities generally associated with the capabilities of the human brain. AI attempts to make it possible for a machine to gain know-how from experiences, acclimate to new inputs, and carry out activities similar to humans. Most of the current AI models—starting from "chess computers" to "self-driving cars"—rely primarily on deep learning (DL) and natural language processing (NLP). With these technologies, the training of computers can be ensured in order to have explicit assignments by processing huge data and perceiving data patterns data.

AI is a widespread area of software engineering that enables a machine to work like a human brain. In the modern era, a lot of technical issues cannot be resolved by utilizing traditional computational techniques, but these same issues can be easily addressed using AI. McCarthy firstly discovered AI in 1956, but unfortunately could not achieve his ultimate goal [1], and the absence of technological advancements made the endeavor less encouraging. Between 1960 and 1970, experts investigated AI across the information-based system (knowledge-based system, KBS) and artificial neural networks (ANNs) [1]. Technical advice utilizing predetermined guidelines was provided using KBS-enabled computers, dependent on the information made available to them by humans. ANNs are neuron connection systems planned in different layers, modeled similar to the brain of humans, that have been utilized in the fields of engineering, law, medicine, manufacturing, science, language interpretation engineering, and regulation, among others [2, 3]. During this time frame, the interest in AI has lessened due to the restricted use of ANNs and the lack of data until the 1980s [4].

Since the 1980s, many explorations have been carried out to limit the errors of prediction using a strategy termed gradient descent. This technique is a backpropagation algorithm used to train ANNs, and it was implemented to address issues in various domains utilizing some hidden layers [5, 6]. Currently, data availability has presented the concept of machine learning (ML) as a subclass of AI. In ML, inferences are drawn from computer coding, enabling computers to act similar to the human brain without being programmed. This gives computers access to big data and to concentrate on significant highlights from these data in order to resolve complex issues [7, 8]. ANN is the most highly recognized AI strategy utilized in various technical tasks. The leading and standard type of ANN is the feed forward neural network, where data move in a single direction from the input layer to the hidden layer to the output layer. Other types of ANNs include the convolutional neural network (CNN) [9–11] and repetitive neural network (RNN) [12–14]. CNNs perform better in picture processing tasks, while RNNs process an arrangement for input data to make them appropriate for certain applications, e.g., for text recognition and writing of language. These are frequently referred to as DL techniques due to the different hidden layers organized in their structures. However, numerous uncertainties and loopholes exist inside the data, which cannot be addressed utilizing conventional methodologies. AI makes use of these uncertainties and models a connection between the cause and effect of several genuine conditions through the combination of available data with speculations and probabilities for a higher-level assessment [15]. The issues in transport networks seem are enormous tasks due to the system and the clients' behavior being too difficult to even consider modeling and predicting travel and transportation patterns. Hence, AI was considered an ideal solution to address the challenges of steadily increasing travel demands, carbon dioxide emissions, safety, and the disturbed ecological balance. These challenges stemmed from the consistent evolution of non-urban and metropolitan traffic in conditions due to the increase in population, specifically in developing areas. Several experts in the modern era have endeavored to achieve a more bankable transportation system with reduced impact on individuals and the climate utilizing smart methods and more dependability on AI approaches. AI offers outstanding and promising applications for drivers, other highway and road infrastructure users, and vehicles. AI-based intelligent transportation systems (ITS) is an updated version that aims to offer innovative service connection with various methods of handling transportation and vehicle congestion and enables users to be accordingly updated and to make further secure, more organized, and more intelligent utilization of transport networks.

Intelligent vehicle system differs in terms of the technology applied, from basic management systems such as vehicle navigation variable message signals, control system for traffic signals, automatic vehicle number rec-ognition, security systems to screen activities such as CCTV, and accident detection to more developed applications that incorporate live data and feedbacks from various sources, such as vehicle parking and information system and weather information, among others. Moreover, predictive methodologies are being developed to permit advanced modeling and comparisons with historical data. At the same time, AI is changing rapidly, improving the efficiency and effectiveness of the healthcare field. It is used to diagnose and treat diseases, predict outcomes, and provide personal-ized care to patients. AI is supportive in enhancing result-oriented patient management through the automation of administrative tasks in hospitals, streamlining patient and medicine data analysis. AI-assisted healthcare solutions are empowering the human race by improving patient outcomes, providing economical treatment and overall better quality of care.

The merging of ITS and e-healthcare can be beneficial for both sectors. By combining these two fields, healthcare providers can utilize ITS toward improving the quality and services of healthcare [15, 105]. ITS can be used to track patients' data, monitor patients' health, and support the provision of better communication between providers and patients, in addition to streamlining the delivery of care and reducing costs.

9.2   Artificial Intelligence

AI is a very popular technology and is currently the main focus as one of emerging fields changing the transportation sector. The ANN shown in Figure 9.1 can be a basic or a more complicated multilayered perceptron model. The perceptron model comprises input and output nodes, where each input node is associated with the output node *via* weight. The con-cept of AI started in the 1950s, and ever since, it has gone through various promising and low periods, where encouraging theories were followed by harsh disappointments. Recently, AI has seen a lot of progress, as ML strat-egies have been combined with technologies utilized to detect and examine a huge quantity of data (also called data mining and big data) as a result of a continually evolving digital world. Further reasons behind its effective development incorporate the improvements in the communication net-work and the Internet of Things (IoT), as well as progress in transportation tools, gadgets, and devices. The next advancements of AI in transport are expected to be considerably more astounding, despite the fact that there is no time frame and specific core area defined as of the moment. AI and ML have shown their capability to revolutionize various industries, public

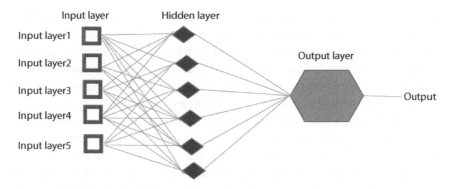

Figure 9.1 Artificial neural network.

administrations, and societies, accomplishing or matching human intelligence in terms of execution and precision in fields such as speech and image recognition [16] and language translation [17]. In any case, their best offering as far as precision is concerned is DL [18], which is similarly often portrayed as a "black box" and opaque [19]. Without a doubt, such models have an enormous number (billions) of parameters that should contain the data gained from the training data. Not only is the quantity of these weights exceptionally huge, but their connection to the physical environments of the issue is very difficult from an isolation point of view. This makes clarification of such types of AI excessively problematic to clients. Utilizing the opaque, black box model is particularly problem-oriented in profoundly sensitive domains such as medical care and in different applications associated with humans, the economy, and security. Since the use of cutting-edge AI and ML techniques, including DL, is presently developing at a rapid pace, enveloping the legal, digital well-being, transport, healthcare, economic, and defense aspects, the issues of transparency and comprehensibility are progressively perceived as fundamentally significant.

9.3 Artificial Intelligence: Transport System and Healthcare

The unexpected occurrence of the coronavirus disease 2019 (COVID-19) pandemic has negatively impacted both the healthcare and transport industries due to the lockdown and the travel restrictions mandated by the state and central authorities. The spread of the pandemic has changed the manner in which patients receive treatment and the use of public transport because of the rising safety concerns and the need to maintain social distance. In any case, incorporating AI in the transport and healthcare sectors proved to be the best answer for the issues faced.

Presently, AI assists in making all transport modes more secure, cleaner, smarter, and more comfort-oriented. AI can be integrated in vehicles and road infrastructures, both for drivers and passengers, enabling an enhanced interface that benefits improved and efficient transport. Moreover, AI assists in the detection of market patterns, in the identification of risks, reducing traffic, reducing the emission of ozone-depleting gases and air pollutants, in planning and designing transportation, and in examining interest in travel and passenger conduct. The majority of huge urban areas globally face challenges related to traffic, transportation, and logistic issues. This is due to the rapid increase in the human population and, consequently, the increase in the number of vehicles on the road. To effectively design and implement a justifiable transportation framework, technologies can prove valuable to a great extent. With the issue of heavy traffic congestion in metropolitan areas, there is a rise in AI systems to obtain constant and live data from vehicles for the smooth management of traffic, with the "mobility on demand" concept being used for better planning of trips through a single user interface. AI-based integrated navigation, traffic management, AI-based guidance and control of traffic flow for efficient and productive management, and transport network administration, as well as other devices contributing to mobility enhancement, are added on conceivable outcomes of efficient and productive traffic management [20]. AI is considered the foremost emerging technology by the World Economic Forum. The AI methodologies that help with transport efficiency enhancement include ANN, genetic algorithm (GA), ant colony optimizer (ACO), simulated annealing (SA), and fuzzy logic model (FLM). In transportation management, these methodologies are specifically utilized to reduce traffic congestion, ensure that travel times are more reliable for passengers, and work on the economic aspect and the efficiency of the whole framework [21]. Vehicles that connect using these technologies enhance the efficiency of driving through the anticipation of traffic conditions [21]. In Mire [22], three viewpoints were addressed, as follows.

1. Precise prediction assessment and detection model targeting the forecasting of the volume of traffic conditions and occurrences;
2. Public transportation as a bankable travel method by exploring the different utilizations of AI; and
3. Connected vehicles targeting to improve utility by reducing the number of accidents on highways and roads.

In parallel, healthcare professionals in developing and developed nations utilize AI for extensive patient care and normal medical care to advance their work. AI has enabled influenced research on intelligent healthcare systems that are oriented on patient care and timely response. AI technologies have a direct and positive impact on how intensive care and administrative tasks are managed in hospitals and clinics [23]. AI offers quick, affordable, and better solutions for cutting-edge prognosis, preventive care, medicine, and several ongoing healthcare research. The medical diagnosis process has welcomed a variety of AI applications to improve disease detection, service delivery, and disease prediction accuracy, among others. Personalized medicine, clinical diagnosis research, robotic surgery, verified prescriptions, prenatal care for pregnant women, imaging, and evaluated patient information are some of the vital areas in which AI is making a big impact and difference. NLP algorithms are used for medical documentation and records. DL algorithms can be used to analyze medical images and to develop systems that can automatically extract relevant data from medical documents. ANN and random forest are utilized to predict the risk of diseases through assessment of a patient's medical history and ECG and MRI data.

For both the transportation and healthcare sectors, AI technologies are very well suited to analyzing data and uncovering patterns and insights that humans could not determine on their own. With various AI tools, e.g., DL, the transport and healthcare industries could utilize algorithms in order to develop a support system that caters to best-in-class transportation solutions and clinical decisions, hence improving the overall quality of experience. There is huge potential in integrating AI into ITS and e-healthcare, zeroing in on how AI could smoothly coordinate and improve insights, expectations, and the challenges of this fusion.

9.4   Artificial Intelligence Algorithms

AI is an arena of software engineering that demonstrates machine intelligence by simulating human-like task performance capabilities. It uses multiple approaches to achieve goals, including supervised learning (SL) [24], unsupervised learning (UL) [25], reinforcement learning (RL) [26], and DL [27], as shown in Figure 9.2. The figure depicts the scientific classifications of AI, displaying cutting-edge AI bandwidths.

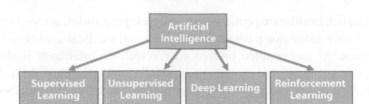

Figure 9.2 Types of artificial intelligence (AI).

1) Supervised learning

The SL model relies on the connection and dependency between the predicted output and the input feature. This is done by inducing a classification or regression from a labeled training dataset. A training dataset is created by models utilized for learning. Labeled data comprise a sample collection that has been tagged with target variables. In view of the capacity gained from the training data, SL could anticipate the output values for fresh data. Regarding its task, a large portion of SL algorithms could be subdivided into two significant types, as follows:

    a. *Classification algorithms* (cognitive load, CL) learn the prediction of categories as the output for new observations based on the labeled training data. Support vector machine (SVM) [28] and AdaBoost, or adaptive boosting [44], are two examples of these algorithms.

    b. *Regression algorithms* (RL) deal with regression issues for which the output variable is continuous or a real value, e.g., weights or remuneration. The basic type is linear regression (LR) [29], which attempts to adjust data with the best hyperplane *via* the training data points. A popular example is support vector regression (SVR) [30].

It has to be noted that a few algorithms are utilized for both classification and regression issues, such as *k*-nearest neighbour (k-NN) [31], random forest (RF) [32], and boosted regression tree (BRT) [33].

2) Unsupervised learning

UL is a technique of knowledge discovery that is data-driven. It can easily work out a function explaining the structure from datasets comprising input data without labeled response. UL could be subdivided into two distinct classes, as follows:

- *Clustering algorithms*: An example is *k*-means clustering [34]. It discovers the inherent grouping in the data.
- *Dimension reduction algorithms*: Examples include principal component analysis (PCA) [35] and independent component analysis (ICA) [36]. These determine the data's top representation with little dimensions.

3) Reinforcement learning

RL determines how to take sequential steps in an environment to cumulatively boost rewards. In RL, learning can be initiated without any data. The functional mechanisms of RL are associated with the ITS environment. The ITS framework incorporates each of its layers and the surrounding environment (e.g., roadway conditions). In RL, the agents are the components that settle the decisions on which actions should be taken. To accomplish this, the agent requires the interactive capability with the environment in order to obtain data (e.g., rewards, state, and actions). Afterward, with the obtained data, the agent may train and update itself in order to make superior decisions. The RL algorithm can be classified into three types, as follows:

- *Value-based algorithms*: In these algorithms, value function is obtained based on temporal difference learning, which gauges the best course for a particular action on a provided state. Q-learning [37], SARSA (state–action–reward–state–action) [38], and deep Q-network (DQN) [39] are examples of value-based RL.
- *Policy-based algorithms*: These algorithms straightforwardly learn optimal policies or attempt to obtain approximately optimal policies depending on observations, e.g., policy gradient (PG) [40] and deterministic policy gradient (DPG) [41].
- *Imitation algorithms* [42]: Also referred to as apprenticeship learning (AL), these algorithms attempt to settle the decision by demonstration, which, most of the time, shows decent performance when the reward function is hard to determine and when it is difficult to directly optimize actions. Imitation algorithms can manage unexplored states (e.g., new states that are not in the training data) and propose a more highly reliable framework for numerous assignments, such as driverless vehicles. The primary AL methodologies include generative adversarial imitation learning (GAIL) and reward augmented imitation learning (RAIL).

Hybrid algorithms combine the value-based and policy-based algorithms. The aim is the same, i.e., to address the policy function using a policy-based algorithm; however, the policy function updates rely on the value-based algorithm. Actor critic (AC) [43], asynchronous advantage actor critic (A3C) [44], and deep deterministic policy gradient (DDGP) [45] are typical hybrid algorithms.

4) Deep learning and neural networks

DL is popularly used in different areas, and its successful execution generally depends on ANNs. ANNs have become a sophisticated technique for the representation of data. An ANN comprises a bunch of interconnected nodes intended to replicate the functioning of the human brain. Each node possesses a weighted association with a few different nodes in the adjoining layers. Ione nodes take inputs from linked nodes and utilize weights along with a basic function for computation of the output values. ANNs, particularly deep neural networks (DNNs), have become attractive inductive methodologies due to their high adaptability, data-driven, and nonlinear model structure.

The major types of neural networks are fully connected neural networks (FNNs), i.e., CNNs and RNNs. CNNs accomplish prevailing execution on visual assignments, e.g., exploitation of the crucial spatial properties of videos and pictures. RNNs could very well portray a data's temporal connection and consequently display the top capacity for time series tasks. Long short-term memory (LSTM) techniques, with units such as RNNs, are equipped for learning order dependencies with regard to issues of sequence predictions. Graph neural networks (GNNs) [46, 47] comprise a type of graph structure that models a bunch of nodes (entities) and their relationship (edges). FNNs, CNNs, and RNNs are formulated based on Euclidean data. Notwithstanding, GNNs utilize non-Euclidean data structures for DL. Neural networks possess a number of extensions, such as deep belief networks (DBNs) [48], error-feedback recurrent convolutional neural networks (eRCNNs), fully convolutional neural networks (FCNs), and spatiotemporal graph convolutional neural networks (ST-GCNNs). DBNs can be portrayed as the stacking of restricted Boltzmann machines (RBMs) [49], which are made up of a two-layered network model comprising both visible and hidden units. Another category, specifically called deep reinforcement learning (DRL), portrays the algorithms that consolidate RL with DL. DDPG, DQN, and multi-agent DRL (MA-DRL) are examples of DRL algorithms.

The combination of ML and ITS data is the primary outcome of the current ITS. Given the range of ITS applications (worldwide, locally, and hybrid applications), data may be gathered from each of the ITS layers. This data-heavy characteristic of ITS anticipates the innate capacity of ML to detect information from data. Clustering, regression, prediction, classification, and decision-making are highlights from ML that are suitable for the upgrade of ITS and lay a strong foundation for the structure blocks of ITS applications. This section incorporates 1) the manner in which AI is merged into ITS, supported by a ML pipeline, and 2) the manner in which harnessing AI is performed by ITS tasks.

9.5   AI Workflow

The AI workflow is discussed in this section. The primary goal of such workflow is to model the ideal ITS components or behaviors that may be coupled with ITS assignments. For instance, mobility modeling of vehicles is important for prediction assignments, although models to classify the transport system framework from pictures may be put into perception. The workflow of AI comprises vital stages, specifically data pre-processing, feature extraction, and modeling.

- *Data pre-processing*: Raw data generally require pre-processing, i.e., data cleaning and normalization. Simply, data pre-processing involves preparing the raw data and making these compatible with the AI model. This is the initial and pivotal stage in the design of an AI model.
- *Feature extraction* (FE): FE from data is a crucial stage. There are two major methods for FE: hand-crafted and DL feature extraction. Hand-crafted features are chosen using human expertise, which are pertinent to the provided tasks. However, even the most experienced individuals cannot distinguish every one of the fundamental features not expressly connected with the captured data [50]. Consequently, the extracted features may reflect limited parts of an issue, the outcome of which is low accuracy. Examples of hand-crafted descriptors for image feature extraction include local binary pattern (LBP), Gabor channel, local ternary pattern (LTP), and histogram of oriented gradients (HOG). While DL shows predominance in the learning of higher-level features, FE may be programmed automatically with next to no manual mediation.

- *Modeling*: AI has reached the highest stage with respect to model training. Specifically, the ML approach enables extraordinary steps to achieve finer visual understanding [27]. AI-trained models could be utilized for regression, clustering, classification, and decision-making, which may be applied into an ITS task.

9.6   AI for ITS and e-Healthcare Tasks

This section presents the AI methodology for performing ITS and healthcare tasks. Firstly, conventional methodologies for ITS perception were generally founded on standard sensors, such as magnetic sensors, global positioning system (GPS), inductive loop detector, and radiofrequency identification (RFID), among others. Due to the extensive use of vision-based devices in ITS frameworks, unusual amounts of video and image data were created, which used vision understanding as the core of the perception task. Conventional procedures could not offer the required speed and accuracy in vision-based perception; however, AI methods could be utilized to work on these metrics. Such advancement is fundamentally carried out with hand-crafted features, which are derived from data in the image. Notwithstanding, considering the increasing variety of items and the little contrast between comparable articles in a few perception issues, the method involved with inferring hand-crafted features may not be discriminatively sufficient. In terms of DL, perception accuracy has been significantly enhanced with deep feature extraction. Furthermore, scientists have studied various parametric and non-parametric techniques for the issue of prediction. When the model design is solid and the parameters are usually gained through data, this approach to modeling is known as parametric. Some examples include time series, gray system model, and Kalman filters. This technique requires a decent model design in the planning, in view of the qualitative analysis of experts. It is exceptionally subjective and limited as significant expense and time are required to obtain results. In a similar manner, non-parametric strategies determine both the parameters and the model design from data *via* training AI-based algorithms, and a standard class of non-parametric techniques is navigated through big data investigation, permitting AI to discover the patterns within the data. Variations of this class of techniques include k-NN, fuzzy logic (FL), and SVM. In particular, with the emergence of parallel processing technologies, neural networks are perhaps the best models for prediction [51], as approximation of almost all functions can be done without previous information on its functional form; at the same time, it is reasonable for use in both linear and nonlinear systems. Through training, i.e., trial and error, AI-based prediction strategies can achieve accuracy with a fast learning pace [52].

Lastly, classical management approaches attempt to determine a succession of activities that move the environment or articles from an initial state to the ideal state with a few objectives. The issues are assumed to be completely discernible (the environment condition is precisely known), finite (the state space and activity space are restricted), deterministic (with prior familiarity with the state transfer rule), and static (the only element for which we control changes the state) in this type of management mechanism [53]. Notwithstanding, the ITS environment is more confounded, not being able to meet every assumption of classical algorithms. AI approaches such as RL, offering strategies to manage an endless state and activity space with uncertain impacts, are more appropriate for ITS management tasks.

In the area of e-healthcare, data collection is the first step carried out using various sources including patient records, medical images, and sensor data. This is followed by data cleaning and pre-processing, which are conducted to remove any noise and ensure accuracy of the data. Subsequently, feature engineering is carried out, where meaningful features from the data that can be used for further analysis and modeling are extracted.

Model building then follows, which is carried out utilizing models such as DL, ML, and NLP. The models are used for the analysis and interpretation of the data. This is followed by model evaluation to ensure accuracy and reliability. Thereafter, the model is implemented in a clinical setting. Finally, accuracy is ensured by monitoring the performance of the model, making necessary changes if required.

Following are a few of the AI-enabled techniques that can be used to improve healthcare services through the intelligent use of transportation networks. By leveraging these technologies, it may be possible to improve the efficiency and effectiveness of medical transportation services and to enhance access to healthcare for communities across the world.

Route optimization: AI algorithms can optimize the routes for ambulances and medical supply deliveries based on real-time traffic conditions, road network conditions, and other factors.

Predictive maintenance: AI algorithms can be utilized to predict when a vehicle is likely to require maintenance, allowing preventive maintenance to be performed before it becomes an issue that affects operations.

Traffic flow optimization: AI algorithms can support improving traffic flow to reduce congestion, minimize travel times, and improve safety for ambulances and other medical vehicles.

Demand-driven dispatch: AI algorithms can match the demand for medical transportation services with the available supply, improving utilization and reducing wait times.

Predictive analytics: AI algorithms can analyze data from various sources, such as traffic flow, weather conditions, and medical data, in order to identify patterns and predict future demand for medical transportation services.

Autonomous vehicles: AI algorithms can be used to develop autonomous vehicles as medical transportation, reducing the risk of human error and improving safety.

Telemedicine in vehicles: Vehicles equipped with ITS technology can be fitted with telemedicine devices such as videoconferencing equipment, allowing patients to receive medical consultations while on the road.

Emergency response coordination: In the event of a medical emergency, ITS technology can coordinate the quickest and most efficient response. For example, an ambulance equipped with GPS technology can be dispatched to the location of an emergency and given real-time updates on traffic conditions in order to reach the patient as quickly as possible.

Health monitoring in public transport: Public transport vehicles such as buses and trains can be equipped with health monitoring devices, making it possible for passengers with medical conditions to receive real-time monitoring and support during their journey.

Remote patient monitoring: Patients with chronic conditions can use wearable devices or telemedicine devices to send real-time data to their healthcare provider, enabling remote monitoring and support.

Integration with electronic health records (EHRs): The data collected from telemedicine devices and health monitoring systems can be integrated into a patient's EHR, providing a comprehensive overview of their health status.

9.7   Intelligent Transportation, Healthcare, and IoT

IoT and AI are empowering another class of ITS not only for roads but also for air, rails, and oceans. The combination of various solutions merges vehicles, traffic lights, tollgates, and other frameworks to facilitate blockage, prevent accidents, reduce emissions of pollutants, and make the transport system more productive. Models incorporate vehicle-to-everything (V2X) technology, fleet management, intelligent traffic management, electric vehicle charging, electronic toll collection, and a wide scope of other mobility-based solutions.

Fleet management officers, operators, various transportation depart-ments, and different organizations utilize IoT and AI approaches to address existing transport system challenges. ITS work on the safety, traffic man-agement, and pollutant emission decrease on roads, rails, aerospace, and sea routes, advancing ecological supportability and monetary development.

With the recent expansion of the use of various innovative devices across different areas, massive amounts of data have been generated. This data accumulation has played a significant role in the quick decision-making of organizations, states, and social administrators. The transport industry, being the existence line of the metropolitan and local area setup cannot be ignored in the data generation drive and use. This domain plays a critical role in the advancements of metropolitan and local cities since it impacts individuals, operations, and the economy. To empower the generation of data, vehicle manufacturers have been actively supporting the production of devices suitable for use in public and service transport vehicles. The data generated by these devices are remotely examined by experts. States and organizations are well suited to make continuous and quick decisions based on the data collected from different applications. Various innovative transportation applications and state-of-the-art technologies have recently become inherent. The application designers center around a process-oriented framework with a specific objective implanted with a response collection criterion to quantify result of the solution connected with trans-portation industries.

Transport management systems (TMS) have a place in the field of trans-port management explicitly concerned with transport operations. The primary goal of these frameworks is to establish convincing route plan, load optimizations, more developed adaptability, and transparency utiliz-ing data. According to De Muynck *et al.*, this field is expected to further develop at a faster speed [54]. The transportation system of a particular city is connected to a data and information framework for better organizational control, which emphasizes data capture, processing, and transmission and data management. In a nutshell, due to the rise of smart technologies in recent years, different data frameworks for logistically coordinated opera-tions, route guiding, mapping, and planning executions have been designed and implemented. These systems now possess expanded data-processing capacities that are beneficial to the transport systems further and better enabling enhancement in ITS execution [55].

The data derived from operators and automobiles are utilized in the design of a proficient ITS. The incorporation of ITS into the vehicle framework will guarantee an enhanced performance attributable to data procurement, exchanges and integrations across vehicles, city infrastructures, and additional correlated exercises. It has been shown that ITS provide an excellent foundation toward quick decision-making processes for urban and semi-urban development authorities and for automobile users.

Hence, ITS form part of TMS. Different strategies comprise the assembly of AI methodologies employed to determine existing challenges in the transport industry toward building an improved transportation framework. The advantages of the different sub-frameworks of ITS have been recognized and examined alongside the uses of AI, positively impacting the transport business. Previous results and further research work help organizations and government agencies in the adoption of the latest technology and in making decisions regarding the best possible solution according to a particular transportation framework condition.

IoT is also doing wonders in the healthcare field, which is being used to provide best-in-class patient care, efficiency, and data security. Moreover, it is used to monitor and track various medical conditions, e.g., diabetes, heart rate, blood pressure, and other vital signs. It can also provide remote monitoring and diagnoses, as well as enable telemedicine. IoT devices collect patient data, and these data are utilized to monitor health trends, detect potential health issues, and provide personalized care.

In addition, IoT is utilized to automate healthcare processes and enable better communication between patients and healthcare providers. Definitely, IoT has enhanced patient care, enabling healthcare providers to monitor the health of patients in real time and allowing them to quickly identify any changes in their health status. This can help reduce the risk of medical errors and ensure that patients receive the best possible care. IoT technology has improved access to healthcare services, particularly in remote or underserved areas. For example, telemedicine and remote monitoring technologies enable healthcare providers to care for patients without having to be physically present. IoT technology also helps in streamlining healthcare processes and in reducing the amount of time needed to complete tasks. The integration of ITS and e-healthcare under the purview of IoT can definitely change the healthcare domain. Figure 9.3 demonstrates the seamless combination of IoT-enabled ITS and the e-healthcare system.

Furthermore, IoT technology elevates the level of security in healthcare settings by providing better control over who has access to patient data and medical records. This helps reduce the risk of unauthorized access and ensures that patient data remain secure.

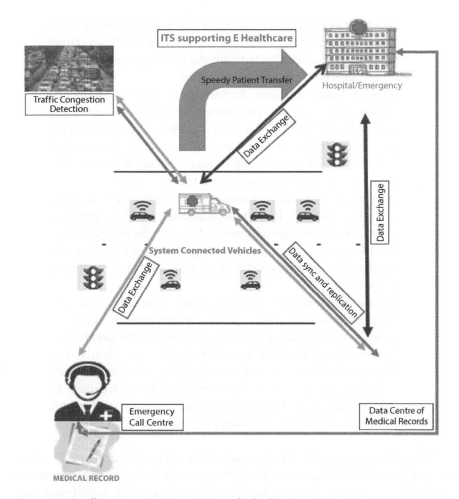

Figure 9.3 Intelligent transport management for healthcare.

9.8 AI Techniques Used in ITS and e-Healthcare

A brief explanation of the AI methodologies ANN, GA, FL, and expert systems (ES) is provided below.

- ANNs are dependent on the mathematical model of neurons proposed in 1943 by McCulloch and Pitts [56], which may be taken as a processing paradigm that functions much the same way as the human brain. ANNs offer a number of features, including adaptive learning, self-organizing capability, and fault tolerance, and these are normally executed to resolve issues connected with data coding, pattern recognition, data mining, and optimization.

- GAs are heuristic search techniques applied to obtain resolutions for issues utilizing natural selection strategies and evolutionary biology [57]. They are often utilized to inspect huge and complex datasets and are exceptionally equipped to tackle optimization issues in areas including telecommunication, medicines, robotics, and transportation.

- FL strategies imitate the human reasoning ability to settle on a rational decision in a vulnerable and imprecise environment [58]. FL is generally applied to address issues such as complex industrial processes, recognizing handwriting and handwritten symbols, driving comfortably, and prediction frameworks [59].

- ES are rule-oriented methodologies dependent on predefined knowledge [60]. They are utilized in decision-making *via* logical deductions. ES imitate the conduct of human experts in order to resolve issues. More clearly, they store information about a specific field and address issues by utilizing logical deduction based on this information. ES are typically utilized in media communications, medication, healthcare, accounts, and transport systems.

The above-mentioned AI approaches have been utilized in ITS and e-healthcare. Following are the key areas connected with transport systems and e-healthcare in which AI has been broadly applied, with promising outcomes.

a) *Vehicle control*: AI is executed to develop novel control frameworks for the automotive industry. These include autonomous driving, anti-lock braking systems (ABS), automobile consumption management, and emission control systems.

b) *Traffic control and prediction*: AI-integrated systems create frameworks that aim to reduce traffic congestion and to predict traffic jams.

c) *Road security and accident prediction*: AI-integrated systems focus on enhancing the road safety aspects, avoid and prevent potential accidents by incorporating systems that independently anticipate these occurrences, and attempt to mitigate the consequences of such events.

d) *Diagnostics*: AI assists in the detection of diseases such as cancer and heart disease. It can analyze medical images and detect patterns that are difficult for humans to accomplish.

e) *Drug discovery*: AI is used to identify potential new drugs more quickly and more accurately compared to traditional methods.

f) *Patient care*: AI supports improving patient care by providing personalized care plans, monitoring patient vitals, and providing better predictions for treatment outcomes.

g) *Clinical decision support*: AI is used to provide clinicians with real-time support in making decisions based on patient data.

h) *Healthcare administration*: AI helps with automating administrative tasks such as scheduling, billing, and insurance claims processing.

9.9   Challenges of AI and ML in ITS and e-Healthcare

AI and ML have consistently shown excellent outcomes in ITS applications and e-healthcare. When incorporated into transport systems and the e-healthcare domain, they could further improve lifestyle and provide safety and health confidence [94]. In any case, these innovations have encountered specific difficulties in the upgrade of the transportation frameworks and e-healthcare, which should be addressed by analysts, developers, and designers. To improve the accuracy of the ML algorithm, an exceptionally large training dataset is required to give relevant and specific information, including patient historical data, updates on medication, vehicle acceleration, the central distance between two vehicles, location details, and distance traveled, among others [95]. These data will lay down the foundation for better outcomes in light of the fact that a bigger dataset will give more precise results. Consequently, it is essential to gather a huge quantity of transport data [96]. In enhancing ITS and e-healthcare, the pressing concern in the development of brilliant procedures utilizing ML is security. With the progress in innovation and the advances in brilliant foundation and smart transport system frameworks, as well as e-healthcare, the developing need to safeguard the overall security of the framework always remains [97]. For instance, a security breach of the traffic detection system may influence the correspondence between cars and may create a delay in the reaction time, and a breach of a patient's personal data can cause personal and professional conflicts. Thus, more developed methods such as big data investigation are expected to guarantee cyber protection and security in smart transport systems [98]. Self-driving cars have demonstrated trustworthiness and better efficiency in driving. AI advancements have changed the way people think about innovations today [99]. The self-driving cars, for example, have shown continuous improvements day by day with the new improvements in AI. Designers and scientists are working on the innovation in self-driving vehicles to make these more secure for movement. Despite that an incredible number of models have already been introduced and multiple improvements have already been done several times, there is yet no legitimate technique available to approve the model's accuracy. In an era of speedy execution of a smart transport system, there are multiple expectations regarding the faster advance of self-driving cars [100]. With the progress of data development, it would be feasible to gather sufficient data for reducing the ratio of current errors in order to establish a more regular utilization of self-driving vehicles in the real world. Another concern is the security and protection of individuals driving from one location to another [101]. Drivers' mobile phones contain data about their movements. These data are significant in assisting with examining the normal travel duration of the vehicles and with obtaining data about crowded locations at specific times. In addition, they may likewise be utilized to gather information about nearby vehicles and to assist with developing a smart framework equipped with sensors that may detect or predict collisions, hence preventing such events through an alarm system [102]. Thus, access of the data from a driver's mobile phone provides vital and valuable information that could support the development and improvement of smart city and transport systems. However, data safeguarding is a necessity, with these data being regularly accessed by actuators, sensors, and huge servers [103]. Data implementation should be done safely and should adhere to all protection guidelines and regulations [104]. The basic need of a smart transportation and e-healthcare framework is a set of suitable ML and AI algorithms that are specific and precise in detecting traffic inconsistencies and in monitoring constant real-time traffic and patient data. Thus, confirm to the security rulings and guidelines as data won't be moved to cloud platforms. The execution of this type of algorithm that could produce real-time data is a challenge-oriented task and, hence, demands effective sample processing and scalability in models. In addition, there are further challenges to the fusion of these algorithms, which are summarized below.

a) *Security* is a major challenge in the ITS and e-healthcare sectors as they involve the handling of large amounts of sensitive data, which need to be protected from unauthorized access and malicious attacks.

b) *Interoperability* between different systems and devices is a challenge in these sectors. This is due to the complexity of the systems and the lack of a common standard.

c) *User adoption* is another challenge in the introduction of new technologies. This is especially true in the healthcare sector, where users may be reluctant to use new technologies due to privacy concerns or the lack of familiarity.

d) *Non-availability of amply vast and complex datasets* for both e-healthcare and ITS, e.g., the lack of curated heath data and integrated transportation data.

e) *Insufficient AI-skilled workforce* for both ITS and e-healthcare tasks.

f) There is a *lack of strong and clear regulatory guidelines* for the ITS and e-healthcare domains, which are necessary in order to boost confidence in the agencies involved in the development and implementation of software.

g) *Cost* is a major challenge in these two sectors. New technologies can be expensive to implement and maintain, and this can hinder their adoption.

9.10 Conclusions

Traffic management authorities worldwide are presented with the chance to change the way road, sea, air, and rail traffic is currently being managed. In the same way, the e-healthcare industry is also entering the IoT- and AI-based era, adding new wings to the sector. This can undoubtedly be accomplished by moving hand in hand with emerging technological innovations. The technologies for traffic management, ITS, and e-healthcare involve a fusion of data and communication systems working together to improve efficiency and safety alongside promising long-term viable transport and healthcare systems. There is no limit to the possible encouraging results. The utilization of data and technologies in the transport system could be the highlight of any transportation organization or business and the force behind the realization of ITS. The technologies that can speed up the development of ITS include electronic-based correspondence, hardware and software upgrade, and atomization. In the same way, new algorithms and software support can introduce new aspects to e-health-care, e.g., AI-based tools for elderly care. Lack of timely and trusted data alongside the lack of system coordination are the fundamental challenges of most transport systems. These challenges may be addressed by gathering data from trusted sources and increasing the bandwidth of data collection. There are a lot of benefits to integrating genuine data and information technologies into systems, empowering organizations to make better synergistic choices and further developing the transportation and e-healthcare sectors.

The combination of ITS and e-healthcare enables better communication between healthcare providers, transport authorities, and patients, as well as improved access to medical information. ITS can provide a secure, efficient, and cost-effective way to deliver healthcare services to patients. In addition, both sectors can help each other in streamlining administrative processes and improving the accuracy of data collection and analysis. Finally, it can be considered as a win–win situation for both sectors. ITS can continue refining the support system for healthcare providers in terms of accessing and sharing information more quickly and easily, improving the quality of medical care. In exchange, the medical care sector can provide better healthcare to society.

References

1. Sadek, A., Artificial intelligence in transportation. *Transp. Res. Circ.*, E-C113, 72–79, 2007.
2. Yegnanarayana, B., *Artificial neural networks*, p. 476, PHI Learning Pvt. Ltd., New Delhi, India, 1999, Sustainability 2019, 11, 189 18 of 24.
3. Abraham, A., Artificial neural networks, in: *Handbook of Measuring System Design*, P.H. Sydenham and R. Thorn (Eds.), John Wiley & Sons, Ltd., Hoboken, NJ, USA, 2005.
4. Minsky, M. and Papert, S., *Perceptron expanded edition*, MIT Press, Cambridge, MA, USA, 1969.
5. Wolpert, D.H., Bayesian backpropagation over I-O functions rather than weights. *Adv. Neural Inf. Process. Syst.*, 6, 200–207, 1993.
6. Parker, D., *Learning logic: Technical report TR-87, center for computational research in economics and management science*, The MIT Press, Cambridge, MA, USA, 1985.
7. Getoor, B. and Taskar, L., *Introduction to statistical relational learning; volume L of adaptive computation and machine learning*, MIT Press, Cambridge, MA, USA, 2007.

8. Bacciu, A., Micheli, D., Sperduti, A., Compositional generative mapping for tree-structured data—Part I: Bottom-up probabilistic modeling of trees. *IEEE Trans. Neural Netw. Learn. Syst.*, 23, 1987–2002, 2012.

9. Krizhevsky, A., Sutskever, I., Hinton, G.E., ImageNet classification with deep convolutional neural networks. *Adv. Neural Inf. Process. Syst.*, 60, 1–9, 2012, Available online: https://papers.nips.cc/paper/4824-imagenet-classification-with-deep-convolutional-neural-networks.pdf (accessed on 27 December 2018).

10. Kim, P., Convolutional neural network, in: *MATLAB Deep Learning*, Apress, Berkeley, CA, USA, 2017. 11. McCann, M.T., Jin, K.H., Unser, M., Deep convolutional neural network for inverse problems in imaging. *IEEE Signal Process. Mag.*, 34, 85–95, 2017.

11. O'Shea, K.T. and Nash, R., An Introduction to convolutional neural networks identification and validation of low-cost, high-throughput microbial and metabolite biomarker assays for lung cancer status, stage and type view project an introduction to convolutional neural networks. *Neural Evol. Comput.*, November, 1–11, 2015, Accessed: Feb. 27, 2023, Available: https://www.researchgate.net/publication/285164623.

12. Zhang, X.Y., Yin, F., Zhang, Y.M., Liu, C.L., Bengio, Y., Drawing and recognizing chinese characters with recurrent neural network. *IEEE Trans. Pattern Anal. Mach. Intell.*, 40, 849–862, 2018.

13. Du, M.N.S. and Swamy, K.L., Recurrent neural networks, in: *Neural Networks and Statistical Learning*, Springer, London, UK, 2014.

14. Caterini, D.E. and Chang, A.L., Recurrent neural networks, in: *Deep Neural Networks in a Mathematical Framework*, Springer, Cham, Switzerland, 2018.

15. Patterson, D., *Introduction to artificial intelligence and expert systems*, Prentice-Hall, Inc., Upper Saddle River, NJ, USA, 1990.

16. Mnih, V., Kavukcuoglu, K., Silver, D., Rusu, A.A., Veness, J., Bellemare, M.G., Graves, A., Riedmiller, M., Fidjeland, A.K., Ostrovski, G., Petersen, S., Beattie, C., Sadik, A., Antonoglou, I., King, H., Kumaran, D., Wierstra, D., Legg, S., Hassabis, D., Human-level control through deep reinforcement learning. *Nature*, 518, 529–533, 2015.

17. Young, T., Hazarika, D., Poria, S., Cambria, E., Recent trends in deep learning based natural language processing. *IEEE Comput. Intell. Mag.*, 13, 55–75, 2018.

18. LeCun, Y., Bengio, Y., Hinton, G., Deep learning. *Nature*, 521, 436–444, 2015.

19. Rudin, C., Stop explaining black box machine learning models for high stakes decisions and use interpretable models instead. *Nat. Mach. Intell.*, 1, 206–215, 2019.

20. Transportation, U.D., 2019, September 23, https://www.transportation.gov/AI, Retrieved October 20, 2019, from https://www.transportation.gov.

21. Abduljabbar, R., Dia, H., Liyanage, S., S.A., Applications of artificial intelligence in transport: An overview. *Sustainability*, 11, 189, 2019. 10.3390/su11010189.

22. Mire, S., 2019, September 30, https://www.disruptordaily.com/future-of-ai-transportation/, Retrieved October 19, 2019, from https://www.disruptordaily.com/.

23. Rani, S., Ahmed, S.H., S.C., Smart health: A novel paradigm to control the Chickungunya virus. *IEEE Internet Things J.*, 6, 2, 1306–11, 2018.

24. Garcia, S., Luengo, J., Saez, J.A., Lopez, V., Herrera, F., A survey of discretization techniques: Taxonomy and empirical analysis in supervised learning. *IEEE Trans. Knowl. Data Eng.*, 25, 4, 734–750, 2013.

25. Hastie, T., Tibshirani, R., Friedman, J., Unsupervised learning, in: *The Elements of Statistical Learning*, pp. 485–585, Springer, 2009.

26. Kaelbling, L.P., Littman, M.L., Moore, A.W., Reinforcement learning: A survey. *J. Artif. Intell. Res.*, 4, 237–285, 1996.

27. LeCun, Y., Bengio, Y., Hinton, G., Deep learning. *Nature*, 521, 7553, 436, 2015. 43. Suykens, J.A., Vandewalle, J., Suykens, A., Vandewalle, J., Least squares support vector machine classifiers. *Neural Process. Lett.*, 9, 3, 293–300, 1999.

28. Freund, Y., Schapire, R., Abe, N., A short introduction to boosting. *J.-Jpn. Soc. Artif. Intell.*, 14, 771-780, 1612, 1999.

29. Seber, G.A. and Lee, A.J., *Linear regression analysis*, vol. 329, John Wiley & Sons, 2012.

30. Smola, A.J. and Scholkopf, B., A tutorial on support vector regression. *Stat. Comput.*, 14, 3, 199–222, 2004.

31. Keller, J.M., Gray, M.R., Givens, J.A., A fuzzy k-nearest neighbor algorithm. *IEEE Trans. Syst. Man Cybern.*, 4, 580–585, 1985.

32. Liaw, A., Wiener, M. *et al.*, Classification and regression by randomforest. *R News*, 2, 3, 18–22, 2002.

33. Elith, J., Leathwick, J.R., Hastie, T., A working guide to boosted regression trees. *J. Anim. Ecol.*, 77, 4, 802– 813, 2008.

34. Steinbach, M., Karypis, G., Kumar, V. *et al.*, A comparison of document clustering techniques, in: *KDD Workshop on Text Mining*, vol. 400, pp. 525–526, Boston, 2000.

35. Jolliffe, I., Principal component analysis, in: *International Encyclopedia of Statistical Science*, pp. 1094–1096, Springer, 2011.

36. Hyvarinen, A., Survey on independent component analysis. *Neural Comput. Surv.*, 2, 4, 94–128, 1999.

37. Watkins, C.J.C.H. and Dayan, P., Q-learning. *Mach. Learn.*, 8, 3, 279–292, May 1992.

38. Singh, S.P. and Sutton, R.S., Reinforcement learning with replacing eligibility traces. *Mach. Learn.*, 22, 1–3, 123–158, 1996.

39. Mnih, V., Kavukcuoglu, K., Silver, D., Rusu, A.A., Veness, J., Bellemare, M.G., Graves, A., Riedmiller, M., Fidjeland, A.K., Ostrovski, G. *et al.*, Human-level control through deep reinforcement learning. *Nature*, 518, 7540, 529, 2015.

40. Sutton, R.S., McAllester, D.A., Singh, S.P., Mansour, Y., Policy gradient methods for reinforcement learning with function approximation, in: *Advances in Neural Information Processing Systems*, pp. 1057–1063, 2000.
41. Silver, D., Lever, G., Heess, N., Degris, T., Wierstra, D., M., Riedmiller, M., Deterministic policy gradient algorithms, in: *ICML*, 2014.
42. Attia, A. and Dayan, S., *Global overview of imitation learning*, 2018, arXiv preprint arXiv:1801.06503.
43. Grondman, I., Busoniu, L., Lopes, G.A., Babuska, R., A survey of actor-critic reinforcement learning: Standard and natural policy gradients. *IEEE Trans. Syst. Man. Cybern. Part C (Applications Reviews)*, 42, 6, 1291–1307, 2012.
44. Mnih, V., Badia, A.P., Mirza, M., Graves, A., Lillicrap, T., Harley, T., Silver, D., Kavukcuoglu, K., Asynchronous methods for deep reinforcement learning, in: *International Conference on Machine Learning*, pp. 1928–1937, 2016.
45. Lillicrap, T.P., Hunt, J.J., Pritzel, A., Heess, N., Erez, T., Tassa, Y., Silver, D., Wierstra, D., *Continuous control with deep reinforcement learning*, 2015, arXiv preprint arXiv:1509.02971.
46. Battaglia, P.W., Hamrick, J.B., Bapst, V., Sanchez-Gonzalez, A., Zambaldi, V., Malinowski, M., Tacchetti, A., Raposo, D., Santoro, A., Faulkner, R. *et al.*, *Relational inductive biases, deep learning, and graph networks*, 2018, arXiv preprint arXiv:1806.01261.
47. Zhou, J., Cui, G., Zhang, Z., Yang, C., Liu, Z., Sun, M., *Graph neural networks: A review of methods and applications*, 2018, arXiv preprint arXiv:1812.08434.
48. Hinton, G.E., Osindero, S., Teh, Y.-W., A fast learning algorithm for deep belief nets. *Neural Comput.*, 18, 7, 1527– 1554, 2006.
49. Hinton, G.E., A practical guide to training restricted boltzmann machines, in: *Neural networks: Tricks of the trade*, pp. 599–619, Springer, 2012.
50. Bejani, M.M. and Ghatee, M., Convolutional neural network with adaptive regularization to classify driving styles on smartphones. *IEEE Trans. Intell. Transp. Syst.*, 2019.
51. Kumar, K., Parida, M., Katiyar, V., Short term traffic flow prediction for a non urban highway using artificial neural network. *Procedia Soc. Behav. Sci.*, 104, 755–764, 2013.
52. Lee, J., Jang, D., Park, S., Deep learning-based corporate performance prediction model considering technical capability. *Sustainability*, 9, 6, 899, 2017.
53. Bartak, R., Salido, M.A., Rossi, F., Constraint satisfaction techniques in planning and scheduling. *J. Intell. Manuf.*, 21, 1, 5–15, 2010.
54. De Muynck, B., Johns, B., Sanchez Duran, O., *Magic quadrant for transportation management systems*, Gartner, Stamford, 2020.
55. He, D. *et al.*, Privacy in the internet of things for smart healthcare. *IEEE Commun. Mag.*, 56, 4, 38–44, Apr. 2018.
56. McCulloch, W.S. and Pitts, W., A logical calculus of the ideas immanent in nervous activity. *Bull. Math. Biophys.*, 5, 4, 115–133, 1943.
57. Mitchell, M., *An introduction to genetic algorithms*, MIT press, 1998.
58. Zadeh, L.A., Fuzzy logic. *Computer*, 21, 4, 83–93, 1988.

59. Wu, C., Chen, X., Ji, Y., Liu, F., Ohzahata, S., Yoshinaga, T., Kato, T., Packet size-aware broadcasting in VANETs with fuzzy logic and RLBased parameter adaptation. *IEEE Access*, 3, 2481–2491, 2015.
60. Mc Cune, B.P., Tong, R.M., Dean, J.S., Shapiro, D.G., RUBRIC: A system for rule-based information retrieval. *IEEE Trans. Soft. Eng.*, 9, 939–945, 1985.
61. Klügl, F., Bazzan, A.L.C., Ossowski, S., Agents in traffic and transportation. *Transp. Res. Part C Emerg. Technol.*, 18, 69–70, 2010.
62. Dogan, E. and Akgüngör, A.P., Forecasting highway casualties under the effect of railway development policy in Turkey using artificial neural networks. *Neural Comput. Appl.*, 22, 869–877, 2013.
63. Budalakoti, S., Srivastava, A.N., Otey, M.E., Anomaly detection and diagnosis algorithms for discrete symbol sequences with applications to airline safety. *IEEE Trans. Syst. Man Cybern. Part C Appl. Rev.*, 39, 101–113, 2009.
64. Dia, H. and Rose, G., Development and evaluation of neural network freeway incident detection models using field data. *Transp. Res. Part C Emerg. Technol.*, 5, 313–331, 1997.
65. Huang, W., Song, G., Hong, H., Xie, K., Deep architecture for traffic flow prediction: Deep belief networks with multitask learning. *IEEE Trans. Intell. Transp. Syst.*, 15, 2191–2201, 2014.
66. Xu, T., Wei, H., Wang, Z.D., Study on continuous network design problem using simulated annealing and genetic algorithm. *Expert Syst. Appl.*, 36 Pt 2, 2735–2741, 2009.
67. Xu, T., Wei, H., Hu, G., Study on continuous network design problem using simulated annealing and genetic algorithm. *Expert Syst. Appl.*, 36 Pt 1, 1322–1328, 2009.
68. Dorigo, M., Gambardella, L.M., Birattari, M., Martinoli, A., Poli, R., Stützle, T., LNCS 4150—Ant colony optimization and swarm intelligence, in: *Proceedings of the 6th International Conference (ANTS 2008)*, Brussels, Belgium, pp. 22–24, September 2008.
69. Dasgupta, D. and Ji, Z., Artificial immune system (AIS) research in the last five years, in: *Proceedings of the 2003 Congress on Evolutionary Computation (CEC '03)*, Canberra, Australia, vol. 1, pp. 123–130, 8–12 December 2003.
70. Lučić, D. and Teodorović, P., Computing with bees: Attacking complex transportation engineering problems. *Int. J. Artif. Intell. Tools*, 12, 375–394, 2003.
71. Voracek, J., Prediction of mechanical properties of cast irons. *Appl. Soft Comput.*, 1, 119–125, 2001.
72. Qureshi, M.F., Shah, S.M.A., Al-Matroushi, G.I.G.A., *Comparative analysis of multi-criteria road network*, pp. 27–47, Eur. Cent. Res. Train. Dev. UK, 2013, Available online: http://www.eajournals.org/wp-content/uploads/A-Comparative-Analysis-of-Multi-criteria-Road-Network.pdf (accessed on 5 July 2018).
73. Murat, N.U.Y., Route choice modelling in urban transportation networks using fuzzy logic and logistic regression methods. *J. Sci. Ind. Res.*, 67, 19–27, 2008.

74. Gu, F., Qian, Y., Chen, Z., From Twitter to detector: Real-time traffic incident detection using social media data. *Transp. Res. Part C Emerg. Technol.*, 67, 321–342, 2016.

75. Aretakis, N., Roumeliotis, I., Alexiou, A., Romesis, C., Mathioudakis, K., Turbofan engine health assessment from flight data. *J. Eng. Gas Turbines Power*, 137, 041203, 2014.

76. Bagloee, M., Sarvi, S.A., Patriksson, M., A hybrid branch-and-bound and benders decomposition algorithm for the network design problem. *Comput. Civ. Infrastruct. Eng.*, 32, 319–343, 2017.

77. Rodrigue, J.P., Parallel modelling and neural networks: An overview for transportation/land use systems. *Transp. Res. Part C Emerg. Technol.*, 5, 259–271, 1997.

78. Li, X., Shi, X., He, J., Liu, X., Coupling simulation and optimization to solve planning problems in a fast-developing area. *Ann. Assoc. Am. Geogr.*, 101, 1032–1048, 2011.

79. Wen, Y. and Li, S.Y., Fastest complete vehicle routing problem using learning multiple ant colony algorithm. *Adv. Mater. Res. Trans. Tech. Publ.*, 217, 1044–1049, 2011.

80. Liu, X., *Deep reinforcement learning for intelligent transportation systems*, 2018, No. Nips, arXivarXiv:1812.00979.

81. Ferdowsi, A., Challita, U., Saad, W., *Deep learning for reliable mobile edge analytics in intelligent transportation systems*, 2017, arXivarXiv:1712.04135.

82. Wang, C., Li, X., Zhou, X., Wang, A., Nedjah, N., Soft computing in big data intelligent transportation systems. *Appl. Soft Comput. J.*, 38, 1099–1108, 2016.

83. Gilmore, N. and Abe, J.F., Neural network models for traffic control and congestion prediction. *J. Intell. Transp. Syst.*, 2, 231–252, 1995.

84. Nakatsuji, T. and Kaku, T., Development of a Self-Organizing Traffic Control System Using Neural Network Models. *Transp. Res. Rec.*, 1324, 137–145, 1991.

85. Choy, M.C., Srinivasan, D., Cheu, R.L., Cooperative, hybrid agent architecture for real-time traffic signal control. *IEEE Trans. Syst. Man Cybern. Part A Syst. Hum.*, 33, 597–607, 2003.

86. Choy, M., Cheu, R., Srinivasan, D., Logi, F., Real-time coordinated signal control through use of agents with online reinforcement learning. *Transp. Res. Rec. J. Transp. Res. Board*, 1836, 64–75, 2003.

87. Stojmenovic, M., Real time machine learning based car detection in images with fast training. *Mach. Vis. Appl.*, 17, 163–172, 2006.

88. Gu, F., Qian, Y., Chen, Z., From Twitter to detector: Real-time traffic incident detection using social media data. *Transp. Res. Part C Emerg. Technol.*, 67, 321–342, 2016.

89. Mahamuni, A., Internet of Things, machine learning, and artificial intelligence in the modern supply chain and transportation. *Def. Transp. J.*, 74, 14, 2018, Available online: https://insights.samsung.com/2018/05/22/

internet-of-things-machine-learning-and-artificial-intelligence-inthe-modern-supply-chain-and-transportation/ (accessed on 27 December 2018).

90. Huang, W., Song, G., Hong, H., Xie, K., Deep architecture for traffic flow prediction: Deep belief networks with multitask learning. *IEEE Trans. Intell. Transp. Syst.*, 15, 2191–2201, 2014.

91. Wu, Y., Tan, H., Qin, L., Ran, B., Jiang, Z., A hybrid deep learning based traffic flow prediction method and its understanding. *Transp. Res. Part C Emerg. Technol.*, 90, 166–180, 2018.

92. More, R., Mugal, A., Rajgure, S., Adhao, R.B., Pachghare, V.K., Road traffic prediction and congestion control using artificial neural networks, in: *Proceedings of the 2016 International Conference on Computing, Analytics and Security Trends (CAST)*, Pune, India, pp. 52–57, 19–21 December 2016.

93. ATOS, *Expecting the unexpected business pattern management*, Atos Scientific Community, 2012, Available online: https://atos.net/content/dam/global/ascent-whitepapers/ascent-whitepaper-expectingthe-unexpected-business-pattern-management.pdf (accessed on 2 October 2018).

94. Voda, A.I. and Radu, L., *How can artificial intelligence respond to smart cities challenges?* Elsevier Inc., 2019.

95. Applications, B.S., Machine learning adoption in the challenges, and a way forward. *IEEE Access*, 1, 2019, https://doi.org/10.1109/ACCESS.2019.2961372.

96. Ullah, Z., Al-turjman, F., Mostarda, L., Gagliardi, R., Applications of artificial intelligence and machine learning in smart cities. *Comput. Commun.*, 154, 313–323, 2020. https://doi.org/10.1016/ j.comcom.2020.02.069.

97. Rajasekaran, M. *et al.*, Autonomous monitoring in healthcare environment: reward-based energy charging mechanism for IoMT wireless sensing nodes. *Future Generation Comput. Syst.*, 98, 565–76, Sept. 1, 2019.

98. Lin, Y., Wang, P., Ma, M., Intelligent transportation system (ITS): Concept, challenge and opportunity, in: *Proceedings of 3rd IEEE international Conference on Big Data Security Cloud, BigDataSecurity 2017, 3rd IEEE International Conference on High Performance Smart Computing HPSC 2017, 2nd IEEE international Conference on Intelligence Data Security 2017*, pp. 167–172, 2017, https://doi.org/10.1109/BigDataSecurity.2017.50.

99. Nishant, R., Kennedy, M., Corbett, J., Laval, U., Prince, P.P., Artificial intelligence for sustainability: Challenges, opportunities, and a research agenda. *Int. J. Inf. Manag.*, 53, 102104, 2020. https:// doi.org/10.1016/j.ijinfomgt.2020.102104.

100. Jo, J.H., Sharma, P.K., Costa, J., Sicato, S., Park, J.H., Emerging technologies for sustainable smart city network security: Issues, challenges countermeasures. 15, 765–784, 2019.

101. Mahdavinejad, M.S., Rezvan, M., Barekatain, M., Adibi, P., Barnaghi, P., Sheth, A.P., Machine learning for internet of things data analysis: A survey. *Digit. Commun. Netw.*, 4, 161–175, 2018. https://doi.org/10.1016/j.dcan.2017.10.002.

102. Conde, M.L. and Twinn, I., *How artificial intelligence is making transport safer, cleaner, more reliable and efficient in emerging markets*, pp. 1–8, IFC-World Bank Gr. 2023, 2019.

103. Chang, M.C., Wei, Y., Song, N., Lyu, S., Video analytics in smart transportation for the AIC'18 challenge. *IEEE Comput Soc Conf Comput Vis Pattern Recognit Work*, pp. 61–68, 2018, https://doi.org/10.1109/CVPRW.2018.00016.

104. Chang, M.-C., Wei, J., Zhu, Z.-A., Chen, Y.-M., Hu, C.-S., Jiang, M.-X., Chiang, C.-K., *AI city challenge 2019-city-scale video analytics for smart transportation*, Open access.Thecvf. Com, pp. 99–108, 2019.

105. Humayun, M. *et al.*, Emerging smart logistics and transportation using IoT and blockchain. *IEEE Internet Things Mag.*, 3, 2, 58–62, June 2020. [12] M. Rajasek.

10

Classification of Dementia Using Statistical First-Order and Second-Order Features

Deepika Bansal[1]* and Rita Chhikara[2]

[1]*Department of Information Technology, Maharaja Agrasen Institute of Technology, Rohini, India*
[2]*Department of Computer Science Engineering, The NorthCap University, Gurugram, India*

Abstract

A neurological disorder called dementia causes memory loss, which interferes with a person's ability to live a normal life. Adults 65 years of age and older are starting to experience it as a global health issue. An early diagnosis can be very helpful to slow down the progress of disease. The purpose of this study is to predict the presence of dementia using magnetic resonance imaging data, which have become a significant tool for the diagnosis of dementia. The publicly available Open Access Series of Imaging Studies cross-sectional MRI data were analyzed. This paper investigates an ensemble of clinical features, first-order features and second-order wavelet features of the magnetic resonance images for classification. Discrete wavelet transform with Haar transform is applied on images for feature extraction. The MRIs of 200 individuals were used for this study, which includes 30 demented, 70 very mild demented, and 100 normal controls. Randomly 75% of the data are used for training and 25% are used for testing purposes. The results with the approximation coefficient using the Haar wavelet and ensembled features outperform with 99.27% accuracy for the two-class (dementia/normal) diagnosis.

Keywords: Dementia, discrete wavelet transform, Haar, feature extraction, support vector machine

Corresponding author: dbansal7@yahoo.com

Akansha Singh, Anuradha Dhull and Krishna Kant Singh (eds.) Blockchain and Deep Learning for Smart Healthcare, (235–256) © 2024 Scrivener Publishing LLC

10.1   Introduction

A cognitive illness called dementia affects memory loss in adults, making them dependent and disabled. Those over 60 are more likely than younger adults to get dementia. A type of dementia that predominates in over 75% of cases is Alzheimer's disease (AD). Frontotemporal dementia, dementia with Lewy bodies, Parkinson's disease, vascular dementia, etc. are among the several types of dementia. According to the World Health Organization (WHO), dementia affects approximately 50 million people worldwide, and an estimated 10 million new cases are predicted to be diagnosed each year [1]. Early dementia treatment is crucial for minimizing the disease's negative social and economic effects [2, 3].

Open Access Series of Imaging Studies (OASIS) [4] and Alzheimer's Disease Neuroimaging Initiative (ADNI) [5] are publicly accessible datasets that cover both longitudinal [6] and cross-sectional studies [7]. The ADNI [8] was founded in 2004 and offers us a variety of data types that are useful in the treatment of dementia, such as clinical data, genetic data, biospecimen data, and a limited amount of neuroimaging data. The neuroimaging data being used comprises single photon emission computed tomography (SPECT), positron emission tomography (PET), and magnetic resonance imaging (MRI). Bansal et al. present a systematic evaluation of the available dementia datasets and the machine learning methods that have been employed to identify the condition [9].

Early accurate disease identification gives patients knowledge of the severity of their ailment and enables them to take preventive actions like taking drugs and improving their lifestyle, among other things [10]. MRI images are frequently utilized for the same purposes. The researchers review the various segmentations, modalities, and machine learning strategies [11, 12]. Additionally, to increase classification accuracy, redundant and unnecessary features are eliminated using effective feature selection approaches [13, 14]. Dallora et al. offer a thorough overview of the use of microsimulation and machine learning for the diagnosis of dementia [15].

For large databases to be stored, the medical MRI picture must be compressed [16]. One method for this objective is the wavelet transformation. This study makes use of the lossy image compression method known as discrete wavelet transformation, which performs admirably on many medical images [15]. The statistical techniques that eliminate redundancy such as discrete cosine transforms (DCTs) and the encoding of sub-band images provide only a little amount of compression. However, in the case of medical picture compression, diagnosis is only effective when compression methods maintain all the necessary relevant and significant image information. The wavelet transform's characteristics, such as multiresolution representation energy compaction, blocking artifacts, and decorrelation, have elevated DWT to the top of the list of the most significant picture compression methods in the past 10 years. The selection of wavelet filter becomes a crucial element to achieve optimal coding performance because there are numerous wavelet filters available with various sets of fundamental functions [16]. Researchers have successfully applied wavelet transformations for feature extraction on images in various other applications as well [17–20].

A set of discriminative features must be extracted from these images to analyze them properly and classify MRI images more accurately. Many feature extraction techniques with different transformations have been put forth in the literature, including Fourier transform [18], wavelet transform [21, 22], and texture-based features [23–25]. It is commonly known that the Fourier transform may be used to extract the frequency content of a signal, but it cannot be used to precisely analyze both the time and frequency contents of a signal at the same time. Wavelet analysis, which uses a fixed-size window to accurately evaluate time information, is suggested to solve the problem. It accurately collects both low-frequency and high-frequency information by employing windows of varying sizes.

Chaplot *et al.* used Daubechies-4 wavelet for extracting the characteristics from MRI for the classification of Alzheimer's disease [21]. According to Dahshan *et al.*, the features obtained using the Daubechies-4 wavelet were overly large and might not be suitable for classification [22]. Principal component analysis (PCA) was employed in the research effort to further reduce characteristics before classification utilizing a level 3 Haar wavelet. Although PCA reduces the feature vector, it has the following drawbacks: (1) the use of transformed feature vectors is limited by the non-trivial task of interpreting the results; (2) the scatter matrix, which is maximized in PCA transformation, maximizes both within-class scatter and between-class scatter, which are undesirable for classification; and (3) PCA transformation requires a significant amount of computation time for high-dimensional datasets.

In the literature [23], features based on first- and second-order statistics that describe textures are also used for image classification. In comparison to features extracted using DWT, features based on texture statistics yield significantly less pertinent, non-redundant, interpretable, and identifiable characteristics. As a result, this study suggests using first- and second-order statistics for feature extraction. The performance of clinical features in combination with first-order and second-order-based wavelet features is compared. Since the classification accuracy can be affected with the selection of a classifier, the MRI brain images are classified using the most popular and widely used classifiers. Classification accuracy has been taken into consideration when evaluating performance.

The rest of the paper is structured as follows: The Materials and Methods are covered in Section 10.2, the Results are covered in Section 10.3, and the analysis is wrapped up in Section 10.4.

10.2   Materials and Methods

10.2.1   Dataset

The OASIS dataset [2] used in this study includes a series of MRI data, which are publicly available to the scientific community for study and analysis. Sample images of a normal and a dementia MR brain are shown in Figure 10.1.

The OASIS-1 dataset consists of N = 416 subjects aged between 18 and 96 years. This study considers 200 samples (including 30 demented, 70 very mild demented, and 100 normal controls). The OASIS-1 study includes only right-handed subjects, consisting of both men and women. A patient with any missing data is excluded from this study, as the unbalanced data may cause difficulty in future recognition. For this study, Washington University's Clinical Dementia Rating (CDR) developed for measuring the severity of dementia is used as the single response variable [26]. The CDR is measured as follows: 0 = non-dementia, 0.5 = very mild dementia, 1 = mild dementia, 2 = moderate dementia. We have considered CDR values as follows: 0 = non-dementia, 1 =very mild dementia, 2 = mild or moderate dementia. For each subject, 3 or 4 individual T1-weighted MRI

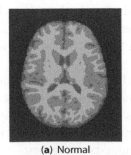
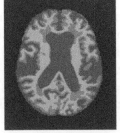

(a) Normal   (b) Dementia

Figure 10.1 Sample images of a normal and a dementia MR brain.

scans obtained in a single scan session are included. The MRI imagery data included [x = 176, y = 208, z = 176] images of the {sagittal(x,y), axial(x,z), coronal(y,z)} planes for each of the 416 observations, respectively.

The clinical features included in the OASIS-1 dataset are as follows:

- Age—age at the time of image acquisition (18–96 years of age)
- Sex—0 = female, 1 = male
- Education—years of education [1 (lowest)–5 (highest)]
- Socioeconomic status (SES)—assessed by the Hollingshead Index of Social position [1 (highest)–5 (lowest)].
- MMSE Score—MMSE is a 30-point questionnaire shown to be valid and reliable for the identification of dementia [27, 28].
- Atlas Scaling Factor (ASF)—one parameter scaling factor allowing the comparison of eTIV based on differences in human anatomy (0.86–1.56) (observed) [28].
- eTIV—estimated intracranial brain volume (1132–1992) mm^2.
- nWBV—volume of the whole brain (0.64–0.90) mg.

10.2.2   Image Pre-Processing

MRI scans are quite complex due to the sheer quantity of features they contain. Pre-processing is therefore essential before extracting features from them. In this investigation, the dataset including the Gray/White/CSF segmentation images created from the atlas image that has been masked is employed. Three or four distinct T1-weighted MRI scans taken during one imaging session are presented for each subject. The Brain Extraction Tool was used at the fMRIDC [29] to remove facial characteristics. A total of 200 PNG images are used in this study for extracting the first-order and second-order features.

10.3   Proposed Framework

The DWT with the Haar wavelet is applied on all the MRI images obtained from the OASIS dataset. The 3rd-level approximation coefficient is used for extracting the first- and second-order features. A total of 10 features are extracted, namely, mean, standard deviation, variance, skewness, kurtosis, entropy, contrast, correlation, homogeneity, and energy. These features are

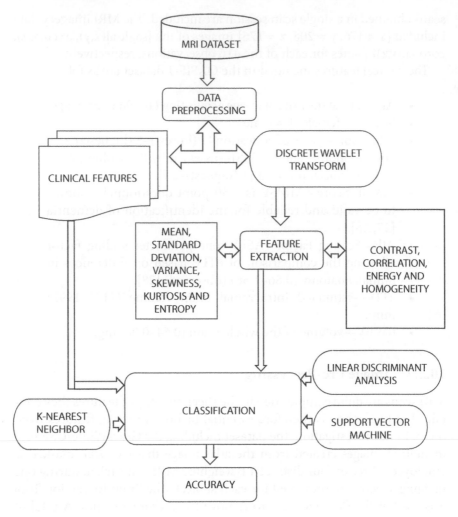

Figure 10.2 Flowchart of the proposed ensemble approach.

classified using 3 classifiers, k-NN, discriminant analysis, and SVM. Figure 10.2 depicts the layout of the proposed ensemble approach.

10.3.1   Discrete Wavelet Transform

The discrete wavelet transform (DWT) is a powerful tool used for analyzing signals and images. In the case of images, the DWT is used to divide an input image into four sub-image components along the frequency axis in both the horizontal and vertical directions. This produces a total of four sub-bands, including the LH, HL, and HH sub-bands, which encode the image features in three directions, as well as an LL sub-band that provides an approximation coefficient [30].

To perform the DWT, a basis function called the mother wavelet [31] is used. The wavelet transform starts by applying this mother wavelet to the input signal to obtain a set of wavelet coefficients, which represent the signal at different scales and translations. The mother wavelet function $\psi(t)$ and its corresponding scaling function $\phi(t)$ are used to generate a sequence of wavelets $\psi_{j,k}(t)$ and binary scale functions $\phi_{j,k}(t)$ through mathematical calculations. Equation (10.1) shows the formula for calculating the wavelet coefficients, while equation (10.2) shows the formula for calculating the scaling coefficients [31, 32].

$$\psi_{j,k}(t) = 2^{\frac{j}{2}} \psi(2^j t - k) \qquad (10.1)$$

$$\varphi_{j,k}(t) = 2^{\frac{j}{2}} \varphi(2^j t - k) \qquad (10.2)$$

Once the wavelet and scaling coefficients are obtained, the original sequence can be expressed as a sum of approximation and detail coefficients, as shown in equation (10.3).

$$os(t) = \sum_{k=1}^{n} c_{j,k} \varphi_{j,k}(t) + \sum_{j=1}^{J} \sum_{k=1}^{n} d_{j,k} \psi_{j,k}(t) \qquad (10.3)$$

The approximation coefficients at scale j and location k, $c_{j,k}$, represent the low-frequency content of the signal, while the detail coefficients at scale j and location k, $d_{j,k}$, represent the high-frequency content of the signal.

To efficiently obtain the sub-bands, the DWT employs multiple low-pass filters (LPFs) and high-pass filters (HPFs) to extract the approximate and detailed sequences under a certain wavelet decomposition level. This allows for the efficient extraction of important information from complex signals and images.

Based on the fast DWT proposed by Mallat [33], the approximate sequence and detailed sequence under a certain WD level can be obtained via multiple low-pass filters (LPF) and high-pass filters (HPF).

Figure 10.3 illustrates the case of three-level decomposition and Figure 10.4 presents the MRI image transformation using level 3 DWT.

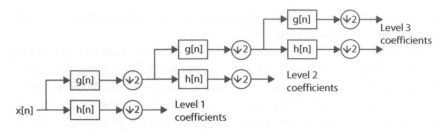

Figure 10.3 A 3-level decomposition of discrete wavelet transform.

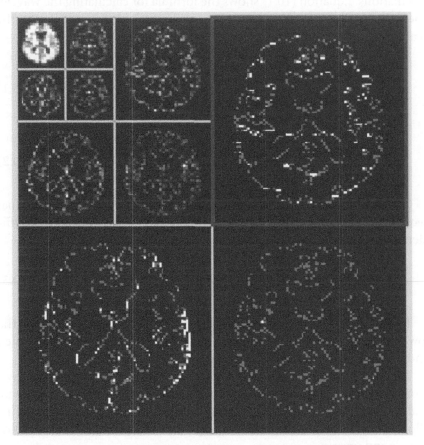

Figure 10.4 A 3-level decomposition of MRI using discrete wavelet transform.

There are several types of wavelets. Few are described below.

- Haar Wavelets: These are the simplest type of wavelets and are based on a step function. Haar wavelets are symmetric and have a compact support, which means that they are only non-zero on a finite interval.

- Daubechies Wavelets: These wavelets are based on a family of orthogonal wavelets, which means that they have a specific mathematical relationship with each other. Daubechies wavelets are commonly used in image compression and feature extraction.
- Symlets Wavelets: These wavelets are similar to Daubechies wavelets but have a slightly different shape. Symlets wavelets are also orthogonal and can be used for image compression and feature extraction.
- Coiflets Wavelets: These wavelets are also based on a family of orthogonal wavelets and are designed to be smoother than other wavelets. Coiflets wavelets are often used in signal and image denoising.

In this study, the Haar wavelet has been utilized.

10.3.1.1   Statistical Features

10.3.1.1.1   First-Order Features
First-order features from an image refer to basic statistical measures that are calculated directly from the pixel values of the image. These features are also known as pixel-based features, as they are calculated on a per-pixel basis without considering any spatial relationships between the pixels. The following features were extracted for this study: mean, standard deviation, variance, skewness, kurtosis, and entropy [34].

Mean: The mean is the average pixel value of the image, calculated by summing all the pixel values and dividing by the total number of pixels.

$$\mu = \sum_{i=0}^{G-1} i p(i) \tag{10.4}$$

Standard deviation: The standard deviation is a measure of the spread of the pixel values around the mean. It indicates how much the pixel values vary from the average.

$$\sigma^2 = \sum_{i=0}^{G-1} (i - \mu)^2 p(i) \tag{10.5}$$

Skewness: Skewness is a measure of the asymmetry of the pixel value distribution. It indicates whether the distribution is more spread out to the left or right of the mean.

$$\mu_3 = \sigma^{-3} \sum_{i=0}^{G-1} (i-\mu)^3 \, p(i) \qquad (10.6)$$

Kurtosis: Kurtosis is a measure of the peakedness of the pixel value distribution. It indicates whether the distribution is more or less peaked than a normal distribution.

$$\mu_4 = \sigma^{-4} \sum_{i=0}^{G-1} (i-\mu)^4 \, p(i) - 3 \qquad (10.7)$$

Entropy: Entropy is a measure of the randomness or uncertainty of the pixel value distribution. It indicates how much information is contained in the pixel values of the image.

$$\text{Entropy:} \quad H = -\sum_{i=0}^{G-1} p(i) log_2 [p(i)] \qquad (10.8)$$

where p(i) is an approximation of the probability distribution of the occurrence of the intensity levels and i = 0, 1,..., G−1 are discrete values of the intensity levels in the image.

10.3.1.1.2   Second-Order Features

The gray-level co-occurrence matrix (GLCM), also known as the gray-level spatial dependency matrix, is used by the second-order features to analyze the spatial relationship between pixels. GLCM is a statistical method used for image analysis and feature extraction. The GLCM method is used to determine the relationship between two adjacent pixels in an image based on their gray-level values. It is used to extract texture information from an image.

The GLCM is a matrix that represents the frequency of occurrence of pixel pairs with certain gray-level values and specific spatial relationships within an image. The matrix is square and its size depends on the number of gray levels in the image. Each element of the matrix represents the frequency of occurrence of a pair of pixels with specific gray-level values and specific spatial relationships in the image.

The GLCM is calculated by defining a sliding window of a certain size that moves across the image. For each pixel in the window, the gray-level value and the gray-level value of its neighboring pixel in a specific direction are recorded. The direction of the neighboring pixel is defined by an offset distance and an angle relative to the current pixel. For example, if the offset distance is one pixel and the angle is zero degrees, the neighboring pixel is the one to the right of the current pixel. Then, the frequency of occurrence of each pixel pair is calculated and stored in the corresponding element of the GLCM matrix.

The GLCM determines the pairs of pixels in a picture that have particular values in a particular spatial relationship. Equations (10.9)–(10.12) show the properties calculated as contrast, correlation, energy, and homogeneity. The contrast is a metric for the GLCM's regional variability. The combined probability occurrences of the chosen pixel pairings are measured through correlation. The GLCM provides energy or angular second moment as the sum of squared elements. Homogeneity measures the closeness of the distribution of elements in the GLCM to the GLCM diagonal.

$$\text{Contrast: } \sum_{I_1 I_2} |I_1 - I_2|^2 \, log \, P(I_1 I_2) \tag{10.9}$$

$$\text{Correlation: } \sum_{I_1 I_2} \frac{(I_1 - \mu_1)(I_2 - \mu_2)P(I_1, I_2)}{\sigma_1 \sigma_2} \tag{10.10}$$

$$\text{Homogeneity: } \sum_{I_1 I_2} \frac{P(I_1, I_2)}{1 + |I_1, I_2|^2} \tag{10.11}$$

$$\text{Energy: } \sum_{i,j} P(I_1 I_2)^2 \tag{10.12}$$

where $P(I_1, I_2)$ is the incidence of a particular gray-level configuration using relative frequencies and I_1, I_2 is the frequency of two pixels.

10.3.2   Classification

10.3.2.1   K-Nearest Neighbor

KNN (K-nearest neighbor) is a simple and widely used machine learning algorithm for classification and regression tasks. It is a non-parametric method, which means that it does not make any assumptions about the underlying distribution of the data. Instead, it uses the training data to find the K closest data points (i.e., neighbors) to a new input data point, and assigns the class or value of the majority of those K neighbors to the new data point. In this study, KNN has been employed for classifying data as normal or suffering from dementia.

In the case of classification, the KNN algorithm determines the class of the new data point based on the class of its K nearest neighbors. For example, if K = 3 and two neighbors belong to class A and one belongs to class B, the new data point would be assigned to class A.

The choice of K is an important parameter in the KNN algorithm and can have a significant impact on the algorithm's performance. A smaller value of K will make the algorithm more sensitive to local variations in the data, while a larger value of K will make the algorithm more robust to noise and outliers but may lead to a loss of accuracy in some cases.

KNN is a simple algorithm that can be implemented easily and works well for small to medium-sized datasets. However, it can be computationally expensive for large datasets, as it requires calculating the distance between the new data point and every other data point in the training set [22, 35].

10.3.2.2   Linear Discriminant Analysis

Ronald A. Fisher created linear discriminant analysis (LDA) in 1963 to solve a two-class problem. It was later made general for three-class problems. LDA is a widely used statistical technique for supervised classification and dimensionality reduction. Its primary goal is to find a linear combination of features that maximally separates two or more classes of data. In other words, LDA seeks to identify a set of features that can be used to discriminate between different groups or categories.

The basic idea behind LDA is to find a projection of the data onto a lower-dimensional space in such a way that the separation between the different classes is maximized. This is achieved by finding the direction that maximizes the ratio of between-class variance to within-class variance. The between-class variance measures the distance between the means of the different classes, while the within-class variance measures the scatter of the data within each class.

Once the optimal projection is found, new data points can be classified based on their projection onto this lower-dimensional space. LDA has been successfully applied to a wide range of applications, including face recognition, text classification, and image analysis [36–38].

10.3.2.3   Support Vector Machine

The most commonly used classifier in the medical area for both binary and multi-class classification is the support vector machine (SVM).

SVM works by finding the hyperplane that best separates the different classes in a dataset. In a binary classification problem, the hyperplane is a line that separates the two classes. SVM aims to find the line that maximizes the margin, which is the distance between the hyperplane and the closest data points from each class. This is done by solving an optimization problem that maximizes the margin while ensuring that the hyperplane correctly separates the data points.

If the data cannot be separated by a linear hyperplane, SVM can use a kernel function to map the data to a higher-dimensional feature space where it can be separated by a hyperplane. This is called the kernel trick. Once the hyperplane is found, new data points can be classified by determining which side of the hyperplane they fall on [39, 40].

10.3.3   Performance Measure

Classification accuracy is a measure of how well a classification model is able to correctly classify instances of a dataset. It is typically expressed as a percentage and is calculated by dividing the number of correctly classified instances by the total number of instances in the dataset. For example, if a classification model correctly classified 90 out of 100 instances in a dataset, the classification accuracy would be 90%. Classification accuracy is an important metric for evaluating the performance of a classification model. The classification accuracy measured by equation (10.13), where TP = true positive, FP = false positive, TN = true negative, and FN = false negative, validates the performance of the proposed approach [41, 42].

$$Accuracy = \frac{(T_P + T_N)}{(T_P + T_N + F_P + F_N)} \qquad (10.13)$$

10.4   Experimental Results and Discussion

For the categorization of two different types of MRI images, namely, normal image and dementia image, various combinations of clinical features, statistical features, and classifiers have been analyzed in this section. The feature extraction techniques being researched are first- and second-order statistics-based features. The three classifiers SVM, k-NN, and LDA have been examined on the extracted features. The most accurate results are identified and presented.

Six first-order statistics (mean, standard deviation, variance, skewness, kurtosis, and energy) and four second-order statistics are used to represent the texture of an image (contrast, correlation, homogeneity, and entropy). The mean and range of the data obtained from the four directions are

Table 10.1 Classification accuracy obtained using original images.

Classifier	Accuracy with clinical features (%)	Accuracy with first-order features (%)	Accuracy with second-order features (%)	Accuracy with clinical + first (%)	Accuracy with clinical + second (%)	Accuracy with first + second (%)	Accuracy with clinical + first + second (%)
k-NN	79.07	72.26	73.27	79.39	79.07	71.79	79.31
LDA	91.32	74.05	74.96	76.49	90.29	77.39	94.51
SVM	79.04	73.48	75.88	79.98	79.05	73.97	80.98

Table 10.2 Classification accuracy obtained using Haar 3rd-level approximation images.

Classifier	Accuracy with clinical features (%)	Accuracy with first-order features (%)	Accuracy with second-order features (%)	Accuracy with clinical + first (%)	Accuracy with clinical + second (%)	Accuracy with first + second (%)	Accuracy with clinical + first + second (%)
k-NN	79.07	80.95	76.14	80.71	79.06	80.96	80.71
LDA	91.32	78.28	76.38	88.90	90.46	83.11	97.24
SVM	89.41	78.55	76.15	79.29	89.41	78.55	**99.27**

determined for each second-order measure since second-order statistics are functions of distance and orientation. Consequently, there are 10 features that have been retrieved using first- and second-order statistics.

The ratio of the training and testing sets in the dataset is 75%:25%, uniformly taken for all experiments. The best outcomes for each classifier for each distinct performance metric are displayed in bold. All experiments have been performed using MATLAB Version 7 utilizing a combination of the Wavelet Toolbox and the Image Processing Toolbox.

The classification accuracy evaluated using original images is depicted in Table 10.1, and classification accuracy obtained from the third-level approximation coefficient upon applying the Haar wavelet is represented in Table 10.2. The values of accuracy obtained with clinical features, first-order features, second-order features, ensemble of clinical and first-order features, ensemble of clinical and second-order features, ensemble of first-order and second-order features, and ensemble of all three features are clearly depicted in both tables. The classification accuracy of the ensemble of all the three features with original images is 79.31% with k-NN, 94.51% for LDA, and 80.98% with SVM. KNN does not perform well when the data are high-dimensional or when the classes are not well-separated.

As observed from Table 10.1, LDA gives the best accuracy with the ensemble of all features. An increase in classification accuracies has been noticed with the third-level approximation coefficient using the Haar wavelet. The best accuracy of 99.27% is obtained with SVM. One of the

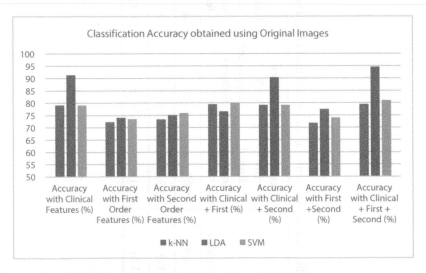

Figure 10.5 Classification accuracy obtained using original images.

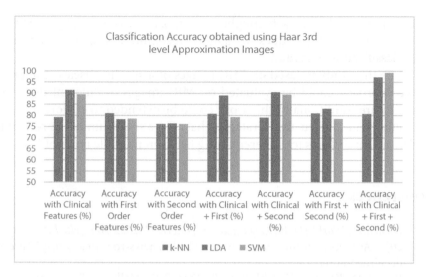

Figure 10.6 Classification accuracy obtained using Haar 3rd-level approximation images.

advantages of SVM is that it is less susceptible to overfitting than other machine learning algorithms, which means that it can generalize well to new data. The values noted in the Tables 10.1 and 10.2 are represented graphically in Figures 10.5 and 10.6.

10.5   Conclusion

This study aimed to compare the performance of statistical features and clinical features for MRI image classification. A pattern recognition system's classification accuracy depends on both the classifier used and the feature extraction technique. In order to classify MRI brain pictures, this study examined the performance of statistical features (first order and second order) in comparison to clinical features. The effectiveness is assessed based on categorization precision.

Statistical features considerably outperform clinical features in terms of classification accuracy for all classifiers. Additionally, it is discovered that neither sensitivity nor specificity is skewed by statistical traits. Additionally, they require substantially less training and testing time than other feature extraction methods recommended in the literature. This is due to the fact that, in comparison to methods suggested in the literature, first- and second-order statistics provides a much lower number of pertinent and distinct features and does not require computationally demanding modification.

The findings in this work highlight the importance of carefully selecting feature extraction techniques for pattern recognition systems to achieve high classification accuracy.

While this study focused on MRI images of a specific disease, the proposed approach could be evaluated on MRI images of different diseases in the future. Additionally, this work could be extended to explore feature extraction and construction strategies that offer a small number of relevant and invariant features for differentiating between multiple types of MRI.

References

1. *Dementia, World Health Organization [Internet]. 2022 Apr. [cited 2022 Apr. 20].* Available from: https://www.who.int/news-room/facts-in-pictures/detail/dementia.
2. Bansal, D., Khanna, K., Chhikara, R., Dua, R.K., Malhotra, R., A superpixel powered autoencoder technique for detecting dementia. *Expert Syst.*, 39, 5, 1–13, 2022.
3. Bansal, D., Khanna, K., Chhikara, R., Dua, R.K., Malhotra, R., Comparative analysis of artificial neural networks and deep neural networks for detection of dementia. *Int. J. Soc. Ecol. Sustain. Dev.*, 13, 9, 1–18, 2022.
4. *OASIS Brains - Open Access Series of Imaging Studies* [Internet]. 2022 Apr. [cited 2022 Apr. 06]. Available from: https://www.oasis-brains.org/.
5. *ADNI-Alzheimer's Disease Neuroimaging Initiative [Internet]. 2022 Apr. [cited 2022 Apr. 20]* Available from: https://adni.loni.usc.edu/data-samples/access-data/.
6. Marcus, D.S., Fotenos, A.F., Csernansky, J.G., Morris, J.C., Buckner, R.L., Open access series of imaging studies: Longitudinal MRI data in nondemented and demented older adults. *J. Cogn. Neurosci.*, 22, 12, 2677–2684, Dec. 2010.
7. Marcus, D.S., Wang, T.H., Parker, J., Csernansky, J.G., Morris, J.C., Buckner, R.L., Open access series of imaging studies (OASIS): Cross-sectional MRI data in young, middle aged, nondemented, and demented older adults. *J. Cogn. Neurosci.*, 19, 9, 1498–1507, Sep. 2007.
8. Jack, C.R. *et al.*, The Alzheimer's disease neuroimaging initiative (ADNI): MRI methods. *J. Magn. Reson. Imaging An Off. J. Int. Soc. Magn. Reson. Med.*, 27, 4, 685–691, 2008.
9. Bansal, D., Chhikara, R., Khanna, K., Kumar Dua, R., Malhotra, R., A study on dementia using machine learning techiniques, in: *Commun. Comput. Syst.*, pp. 414–426, 2019.
10. Roberson, E.D. and Mucke, L., 100 years and counting: Prospects for defeating Alzheimer's disease. *Science (80-.)*, 314, 5800, 781–784, 2006.

11. Mirzaei, G., Adeli, A., Adeli, H., Imaging and machine learning techniques for diagnosis of Alzheimer's disease. *Rev. Neurosci.*, 27, 8, 857–870, 2016.

12. Ahmed, M.R., Zhang, Y., Feng, Z., Lo, B., Inan, O.T., Liao, H., Neuroimaging and machine learning for dementia diagnosis: Recent advancements and future prospects. *IEEE Rev. Biomed. Eng.*, 12, 19–33, 2019.

13. Bansal, D., Chhikara, R., Khanna, K., Gupta, P., Comparative analysis of various machine learning algorithms for detecting dementia. *Procedia Comput. Sci.*, 132, 1497–1502, 2018.

14. Bansal, D., Khanna, K., Chhikara, R., Dua, R.K., Malhotra, R., Analysis of classification & feature selection techniques for detecting dementia. *In Proceedings of International Conference on Sustainable Computing in Science, Technology and Management (SUSCOM), SSRN Electron. J.*, 1768–1773, Amity University Rajasthan, Jaipur-India, 2019.

15. Dallora, A.L., Eivazzadeh, S., Mendes, E., Berglund, J., Anderberg, P., Machine learning and microsimulation techniques on the prognosis of dementia: A systematic literature review. *PLoS One*, 12, 6, 1–17, 2017.

16. Singh, R. M., Singh, A.R., and A. R. Singh, Compression of medical images using wavelet transforms. International, *Journal of Soft Computing and Engineering (IJSCE)*, 2, 2, 2231-2307, 2012.

17. Udomhunsakul, S. and Hamamoto, K., Wavelet filters comparison for ultrasonic image compression. *IEEE Reg. 10 Annu. Int. Conf. Proceedings/TENCON*, vol. A, pp. 171–174, 2004.

18. Osgood, B., EE261 - fourier transform and its applications, in: *Lect. Notes EE 261 - Fourier Transform its Appl.*, pp. 26–33, 2014.

19. Bhasin, H. and Agrawal, R.K., A combination of 3-D discrete wavelet transform and 3-D local binary pattern for classification of mild cognitive impairment. *BMC Med. Inform. Decis. Mak.*, 20, 1, 1–10, 2020.

20. Aggarwal, N., Rana, B., Agrawal, R.K., Role of surfacelet transform in diagnosing Alzheimer's disease. *Multidimens. Syst. Signal Process.*, 30, 4, 1839–1858, 2019.

21. Chaplot, S., Patnaik, L.M., Jagannathan, N.R., Classification of magnetic resonance brain images using wavelets as input to support vector machine and neural network. *Biomed. Signal Process. Control*, 1, 1, 86–92, 2006.

22. El-Dahshan, E.S.A., Hosny, T., Salem, A.B.M., Hybrid intelligent techniques for MRI brain images classification. *Digit. Signal Process. A Rev. J.*, 20, 2.

23. Begg, R.K., Palaniswami, M., Owen, B., Support vector machines for automated gait classification. *IEEE Trans. Biomed. Eng.*, 52, 5, 828–838, 2005.

24. Matreka, A. and Strzelecki, M., Texture Analysis Methods – A review. *Spectrochim. Acta A Mol. Biomol. Spectrosc.*, 67, 1, 172–177, 2007.

25. Haralick, R.M., Shanmugam, K., Dinstein, I., Textural features for image classification. *IEEE Transactions on Systems, Man, and Cybernetics*, 6, 610–621, 1973

26. Morris, J.C., The clinical dementia rating (cdr): Current version and scoring rules. *Neurology*, 43, 11, 2412–2414, 1993.

27. Folstein, M., Folstein, S., Mchugh, P., Mini-mental state" A practical method for grading the cognitive state of patients for the clinician related papers 'MINI-MENTAL STATE' a practival method for grading the cognitive state of patients for the clinician. *J. Gsychiaf. Res.*, 12, 189–198, 1975.

28. Fotenos, A.F., Snyder, A.Z., Girton, L.E., Morris, J.C., Buckner, R.L., Normative estimates of cross-sectional and longitudinal brain volume decline in aging and AD. *Neurology*, 64, 6, 1032–1039, 2005.

29. NITRC: The fMRI Data Center Tool/resource info [Internet]. 2022 Apr. [cited 2022 May 16] Available from: https://www.nitrc.org/projects/fmridatacenter/.

30. Cheng, J.Z. *et al.*, Computer-aided diagnosis with deep learning architecture: Applications to breast lesions in US images and pulmonary nodules in CT scans. *Sci. Rep.*, 6, 1–13, April, 2016.

31. Lahmiri, S. and Boukadoum, M., Hybrid discrete wavelet transform and gabor filter banks processing for mammogram features extraction. *2011 IEEE 9th Int. New Circuits Syst. Conf. NEWCAS 2011*, vol. 2013, pp. 53–56, 20117.

32. Aggarwal, N., Rana, B., Agrawal, R.K., 3D discrete wavelet transform for computer aided diagnosis of Alzheimer's disease using t1-weighted brain MRI. *Int. J. Imaging Syst. Technol.*, 25, 2, 179–190, 2015.

33. Mallat, S.G., A theory for multiresolution signal decomposition: The wavelet representation, in: *Fundam. Pap. Wavelet Theory*, vol. I, pp. 494–513, 2009.

34. Aggarwal, N. and Agrawal, R.K., First and second order statistics features for classification of magnetic resonance brain images. *J. Signal Inf. Process.*, 03, 02, 146–153, 2012.

35. Gupta, Y., Lee, K.H., Choi, K.Y., Lee, J.J., Kim, B.C., Kwon, G.R., Early diagnosis of Alzheimer's disease using combined features from voxel-based morphometry and cortical, subcortical, and hippocampus regions of MRI T1 brain images. *PLoS One*, 14, 10, 1–30, 2019.

36. Zheng, C., Xia, Y., Pan, Y., Chen, J., Automated identification of dementia using medical imaging: A survey from a pattern classification perspective. *Brain Inform.*, 3, 1, 17–27, 2016.

37. Świetlik, D. and Białowąs, J., Application of artificial neural networks to identify Alzheimer's disease using cerebral perfusion SPECT data. *Int. J. Environ. Res. Public Health*, 16, 7, p. 1303, 2019.

38. López, M. *et al.*, Neurological image classification for the Alzheimer's disease diagnosis using kernel PCA and support vector machines. *IEEE Nucl. Sci. Symp. Conf. Rec.*, 4, 2486–2489, 2009.

39. Cortes, C. and Vapnik, V., Support vector networks. *Mach. Learn.*, 20, 273–297, 1995.

40. Magnin, B. *et al.*, Support vector machine-based classification of Alzheimer's disease from whole-brain anatomical MRI. *Neuroradiology*, 51, 2, 73–83, 2009.

41. Lu, D., Popuri, K., Ding, G.W., Balachandar, R., Beg, M.F., Multiscale deep neural network based analysis of FDG-PET images for the early diagnosis of alzheimer's disease. *Med. Image Anal.*, 46, 26–34, 2018.

42. Plant, C. *et al.*, Automated detection of brain atrophy patterns based on MRI for the prediction of alzheimer's disease. *Neuroimage*, 50, 1, 162–174, 2010.

11

Pulmonary Embolism Detection Using Machine and Deep Learning Techniques

Renu Vadhera[1]*, Meghna Sharma[1] and Priyanka Vashisht[2]

[1]The Northcap University, Gurugram, India
[2]Amity University, Gurugram, India

Abstract

Pulmonary embolism (PE) is a disease that occurs due to blood clot in pulmonary arteries. Various methods are available for pulmonary embolism detection. The primary method to detect PE is computed tomography pulmonary angiogram (CTPA). One CTPA contains hundreds of images. It is very difficult for a radiologist to study such a CTPA on time. The radiologist's accuracy and efficiency are also affected by other human factors such as attention span and eye fatigue. This delayed study of PE detection may cause serious illness or death. Many research efforts have been made to solve this problem with computer-aided detection (CAD) systems. The pulmonary embolism CAD system helps the radiologist for a better and timely diagnosis. This system uses light from various machines and deep learning-based CAD models designed for PE detection. In PE detection, we can perform classification, detection, and segmentation. A comparative analysis of various proposed models of PE detection is also conducted in this study.

Keywords: Pulmonary embolism detection, CAD, CTPA, segmentation, deep learning, CNN, UNET, pulmonary embolism

11.1 Introduction

Pulmonary embolism (PE), which is associated with significant morbidity and humanity, is the third most prevalent cardiovascular disease in the United States [1]. PE is brought on by a blood clot in the pulmonary arteries,

---

*Corresponding author: renu19csd@ncuindia.edu

Akansha Singh, Anuradha Dhull and Krishna Kant Singh (eds.) Blockchain and Deep Learning for Smart Healthcare, (257–276) © 2024 Scrivener Publishing LLC

which goes from the legs or other regions of the body to the lungs through deep veins. This blockage in the pulmonary arteries may lead to lack of oxygen in the human body. In severe cases, a person may have abnormally low blood pressure and sudden death [2]. Therefore, early diagnosis is necessary so that timely treatment can save lives [3]. Each PE in pulmonary arteries can be classified into different types as shown in Figure 11.1, which can be recognized based on its location and based on severity.

The main problem is to detect subsegmental pulmonary embolism because it occurs thinly in the subsegmental part of the pulmonary artery [4]. Because its symptoms are similar to those of a cold, and for the timely detection of PE [5], doctors have to check different methods of diagnosis to confirm the PE condition. PE can be diagnosed with various methods as shown in Figure 11.2.

The most common and most effective method is computed tomography pulmonary angiogram (CTPA) because of its greatly enhanced visualization [7], easy management, wide availability, and good accuracy [2]. CTPA provides evidence on other probable reasons of severe chest pain as well. Lung perfusion variances can also be seen and assessed with dual-energy CT [1]. CTPA is the gold standard in detecting PE. One CTPA is composed

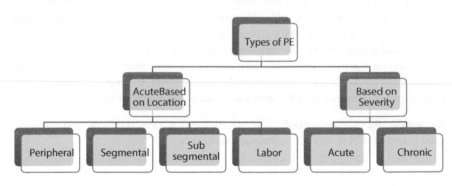

Figure 11.1 Types of PE.

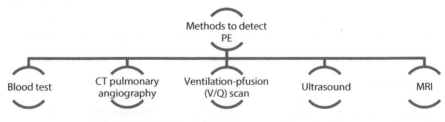

Figure 11.2 Methods used to detect PE [6].

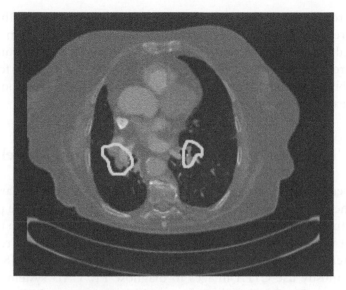

Figure 11.3 Marked PE in CTPA.

of hundreds of slices. It takes a lot of time to study such slices in one CTPA [2]. Figure 11.3 shows an example of CTPA with marked PE.

The growing patient population and physician shortage may have an impact on both medically underprivileged individuals and contemporary healthcare organizations [3]; this may delay the diagnosis [4] and patients may die [5]. Complexities in imaging studies also decrease manual diagnosis accuracy [6]. To reduce mortality during the waiting period, a study is conducted to develop an automated system for sorting patients with pulmonary embolism. In this study, CTPA is used for PE diagnosis and results show that the automated system performs well as compared to the expert panel. As per the study, the normal radiologist has a sensitivity of between 77% and 94%, but the automated system can help the radiologist in detecting PE with a higher sensitivity but with less time [7]. Currently, along with Artificial Intelligence, Machine Learning (ML) and Deep Learning (DL) are widely used to detect PE. In this study, we show a literature review of various computer-based techniques and algorithms used for PE detection on CTPA.

Although many studies have been conducted to develop computer-aided detection (CAD) for detecting PE in CTPA, little efforts have been put to review their work under one heading. The objectives of this chapter are to deliver the insights, scope, and outcomes of several studies done in the field; to analyze the advantages and shortcomings of the techniques used;

and to provide suggestions that would enhance future research. The study is prepared as follows: Firstly, the state of the art of PE detection models is defined. Then, literature survey is explained in detail, and a summary of the different proposed models is explained in tabular form. This is followed by a publication analysis presented in chart form. Lastly, the conclusion and future scope are summarized.

11.2   The State-of-the-Art of PE Detection Models

It has been seen that various automated systems for PE detection are available to help radiologists. However, because of the very high false positive rates in these systems, they have not been implemented yet in the medical field, but with the emergence of new methods and techniques in research, researchers are trying to reduce the number of false positives [8]. CAD systems mostly use CTPA images to diagnose PE. CAD systems generally perform classification, detection, and segmentation of PE as shown in Figure 11.4. Detection means finding the location of PE in the image. Classification [9] means classifying images with and without PE and segmentation means extracting the area of PE from an image. Segmentation

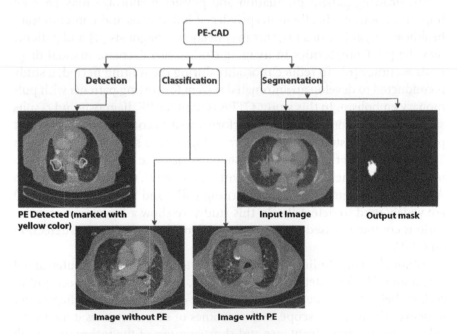

Figure 11.4 Tasks performed by PE CAD systems.

aims to extract a specific part or object in the image. Some other models are also proposed to calculate the number of emboli and segment the complete arteries, veins, etc., which may help to improve the performance of the computer-aided detection system [10]. In this chapter, results of PE-CAD are also compared with manually extracted results provided by the radiologist. Some studies are also conducted to check the impact of the dataset in terms of size and other characteristics on PE diagnosis with CAD.

11.3   Literature Survey

Many machine and deep learning methods have been used to detect or segment PE. An adaptive 3D voxel cluster model that separates blood vessels from surrounding tissues was developed primarily to facilitate PE detection. Connected Component Analysis (CCA) was used to reconstruct a vessel tree to detect the suspicious PE areas [11]. The performance of AI-based CAD is evaluated, and its benefits for general radiologists are explained [12]. A total of 104 pulmonary CTPAs to detect PE were studied by radiologists and a CAD system (Image Checker CT V 2.0). The results of the CAD system were analyzed, obtaining a sensitivity of 53% and a specificity of 77%. The right prediction of the CAD system was 28.5% and the wrong prediction was 90% [13]. Another CAD system was proposed to detect PE using CTPA. This technique helps radiologists to detect acute and chronic PE with 80% sensitivity with 4 false detections [14]. To identify and classify pulmonary embolisms (PEs) on computed tomography angiography (CTA), another automatic genetic algorithm (GA)-based method is proposed [15]. To test the performance of the CAD system with different datasets, research has been conducted on individual datasets of United Methodist (UM) with 59 studies and Prospective Investigation of Pulmonary Embolism Diagnosis (PIOPED) data with 69 patients. They applied a multiscale vessel segmentation technique, a parallel multi-pre-screening method, and Linear Discriminant Analysis classifier to reduce the false positives. They obtained a sensitivity of 80% at 18.9 false positives per case when used with the PIOPED dataset. It concludes that the CAD system can be used to any unknown dataset to detect PE [16]. A new model using logistic regression was developed to extract important projecting features that was fed to the Binarized Neural Network (BNN) as input. The results show that, together, logistic regression with BNN performs better [17].

In comparison with inexperienced readers, the sensitivity of CAD to detect PE was calculated as 78%. It means that CAD can assist them for better diagnosis [18]. Still, it is very difficult to detect central PEs with CAD.

If the pulmonary artery can be distinguished from the vein, then results can be improved. For this, an ML-based model was proposed that can automatically extract the pulmonary trunk. An AdaBoost classifier that extracts Haar features was used to identify the pulmonary trunk and classify it. This approach outperformed other approaches and obtained 100% accuracy when evaluated using different datasets [19]. The performance of another CAD system in detecting peripheral pulmonary embolism (PE) was evaluated; the CAD system and the dual-energy software ("Lung PBV", "Lung Vessels") were then tested, obtaining good results. This concludes that the computer-aided detection system, Lung Vessels, and Lung PBV can be used for detection of peripheral PE [20]. It is also verified that CAD's performance is not dependent on the type of scanner used to take the CTPA. Only the superiority of an image and some scanning protocols matter while selecting the CTPA for the CAD system [21]. Iterative reconstruction can also improve the results of the CAD system by improving image quality. It also decreases false positive detection and sensitivity [22]. A new hybrid approach based on the Neural Hypernetwork has been used to detect PE, showing 93% of the AUC of the ROCT [23].

To develop new CAD systems, researchers are facing many problems due to lack of publicly available datasets. Thus, to solve this problem, a new dataset for Ferdowsi University of Mashhad's PE (FUMPE) was introduced. It contains 3D Pulmonary Embolism CTA of 35 patients with 8792 slices (images). This dataset also provides ground truths that are marked by the radiologist. This is a public dataset that initially can be used for the study of humanity and morbidity risks related to PE [24].

Many CAD systems are there for PE detection but it is difficult and time-consuming to analyze all vessels to detect the present PE. To overcome this issue, another model was proposed for automatic separation of arteries and veins. It also improves the efficiency of the CAD system [10]. 33 patients' data were used to automatically distinguish arteries and veins from a chest CT scan. This is done using three steps: (i) segmentation was carried out to separate vessels; (ii) 3D convolutional neural network (3D CNN) was used to obtain first classification of vessels; and (iii) Graph Cuts optimization was used to improve the accuracy, which shows a value of 94% [25].

Another multimodal fusion model is developed that uses pixel data from volumetric CTPA scans and electronic medical record data for PE classification. Its results show an AUROC of 0.947 on testing data. It outperforms imaginary data and EMR data for a model used separately [26, 27]. Sometimes, the CAD system shows poor sensitivity and more false positives. Thus, it cannot be used as a stand-alone system but it can be used as a second reader. Another AI prototype algorithm is developed that balances sensitivity and specificity [28]. To segment the PE in CTPA, a deep learning-based UNET model was trained and tested with 590 patients and shows 94.6% sensitivity and 76.5% specificity, while the AUC was 0.926. Lastly, the burden of clot was calculated with the UNET model [29].

To overcome the problem of detection of small emboli, a new probability-based Mask Region Convolution Neural Network (P-RCNN) model is suggested for PE detection. It also overcomes the shortcomings of RCNN and improves the local data of the small objects to extract anchors at a complex density by firstly upsampling the feature map [30]. To examine its predictive value in patients suffering from acute PE, an automated calculation was done to get the right ventricle (RV)-to-left ventricle (LV) ratio in CTPA, and to measure the risk of acute PE in patients. This can be used in automated analysis to gather prognostic details of patients with acute pulmonary embolism [31].

Because the dataset plays a major role in the PE detection system and its generalization can be increased by dual-energy data augmentation, it will be more robust to contrast dissimilarities, which may empower the transition to non-PE protocols and the detection of incidental PE [32]. A new multinational large dataset was introduced. This dataset was composed of annotated CTPA related to pulmonary embolism. It was hosted by Kaggle for the Society of Thoracic Radiology PE Detection competition. This dataset solved the problem of small datasets, and this large dataset can be used for machine and deep models to diagnose PE in CTPA [2]. In the literature, various deep learning models exist, but which one should be used for CAD PE development remains unanswered. To report this problem, researchers show a study of various deep learning solutions used for PE diagnosis using CTPA. Both image- and exam-level diagnosis were carried out. Convolutional Neural Networks (CNNs) were used for image-level examination. Various other methods with vision transformers and self-supervised learning contrasted with supervised learning (SL) were also used. These are followed by results of Transfer Learning (TL) is compared and at exam level, conventional classification (CC) with Multiple Instance Learning (MIL) is compared. Results show that transfer learning boosts performance, TL with SSL beats its supervised counterparts, CNN is best for vision transformations, and CC performed better than MIL. Thus, AUC gains of 0.2% for the image level and 1.05% for the exam level were obtained compared to previous methods used in literature [33].

Many models are available for segmentation or classification. However, the new CAD system is designed not only for classifying the images but also for segmentation of PE images after classification [5]. Researchers mostly used

Table 11.1 Comparative analysis of the proposed models for PE detection.

Paper	Dataset used	Dataset size	Method	Performance	Research gaps
[16]	Private Dataset	38 CTA	Feature computation and classification methods	Sensitivity of 63% at 4.9 false positive (FP) per dataset	• Did not find a difference between PE in large proximal and small peripheral vessels.
[36]	Private Dataset	20 CTPA	Tobogganing, ANN with k-Nearest Neighbor and GA	Sensitivity of 63.2% with 18.4 false positive per investigation	• Only detected 66% of TP PE regions. • Other optimization methods can be used to improve performance. • The size of the dataset is very small.
[10]	Private Dataset	12 CT	Tobogganing, ANN and kNN	Sensitivity of 62.5% with 17.1 FP per inspection.	• Additional segmentation of the vessel tree slows down the total performance of the CAD system.
[46]	Public Dataset (PE challenge) and Private Dataset	141 CTPA	Tobogganing and CNN	Sensitivity of 83% with 2 false positives per volume.	• On the PE challenge dataset, CNN did not perform well to remove false positives.
[37]	Private Dataset	33 CTA	ANN, kNN. Support Vector Machine (SVM)	Sensitivities calculated are 98.3% with 10.2 FPs, 57.3% with 5.7 FPs, and 73% at 8.2 FPs per dataset.	• A small dataset is used.

(Continued)

Table 11.1 Comparative analysis of the proposed models for PE detection. (*Continued*)

Paper	Dataset used	Dataset size	Method	Performance	Research gaps
[26]	Private Dataset	2592 CT studies	2D U-Net and 2D Conv-LSTM	For Validation Dataset, AUC of 0.94, and for test data, AUC of 0.85	• Used fewer parameters for the model.
[38]	Public Dataset (PE challenge) and Private Dataset	149 CTPA	Public Dataset (sensitivities of 75.4%, 75.4%, and 75.4% at two FP per CT scan at 0 mm, 2 mm, and 5 mm error) Private Dataset (sensitivities of 76.3%, 78.9%, and 84.2% at two FP per scan at 0 mm, 2 mm, and 5 mm error)	Two-stage CNN	• Obtained low sensitivity with the PE challenge dataset because of the large number of small PEs. • Problem in detection of subsegmental emboli.
[29]	Private Dataset	590 CTPA	DL-CNN (UNET)	Sensitivity of 94.6% and specificity of 76.5%	• Does not include the CTPA of chronic pulmonary embolism as it used only acute PE and non-APE • CTPA

(Continued)

Table 11.1 Comparative analysis of the proposed models for PE detection. (*Continued*)

Paper	Dataset used	Dataset size	Method	Performance	Research gaps
[3]	Private Dataset (Kinetics-600 dataset)		3D CNN	AUROC of 0.84	• Chronic and subsegmental types of pulmonary embolism were not involved in this study • Performance with imaging artifacts didn't check.
[7]	Public Dataset (PE challenge)	80 CTPA	2D, 2.5D, and 3D UNET	Sensitivity of 68% with one FP per scan	• Not able to find emboli less than 0.5 ml efficiently. • To train the system, 60 scans are used. • Only detects emboli but did not classify into an obstructive and non-obstructive type.
[39]	Public Dataset (RSNA)	Training 7279, test 650, Evaluation 1517	Xception Net based on CNN	Accuracy of 92% on validation test set	• First, the feature extractor can be ensembled with RNN units treating the set of images in a study as a series and improve the accuracy, and the data can be further pre-processed to create a better balance between the labels.

(Continued)

Table 11.1 Comparative analysis of the proposed models for PE detection. (*Continued*)

Paper	Dataset used	Dataset size	Method	Performance	Research gaps
[40]	Private Dataset	5856 positive and 5196 negative volumetric images	CNN and RCNN	AUC of 0.812.	• A slice thickness of 2.5 mm is taken for fast training with the lack of GPU and more memory, which may lead to problems in detecting subsegmental PEs.
[41]	Private Dataset	85 (CTA)	Deep Learning	Sensitivity of 90.9% with an average false positive of 2.0	• Not able to detect pulmonary embolism below three levels.
[42]	Public Dataset (RSNA-STR Pulmonary Embolism CT, RSPECT)	7279 CTPA	CNN and LSTM	AUC of 0.95	• Model does not perform well for detecting bilateral PE.

(*Continued*)

Table 11.1 Comparative analysis of the proposed models for PE detection. (*Continued*)

Paper	Dataset used	Dataset size	Method	Performance	Research gaps
[43]	Public Dataset (CHAOS dataset) and Private Dataset	70 CTPA	Res-Unet	For the Private Dataset, Dice coefficient = 0.98, Precision = 97.6%, and Recall = 0.983 For the CHOAS dataset, Dice coefficient = 0.965, Precision = 96.9%, and Recall = 0.96.1	• Model only segments the pulmonary arteries to detect PE but does not define anything for the classification of CTPA.
[44]	Public Dataset (CHAOS dataset) and Private Dataset	120 CTPA	ResD-Unet	With the Private Dataset, DSE is 0.982, Precision is 0.985, Recall is 0.980, and SSIM is 0.961 With the Public Dataset, DSE is 0.969, Precision is 0.966, Recall is 0.968, and SSIM is 0.951	• Model only segments the pulmonary arteries to detect PE but does not define anything for the classification of CTPA.

(Continued)

Table 11.1 Comparative analysis of the proposed models for PE detection. (*Continued*)

Paper	Dataset used	Dataset size	Method	Performance	Research gaps
[45]	Private Dataset	800 CTPA	CNN and LSTM (classification)	Stack level sensitivity of 93.5% and specificity of 86.6% Image level sensitivity of 83.5% and specificity of 90.7%	• Models do not provide specific information about the location of emboli. • Dataset from one vendor is used. • The number of PE CTPA is less than that of non-PE CTPA.
[5]	Public Dataset (FUMPE) and Private Dataset (NCKUH)	200 CTPA	Classification (DRN and MIxNet) and segmentation (ARUX-Net architecture)	Accuracy is 85% and mean intersection over union is 0.689	• Solitary small lesions are misdiagnosed.
[34]	Public Dataset (FUMPE) and Private Dataset NCKUH	132 CTPA	HRNet-based architecture	Sensitivity of 68.56% on FUMPE, 2.53% on the CMUH dataset, and 49.67% on the CMUH dataset	• With the FUMPE dataset, the model did not improve the accuracy on the testing data because training is done using the supervised method.

supervised learning techniques for PE detection. A new feature-enhanced adversarial semi-supervised method of semantic segmentation network is prepared to mark the PE lesion area in CTPA. It shows very good results when applied on three different datasets [34]. Along with detection of PE, it is also important to find patients with a higher risk of PE in an inpatient population. PE is predicted from data of 63,798 medical and surgical patients with logistic regression (RL)-, gradient boosted tree (XGBoost)-, and neural network (NN)-based models. It was concluded that out of these models, XGBoost outperforms the others in terms of predicting PEs with a sensitivity of 81% and a specificity of 70% [35]. A comparative analysis of the proposed models for PE is shown in Table 11.1.

11.4   Publications Analysis

In this chapter, Google Scholar is used to gather various research papers from 2005 to 2022 with different keywords like "Pulmonary Embolism", "Detection of Pulmonary Embolism using Machine Learning", "Detection of Pulmonary Embolism using Deep Learning", "CAD for PE detection", etc. These titles are used as a part of the titles or abstracts of the identified papers. We identified 315 papers in total, but after screening and the eligibility process, we obtained 50 papers for this literature review, and from them, we used 19 papers for qualitative analysis. Figure 11.5 shows the search and inclusion process of papers.

We selected the papers mostly from Nature, Wiley, IEEE Access, Springer, ACM, and BioMed central. The bar chart in Figure 11.6 shows the number of papers selected for this study from various databases.

The top journals and conferences such as the International Society for Optical Engineering-Medical Imaging (SPIE-MI), Academic Radiology, Medical Imaging, European Journal of Radiology (EJR), American Journal of Roentgenology (AJR), and Radiological Society of North America are used for paper selection.

11.5   Conclusion

In this study, we found that various machine learning models, such as k-Nearest Neighbor (kNN) and Support Vector Machine (SVM), and deep learning models, such as Convolution Neural Network (CNN), Residual Net, UNET, and Region-based CNN (R-CNN), have been used to develop the CAD system for pulmonary embolism (PE) detection. We analyzed

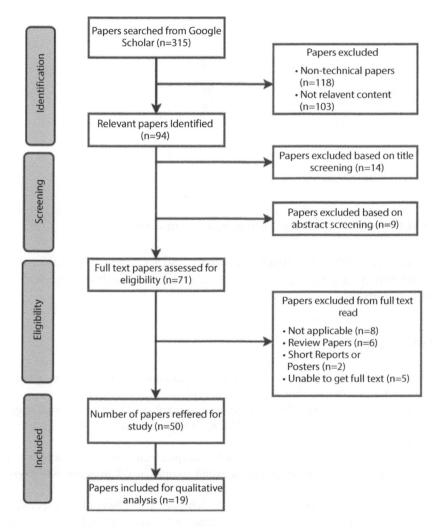

Figure 11.5 Study and insertion method of papers.

their performance in terms of sensitivity. Both the advantages and disadvantages of the proposed models were also recognized. From the state of the art, we conclude that the proposed CAD systems for PE detections perform satisfactorily and can assist the radiologist for timely diagnosis and treatment. In the future, research related to this topic should mainly focus on the development of CAD systems that can reduce the number of false positives (FP) and help in the detection of subsegmental and small pulmonary embolism more accurately. The performance of the models can be determined using different datasets. We believe that a vast improvement in

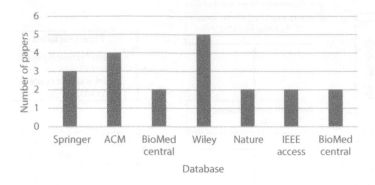

Figure 11.6 Selected databases and corresponding paper count.

this area will enable automated, consistent, and accurate PE detection and deliver timely diagnosis and treatment that can help with the survival of patients with PE.

References

1. Moore, A.J.E. *et al.*, Imaging of acute pulmonary embolism: An update. *Cardiovasc. Diagn. Ther.*, 8, 225–243, 2018.
2. Colak E., *et al.*, The RSNA pulmonary embolism CT dataset. *Radiology: Artificial Intelligence*, 3, 2, e200254, Radiological Society of North America, 2021.
3. Huang, S.C. *et al.*, PENet—A scalable deep-learning model for automated diagnosis of pulmonary embolism using volumetric CT imaging. *NPJ Digit. Med.*, 3, 1, 1–9, 2020.
4. Rufener, S.L., Patel, S., Kazerooni, E.A., Schipper, M., Kelly, A.M., Comparison of on-call radiology resident and faculty interpretation of 4- and 16-row multidetector CT pulmonary angiography with indirect CT venography. *Acad. Radiol*, 15, 71–76, 2008.
5. Yu, C.-Y., Chang, M.-C., Cheng, Y.-C., Kuo, C., *Convolutional neural network for early pulmonary embolism detection via computed tomography pulmonary angiography*, arXiv preprint arXiv:2204.03204, pp. 1–7, 2022.
6. Bělohlávek, J., Dytrych, V., Linhart, A., Pulmonary embolism, part I: Epidemiology, risk factors and risk stratification, pathophysiology, clinical presentation, diagnosis and nonthrombotic pulmonary embolism. *Exp. Clin. Cardiol.*, 18, 129–138, 2013.
7. Cano-Espinosa, C., Cazorla, M., González, G., Computer aided detection of pulmonary embolism using multi-slice multi-axial segmentation. *Appl. Sci.*, 10, 8, 2945, 2020.

8. González, G. *et al.*, *Computer aided detection for pulmonary embolism challenge (CAD-PE)*, arXiv preprint arXiv:2003.13440. p. 13440, 2020.
9. Serpen, G., Tekkedil, D.K., Orra, M., A knowledge-based artificial neural network classifier for pulmonary embolism diagnosis. *Comput. Biol. Med.*, 38, 204–220, 2008.
10. Wang, X., Song, X., Chapman, B.E., Zheng, B., Improving performance of computer-aided detection of pulmonary embolisms by incorporating a new pulmonary vascular-tree segmentation algorithm. *Med. Imaging 2012 Comput. Diagnosis*, vol. 8315, p. 83152U, 2012.
11. Zhou, C., Chan, H.P., Patel, S., Cascade, P.N., Sahiner, B., Hadjiiski, L.M., E.A., Preliminary investigation of computer-aided detection of pulmonary embolism in threedimensional computed tomography pulmonary angiography images. *Acad. Radiol.*, 12, 782, 2005. Kazerooni.
12. Buhmann, S. *et al.*, Clinical evaluation of a computer-aided diagnosis (CAD) prototype for the detection of pulmonary embolism. *Acad. Radiol.*, 14, 651–658, 2007.
13. Maizlin, Z.V., Vos, P.M., Godoy, M.B., Cooperberg, P.L., Computer-aided detection of pulmonary embolism on CT angiography: Initial experience. *J. Thorac. Imaging*, 22, 324–329, 2007.
14. Jianming, L. and Jinbo, B., Computer aided detection of pulmonary embolism with tobogganing and mutiple instance classification in CT pulmonary angiography, in: *Lect. Notes Comput. Sci. (including Subser. Lect. Notes Artif. Intell. Lect. Notes Bioinformatics)*, vol. 4584 LNCS, pp. 630–641, 2007.
15. Myers, M.H., Beliaev, I., Lin, K.I., Machine learning techniques in detecting of pulmonary embolisms. *IEEE Int. Conf. Neural Networks - Conf. Proc*, pp. 385–390, 2007.
16. Zhou, C. *et al.*, Computer-aided detection of pulmonary embolism in computed tomographic pulmonary angiography (CTPA): Performance evaluation with independent data sets. *Med. Phys.*, 36, 3385–3396, 2009.
17. Tang, L., Wang, L., Pan, S., Su, Y., Chen, Y., A neural network to pulmonary embolism aided diagnosis with a feature selection approach. *Proc. - 2010 3rd Int. Conf. Biomed. Eng. Informatics, BMEI 2010*, vol. 6, pp. 2255–2260, 2010.
18. Blackmon, K.N. *et al.*, Computer-aided detection of pulmonary embolism at CT pulmonary angiography: Can it improve performance of inexperienced readers? *Eur. Radiol.*, 21, 1214–1223, 2011.
19. Wu, H., Deng, K., Liang, J., Machine learning-based automatic detection of pulmonary trunk. *Med. Imaging 2011 Comput. Diagnosis*, vol. 7963, p. 79630K, 2011.
20. Lee, C.W. *et al.*, Evaluation of computer-aided detection and dual energy software in detection of peripheral pulmonary embolism on dual-energy pulmonary CT angiography. *Eur. Radiol.*, 21, 54–62, 2011.
21. Wittenberg, R. *et al.*, Stand-alone performance of a computer-assisted detection prototype for detection of acute pulmonary embolism: A multi-institutional comparison. *Br. J. Radiol.*, 85, 758–764, 2012.

22. Lahiji, K., Kligerman, S., Jeudy, J., White, C., Improved accuracy of pulmonary embolism computer-aided detection using iterative reconstruction compared with filtered back projection. *Am. J. Roentgenol.*, 203, 763–771, 2014.

23. Rucco, M. *et al.*, Neural hypernetwork approach for pulmonary embolism diagnosis. *BMC Res. Notes*, 8, 1–11, 2015.

24. Masoudi, M. *et al.*, Data descriptor: A new dataset of computed-tomography angiography images for computer-aided detection of pulmonary embolism. *Sci. Data*, 5, 1–9, 2018.

25. Nardelli, P. *et al.*, Pulmonary artery-vein classification in ct images using deep learning. *IEEE Trans. Med. Imaging*, 37, 2428–2440, 2018.

26. Rajan, D., Beymer, D., Abedin, S., Dehghan, E., *Pi-PE: A pipeline for pulmonary embolism detection using sparsely annotated 3D CT images*, pp. 220–232, PMLR, 2020.

27. Huang, S.C., Pareek, A., Zamanian, R., Banerjee, I., Lungren, M.P., Multimodal fusion with deep neural networks for leveraging CT imaging and electronic health record: A case-study in pulmonary embolism detection. *Sci. Rep.*, 10, 1–9, 2020.

28. Weikert, T. *et al.*, Automated detection of pulmonary embolism in CT pulmonary angiograms using an AI-powered algorithm. *Eur. Radiol.*, 30, 6545–6553, 2020.

29. Liu, W. *et al.*, Evaluation of acute pulmonary embolism and clot burden on CTPA with deep learning. *Eur. Radiol.*, 30, 3567–3575, 2020.

30. Long, K. *et al.*, Probability-based Mask R-CNN for pulmonary embolism detection. *Neurocomputing*, 422, 345–353, 2021.

31. Foley, R.W. *et al.*, Automated calculation of the right ventricle to left ventricle ratio on CT for the risk stratification of patients with acute pulmonary embolism. *Eur. Radiol.*, 31, 6013–6020, 2021.

32. Hofs, C. *et al.*, *PE detection with dual-energy CT Data augmentation*, pp. 3–5, 2022.

33. Islam, N.U., Gehlot, S., Zhou, Z., Gotway, M.B., Liang, J., Seeking an optimal approach for computer-aided pulmonary embolism detection, in: *Lect. Notes Comput. Sci. (including Subser. Lect. Notes Artif. Intell. Lect. Notes Bioinformatics)*, vol. 12966 LNCS, pp. 692–702, 2021.

34. Cheng, T., Chang, J., Huang, C., Kuo, C., Feature-enhanced adversarial semi-supervised semantic segmentation network for pulmonary embolism annotation. *Heliyon.*, Elsevier, 9, 5, 2023.

35. Ryan, L. *et al.*, Predicting pulmonary embolism among hospitalized patients with machine learning algorithms. *Pulm. Circ.*, 12, 1–9, 2022.

36. Park, S.C., Chapman, B.E., Zheng, B., A multistage approach to improve performance of computer-aided detection of pulmonary embolisms depicted on CT Images: Preliminary investigation. *IEEE Trans. Biomed. Eng.*, 58, 1519–1527, 2011.

37. Ozkan, H., Tulum, G., Osman, O., Sahin, S., Automatic detection of pulmonary embolism in CTA images using machine learning. *Elektron. ir Elektrotechnika*, 23, 63–67, 2017.
38. Yang, X. *et al.*, A two-stage convolutional neural network for pulmonary embolism detection from CTPA images. *IEEE Access*, 7, 84849–84857, 2019.
39. Aditya Mohan, O.C.G., *Pulmonary embolism detection*, pp. 1–6, MALIS PROJECT, FALL, Github, 2020.
40. Shi, L. *et al.*, Medical Imaging with deep learning, *Automatic diagnosis of pulmonary embolism using an attention-guided framework: A large-scale study*, pp. 743–754, 2020.
41. Li, X., Wang, X., Yang, X., Lin, Y., Huang, Z., Preliminary study on artificial intelligence diagnosis of pulmonary embolism based on computer in-depth study. *Ann. Transl. Med.*, 9, 838–838, 2021.
42. Suman, S. *et al.*, Attention based CNN-LSTM network for pulmonary embolism prediction on chest computed tomography pulmonary angiograms, in: *Lect. Notes Comput. Sci. (including Subser. Lect. Notes Artif. Intell. Lect. Notes Bioinformatics)*, vol. 12907 LNCS, pp. 356–366, 2021.
43. Liu, Z. and Yuan, H., An res-unet method for pulmonary artery segmentation of CT images. *J. Phys. Conf. Ser.*, 1924, 1, 012018, 2021.
44. Yuan, H., Liu, Z., Shao, Y., Liu, M., ResD-unet research and application for pulmonary artery segmentation. *IEEE Access*, 9, 67504–67511, 2021.
45. Huhtanen, H. *et al.*, Automated detection of pulmonary embolism from CT-angiograms using deep learning. *BMC Med. Imaging*, 22, 1–10, 2022.
46. Tajbakhsh, N., Gotway, M.B., Liang, J., Computer-aided pulmonary embolism detection using a novel vessel-aligned multi-planar image representation and convolutional neural networks, in: *Medical Image Computing and Computer-Assisted Intervention–MICCA 2015: 18th International Conference*, Munich, Germany, vol. 18, pp. 62–69, 2015.

12

Computer Vision Techniques for Smart Healthcare Infrastructure

Reshu Agarwal

Amity Institute of Information Technology, Amity University, Noida, India

Abstract

This Chapter discusses the use of computer vision for optical character recognition (OCR) of cursive writing; that is, the aim was to identify cursive style texts that were destroyed due to motion blur while in a slow-moving vehicle. The field of application is transportation, one of the many fields where the use of machine learning for OCR has been found extremely useful. OCR helps identify destroyed vehicle nameplates, read messages and texts displayed through printed means such as billboards and visual electronic means such as TV, and read traffic signs and boards, which are just some of its wide range of applications. When we click a picture of a billboard or any printed poster from a moving vehicle, various disturbances, particularly the motion blur effect, influence the image acquired, which makes it hard to read the text or make out the image. The OCR carried out by machines can easily read and predict such non-readable texts. Modern research studies have proposed powerful techniques such as deep learning, machine learning, binary format matrix techniques, and Internet of Things (IoT), among others. The idea behind this project was highly influenced by such techniques, which uses a line detection method combined with a circular empty mask to detect and identify the edge pixels of targeted texts, crops the selected regions, and converts them to binary number matrices in order to recognize features of the character. This research covers the segmentation and feature extraction of the characters for OCR. This technique can be used further in convolutional neural networks to classify the extracted features into appropriate character groups by comparing them with predefined character rules. In the course of this project, many new things were learned as this domain of research is completely new to me. The original names of five major lines used to segment cursive letters in the standard line detection technique were changed. This study, the idea of which is simple yet efficient, was

Email: agarwal.reshu3@gmail.com

Akansha Singh, Anuradha Dhull and Krishna Kant Singh (eds.) Blockchain and Deep Learning for Smart Healthcare, (277–322) © 2024 Scrivener Publishing LLC

inspired by a research work that used global parameters such as stroke, slant angle, baselines, size to segment cursive letters, and the hidden Markov model (HMM) for shape recognition and for ranking the candidate letters. Finally, information from the lexicon and the HMM ranking were combined in graph optimization problems to recognize words [1].

Keywords: Optical character recognition, baseline, blind deconvolution, tangent lines, binary format, neural network, IoT

12.1   Introduction

Computer vision is the eye of artificial intelligence (AI) that enables machines to see or detect objects correctly in their field of vision, observe and learn the different properties of these objects, and classify them by finding similarities and differences between them.

The implementation of computer vision in the transportation domain denotes its application to help humans read and understand texts related to vehicles on the road and to read traffic signs and posted messages alongside roads and streets. Computer vision is like a third eye that assists people to see things that are difficult or not possible through the naked eye.

This study proposes an idea that can be used to segment and extract primary features from the texts that define them. Firstly, the captured image is deconvolved using the blind deconvolution technique to reduce noise and the motion blur effects on the image. This deblurring technique was chosen as it is one of the most readily available and efficient standard deblurring algorithms. Matlab tools were utilized for image processing tasks. Deconvolution is a pre-processing step, during which weights can also be used to reduce the noisy high-frequency waves around the edges of objects that define the image. At present, the potential region of interest (ROI) is determined and the textual parts detected are cut out and converted to gray-level images, which are then converted to the binary format.

Cursive writing has many variations, such as looped character style, calligraphy style, formal plane cursive, or simple italic writing. Italic formal cursive writing means that the letters in a word tend to slant toward a certain direction. Closed loop, slope, aspect ratio, intersection points, and U shape are some of the common features used to identify cursive writings. Almost all of the modern curly font styles were based on and modified from the old cursive writing. After establishing the ROI, line detection techniques are used to determine the baselines, which are then utilized to compare the height and width of the letters. A line detection technique can help in the segmentation of the word into sub-regions through detection of the edges and the intersection points. This method extracts the outer features of texts. It segments words by considering that most letters have some common sizes, and it also compares the height and width of letters to determine the baselines. The size of a word is calculated by comparing the horizontal distance between the leftmost first point and the rightmost last point. To segment characters, it is necessary to determine the baselines of the word. Baselines are the ground line, underground line, top and middle lines, and the topmost line. After determining the baselines, the slant angle, the angle at which the word is slanted to the ground line, is calculated. The slant angle can help predict the position of the letters. Each letter is connected by a small link or curve that comes after touching the ground line, but is not necessary for every letter. For example, the letter O usually connects to the next right-side letter without touching the ground line. After the first segmentation, each letter is compared against a number of known attributes or global parameters of cursive writing style for further segmentation. Circular masks are used for edge detection, the sub-regions are cropped, and a binary number matrix further applied to recognize unique features.

It is extremely difficult to establish the location of baselines, especially when there are many loops surrounding the word, as shown in Figure 12.1. One popular edge detection method uses a combination of the tangent line and circle mask, which appears similar to a compass that can detect continuous loops and broken edges. At the intersection points, where one line is split into multiple paths, the tangents moving in that direction are also split. At any point, if two tangent lines meet, then they cancel each other out. The tangent that reaches one end of a branch uses a circle algorithm, such as polar circle, to locate the next nearby pixel within the circle's range. This works like a radar system. Then, a tangent line is drawn at the new location jump. This technique is very creative and powerful, but lacks the ability to detect all pixels. Wide loops can be easily found by comparing

Figure 12.1 Cursive style text.

the pixel positions, but this technique becomes complex and cumbersome when there are a lot of intertwined loops. Therefore, this study did not consider such complex loops.

After establishing the baselines, the intersection points are determined to create sub-regions. Once a slanting link line (the line that connects the letters) is found, the median value of the slant line is calculated to divide the letters into small regions. The slant line must touch the ground line; otherwise, it is not considered. In some instances, some letters do not touch the ground line. To solve this, the letters can be brought down to the line, which can be achieved by equally changing the x and y coordinates of all pixels around the rectangular regions and using transformation functions such as rotation and translation. Pixels are moved in a direction where they do not lose the original structure and are fitted right to the correct position on the line.

This study has seven parts. Section 12.1 provides the introduction. Section 12.2 includes a literature survey, providing insights on the techniques used by computer vision in transportation. It gives detailed information on the various techniques used for optical character recognition (OCR). A number of in-depth research works were selected due to the variety of techniques they proposed and the innovative ideas in these studies. The convolutional neural network (CNN) of deep learning is the best technique that can classify visual texts. Section 12.3 presents the proposed method that describes the line detection binary matrix and the masks used for segmentation and feature extraction. These are the two major phases in OCR: *segmentation*, which is the technique used to divide big words into letters and letters into patterns, and *feature extraction*, which is the process of comprehension or machine learning of the feature or the unique patterns of letters that can be used for definition. Section 12.3 discusses the results found, or those that could happen. Section 12.4 presents conclusion.

12.2　Literature Survey

12.2.1　Computer Vision

Computer vision is used in transportation to provide solutions to several key problems related to safety, law enforcement, and security. The use of computer vision has been proven to be very efficient in solving the many problems faced by transportation infrastructure authorities and those who avail of transportation services. Technology is a part of daily life, and there are a lot of high-technology software and devices that assist humans. For example, advanced driver assistance system (ADAS), safer autonomous navigation, and vehicles with autonomous navigation system can navigate and monitor the environment. However, the main issue is safety; therefore, a human driver is still required. ADAS is an advanced technology developed for the safety of drivers and everyone in view of the system scanner. Lane change assistance, adaptive cruise control, automatic parking, automatic night vision, driver monitoring, and collision avoidance are some advance features that use computer vision. The aim of all these is to assist drivers without compromising their safety [2].

12.2.1.1 Computer Vision Techniques for Safety and Driver Assistance

The use of computer vision for driver assistance involves assessing the surroundings of the vehicle and providing warning to avoid road accidents. However, every type of assistance, to some extent, is compromised due to the presence of a high amount of noise or problems. A lot of image preprocessing techniques are available, but every algorithm has limitations. If a vehicle is moving faster than a certain level, then this definitely can affect the performance of any driver assistance. Noise comes in many forms: natural noise, which is due to weather and pollution such as large sunlight reflection and illumination, fog and smoke, snow, and rain, and manmade noise, comprising various blur effects due to camera shaking or motion. Noise can be an unwanted object in an image, such as water (unwanted object) flooding the streets. It can be problematic if any unwanted object is covering the object that the computer wants to detect. Excess shadow also affects image processing.

12.2.1.1.1 Lane Departure Warning System
A video camera is used to detect lanes. It is mounted on the car, near the rear view mirror or on the dashboard. A camera is also used to cover the front view of the car. The system will immediately warn the driver if the car unintentionally gets close to a certain range of the lane marks. Light displays, vibration, and sounds are the warning signals used by the system. Different lane departure warning (LDW) systems have different warning thresholds related to speed and road curvature. LDW cameras provide an approximately 4,040-mm view with a 50° angle range in front of the car. An algorithm can detect broken lines, double lines, hatched lines, the particular entrance and exit lines, lines other than the lane mark, yellow lines

with different hue values, and Bott's dots. The system is programmed to detect lines in harsh weather conditions, but detecting lines with many variations due to water reflection, darkness, and other distractions can be problematic. The LDW system detects a line by dividing it into frames. This system comprises two modules: data acquisition and time to lane crossing (TLC) estimation. In the first module, image frames are used to estimate the lane boundary parameters and the orientation of the vehicle relative to the lane, and then the distance to TLC is calculated. TLC is the time at which the vehicle will cross the lane mark. This is determined by calculating the speed, trajectory, and kinematic data of the car, the model of the lane boundary [3]. It estimates the lane boundary and the orientation of the car relative to the lane. The lane detection algorithm uses pre-processing techniques such as denoising and morphological operations and image segmentation techniques such as line detection, edge detection, and ROI to obtain the interest points or edge points [3].

In the second module, TLC estimation is divided into two phases: lane detection and lane tracking. Lane detection comprises five parts, as follows:

- *Data (frame) acquisition*: In this process, the input video image is converted into frames.
- *Inverse perspective mapping*: In this phase, pixels under a 2D perspective view relative to a bird's view from 3D are remapped on a new plane.
- *Edge detection*: The algorithm uses a second derivative of the image to determine the zero crossing of the Laplacian operator in order to detect smoothed edges.
- *Line identification*: The algorithm identifies the correct form of line using steerable filters. It uses a threshold to binarize the high-intensity pixels from lower-intensity ones.
- *Line fitting*: The algorithm uses a Kalman filter to quantify the parameters of the parabolic model used to form curved edges.

Lane tracking involves estimating the kinematic information of a vehicle, which is sensed by sensors attached on the steering wheel and the rear wheel. The kinematic and vehicle model information are combined using a data fusion algorithm to calculate the TLC.

12.2.1.1.2   Detection of Pedestrians and Animals on the Street

To avoid accidents involving pedestrians, they can be detected at different challenging poses, wearing colorful clothes, from varying distances from the camera and occlusions can be determined. The device uses a motion sensor to predict pedestrians moving and crossing within the camera's vision. A method called optical flow to find the ROI (region of pedestrian) is utilized, and a clustering algorithm to classify the pedestrian's gait is employed. This divides the video into frames and analyzes the shape, size, and direction of motion of the object (pedestrian) in order to identify, relate, and classify them. Many pedestrian detection techniques are available, with the histogram of oriented gradients having been widely used for some time [4]. The algorithm was improved using a framework proposed by Felzenszwalb *et al.* [5]. This framework detects small parts of the target object and matches them with statistically learned deformable models. Furthermore, many algorithms and improvements, as well as research, have been developed and accomplished in the field of pedestrian detection [6].

12.2.1.1.3   Driver Monitoring

Most accidents occur due to the carelessness of the driver, including drowsiness, getting distracted, and looking at different directions while behind the wheel, among others. Systems use infrared sensors and cameras to track eye motion and direction to indicate the driver's attention. The system then scans all obstacles nearby, reacting when the driver does not appropriately react to them. The detection of drowsiness relies first on locating the eye and then detecting its state, whether open or closed. The most common approach is to use binary classifiers to identify and classify the state of the eye, while the shape model is used to locate the eye. The speeded up robust features (SURF) algorithm is combined with the binary support vector machine (SVM) to detect features. A near-infrared (NIR) camera is utilized for detection under shadow effects of night and when the driver is wearing sunglass. The system estimates four basic features, namely, compactness of points, eccentricity of eye points, Hu's seventh moment, and the ratio of the number of eye pixels in the top hat transform to the number of eye pixels in the bottom hat transform [7]. Once the eye state is determined, the drowsiness rate is calculated, which is the percentage of eye closure over time [7, 8].

12.2.1.1.4   ADAS-Adaptive Cruise Control

This adjusts the vehicle in traffic from a leading vehicle. It accelerates and de-accelerates automatically to maintain distance from the leading vehicle. The method measuring the distance involves millimeter wave radars, light detection and ranging (LIDAR), and stereo imaging, proposed by Saneyoshi [9].

12.2.1.1.5   ADAS Automatic Parking

This facilitates automatic acceleration, steering, and braking, among others, and estimates the relative space between the vehicle and surrounding obstacles. Automatic parking uses computer vision for pedestrian detection, vehicle detection, parking line detection, and free space detection [10].

12.2.1.1.6   Street Sign Recognition

The detection algorithms for street signs, such as traffic signs and paintings, are categorized into two types: shape-based and color-based. The color-based technique requires knowledge of discrete values of the colors to be detected. A widely popular pattern detection algorithm uses a multilayer perceptron data training and testing approach to detect and analyze the colored pixels of traffic and non-traffic signs [11]. The spatiotemporal attentional neural network is another sign detection algorithm [12].

The shape-based approach is dependent on basic point and line detection algorithms such as Hough transform. Many other algorithms have been introduced in this field, such as fast radial symmetric transform [13], Harris corner detector to detect corners in predefined spatial configurations [14], space vector machine to detect circular shapes in RGB (red, green, blue) color space [15]. The recognition of signs is categorized into two: template-based and classifier-based. Neural network, CNN, and deep learning are some examples of classifiers.

12.2.1.1.7   Prediction of Road Damage

Estimation of the polarization of light on a water surface caused by reflection is less accurate when compared to NIR detection, but NIR is rather costly. Computer vision scans the conditions of the road using thermal scanners to check the amount of water droplets present within the tiny holes and crevices on roads. Water penetrates deep within roads, and as more water ingress and enter the crystalline state, this causes roads to begin to crack. Water temperature changes from positive to negative, and *vice versa*, as the weather changes, and a change in temperature weakens the binding of the mixed materials used to construct the road. Asphalt is a popular material as it gives a smooth surface structure and makes laying the road much more effortless and inexpensive. However, asphalt roads are generally prone to potholes [16].

12.2.1.1.8   Prediction of Traffic Flow

Prediction of traffic flow is important and beneficial as it helps maintain safety and provides a warning to drivers about upcoming unexpected dangers. Traffic prediction utilizes spatiotemporal data, which refers to data at a specific space during a time period. Some examples of spatiotemporal data are historical regional traffic flows, transportation service demand, speed and travel time of vehicles, date, and holidays [17]. Main roads such as highways are prone to accidents, especially crossroads or the junction of multiple roads. Traffic flow can be forecast by determining the number of vehicles moving at a direction, their speed, and the travel time. Regression is generally used to calculate these data. Another way of predicting congestion of roads is to use continuous intervals of traffic speed to calculate the future traffic flow at a direction. Many algorithms have been developed to forecast the flow of traffic, which can be broadly categorized into two groups relative to time: short-term and long-term forecasting. Short-term forecasting predicts the flow of traffic at a direction for the next 5–30 min, while long-term forecasting predicts the traffic flow for over months or years ahead.

Short-term prediction mostly uses neural network, fuzzy model, and linear regression to classify traffic flows. Good prediction depends on good techniques for data collection and storage, but even the best of the best prediction algorithms can fail if the data are incorrect or insufficient. Linear regression is used to predict traffic flow, and most traffic flow detection technologies use induction loop and video processing. Short-term traffic flow prediction using improved data detection technology [which uses infrared (IR) cameras] follows a fundamental framework. In this framework, the data acquired *via* IR cameras are converted into data frames for data processing.

There are two types of frames: background data frames (abstract background data of the image) and thermal frames. Thermal frames are thresholded using a binarization technique, and the raw data collected are denoised (removal of noise). The points of interest (i.e., relevant data) and the background data (less important data) are separated, the object is detected (the point of interest), and a region filling algorithm is used to detect the boundary points and to fill areas with inefficient pixels. After pre-processing, the generated output is used to calculate traffic information, which is then combined with historical records. Subsequently, relevant data are filtered out and the short-term traffic flow prediction algorithm applied on the filtered data to accurately estimate the traffic flow information. If the obtained information is insufficient to predict traffic, then more input frames are processed until prediction is made.

Traffic data can be calculated using two methods: manual and automatic. The manual method involves more human intervention, and data are collected from busy streets using handheld sensors. In contrast, the automatic method uses induction coils that are laid on the ground. Induction coils have many limitations, including physical damage due to weather, cuts, etc. Weather is not an issue if IR cameras are used, but these cannot be utilized for long distances and for long-term forecasting. The fuzzy model, neural network, and linear regression methods use an improved data prediction technology. The fuzzy prediction system uses subtractive clustering to determine the number of rules. It uses six rules to estimate the flow of traffic, as follows: M (small traffic flow), N (little traffic flow), DV (medium traffic flow), LM (very small traffic), and LD (very big traffic flow). This method takes as input clusters of data points. Each cluster has a center point based on the density of all data points. Prediction using the simplest feed forward neural network (FNN) model involves an input layer, hidden layers, and an output layer. This algorithm uses regression and correlation to calculate the correlation between the output and the target (the input). Forecasting using linear regression uses a heuristic approach to forecast traffic flow. Root mean square error is used to determine the accuracy of the results.

Traffic flow can be distinguished into network-based and region-based classification. Network-based techniques use a loop detector at both ends of roads to detect traffic, whereas region-based classification techniques divide wide areas into small regions and calculate the inflow and outflow traffic of vehicles in that region. Travel demand prediction can help predict the traffic flow in a region. The travel demand of passengers for transportation services such as the metro, bus, train, and plane at particular time intervals is also a factor that determines traffic flow, for example during the morning rush hour when there is more demand for taxies and the metro in the rush to get to the workplace.

In traditional traffic learning methods, the hidden Markov model (HMM) is a stochastic classification model for predicting traffic flow in different regions. The classification of traffic is difficult, as people often change their mode of transport and different transportation modes use different paths; for example, if a person walks, then the path can be narrow. Vehicles such as buses need a broader area compared to a taxi. Moreover, buses have different routes and bus stop arrival times, while taxis can use any direction (most probably the shortest route) to reach a destination. The hidden Markov chain rule is also used for probability estimation of the next location relative to the previous one. It is a greedy method that selects the highest probable route as the next route.

Conditional random field and decision trees are other traditional methods. Spatiotemporal data are obtained, after which they are pre-processed. One of the main techniques used is map matching, which converts longitude/latitude coordinates into road networks.

12.2.1.1.9   Automated Tolling

Automated road tolling is a road use fee collection system. Each vehicle has an RFID (radiofrequency identification) tag, which is a unique identification number assigned by the traffic governing authority. An RFID tag or transponder consists of a chip, which stores the unique ID and other information, and an antenna. Computer vision in automated road tolling uses video frames to classify vehicles. The system scans the vehicle number plate in conjunction with the RFID [18].

There are many other applications of computer vision in transportation. This project mainly focuses on OCR, which is used to recognize texts.

12.2.1.2   Types of Optical Character Recognition Systems

The OCR system is divided into two types based on the input: handwriting recognition and printed character recognition. Handwriting recognition requires much more intelligence compared to printed character recognition because handwritten characters have irregular dimensions and sizes [19]. Handwritten character recognition is subdivided into two categories, i.e., on-line and off-line systems. The former is executed in real time, while a person is writing. Such system is less complex as it can observe time-based information such as speed, velocity, number of strokes, and direction. On the other hand, the off-line system works on static data such as a bitmap; hence, comparatively, it is much more difficult to recognize [20].

12.2.1.3   Phases of Optical Character Recognition

Before an image is accurately recognized in the final stage, a lot of processes are performed beforehand, which are outlined as follows:

1) *Image acquisition*: This is the first phase in OCR, the aim of which is to transform an optical image (real-world data) captured using hardware into an array of numerical data for the purpose of image processing and manipulation. In this stage, analog images are converted into digital images [21]. Images are digitized, as digital images allow a wide range of algorithms to be performed and can avoid noise and distortions [22–24].

2. *Pre-processing*: This is the second stage that involves assessment and processing of the input image in order to improve its quality. The input image comes with a lot of noise and distortions, it can be skewed, and its structure can be rough or broken. Some of the processes executed during this stage are listed below:

- Skewness removal
- Denoising
- Normalization
- Compression
- Morphological operations

Skewness removal is performed to transform or change the position of the pixels in an image. Roughly or hastily done handwriting can be skewed and cursive handwriting is naturally slanted, making it difficult to detect the written output. Hence, these are transformed to a possible extent, in which each text together appears to form a horizontal line.

Denoising is the process of reducing the noise present in images. Filtering is used to execute many tasks such as denoising, resampling, and interpolation. Denoising is mainly divided into two parts: spatial domain and transform domain. In the spatial domain, the input image is processed and then the output image matrix is created. In the transform domain, the rate at which the neighboring pixel values are changing in the spatial domain is determined. Transformation is the process of converting signals in the time–space domain into the frequency domain.

Spatial domain filters are further subdivided into linear and nonlinear types. The selection of a filter depends on the quality of the image and the task to be performed. Nonlinear filters do not have any inbuilt function to identify the nature of noise and therefore are mainly used to filter digital images. These filters also make the edges hidden and the image blurry after processing. Linear filters, on the other hand, generate outputs that are a linear combination of the neighboring input pixels. This can be done with convolution, which is not applicable for nonlinear filters [24]. An example of a linear filter is median filter, while mean filter and weighted mean filter are examples of nonlinear filters.

The transform domain is further subdivided into non-data-adaptive and data-adaptive transformation. Non-data-adaptive transformation uses the same set of parameters to reduce dimensions regardless of the underlying data. This type of transformation is further subdivided into a spatial frequency domain and a wavelet domain. An earlier work conducted by Agarwal *et al.* on this topic used discrete Fourier transform, which applies the idea that any time sequence is the superposition of sinusoidal waves. It is used to project time series in the frequency domain by decomposing series into sinusoidal waves, and it uses the dominant waves for reconstructing the image and for omitting other insignificant waves. There are differences between Fourier transform and wavelet transform, as follows: 1) In Fourier transform, basic functions supported with infinity values are assumed to be periodic, and Fourier transform breaks the rules of periodicity multiple times. However, this does not apply in wavelet transform. 2) Spatial information is completely lost in Fourier transform, while it is retained on all levels in wavelet transform. 3) Fourier transform uses only frequency information, whereas the filters in wavelet transform can apply adaptive filter schemes and use *a priori* shape information [25–27]. The wavelet domain is further subdivided into linear and nonlinear filtering.

A normalization technique is applied to reduce the number of data used in character classification. The aim is to reduce the size of the image without effecting or destroying the real meaning or essential attribute of the characters. Normalization resizes the image into a certain size. Large normalization sizes increase the training time of the image, while a too low normalization size can destroy the essence of the image.

Compression is carried out by the encoder, producing a compressed image as the output. This is done by mathematically transforming an image, and it helps in reducing the storage space without losing any characteristic of the image. Space domain techniques such as thinning and threshold are mainly used for compression. Binarization is also a compression process of transforming an image in grayscale from the (0–255) spectrum to the (0–1) spectrum.

Morphological operations are performed to remove imperfections on the structure of the image. It is especially used in binary images due to the presence of a lot of blocks and broken edges. This is performed by combining two basic processes: dilation and erosion. Dilation adds pixels onto the boundaries, whereas erosion removes pixels from the boundaries. Many large noises are reduced by combining both, which is called an opening operation.

3) *Segmentation*: This is the third phase in OCR, which is the process of subdividing the image into constituent parts until the problem is resolved. In OCR, segmentation first finds the required object (text) in an image, which is then further subdivided, e.g., from paragraphs to lines, lines to words, words to letters, and letters to patterns, until the parts are isolated and ready for recognition. Segmentation techniques can be implicit or explicit.

In explicit segmentation, the binary word image is scanned from top to bottom using a vertical histogram projection profile technique, and then the cut points of the characters are determined. There is a minimum constant distance between each character cut point. In implicit segmentation, words are segmented into letters and then recognized using heuristic rules. If the recognition process fails, then using a feedback method, that letter or group of letters is again segmented and classified; that is, word segmentation and character recognition take place simultaneously. This is also a limitation of implicit segmentation, in which the segmentation process is completely dependent on the recognition process and complete segmentation is acquired only along with the recognition process of features of the text. This issue can be handled using a sequence of improved heuristic rules to determine the segmentation points [28].

A lot of image segmentation techniques are used for text segmentation. To segment large paragraphs into sentences, then to words, and then to letters, similar segmentation techniques are used, differing only in terms of the real purpose or the algorithm used. Image segmentation techniques are used in OCR segmentation, where text is the object of the image of interest. There are many other different techniques that use basic image segmentation methods.

Image segmentation is an image processing method that separates or partitions an image into multiple fragments or objects. Text is an entity or a form of an image object. Broadly, image segmentation techniques can be categorized as follows:

- Approach-based segmentation
- Technique-based segmentation

Approach-based segmentation is used when an image is completely unknown. It processes every pixel using a general approach without particularly focusing on any structure or feature. This method is further divided into two types: region-based approach (detects similarity) and boundary-based approach (detects dissimilarity).

Region-based segmentation is a general approach to segmentation. This approach segments every pixel in the image into groups, aiming to find pixels that are similar. On the other hand, boundary-based segmentation aims to find two edges, two lines, or two points that are dissimilar to each other; that is, it selects the outermost pixels. Edge detection and line detection are boundary-based approaches.

Technique-based segmentation is not commonly used to detect unknown images. Algorithms are developed particularly depending on the type of image and focus on a particular feature or structure of the image. Technique-based segmentation is further divided into three broader categories: structural segmentation, stochastic segmentation, and hybrid technique.

Structural segmentation techniques require structural information of the image such as pixel density, distribution, and histogram. Stochastic segmentation techniques require discrete pixel values of the image rather than structural information. This technique is efficient and gives accurate segmentation of objects, especially when the structure of a portion of the image is highly uncertain. The k-means algorithm and ANN using k-means employ this technique to segment objects.

Some of the most commonly used image segmentation techniques in OCR are as follows:

- Threshold segmentation
- Edge detection or line detection
- Simple clustering
- Holistic approach
- Histogram projection

Threshold segmentation is considered as one of the simplest and efficient methods of segmentation. It converts an image into a binary image (black and white). In this process, it is assumed that the object pixels have high pixel intensity compared to the background pixels. This technique works best when there is a high contrast between the required object pixels and the unwanted background pixels of an image. Recently, a method has been developed for CT images, which uses radiographs instead of reconstructed images [29, 30].

Edge detection is the process of detecting the edges or points where the rate of change intensity is rapid. It also involves convolving a 2D image into a set of points or edges. Hough transform and convolution-based techniques for detecting lines are some of the methods used for segmentation. The edges found using edge detection are always disconnected, but requires a closed path to segment an object from the image. Edges are the spatial taxa or boundaries between objects [31, 32].

Each stage of OCR is not completely separate or unique from each other. Implicit segmentation is a general term for a segmentation method that uses an algorithm from the segmentation process to the recognition stage. It is executed in cycle multiple times. K-means clustering can be used for both explicit and implicit segmentation. The k-means algorithm divides each close point into one cluster and likewise creates many clusters. It randomly initializes several k-mean values to each cluster and assigns non-clusters or new points to the group of the nearest k-means. This is an example of explicit segmentation. However, if the same technique is used within the feature extraction and classification phases of OCR for the segmentation of patterns based on some heuristic rules of character, then it is called implicit segmentation. Heuristic rules can be based on the aspect ratio, curve, slope, and skewness of predefined letters, among others.

Holistic segmentation is an approach that employs a word or part of a word from a string as a unit. When the approach is focused on words rather letters, then the word is a unit. Since it is not further segmented, this unit is segmentation-free. Detection of white spaces between successive characters can be used to dissect block letters or machine-typed fonts. Pitch is represented as the number of characters per unit, which gives a global basis that each segmentation point is equally spaced from each other at a distance corresponding to the pitch.

Vertical projection, also called histogram projection, is a technique that counts the number of running black pixels in each column in order to detect a line. White spaces are counted to detect separation between letters.

4) *Feature extraction*: This is the fourth phase, in which information about the body parts (patterns) of letters is extracted. This is where the character is recognized by comparing its

features with some predefined features stored in a library. The curves, loops, and moments of a letter are compared in order to recognize it. Some of the feature extraction methods are as follows:

- Zoning
- Intersections
- Projections
- Geometrical representation
- Moments

Zoning is a feature extraction technique that divides a character into overlapping and non-overlapping zones. The character is divided into a matrix, and the density and the formation of points are examined to recognize characters.

Intersection is the point where multiple line segments cross each other, i.e., the meeting point of multiple lines. Continuous loops have intersection points that create a cross shape. These intersection points are used to identify the number of loops, branches of characters, etc.

Projection is used to create a 1D signal from a 2D character. Projecting a part of a character onto a curve or a line provides an idea about the identity of the character.

In geometrical representation, the features of a character are compared to geometrical shapes and curves. This technique identifies the small patterns or shapes of characters.

Moments are defined with respect to a fixed reference point, which is calculated using the distance of the neighboring points from the fixed reference point. The mean, variance skewness, and kurtosis are high-order moments. Mean is the crude moment, while variance is the central moment. Researchers suggested that characters can be recognized by observing the distance of the various pixels from the centroid of the character. Standardized moments that have an asymmetric distribution of pixels indicate skewness. The fourth central moment is the product of kurtosis and standard deviation. Kurtosis is the measure of the tailedness of the distribution of pixels. There are Legendre moments and Zernike moments.

This paper described the development of an OCR system in Java. For character recognition, the study used a character model and compared it with a pre-generated database of generic characters. The character model was basically a collection of many related or similar attributes that represent a character. The attributes were divided into parts and were compared and studied. The two major attributes used were gap vector and sector vector. The gap vector determined the gaps between line segments in a letter. A gap was defined as the breakage of pixels between four edges: top, right, bottom, and left. The sector vector had two steps: sector parsing and slope field parsing. This algorithm divided a letter into sectors. Sector parsing was used to perform a vertical line test, where one line is one segment. On the other hand, slope field parsing was used to calculate the slope of the line segments.

5) *Classification*: This is the fifth phase where unknown letters are classified into clusters due to the similarities found in their features. Each cluster is further segmented and the features extracted, which, again, are clustered into groups until the letter is identified. This is the phase where actual recognition takes place. There are two main classification techniques: classical and structural. Template matching, statistical techniques and structural techniques are classical techniques. Neural network, k-nearest neighbor, Bayesian statistics, fuzzy logic, and evolutionary computing are some of the soft computing techniques. Outlined below are some of the classification techniques.

- Kernel method
- Artificial neural network
- HMM approach and neural network
- K-nearest neighbor
- Bayesian model
- Fuzzy logic
- Evolutionary computing
- Template matching

Support vector machine (SVM), kernel principal component analysis (KPCA), and kernel Fisher discriminant analysis (KFDA) are three of the most widely used kernel methods. SVM is a supervised learning model used for classification and regression analysis. The SVM training algorithm builds a model and classifies all the new training examples into two major groups, behaving like a non-probabilistic binary linear classifier. This algorithm maximizes the gap between two categories and maps the training examples in space.

ANN is a network of neurons that works similar to a human brain. It completes a given task by training itself and gathering information from databases. There are many types of neural networks for training data, such as FNN, CNN, and radial basis function (RBF).

HMM is used along with neural network. It is a doubly stochastic process that contains a hidden stochastic process within it. These processes are not observable, but can be observed using another stochastic process that produces a sequence of observations [33–36]. The hidden process has many transition states with probabilities. The observed processes generate outputs and observations that are caused by different states according to some probability density function [37, 38].

K-nearest neighbor is a type of supervised learning method used for classification and regression. The algorithm calculates the distance between the training and the test data and finds the k number of neighboring points. All neighbors have a category, which will assign the training data into the category that matched the maximum number of neighbors.

The Bayesian model is based on probability distribution. It is used to determine the relationship between multiple events or variables and for several predictions of any anomaly. Among some of its other uses are to make a diagnosis, to obtain automated insight, and, under uncertainty, to predict the probability of occurrence of an event. The Bayesian network is made up of nodes and arcs. The nodes represent variables, while arcs indicate the casual relationship between them.

Fuzzy logic is a type of AI that assigns an output value by taking as input incomplete, distorted, and inaccurate data. It makes a decision similar to the human brain by considering all the possible intermediate problems and comparing all possible solutions in a binary format of "YES" or "NO." It consists of four main parts, as given below:

- Fuzzification module: This splits the input data into fuzzy sets, such as large positive, medium positive, large negative, medium negative, and small.
- Knowledge base: This contains the expert knowledge in the format of "IF" conditions.
- Inference rules: This is used to make fuzzy inference or conclusion on the decision of the output using knowledge base.
- Defuzzification module: This transforms the fuzzy value set generated using inference rules into crisp output values.

The evolutionary computing OCR algorithm is inspired by biological evolution. This algorithm initially finds some sets of candidate solutions for a set of input values and iteratively updates a new generation until the best solution is found. Each new solution is found by stochastically removing the less desired attributes.

Template matching is a high-level machine learning technique and also the most favored due to its simplicity. The idea is to match the parts of the input image with predefined templates, which helps in locating the input image among many other images regardless of variations such as brightness, orientation, and size.

6) *Post-processing*: This is the final stage of OCR, where the identified letters are compared with each other and examined using a set of rules to obtain the real meaning of the text. In this stage, correction of errors is performed, with the error calculated as the difference between the predicted value and the real value. The cost of the system is deducted to measure its performance. Good performance is based on the accuracy of the estimation and the cost, and performance is dependent on the time complexity of the algorithm: as the time complexity of the algorithm increases, the cost also increases and the performance level falls. The dictionary-based, lexicon-based, multi-knowledge approaches are some of the techniques used in the post-processing stage. Some letters are poorly recognized due to the use of a poor classification algorithm or the poor quality of the image. It is assumed that most words have some logical meaning; hence, a word is compared to words in the dictionary and lexicon in order to correctly identify it. The multi-knowledge approach combines the knowledge obtained through classification with lexicons to recognize meaningful words.

12.2.1.4   *Threshold Segmentation*

The thresholding method was developed by Nobuyuki Otsu. Global thresholding uses a constant threshold value, but the best thresholding technique uses a dynamic threshold value, which changes for different portions of the image as per the nature of the image for the best output. The image is converted into a histogram. The peaks and valleys in the histogram show the high and low intensity levels of the pixels. If a histogram image has two peaks, one for object and another for the background (bimodal-shaped histogram), then the threshold value is set in the middle of the two peaks. The threshold point is determined by finding the point at which two neighboring pixels (left and right) have maximum variance. Otsu's method works well with a bimodal-shaped histogram, but performs badly when the image has heavy noise, when the size of the required object is small, when there are light reflection variations on the colors of the image, and when there are large intra- and inter-class variations [39].

Variable thresholding, also known as adaptive thresholding, uses different threshold values for different regions. When an image has many light reflection variations and high inter- and intra-class variations, the image is then divided into parts and a threshold value for each part is calculated. The threshold point is determined by calculating the mean value of the neighboring areas or the weighted sum of neighboring values. A histogram image has many peaks and valleys, Some factors listed below should be considered while using histograms are:

- Separation between peaks
- High noise content in image
- When the relative size of the object is very small
- Reflection and luminance of light in some portions

Otsu's method is used to segment gray-level images. Hue, saturation, and value space (HSV) segmentation is used for images with colored channel distribution. HSV space segmentation uses three different channels, namely, hue, saturation, and value. Firstly, the required object is determined from the input image using an appropriate technique to find the ROI. Then, the pixel color component values (i.e., hue, saturation, and value) are calculated. In the next step, using graphical user interface-based taskbar, the color values are adjusted. The pixels are isolated from the background pixels for further processing (feature extraction).

12.2.1.5 Edge Detection Operator

The edge of a small region is defined as the points where there is a rapid rate of change in pixel intensity. Edge detection includes detecting a curve or a set of points and the corner points. This is done by finding the derivative of a continuous function, which is the rate of change in the function. The local extrema of the first derivative of function of any curve indicates the edge. The location of the peaks gives the location of the edge, while the height of the peaks indicates the strength of the edge. Derivatives are implemented using finite difference approximation or using convolution kernels or masks. The second derivative is also utilized to detect the edge, while zero crossing of the second derivative of the function (edge) denotes the location of the edge. The first derivative of the image gives the location and direction of the edge, while the second derivation gives only the edge's location.

The two basic operators used for edge detection are gradient operator and Laplacian operator, discussed in the following sections.

1) Gradient operator

Basic edge detection of texts in a 2D image is performed using the gradient operator, which is represented as a del operator (∇I). In calculating the gradient edge, the partial derivative is used to determine the edge or the direction of the most rapid rate of change of pixel intensity along both dimensions. The derivatives of pixel intensity with respect to the x and y coordinate values of the pixel are calculated to obtain the gradient magnitude and gradient orientation. Magnitude is the absolute value of the detected edge. It is the square root of the sum of squares of two partial derivatives, while orientation is the slope of the tangent line to the point. The first derivative is used to detect the presence of an edge, while the second derivative helps determine in which region the pixel lies (two regions are separated by an edge).

$$h(x, y) \simeq ((\Delta x)^2 + (\Delta y)^2)^{\frac{1}{2}}$$

$$\theta(x, y) \simeq \tan^{-1}(\frac{\Delta y}{\Delta x})$$

where $h(x,y)$ is the function magnitude and $\vartheta(x,y)$ is the angle of orientation.

Finite difference or convolution mask can be used to find Δx and Δy.

Gradient operator is further divided into three types, as follows:

- Roberts operator
- Prewitt operator
- Sobel operator

The Roberts operator computes the sum of squares of the difference of the diagonally adjacent pixels using discrete approximations and then finds the gradient approximations using 2×2 kernel masks. The biggest disadvantage of this method that it is extremely sensitive to noise and gives bad results.

$$R_x = \begin{vmatrix} 1 & 0 \\ 0 & -1 \end{vmatrix} \quad R_y = \begin{vmatrix} 0 & 1 \\ -1 & 0 \end{vmatrix}$$

where R_x and R_y are the masks along two dimensions.

The Prewitt operator is considered as the best operator for determining the orientation. However, it has limitations in that the magnitude of coefficient is fixed and the mask does not preserve the diagonal direction points.

$$P_x = \begin{vmatrix} -1 & 0 & 1 \\ -1 & 0 & 1 \\ -1 & 0 & 1 \end{vmatrix} \quad P_y = \begin{vmatrix} 1 & 1 & 1 \\ 0 & 0 & 0 \\ -1 & -1 & -1 \end{vmatrix}$$

The Sobel operator is the most extensively used. It can be implemented using a kernel size of either 3×3 or 5×5.

$$S_x = \begin{vmatrix} -1 & 0 & 1 \\ -2 & 0 & 2 \\ -1 & 0 & 1 \end{vmatrix} \quad S_x = \begin{vmatrix} -1 & 2 & 1 \\ 0 & 0 & 0 \\ -1 & -2 & 1 \end{vmatrix}$$

or

$$S_x = \begin{vmatrix} -1 & -2 & 0 & 2 & 1 \\ -2 & -2 & 0 & 3 & 2 \\ -3 & -5 & 0 & 5 & 3 \\ -2 & -3 & 0 & 3 & 2 \\ -1 & -2 & 0 & 2 & 1 \end{vmatrix}$$

$$S_y = \begin{vmatrix} 1 & 2 & 3 & 2 & 1 \\ 2 & 3 & 5 & 3 & 2 \\ 0 & 0 & 0 & 0 & 0 \\ -2 & -3 & -5 & -3 & -2 \\ -1 & -2 & -3 & -2 & -1 \end{vmatrix}$$

The biggest disadvantage of the Sobel operator is that it responds to steps having a width of either 2 or 3 pixels; hence, to reduce the computational complexity in further image processing, post-processing operations such as thinning and thresholding are performed. Another limitation is that it does not always preserve the diagonal direction points.

As the kernel size of the gradient operator increases, the localization of the edge pixels becomes poor due to the influence of neighboring pixels. Bigger masks are less noise-sensitive because a kernel performs a smoothing operation to diminish noise, which makes edge detection more efficient.

2) Laplacian operator

The Laplacian operator is represented by a del square operator. It calculates the second derivative of every edge point in the image, which produces two values: negative and positive. It creates an imaginary straight line that joins the extreme positive and negative values and, in the middle, crosses the zero value of the horizontal axis. In the line that passes through the horizontal axis, this point of crossing is called zero crossing. It is extremely useful to find the midpoint of a thick edge. Laplacian is the sum of two second derivatives. It does not estimate the direction of the edge. The two derivatives found using finite difference approximations are:

$$\frac{d^2I}{dx^2} \approx \frac{1}{\in^2}(I_{i-1,j}) - 2I_{i,j} + I_{i+1,j})$$

$$\frac{d^2I}{dy^2} \approx \frac{1}{\in^2}(I_{i,j-1}) - 2I_{i,j} + I_{i,j+1})$$

The convolution masks to find the derivatives are:

$$\nabla^2 \approx \frac{1}{\epsilon^2} \cdot \begin{vmatrix} 0 & 1 & 0 \\ 1 & -4 & 1 \\ 0 & 1 & 0 \end{vmatrix} \; or \; \frac{1}{\epsilon^2} \cdot \begin{vmatrix} 1 & 4 & 1 \\ 4 & -20 & 4 \\ 1 & 4 & 1 \end{vmatrix}$$

The gradient operator performs a nonlinear operation and requires two convolution masks, which are convolved to produce the output, whereas Laplacian uses only one convolution mask.

The Marr–Hildreth operator or Laplacian of Gaussian (log) is a Gaussian-based operator that uses a Laplacian operator to detect the edge.

$$Gaussian - G(x, y) = \frac{1}{\sqrt{2\pi\sigma^2}} \exp\left(\frac{x^2 + y^2}{2\sigma^2} \right)$$

$$(log) \rightarrow \frac{d^2}{dx^2} G(x, y) + \frac{d^2}{dy^2} G(x, y)$$

The advantages of using a combination of Gaussian kernel and Laplacian are: it diminishes noise and performs good edge detection. The Laplacian operator alone is highly susceptible to noise.

3) Canny edge detector

The Canny edge detector uses the combined properties of the gradient operator and the Laplacian operator. Its main objective is to minimize the error rate, which is the difference between the total number of edges and the number of edges found. A second aim is to localize the edge points properly, which indicates that the difference between the distance of the pixel found at a direction and the actual distance should be minimum. A third aim is to ensure that each edge gets only a single response.

The Canny edge detector first smoothens the input image with a 2D Gaussian filter using a convolution operator, $\rightarrow n\sigma * \sigma * I$. Then, it computes the image gradient function using the Sobel operator, $\rightarrow \nabla n_\sigma * I$, and finds the magnitude of the edge pixels (gradient maxima), $||\nabla n_\sigma * I||$.

It then determines the direction of the edge: $\hat{c} = \dfrac{\nabla n_\sigma * I}{||\nabla n_\sigma * I||}$.

The Canny operator uses 1D Laplacian along the direction of the edge: $\dfrac{d^2(n_{\sigma*}I)}{d\hat{c}^2}$.

Zero crossing in Laplacian is used to detect the location of the edge: $\rightarrow |\nabla n_{\sigma} * I|$.

The end or starting point of the edge is determined by its corner points. Corner detection in edge detection is the process of determining the points where two edges meet or those where there are local maxima of small curvature or a region of edge. Broadly, corner detection techniques fall into three categories.

- Intensity-based methods: These techniques identify corners by comparing the rate of change in the intensity of the points. They recognize corners as points that confer a large change in intensity along all dimensions. There is no change in intensity on uniform regions, and there is low change in the adjoining pixels of edges.
- Contour-based methods: These techniques use an edge detector method to obtain the points of planar curves and then analyze the properties of the curves (edges) to detect corners. Properties such as closed or open contours are extracted, and the corner is determined as the point with large local maxima of curvature.
- Model-based methods: These techniques detect corners by fitting (matching) a pattern (template) to predefined models (template). Deviations between them are calculated using various techniques, and if any one template is matched, then it is considered as the corner.

Moravec's corner detection algorithm is one of the earliest techniques developed. He defined corner as the point with low self-similarity. One of the limitations of this method is that it is not isotropic. If an edge is present, but not in the direction of the neighbors, then the sum of the squared differences will be large and a false interest point will be given. A corner point is an interest point. The Harris and Stephens intensity-based corner detector is an improved version of Moravec's algorithm, which is also very popular.

Harris' corner detector recognizes points by looking through a small window. It is shifted in all directions to determine the regions that give a large change in intensity. Harris improved Moravec's algorithm by using a differentiation of the Moravec corner score with respect to the change in direction. The algorithm first converts the image into a grayscale level, and then it uses patches (small window) and calculates the weighted sum of the squared differences or the change in intensity for the shift, as given below:

$$E(u,v) = \sum_{x,y} (\text{weighted value of window} * (shifted\ intensity - intensity)^2$$

Weighted values: $\rightarrow \Sigma_{xy}\ W(x, y)$
Shifted intensity: $\rightarrow I(x + a, y + b)$
Intensity: $\rightarrow I(x,y)$
Taylor expansion is used to approximate $E(u,v)$.

$$E(u,v) \cong [u,v]\ C \begin{bmatrix} u \\ v \end{bmatrix} = \text{constant}$$

where $C = \Sigma_{xy} W(x,y). \begin{bmatrix} I^2 x & I_x I_y \\ I_x I_y & I^2 y \end{bmatrix}$

Harris uses a Gaussian window to obtain the autocorrelation matrix C. The edge and corner points form the gradient vectors or long linear clusters with intensities I_x and I_y, while the flat region will form a compact cluster that is close to the origin in the coordinate system. I_x and I_y are two intensity parameters that are quantified, and each region is classified by fitting an ellipse *via* a scatter matrix.

Eigenvalues are used to determine the two dominant directions of changes.

λ_1, λ_2 are eigenvalues, the major and minor axis of an ellipse. Eigenvalues are also known as principal component analysis. The largest vector gives the direction of the highest data distribution. These gradient vectors are sets of d_x, d_y points that have a center of mass at (0,0).

Harris and Stephen also proposed an alternate method that is less complex, which is also called the Kanade–Tomasi corner detector.

$R = \det M - k(\text{trace } M)^2$, where $\det M = \lambda_1, \lambda_2$
Trace $M = \lambda_1 + \lambda_2$ and k are constant between 0.04 and 0.15.
If λ_1, λ_2 is large $\rightarrow$ it is a corner point.
If $\lambda_1 \gg \lambda_2$ and vice versa $\rightarrow$ it is an edge.
If λ_1, λ_2 are small $\rightarrow$ is a flat region.

Optimal values to indicate corners are determined, while non-maximum points (other than corners) are suppressed.

Two partial derivatives of Harris' corner detector cannot completely describe local grayscale variations. However, they indicate L-type corners well. A selection of non-maximum suppression points decreases the accuracy of corner detection.

12.2.1.6   Use Cases of OCR

1) *Banking*: Checks are scanned to obtain account information, and the signature is also scanned for authentication. Mortgage-related documents are scanned, and payslips and other disposable income information are also scanned, taken account of, and stored in a database.

2) *Insurance*: Insurance claims are handled using OCR.

3) *Legal documents*: Legal documents such as affidavits, certificates, Aadhaar, are verified through OCR.

4) *Healthcare*: Skin diseases and rashes are diagnosed using OCR, and medicines are checked for authentication and expiry date. Large amounts of forms, such as patient data, insurance, and healthcare forms, are digitized through OCR. Every patient's data are stored in a database, which can be accessed as and when needed, which makes storing and accessing information very efficient and secure.

5) *Asset protection and management*: OCR is used in business to protect and manage assets. Assets can be employees or things. The IDs of workers on site and the transport of goods to their destination, for example, will all be scanned, digitized, and kept as records.

6) *Transportation*: Travel tickets and metro travel cards are scanned using OCR. OCR is widely used for automated vehicle nameplate recognition to retrieve information about the owner and the vehicle.

7) *Retail shops*: Items bought are verified using OCR.

8) *Tourism*: Check-in to a website or an app or places visited can be done by scanning passports.

9) *Communication*: Storytelling apps use OCR to scan images and read out sentences, which is especially useful for those who are physically impaired.

10) *Recommender system*: Google lens uses OCR to scan, copy, and paste texts. It gives recommendations of similar documents found on the Internet. Scanning of images from a paused video can also be very easy.

11) *Breaking CAPTCHA*: CAPTCHA stands for completely automated public Turing test, which is used to tell computers and humans apart. Almost all websites use CAPTCHA in their registration or login form. There are many CAPTCHA varieties, but the text-based one is considered as the most efficient. Hackers use OCR to digitize the image and break the CAPTCHA.

12) *Handwriting recognition*: Intelligent writing such as cursive is ambiguous in nature and requires extra effort and calculation for recognition, as well as many other types of handwriting.

13) *Optical music recognition*: Large amounts of musical notations are digitized so that computers can understand them.

14) *Digital libraries*: Students or teachers can issue books from the library and scan them, with the user records stored. A lot of documents can be scanned through OCR.

15) *Invoice imaging*: This is widely used in business to keep track of financial records. Large amounts of payment slips are also scanned.

12.2.1.7   List of Research Papers

1) Title: *A Comparative Study of Persian/Arabic Handwritten Character Recognition*
Authors: Alireza Alaei, Umapada Pal, and P. Nagabhushan
This is a comparative study on Persian handwritten character recognition using feature sets. The feature sets were based on gradient; shadow features (which observe the projection of black characters at a particular direction); directional chain code (which gives information regarding the direction of contour points on the character); undersampled bitmap (a feature that determines the total number of non-overlapping blocks of pixels with the same size, basically identifying colored pixels); intersection/junction endpoints (the image is normalized and then thinned before finding the intersection points, the intersections being the pixel points where there are more than two neighboring pixels and the endpoints the pixel points that have one neighboring pixel); and line fitting information (the image

is normalized and then thinned, calculating the slope of the line using the least minimum square method of line fitting). For classification, the study used *k*-nearest neighbor (3-NN and 5-NN), nearest neighbor, and SVM. The best correct recognition percentage was 96.91%.

2) Title: *Research Report on Bangla OCR Training and Testing Methods*
Author: Md. Abul Hasnat
The central idea was to separate the HMM models for each character. The study used HTK (hidden Markov model toolkit) for data preparation, training, and recognition. The characters were divided into frames and the discrete cosine transform function used on each pixel on the frames. These frames were used as input to the HMMs. Character models were built for recognition, and these models were input into HTK for character recognition, which used the Viterbi algorithm. The results of the experiment showed significant performance over models based on neural networks.

3) Title: *A multi-Evidence, Multi-Engine OCR System*
Authors: I. Zavorin and E. Borovikov
Every OCR system has strengths and weaknesses, and different OCR engines generate different outputs with varied accuracy rates on the same document. Multi-engine OCR used the output streams generated by different engines and combined them. The idea of this project was to combine the multiple output streams produced with all the pieces of evidence extracted from different engines for recognition. The multi-evidence, multi-engine OCR (MEMOE) system took the original document images, output stream, and some input configuration parameters as the input. The types of evidence used in the project are as follows:

Character confusion matrices: These recorded information about characters.

- Language models: Bigram statistics for character-level recognition and dictionary for word level.
- Assuming that characters are deformable shapes, the idea of confusion matrices to transform one skeleton character to another was used.
- Co-location: For word correction, other words in the document were used as the source.
- OCR confidence indicators were used to determine unrecognized character markers in the output stream.

4) Title: *A Multi-Stage Approach to Arabic Document Analysis*
Authors: E. Borovikov and I. Zavorin
The multi-filter document processing framework was used to analyze electronic documents. This project presented a multistage solution to multi-engine Arabic OCR and Arabic handwriting recognition. It used an image cleanup system called ImageRefiner.

5) Title: *A Novel SIFE-Based Codebook Generation for Handwritten Tamil Character Recognition*
Authors: A. Subashini and N.D. Kodikara
In the pre-processing stage, morphological operations were performed to remove noise. For segmentation, histogram profile and connected component analysis were used. Features were extracted using the scale-invariant transformation method, and the k-means clustering algorithm was used to create a code book for each character, centroid condition and two feature conditions of the nearest neighbor. For classification, it used a bag of key points to count the number of patches, also using the k-means clustering algorithm. The Linde–Buzo–Gray (LBG) algorithm was utilized to create an initial codebook. The experiment used 6,000 training and 2,000 test images of 20 characters, which achieved an accuracy of 87%. However, a limitation is that it showed problems in recognizing similar characters with abnormal shapes.

6) Title: *Handwritten Tamil Character Recognition Using Artificial Neural Networks*
Authors: P. Banumathi and G.M. Nasira
In the pre-processing stage, the binarization technique was applied to threshold white background pixels from the foreground pixels. High peaks were made of background pixels, while lower peaks were made of foreground pixels. The study used a skew detection algorithm, with detection ranges from −15° to +15°. The scanned image was segmented into multiple paragraphs, with the paragraphs further segmented into lines, the lines further segmented into words, and the words into a character image glyph. It considered features such as height and width, slope, number of circles present, number of horizontal and vertical lines, number of horizontally and vertically oriented curves, special dots, and image centroid. The character features were extracted as vectors. Kohonen's self-organizing feature map was used for classification. The study analyzed the weight assigned to each feature node and attempted to find the best match. Moreover, it compared neighboring characters for recognition.

12.2.2   How is IoT Changing the Face of Information Science?

As the popularity of the Internet of Things (IoT) expands, a flood of information will soon follow. Undoubtedly, this technology will meaningfully impact the manner in which people see data science. This surge in information is not only for the need of a better framework, but more for an infrastructure that could reliably process a continuing stream of complex data. Therefore, this new technology should be used to its full advantage, and this explosion of information is a chance for data scientists. By taking the advantages of information science for IoT, we are not only helping businesses in terms of higher performance and profits, but we are also able to create a much better world. With smarter analytics, multiple problems faced globally can be resolved.

12.3   Proposed Idea

This project proposed the idea to use the line detection method with circular masks and a binary number matrix formation technique to segment and extract the features of letters. This can be used in CNN for the classification of sub-patterns or features similar to predefined features of alphabets into groups that belong to a particular character of the detected word. Each feature, when joined together, can uniquely identify its parent pattern or letter. Initially, the captured image is denoised, and then the image is pre-processed or deconvolved using blind deconvolution, during which weight function can be used to improve the quality of the image. Subsequently, the image is converted into grayscale and the ROI is determined, followed by the conversion of the text region into a binary image. Thereafter, the edge pixels are calculated applying a combination of a standard line detection algorithm using a circular empty mask that stores the location of the edge pixels. One circular mask can detect edges by moving along eight coordinating directions, detecting vertical, horizontal, and diagonal edges. While establishing the image boundary according to the direction of edge detection, previous locations of the mask curves are determined and then divided into sub-regions. The regions are cropped and stored in binary number matrices for further feature extraction. The ROI can be found by extracting the wave-like feature, which is a gradient effect or the high-frequency noise created due to blind deconvolution.

12.3.1   Phases of OCR Processing

12.3.1.1   Pre-Processing

Blind deconvolution was used to deblur the acquired image with noise. It can estimate the optimal unknown point spread function (PSF) and then recover the unknown target image. After deconvolving, a proper weight function can be used to reduce the rigging effect or the high-frequency waves (rings) around the image pixels produced due to blind deconvolution. Another technique, called total variation deconvolution, can be used for better results. This deconvolution technique has a drawback, however. When the word in the image to be recognized is thin like a pencil stroke or if the width of a character is less than it should be, then it is difficult to

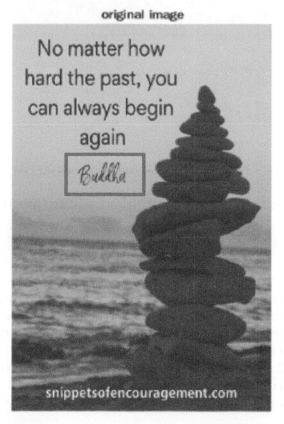

Figure 12.2 Original image.

Figure 12.3 Image blurred using a point spread function (PSF) of len = 11 and theta = 100.

recover the texts properly, leading to broken edges and incomplete letters. Incomplete letters can interfere with the recognition of words. Finally, the image was converted into a binary image to remove the traces of noise waves around it.

Figure 12.2 shows original image and Figure 12.3 shows the image was manually blurred to deblur it, which used a PSF of length 11. Since the text was very thin, a mild motion blur effect at an angle of 100° was used.

12.3.1.2   Segmentation

I) Baseline detection: In this stage, the edge pixels were detected using the combined line detection and circular mask. Firstly, a random colored pixel A was selected, and then four imaginary lines were extended from the colored pixel toward the top, bottom, left, and right. Lines were extended to the endmost edge pixel in that direction, and all endmost edge pixels were marked.

Point *A* was the first random point. Initially, imaginary lines were extended from point *A* in four directions until the endmost pixels *a*, *b*, *c*, and *d* were found, which are the leftmost, rightmost, bottom, and topmost edge pixels, respectively, along the direction of the line. Along with determining the edge pixels, the total number of colored pixels that form the lines was calculated. The lines were extended in order to determine the baseline for the unknown word whose size and orientation are not yet clear. This process attempted to determine an imaginary preliminary baseline that connects the most number of colored pixels (not necessarily edge pixels), which gives information on the orientation of the word, i.e., in which direction the unknown word is tilted. Less than or equal to four random pixels were initially found, and the distance between these random pixels was calculated, as shown in Figure 12.4. Each random pixel was connected to form a shape and the longest distance established.

It was assumed that the direction provided by the longest line shows the direction of the word (direction of the length of the word), while the shortest line is the height of the letter. The longest line was considered as the preliminary line, until it is confirmed. There are hundreds of ways to find the baseline. The aspect ratios of most letters are close to each other. The aspect ratio refers to the ratio of the height of a letter to its width;

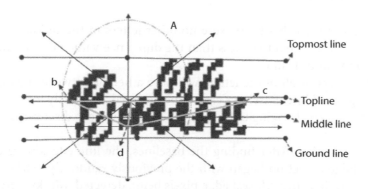

Figure 12.4 Baseline detection of a binary image (the image is zoomed in).

therefore, by following this assumption, an imaginary line *EF* was drawn parallel to the direction of the longest line by passing through the bottom point *d* to detect the bottom line or the lower baseline. It was much easier to find the bottom line compared to the lines that appear in the middle, as this line was shifted downward to the position of the last pixel (bottom). The bottom pixel is the last colored pixel closer to the ROI of the text at one side or edge. This line was rotated around to establish a straight line that touches the most number of bottom pixels. Then, the slope of the line was calculated to determine the rotation angle of the word. This detects 2D texts only, but does not confirm it. To confirm the position of the bottom line, the ROI boundary can be used for comparison by extending many adjoined lines from the ROI boundary toward the text. After establishing the bottom line, other lines can be detected, in no particular order.

There are five types of baselines, the definitions provided for which are from my own knowledge, which can be different from the standard.

a) *Ground line* is the bottom line that touches the most number of points or pixels in most letters of the English alphabet.

b) *Top line* is the topmost line that touches the most number of colored points in most letters of the English alphabet.

c) *Middle line* is the centerline that touches the most number of points between the top line and the ground line in most letters of the English alphabet.

d) *Underground line* is the bottom line that is below the ground line that touches the maximum number of points of the lowest part of most letters.

e) *Topmost line* is the line topmost of the top line that touches the maximum number of points of the upper part of most letters.

It was assumed that there were no other letters in the unknown word whose height is equal to or less than the difference value between the top line and the middle line.

Most letters or all of the letters will have a height between the top line and the ground line. Baselines cannot be detected accurately for every letter, as they keep changing until the most accurate line is discovered.

II) Edge detection: After finding the baselines, the line edges were determined. Edge detection began with the previously randomly marked edge pixels, with their next closest edge pixels being detected. Masks were used in parallel, and parallel processing was performed for faster results. Edges were detected by estimating the change in the intensity of pixels, which varied from white-1 to black-0 and *vice versa*. There were two major regions, the white and black regions, and edge was the boundary that separated these two regions.

After establishing the baselines, random pixels that were far from each other were selected. Eight circular masks started from a certain location and moved in eight different directions. A circular empty mask detected the edge pixels at the current location. Since the image was binarized, a simple mask was used, as shown in Figure 12.5. Binary images have either 0 or 1 values; therefore, the basic AND, NOT, and OR operators can be used to determine the edge pixels. A circular mask detected a line that connected two regions by moving from one region to another. Masks moved in the direction of the edge line.

Each mask stored the location of the edge pixels in a 2D array. The masks can move in any direction, i.e., there was no order for the combination of edge pixels. There are four different types of edges: horizontal, vertical, and two diagonal edges. A new line was detected by determining the changes in the direction of the edges detected. When multiple straight lines with different slope values are joined together, a curve is formed. Masks were

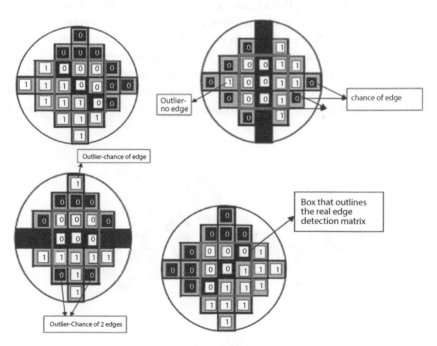

Figure 12.5 Empty circular masks that determine the image pixels.

created to find these curves in order to extract features and segment them. Curves are not straight, but form a pattern.

An intersection point is a point where multiple lines meet, or is a junction where multiple lines from different directions appear to join at a point or a center. It is easy to find the intersection points when the width of the letters is very thin; however, for bigger widths, binary number matrix is the best suitable method to detect intersections. The outliers shown in the above figure were candidate edge pixels. Masks will move toward the direction of the line; if a mask is stuck, where it could not determine the next edge pixel, then it will move to the location of the outlier. Not every outlier is an edge pixel. If the mask is again stuck, then its size was doubled. If the edge was not found after two to three times, then the mask will diminish in size. The English lowercase letters *i* and *j* have a small dot above them, which can be detected as a small group of outliers due to outliers not being discarded and their locations instead stored.

III) Splitting words into letters: Curves were divided into sub-curves using a cut. While determining the edge pixels, a mask also stored their locations in 2D matrices for the *x* and *y* coordinates. The easiest way to find the cut mark is to examine the directions of almost straight lines or a curve. This was done by comparing the locations of the curve pixels and marking the pixel locations whose *x* or *y* coordinates were the same or were parallel to each other. This technique is much more efficient when the shapes of letters are distorted, as shown in Figure 12.6. By observing the letter *u* from the figure, three different patterns can be determined: the left one whose slope is moving up or down, another curve or line that is more horizontal in the middle, and the right one whose slope increases similar to the left

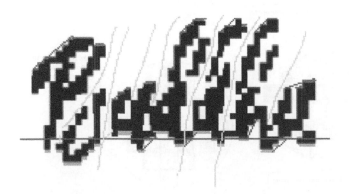

Figure 12.6 Segmentation into sub-regions.

one. The more horizontal pattern in the middle was cut. This technique can be used to semi-segment words into letters by cutting links that connect letters. Generally, these links are detected through the intersection points of letters. This technique works for formal cursive writing, but not for distorted words like the one shown below.

The standard line detection technique of cursive writing was used to find the segmentation points. In the above figure, the long and flesh-colored light lines were the longest-running white-colored pixels detected from the topmost line toward the bottom line, until these were obstructed by a colored pixel. The red marks in the figure are the top edge pixels, the green marks the bottom edge pixels, and the violet line touching the green edges is the roughly estimated ground line determined using green points. The flesh-colored lines help determine the direction of the cut. Shapes or curves that form a closed loop were not cut; hence, links were cut to create sub-regions.

The regions were cropped and the binary number matrix technique was used on sub-regions. Matrices can help to better understand and extract the features that represent the English alphabet. Regions were cropped using the edge pixels found. This started from the location of the cut and went around cropping white pixels moving in the direction of the edge pixels, which were covered by white pixels. Cropping indicates selecting regions and storing values of the white and black pixels found within those regions in the matrices. One region will use one matrix.

The largest values obtained were decimal number = 31,718,912, most significant bit (MSB) = 23, and least significant bit (LSB) = 0, while the least values were decimal number = 2,60,604, MSB = 17, and LSB = 2.

The algorithm used to calculate the decimal value was $2^n + \ldots\ldots\ldots 2^3 + 2^2 + 2^1 + 2^0$. Every letter has unique features, one of which is unique edge or curve slope direction.

Binary matrix compares patterns by calculating the directions of the slope of curves, as shown Figure 12.7. The middle pixels along the horizontal direction (blue-filled rectangles) and the vertical pixels (red boundary rectangles) were marked and compared. If all rectangles were joined by linking one to the next closest rectangle, then the direction of the letter can be identified.

Character recognition is extremely difficult, and a letter is better identified if CNN is used. Combining line detection and binary number matrix can help with extracting the features of letters. Line detection or edge detection determines the similarity among letters. Another method that can distinguish patterns is to compare the lower and upper parts, the lower part being the area below the middle line and the upper part the area above the

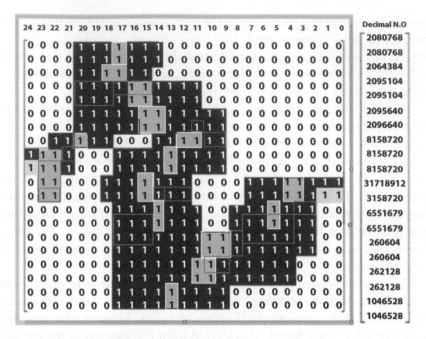

Figure 12.7 Binary number matrix of the letter *r*.

middle line. Another main purpose of using line detection is to find similar patterns. When similar patterns are found, then their region is separated or excluded from the binary number matrix test. Finding repeated words, letters, and patterns (sub-regions) therefore avoids having duplicates.

12.4   Results

The table below shows the baselines of the letters in the English alphabet. These letters were grouped according to the results of baseline detection and binary number matrix feature extraction.

Group no	Baselines	Probable to be
1	Height touches ground line and underground line	*f*
2	Height is between the top line and the ground line	*b, d, h, k, l, t*
3	Height is between top line and underground line	*g, y, z, p, q, j*
4	Height is between the top line and the ground line	*a, u, w, c, e, o, r, s, x, i, m, n, v*

In group 1 are the letters a, c, e, r, s, x, n, m, and i.

In the upper part test, the letters n and m are mostly similar, except for n having one increasing and decreasing slope and m having two increasing and decreasing slopes. The letter c has a semi u shape. The letter a is u-shaped and e has a closed shape, while the letter i has a dot.

In the lower part test, the letters a, c, and e are generally similar to a u shape or a quadratic curve.

Group 2 comprised the letters u, v, and w. The similarity between them is the area above the half part being wide open, while the dissimilarity is the lower part of the letter u having a shape similar to a parabola; that is, if the letter u is placed on a parabola of any width, then it will touch most of the parabola compared to the letter v. The lower part of w is similar to two parabolas joined together, or with a common side facing the same direction. The lower part of the letter v is less similar to a parabola compared to u.

Group 3 has the letters g, y, z, p, q, and j.

In the upper part test, g, p, and q generally have a shape similar to u, or a negative quadratic curve. The upper part of g is similar to that of a. The letters z, j, and y are uniquely identified, with only the letter y looking like a u shape, or a positive quadratic curve. Letter j has a dot. The upper part of g and p mostly looks similar to that of letter a.

In the lower part test, unlike y, z, j, and g, the letter q usually has a v-shaped leg. The letter p has one leg.

Group 4 is composed of the letters b, d, h, k, l, and t.

In the upper part test, t and k are unique.

In the lower part test, the letter d has a tail, but b does not. The letter k is unique.

This technique helps decrease the cost of using binary matrix alone and reduces the complexity of using line detection and the mask technique alone.

12.5 Conclusion

Cursive letters are such ambiguous letters that their recognition requires much more effort and patience. A small mistake in the observations and calculations can completely ruin the effort. The assumptions and ideas provided in research papers can be applied in real scenarios only if the errors are minimal. There is no perfect algorithm. In this paper, I have included what I have learned. Line detection with binary images has limitations. When using the edge detection technique, it will not give clean, accurate, and complete detection. Moreover, cropping an image limits the use of the binary matrix method, which can easily and efficiently detect small details. The major advantage of this method is the reduction in the complexity of recognizing characters, and parts that are extremely sensitive and crucial are cropped out for further evaluation using the binary matrix method. Line detection techniques can recognize similar patterns, reducing the workload as well.

Many marvelous works have been accomplished for OCR for decades. A lot of baseline-based techniques work based on different types of neural networks, such as CNN and RNN, and AI is emerging on top. In the future, AI in OCR can overcome many of the limitations faced by the current techniques. This field of research is new for me, and I hope to continue learning more about OCR and the many techniques developed by researchers around the world. It is my hope that, in the future, I could contribute something valuable to society.

References

1. Arica, N. and Yarman-Vural, F.T., Optical character recognition of cursive handwriting. *IEEE Trans. Pattern Anal. Mach. Intell.*, 24, 801 – 813, Jun 2002.
2. Abdul Hamid, U.Z., Ahmad Zakuan, F.R., Zulkepli, K., Azmi, M.Z., Zamzuri, H., Abdul Rahman, M.A., Zakaria, M., Autonomous emergency braking system with potential field risk assessment for frontal collision mitigation. *2017 IEEE Conference on Systems, Process and Control (ICSPC)*, pp. 71–76, 2017-12-01.
3. Cario, G. *et al.*, Data fusion algorithms for lane departure warning systems. *Presented at American Control Conference (ACC)*, pp. 5344–5349, 2010.
4. Dalal, N. and Triggs, B., Histograms of oriented gradients for human detection, in: *IEEE Computer Society Conf. on Computer Vision and Pattern Recognition*, pp. 886–893, IEEE, 2005.
5. Felzenszwalb, P. *et al.*, Object detection with discriminatively trained part based models. *IEEE Trans. Pattern Anal. Mach. Intell.*, 32, 9, 1627–1645, 2010.
6. Ding, Y. and Xiao, J., Contextual boost for pedestrian detection, in: *IEEE Computer Society Conf. on Computer Vision and Pattern Recognition*, pp. 2895–2902, IEEE, New York, 2012.

7. Sharma, P., Singh, A., Raheja, S., Singh, K.K., Automatic vehicle detection using spatial time frame and object based classification. *J. Intell. Fuzzy Syst.*, 37, 6, 8147–8157, 2019.

8. Bhowmick, B. and Kumar, K.S., Detection and classification of eye state in IR camera for driver drowsiness identification, in: *Proc. 2009 IEEE Conf. on Signal and Image Processing Algorithms*, pp. 340–345, IEEE, 2009.

9. Saneyoshi, K., Drive assist system using stereo image recognition, in: *Proc. of the Intelligent Vehicles Symp*, pp. 230–235, IEEE, New York, 1996.

10. Heimberger, M., Horgan, J., Hughes, C., McDonald, J., Yogamani, S., Computer vision in automated parking system: Design, implementation and challenges. *Image Vis. Comput.*, 68, 88–101, 2017.

11. Nguwi, Y.Y. and Kouzani, A.Z., Detection and classification of road signs in natural environments. *Neural Comput. Appl.*, 17, 3, 265–289, 2008.

12. Fang, C.Y. *et al.*, An automatic road sign recognition system based on a computational model of human recognition processing. *Comput. Vis. Image Underst.*, 96, 2, 237–268, 2004.

13. Sharma, P., Singh, A., Singh, K.K., Dhull, A., Vehicle identification using modified region based convolution network for intelligent transportation system. *Multimed. Tools Appl.*, 81, 24, 1–25, 2021.

14. Paulo, C. and Correia, P., Automatic detection and classification of traffic signs. *Presented at Eighth Int. Workshop on Image Analysis for Multimedia Interactive Services, European Association for Signal Image Processing (EURASIP)*, Santorini, 6–8 June 2007.

15. Kaul, S., Joshi, G., Singh, A., Automated vehicle detection and classification methods, in: *Recent Trends in Communication and Electronics*, pp. 326–332, 2021.

16. Sharma, P., Singh, A., Dhull, A., Applications of deep learning for vehicle detection for smart transportation systems, in: *Proceedings of Academia-Industry Consortium for Data Science*, pp. 307–321, Springer, Singapore, 2022.

17. Xie, P., Li, T., Liu, J., Du, S., Yang, X., Zhang, J., Urban fow prediction from spatiotemporal data using machine learning: A survey. *Inf Fusion*, 59, 1–12, 2020.

18. Kommey, B., GhanaToll: Barrier-Free RFID Toll Collection and Management System for GhanaToll. *International Journal of Computer Applications*, 176, 27, June 21–29, 2020.

19. Bhansali, M. and Kumar, P., An alternative method for facilitating cheque clearance using smart phones application. *Int. J. Appl. Innov Eng. Manag. (IJAIEM)*, 2, 1, 211–217, 2013.

20. Shen, H. and Coughlan, J.M., Towards a real time system for finding and reading signs for visually impaired users, in: *Computers Helping People with Special Needs*, Springer International Publishing, Linz, Austria, 2012.

21. Chakravorty, P., What is a signal? Lecture notes. *IEEE Signal Process. Mag.*, 35, 5, 175–177, 2018.

22. Gonzalez, R., *Digital image processing*, Pearson, New York, NY, 2018.
23. Ahmed, N., How I came up with the discrete cosine transform. *Digit. Signal Process.*, 1, 1, 4–5, January 1991.
24. Koundal, D. and Gupta, S., *Advances in computational techniques for biomedical image analysis*, *Methods and Applications*, 1st Edition, Elsevier, Netherlands, 2020.
25. Vaseghi, S.V., *Advanced digital signal processing and noise reduction*, second edition, John Wiley & Sons Ltd. chrome-extension://efaidnbmnnnibpcajpcglclefindmkaj/https://www.iz3mez.it/wp-content/library/ebook/Advanced%20Digital%20Signal%20Processing%20And%20Noise%20Reduction%202nd%20ed.%20%20-%20S.%20Vaseghi%20(2000)%20WW.pdf
26. Hansen, P.C., Naqy, J.G., OLeary, D.P., *Fundamentals of algorithms deblurring images*, Deblurring images: Matrices, spectra, and filtering, SIAM, Philadelphia, 2006.
27. Gurney, K., *An introduction to neural networks*, UCL Press, London, 1997.
28. Rehman, A., Mohamad, D., Sulong, G., Implicit vs explicit based script segmentation and recognition: A performance comparison on benchmark database. *Int. J. Open Problems Compt. Math.*, 2, 3, 354–364, September 2009.
29. Batenburg, K.J. and Sijbers, J., Adaptive thresholding of tomograms by projection distance minimization. *Pattern Recognit.*, 42, 10, 2297–2305, 2009.
30. Batenburg, K.J. and Sijbers, J., Optimal threshold selection for tomogram segmentation by projection distance minimization. *IEEE Trans. Med. Imaging*, 28, 5, 676–686, June 2009.
31. Kimmel, R. and Bruckstein, A.M., Regularized Laplacian zero crossings as optimal edge integrators. *Int. J. Comput. Vis.*, 53, 3, 225–243, 2003, https://www.cs.technion.ac.il/~ron/PAPERS/Paragios_chapter2003.pdf.
32. Kimmel, R., *Geometric level set methods in imaging, vision and graphics*, S. Osher and N. Paragios (Eds.), Springer Verlag, New York, 2003, https://www.cs.technion.ac.il/~ron/PAPERS/laplacian_ijcv2003.pdf, chapter.
33. Impedovo, S., Ottaviano, L., Occhinegro, S., Optical character recognition. *Int. J. Pattern Recognit. Artif. Intell.*, 5, 1–2, 1–24, 1991.
34. Plamondon, R. and Srihari, S.N., On-line and off- line handwritten character recognition: A comprehensive survey. *IEEE. Trans. Pattern Anal. Mach. Intell.*, 22, 1, 63–84, 2000.
35. Arica, N. and Yarman-Vural, F., An overview of character recognition focused on off-line handwriting. *IEEE Trans. Syst. Man Cybern. C. Appl. Rev.*, 31, 2, 216–233, 2001.
36. Imtiaz, H. and Fattah, S.A., A wavelet-domain local dominant feature selection scheme for face recognition. *Int. J. Comput. Bus. Res.*, 3, 2, 1–13, 2011.

37. Tsantekidis, A., Passalis, N., Tefas, A., Kanniainen, J., Gabbouj, M., Iosifidis, A., Forecasting stock prices from the limit order book using convolutional neural networks. *2017 IEEE 19th Conference on Business Informatics (CBI)*, pp. 7–12, Thessaloniki, IEEE, Greece, July 2017.
38. Juneja, M. and Sandhu, P., Performance evaluation of edge detection Techniques for images in spatial domain. *IJCTE*, 1, 5, 1793–8201, December, 2009.
39. Bangare, S.L., Dubal, A., Bangare, P.S., Patil, S.T., Reviewing Otsu's method for image thresholding. *Int. J. Appl. Eng. Res.*, 10, 9, 21777–21783, 2015.

13

Energy-Efficient Fog-Assisted System for Monitoring Diabetic Patients with Cardiovascular Disease

Rishita Khurana[1], Manika Choudhary[1], Akansha Singh[2]*
and Krishna Kant Singh[3]

[1]Department of Computer Science and Engineering, Amity School of Engineering and Technology, Amity University, Noida, Uttar Pradesh, India
[2]School of Computer Science Engineering and Technology, Bennett University, Greater Noida, India
[3]Delhi Technical Campus, Greater Noida, India

Abstract

The Internet of Things (IoT) is a nascent technological advancement aimed at establishing connectivity between a wide array of devices and sensors, encompassing wearable sensors, medical care sensors, cameras, home appliances, and smartphones, through the utilization of the Internet. The interconnectivity of this network results in the generation of substantial volumes of data, thereby requiring the presence of effective storage and processing capabilities. Fog computing has been identified as a viable solution to tackle this particular challenge. Nevertheless, specific use cases, particularly within the healthcare industry, necessitate the processing of data in real-time to optimize performance while simultaneously minimizing latency and delay.

Within the domain of healthcare, fog computing presents a viable and effective approach for enhancing the provision of superior facilities. This study presents a novel framework that utilizes fog computing to facilitate remote health monitoring. The framework is specifically designed to monitor blood glucose levels in patients diagnosed with diabetes and cardiovascular disease. The framework additionally underscores the significance of constraining energy consumption. The experimental findings provide evidence that the proposed framework demonstrates effective management of network delay and efficient utilization of energy resources.

Corresponding author: akanahasingh@gmail.com

Akansha Singh, Anuradha Dhull and Krishna Kant Singh (eds.) Blockchain and Deep Learning for Smart Healthcare, (323–352) © 2024 Scrivener Publishing LLC

In general, the Internet of Things (IoT) endeavors to establish connectivity between a diverse array of devices and sensors with the internet. Fog computing, as a novel approach, addresses the challenge of managing the substantial volumes of data that are produced. A framework based on fog computing has been developed in the healthcare domain to facilitate the remote monitoring of patients' blood glucose levels. This framework aims to optimize energy consumption and enhance network performance for improved efficiency.

Keywords: IoT, fog-computing, diabetes monitoring, healthcare, ECG, glucose, hyperglycemia, technology

13.1   Introduction

Glucose serves as the primary energy substrate for the brain and plays a pivotal role in sustaining physiological processes within the body. Nevertheless, deviations from normal blood glucose levels can result in significant ramifications. Hypoglycemia, characterized by abnormally low levels of blood glucose, has the potential to induce cardiovascular arrhythmia and may ultimately result in sudden cardiovascular mortality [1]. In contrast, diabetes, which is characterized by prolonged elevated levels of blood glucose, presents substantial hazards including heart attacks, strokes, cardiovascular failure, and other potentially fatal ailments.

In order to address the significant consequences linked to diabetes and hypoglycemia, it is imperative to engage in continuous monitoring of blood glucose levels to facilitate timely intervention. Furthermore, it is crucial to closely monitor data pertaining to glucose levels, including Electrocardiography (ECG), due to the significant correlation between these variables [2, 3]. When blood glucose levels decrease to less than 60 mg/dl, it initiates the occurrence of hypoglycemia, a condition that interferes with the repolarization of the heart and has the potential to result in cardiovascular arrhythmia. This particular arrhythmia is recognized as a primary contributor to instances of sudden cardiovascular deaths, particularly among individuals who are 60 years of age or older.

Recent research has put forth the notion of utilizing electrocardiogram (ECG) readings to forecast the occurrence of hypoglycemia through the analysis of QT interval and T-Wave patterns. In a similar vein, the occurrence of hyperglycemia, denoting elevated levels of glucose in the bloodstream, can be anticipated through the assessment of the duration required for the ventricles of the heart to undergo contraction and relaxation [4]. Diabetes has the potential to impact individuals across various age groups and genders, extending beyond the boundaries of developed nations.

Based on data from the National Vital Statistics Reports, it was observed that diabetes occupied the seventh position within the list of the top 15 causes of mortality in the year 2014. In addition, diabetes is known to have a direct or indirect impact on various health conditions, including strokes, cardiovascular failure, kidney failure, blindness, and other severe illnesses that frequently lead to mortality [5]. While it is currently understood that diabetes is not curable, the ongoing monitoring of blood glucose levels and the necessary adjustments to insulin administration are essential components in effectively managing this condition.

There exists a significant interconnection between diabetes, cardiovascular diseases, falls, and the elderly population. Existing research has demonstrated a positive correlation between diabetes and an elevated susceptibility to falls, particularly within the demographic of individuals aged 65 years and above [6, 7]. Moreover, this age group is also more prone to experiencing cardiovascular ailments. A significant proportion, specifically over 25%, of individuals belonging to this particular age demographic are afflicted with diabetes. Furthermore, an excess of 30% of these individuals encounter instances of falls on an annual basis, which may lead to potentially fatal outcomes. Moreover, a significant proportion of individuals diagnosed with diabetes, specifically over 68%, experience mortality as a result of cardiovascular ailments [8]. Hence, the development of a system that can consistently monitor diabetes, ECG, and identify anomalies such as falls, abnormal blood glucose levels, and irregular heart rate in real-time, while minimizing interference with the patient's routine, is of utmost importance [9].

The Internet of Things (IoT) offers a feasible resolution to tackle these challenges. The term "Internet of Things" (IoT) pertains to a system in which both tangible and intangible entities are interconnected, facilitating the remote monitoring of health conditions while simultaneously upholding the overall standard of living. Internet of Things (IoT) systems have the capability to gather and store data in cloud servers through the utilization of sensing, sensor networks, internet connectivity, and cloud computing technologies. Moreover, Internet of Things (IoT) systems have the capability to initiate immediate and timely responses or execute actions in real-time. An instance of an insulin pump that is linked to an Internet of Things (IoT) framework has the capability to autonomously or remotely deliver insulin injections in response to low blood glucose levels.

Nevertheless, despite the numerous benefits associated with glucose monitoring Internet of Things (IoT) systems, including the ability to remotely monitor glucose levels in real-time and store data globally, there are also certain constraints that need to be acknowledged. Many systems exhibit a deficiency in security measures, thereby rendering transmitted data susceptible to interception and manipulation by unauthorized enti-ties. In addition, a considerable number of current healthcare monitoring Internet of Things (IoT) systems lack the capability to facilitate distributed local storage. Consequently, this deficiency may give rise to the loss of data in the event of a disruption in the connection to cloud servers. As a con-sequence, this can lead to the generation of erroneous disease diagnoses.

In order to tackle these challenges, it is possible to introduce an addi-tional layer known as "Fog" within Internet of Things (IoT) systems. The Fog layer is positioned above smart gateways and offers advanced services aimed at improving the quality of healthcare services. One example is the utilization of fog computing to effectively preserve network bandwidth between gateways and cloud servers through the implementation of data processing and compression techniques. Furthermore, the offloading of data pre-processing tasks to intelligent gateways can effectively reduce the workload on cloud servers [7, 9]. This results in the establishment of a uni-fied network of interconnected gateways that effectively mitigate service disruptions and greatly improve service quality.

This chapter introduces an Internet of Things (IoT) system that utilizes Fog computing to enable real-time remote healthcare monitoring. The sys-tem is capable of monitoring various physiological parameters, including blood glucose levels, electrocardiogram (ECG) readings, patient move-ments, body temperature, as well as environmental factors such as room temperature, humidity, and air quality. The device has the capability to identify instances of falls, elevated blood pressure, and atypical glucose lev-els. The data that has been gathered is safeguarded through the utilization of cryptographic algorithms, which guarantee that encryption takes place at the sensor nodes prior to transmission, and subsequently, decryption occurs at the smart gateways. Finally, a sensor node with high energy effi-ciency is presented for the purpose of monitoring vital signs.

In the realm of healthcare, the diligent surveillance of blood glucose levels and associated data in real-time plays a pivotal role in the manage-ment of medical conditions such as diabetes and hypoglycemia. Internet of Things (IoT) systems, when augmented by the Fog layer, offer a robust solution for enabling remote monitoring, ensuring data security, and enhancing the quality of healthcare services.

13.2   Literature Review

A proposal of real-time and remote health monitoring IoT-based systems has been made. An IoT system with a smart gateway for e-health monitoring has been presented by Rahmani. The gateway supports interoperability. Also, many advanced services such as data compression, data storage, and security have been provided by gateway. A proposal of an ECG monitoring IoT-based system using 6LoWPAN that consist of smart gateways and sensor nodes which are energy efficient. IoT systems have been presented by the authors for detecting falls [10].

For determining the 3-D acceleration and 3-D angular velocity, wearable sensor nodes are utilized by the frameworks. Push notification services are offered to the caregivers for letting them know about the status of a fall. A glucose-observing IoT-based framework which shows a few degrees of energy effectiveness by implementing 6LoWPAN and RFID is presented by the authors. The framework can recognize non-fasting and fasting cases for a precise determination. Additionally, an IoT framework is proposed for detecting & sensing non-intrusive glucose levels. The framework utilizes a PC as a door for getting information from 6LoWPAN nodes and sending the information to Cloud workers. Some of the works do not support interoperability which limits the flexibility and ubiquity of the health monitoring system [11].

IoT frameworks for monitoring health have been proposed by researchers with the help of Fog Computing technology. The Fog-based frameworks have points of interest, for example, data transfer capacity saving, energy proficiency, and an undeniable degree of security. Authors apply a savvy entryway and Fog computing into an ECG observing IoT framework. The framework offers numerous types of assistance, for example, pop-up message or push-notification service and distributed local storage. Authors also proposed an IoT framework with Fog Computing for ceaseless glucose observing framework. The framework utilizes a versatile based door for preparing and breaking down information.

Fog approach for ECG monitoring frameworks is proposed by the authors. The frameworks can separate ECG highlights at Fog and accomplish a few degrees of energy effectiveness at sensor nodes. Wellbeing observing IoT frameworks with Fog processing are proposed. These frameworks give many progressed Fog administrations like information examination, information combination, distributed local storage, and compression of data.

In the system, a new set of fall detection algorithms is investigated and developed for improving the results of fall detection. Craciunescu *et al.* applied Fog computing for reliable e-health applications. The system has both e-health and contextual sensor nodes which are built from general-purpose devices. These sensor nodes transmit the collected data to a computer for processing. The Fog-based approaches which have been referenced or mentioned provide many advanced services to enhance the health monitoring frameworks, but none of them considers parts of sensor node's energy productivity, security, and the relationship of e-health data (i.e., diabetes, ECG, body motion, and body temperature).

At the point when a sensor node isn't energy effective, it can cause administration interference which is one reason for lessening the precision of sickness investigation [12]. Patient's information can be stolen or the system can be instructed for doing unacceptable actions when the system is not secured. The analysis and diagnosis of disease might be not accurate when independent e-health information is utilized without thinking about logical information or action status. The framework not just screens e-health (i.e., blood glucose, ECG, and internal heat level), everyday action, and context-oriented information (i.e., room temperature, stickiness, and air quality) yet in addition offers progressed types of assistance for improving the precision of disease investigation and educating anomalies (i.e., hypoglycemia, hyperglycemia, and heart infection) continuously [11, 12].

13.3   Architectural Design of the Proposed Framework

The design of the proposed framework has 3 layers as follows:

Sensor layer: The sensor layer incorporates various kinds of sensor nodes, for example, context-oriented nodes, e-wellbeing hubs, and actuator nodes. Context-oriented nodes can be fixed in a solitary space for social occasions relevant information from general conditions, for example, room temperature, moistness, time, area, and air quality. The relevant information assumes a significant part in accomplishing the exact investigation.

E-health nodes can be ordered into various sorts relying upon the given well-being observing application. There are 3 sorts of e-health sensor nodes as follows:

- low information rate sensor nodes
- high information rate sensor nodes
- mixed or hybrid sensor nodes (outfitted with both low and high information rate sensors)

Low information rate sensor nodes can be utilized for obtaining blood glucose, body temperature, and dampness. High information rate sensor nodes can be utilized for gathering ECG and body movement. Mixed sensor nodes can be utilized for gathering all referenced information [13].

Actuator nodes are utilized for controlling activities identified with the well-being or the general climate. Actuator nodes frequently get guidelines from a smart door. For instance, an environment-controlling actuator can change a room's temperature and mugginess. The gathered information from sensors is shipped off to smart doors by means of one of a few remote conventions. A decision of a particular remote convention relies upon the application's necessities. For instance, Wi-Fi is utilized for high information rate checking applications. A nRF convention, which is an ultra-low force 2.4 GHz ISM band remote convention, is used in the proposed framework because of its adaptability of information rate backing and energy proficiency. The nRF convention upholds information paces of 250 kbps, 1 Mbps, and 2 Mbps. The gathered information can be kept flawless or pre-handled prior to being communicated [14].

Fog computing layer: The next layer is the fog computing layer which consists of fog-assisted various smart entryways. These entryways can be fixed or mobile relying on the given application. As of now, it is discovered that fixed entryways are preferable because of their flexibility. Furthermore, they offer progressed administrations running weighty computational calculations while portable entryways are not proficient because of restricted battery limits. Synchronized and intact databases are the two prime components of dispersed local storage wherein context-oriented data and e-health data are stored in the synchronized database and information which is required for calculations and important information such as the username and password of the system if stored in the intact databases. Compressing the Information helps in saving the bandwidth of the network despite the fact that compacting and decompressing cost a few assets and idleness; they don't influence the exhibition of different administrations and just increment the complete dormancy marginally [15].

Neighborhood clients and outer clients are categorized using the categorization services. The categorization service particularly screens the Wi-Fi devices at the point when a client attempts to interface with keen entryways; the framework checks the data set. In the event that the client is a nearby client, the shrewd entryways send constant information straightforwardly to the client's terminal without experiencing Cloud workers.

Cloud server layer: The cloud servers give numerous advantages, for example, stockpiling, adaptability, information security, and information handling. Substantial computational undertakings, which can't be run at

Fog, can be prepared easily in Cloud servers. Various advancements can be introduced at Cloud for facilitating a thorough site indicating ongoing information in both printed and graphical interfaces. Besides, Cloud workers uphold message pop-ups sending the texts to an end client continuously. In this proposed framework which is presented in this chapter, the abnormalities are informed to the system administrator through the push notification feature [16].

13.4   Fog Services

Fog processing can offer many progressed administrations and consequently, possibly upgrade the nature of medical care administrations. In this chapter, interoperability, security, and information preparing are examined and clarified as follows.

13.4.1   Information Processing

In fog-assisted health monitoring systems, data processing and data analysis play a major role in monitoring the health of the patients. Along with reducing the burden of cloud servers, they also play an important role in extracting the significant data which is required for making decisions and push notifications. The ECG waveform is used for extracting the data for the pulse rate and QT intervals. The data extracted from ECG waveform is combined with other e-health information, for example, blood glucose level, internal heat level, and movement of the body is utilized for recognizing hypoglycemia.

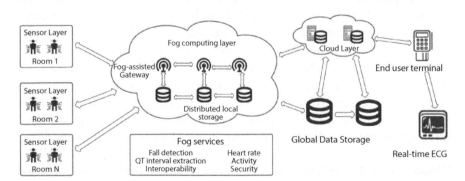

Figure 13.1 Architecture of the fog-assisted IoT framework for monitoring patients with diabetes and cardiovascular disease.

13.4.2   Algorithm for Extracting Heart Rate and QT Interval

Electrocardiography (ECG) is basically characterized as a periodic signal in which every ordinary waveform addresses the electrical occasions in a single heart cycle. An ordinary ECG waveform, shown in Figure 13.2, regularly comprises a few waves that are named as P, Q, R, S, T, and U. Out of these waves, waves P, R, and T frequently have positive peaks when the baseline of ECG is zero whereas Q, S have negative peaks.

We can calculate the heart rate from ECG waveform using the formula: HR = 60/RR interval, where HR stands for Heart rate, RR interval stands for the time between QRS waves. The heart rate can be determined by taking the time between 2 QRS waves or complexes. We can easily calculate the RR interval because R waves have the highest amplitude among the other waves.

A linear time algorithm which requires the determination of local extreme can be used for computing the peak waves. QT interval can be determined by using the algorithm in which we first locate the lowest interval IP in which P wave reaches its maximum value. Similarly, the other intervals i.e. IR, IS, IT are also calculated where P, R, S, and T are the different kinds of waves. IQT = IR + IQ + IS + IT is the formula for calculating the length of QT interval. In the algorithm discussed below, function f(x) reaches its local maximum. Two inputs i.e. xi = f (ti) are taken in this algorithm where ti refers to the instant of time. Also, this algorithm does not require any memory which makes it suitable for tiny devices [17].

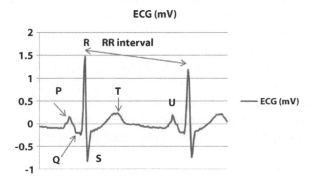

Figure 13.2 Generation of ECG signal in excel using a database.

Algorithm 1: To compute local maximum of a function.

Procedure: We take two inputs here (xi, ti), where x: value of ECG and t: specific time.

If (xi-1 = 0 and xi > 0) then

I1←ti

M ←xi

else if (I1 not equal to 0 and xi > 0) then

M = Max (xi , M)

else if (I1 not equal to 0 and xi = 0) then

I2 ← ti

Break

return M, [I1, I2]

13.4.3   Activity Status Categorization and Fall Detection Algorithm

An ECG cannot be analyzed without considering an activity status because the status of ECG changes on the current activity status. ECG of an individual is different during rest and motion. Hence, ECG and movement status should be observed and investigated at the same time. Movement status addressing day-to-day proactive tasks of an individual can comprise of three essential groups, for example, immobile/resting, strolling, and workouts. There can be numerous activities in each group such as sleeping, lying, etc. The resting group comprises standing and sitting. Whereas, the training group consists of running, push up, weight lifting, and other heavy activities. Activities belonging to the same group have comparative impacts to the ECG waveform. Camera or wearable movement sensors are utilized to identify an individual's action status. The calculation incorporates numerous means like the securing of 3-D increasing speed (acceleration) and 3-D precise speed (angular velocity), information separating, and fall recognition. The calculation utilizes both 3-D speeding up and 3-D rakish speed since they help to improve the exactness of a fall calculation [18].

Signals are affected by surrounding noise. Therefore, noise must be removed by using filters to achieve a high quality of signals:

SV Mi = $\sqrt{x^2 + yi2 + zi2}$

Φ = arctan {$\sqrt{yi2 + zi2}$ / xi } 180 / pi SVM: Sum vector magnitude

Table 13.1 Formulas for calculating corrected QT interval.

Algorithm	Formula
Bazett (QTcB)	QTc = QT/(√RR)
Fridericia (QTcFri)	QTc = QT/(√3 RR)
Framingham (QTcFra)	QTc = QT + 0.154 x (1 - RR)
Hodges (QTcH)	QTc = QT + 0.00175 x ([60/RR] - 60)
Rautaharju (QTcR)	QTc = QT - 0.185 * (RR-1)+k

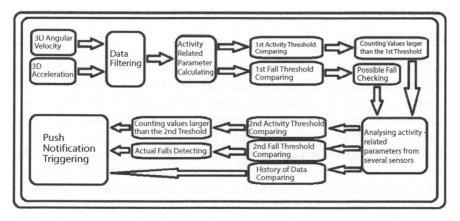

Figure 13.3 Algorithm of fall discovery and activity status.

i: number of sample
x, y, z: value of accelerometer
Φ: the angle between y-axis and vertical direction

The limits that we get after calculation are compared with the first set of thresholds and fall detection threshold [19]. Table 13.1 lists the formulas for calculating corrected QT interval.

13.4.4 Interoperability

A specific type of sensor node has been supported by traditional monitoring system that includes Wi-Fi-based node which monitors EMG, 6LoWPAN-based node which monitors ECG, Bluetooth-based node which monitors ECG, EMG or BLE-based node for detecting human fall. These frameworks are not appropriate for sensor nodes utilizing other conventions like Zigbee or nRF and LoraWan. Fog computing along with its potential offers interoperability to tackle these difficulties. The interoperability can be referred to as a potential of supporting various sensors from different makers as well as various conventions which includes both wire and wireless conventions. As per the application, other wire or wireless communication conventions can be combined into Fog-assisted brilliant entryways. For example, long-range distance-related applications can be supported by LoraWan so they can be added to Fog-assisted smart gateways. The sensor nodes utilized in the Fog-based framework can work in both ways i.e. independently and cooperatively and can also speak with one another through Fog-assisted smart gateways.

13.4.5 Security

In IoT based healthcare monitoring frameworks, the association between sensors and passages is probably the weakest point of the framework. The fundamental reason is that the sensors are wearable. Accordingly, they can't run complex security calculations. Despite the fact that unpredictable security calculations can be run effectively at sensor nodes, they are definitely not applied in light of the fact that inactivity prerequisites of the framework may be encroached and their battery is drained. In numerous IoT frameworks, crude information is frequently sent for saving battery life of sensor nodes. This methodology is hazardous since information can be tuned in by unapproved parties. In the most pessimistic scenario, they can educate orders to make damage to a patient. For instance, Klonoff utilizes his product to take the security qualification of the glucose observing framework. Therefore, he has full access and control to an insulin pump. To evade such cases, lightweight security calculations should be run at sensor nodes.

The calculation should give a few degrees of security while the sensors' battery life can't be diminished essentially. AES calculations are applied in this chapter which comprises of four essential operations: SubBytes, ShiftRows, MixColumns, and AddRoundKey. Each sensor node has its private keys for scrambling the information while a passage has all private keys of all sensor nodes. In detail, every sensor node has three diverse private keys where every private key has an ID and is utilized during a timeframe. The sensor node sends messages to illuminate a related door about the key ID before another key is applied. At a savvy passage, the encoded information got will be unscrambled by the right private key which has been recovered from a table of all private keys based on the given ID [20].

13.4.6   Implementation of the Framework and Testbed Scenario

A total IoT-based framework with Fog processing for consistent glucose, ECG, internal heat level and body movement observation is actualized. The framework incorporates the following:

a) 4 savvy passages
b) 6 relevant sensor nodes
c) 4 well-being sensor nodes
d) Cloud workers, and end-client terminals, for example, versatile applications.

Two entryways are set in two adjoining rooms while the other two are set at passageways. These entryways are associated with the Internet. Every one of the rooms has 3 logical sensor nodes set at the center, top and back corners of the room. The ECG data is collected by the e-health sensor nodes via electrodes. The tested rooms are office rooms comprising PCs and furniture, for example, tables and seats. Definite data of the framework's segments are clarified as follows:

13.4.7   Sensor Layer Implementation

The system presented in this chapter has two types of sensor nodes:

- Context-oriented or logical
- e-health

Each sensor node consists of five primary components which include:

- sensors
- energy harvesting unit
- wireless communication chip
- power management unit
- microcontroller

ATmega328P-8-bit AVR which is an ultralow power microcontroller, is utilized in sensor nodes. This microcontroller deftly assists various frequencies and different rest modes for saving energy. In the framework presented in this chapter, a sensor node just performs straightforward computational work while weighty computational works are handled at Fog. Subsequently, the sensor node doesn't have to run at a high clock recurrence for saving energy utilization. 1 MHz clock frequency is applied to all sensor nodes in its execution. The microcontroller underpins distinctive correspondence interfaces also. Moreover, the microcontroller has 1 KBytes EEPROM and 2 KBytes inward SRAM. Therefore, it is fit for supporting numerous libraries for gathering information from various sensors. It is discovered that SPI is more energy-efficient and has a higher transmission capacity than different interfaces. Therefore, SPI is utilized in the majority of the cases [21].

Context-oriented sensor nodes are outfitted with the following sensors:

- BME280
- SNS-MQ2
- SNSMQ7
- SNS-MQ135

These sensors are utilized for gathering the temperature of the room, dampness, and air quality levels. DHT22 is a little size moistness and temperature sensor which yields the aligned advanced signs. With a high working reach, the sensor can work in unforgiving conditions. The sensor has a high goal and it is exact. Air sensors (SNS-MQ2, SNS-MQ7, and SNS-MQ135) are used for gathering LPG, hydrogen, propane, CO, methane, NH3, liquor, NO, smoke, benzene, and CO2 from the air. These context-oriented sensor nodes are fixed in a room.

E-health sensors can be ordered into low information rate, high information rate, and hybrid nodes where half and half nodes comprise both low and high information rate sensors. Low information rate sensor nodes are furnished with a glucose sensor and an internal heat level sensor. An implantable sensor under a patient's skin and a transmitter put on top of the skin is incorporated by the glucose sensor. In the execution, the transmitter is associated with the microcontroller through SPI. The glucose sensor gathers the level of glucose at regular intervals as it doesn't change quickly. Likewise, the internal heat level sensor is associated with the microcontroller through SPI. The temperature information is gathered at regular intervals i.e. in every 120 seconds [13, 21].

E-health sensors that have high information rates are outfitted with a movement sensor and an ECG simple front-end. An ultralow power movement sensor i.e. MPU-9250 is for gathering 3-D speeding up (acceleration), 3-D precise speed (angular velocity), and 3-D attraction. The information pace of the movement sensor is 50 samples/s. A low-power Schmitt trigger-based circuit is the power managing unit having a few super-capacitors. The unit which manages power can distinguish the energy level

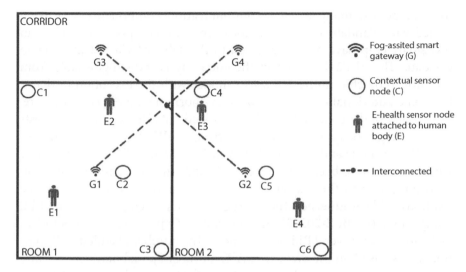

Figure 13.4 Scenario of test-bed implementation.

of the battery, current, and force by means of INA226. INA226 is a current shunt and power screen created by TI. The remote correspondence chip is nRF24L01. This chip is an ultralow power RF handset which supports many-to-numerous interchanges. The nRF24L01 chip underpins up to 2 Mbps. Nonetheless, 250 kbps is utilized for conserving the utilization of energy. The chip can work with low-power, normal or greatest power. The framework presented in this chapter is designed to run at low-power mode and is associated with the microcontroller through SPI.

13.5   Smart Gateway and Fog Services Implementation

Pandaboard which has a 1.2 GHz dual-core Arm Cortex microprocessor and 1 GB low-power DDR2- RAM has been used to build a smart gateway of the system. Various communication interfaces has been supported by Pandaboard which includes Wi-Fi, Bluetooth, and Ethernet by built-in components. A 32 GB SD-card which can be used for installing embedded operating systems has also been supported by it.

A lightweight version of Ubuntu based on Linux is used in the execution. Various services including information decompression, information handling, information examination, and security have been based on the working framework or the OS (operating system). To provide interoperability, many wireless communication components have been joined with Pandaboard. Sensor nodes that are equipped with nRF, an nRF24L01 chip have been connected to Pandaboard via SPI in order to get data. The nRF24L01 chip in the entryway is indistinguishable from the nRF24L01 chip utilized in sensor nodes with the exception of that it has some additional circuits and uses an enormous outer receiving wire. The quality of the collected signal is increased but also large antenna costs higher energy consumption. For supporting 6LoWPAN, a composition of a CC2538 module and a SmartRF06 board is added to Pandaboard. These various parts have been connected to Pandaboard through Ethernet and USB ports due to the reason that high transmission bandwidth can be made available by Ethernet. The smart gateway has been provided with BLE components (CYBLE-202007-01 provided by Cypress Semiconductor) in order to support several BLE sensor nodes. The number of added BLE components is based on the available UART ports of Pandaboard. So, because of the above reason these UART ports are finite. In order to conquer this problem, an FTDI chip and an ATmega328P microcontroller have been joined to Pandaboard. These segments can encourage BLE parts that are associated with programming-based or equipment-based UART [22].

AES algorithm has been run by Sensor nodes for encrypting transmitted messages and also the same is used by the smart gateway for decrypting the received messages. For various services to get cooperative the AES algorithm has been run in the smart gateway and is executed in Python. The smart gateway's database which has been built from MongoDB and JSON objects are used to store decrypted messages. The database has been combined with various languages such as HTML5, XML, Django, CSS, and JavaScript so as to provide a local host with a user interface.

Iptables and a part of our advanced security methods have been executed in the framework in order to protect the smart gateways. A part of these methods has been applied for the protection of connection between the smart gateways and the Cloud. Many parts have been not employed due to the reason of an increase in latency and energy consumption of sensor nodes. The implementation of smart gateways is in Python because it remains consistent with other services.

13.6 Cloud Servers

Google Cloud workers, API, and Cloud administrations are utilized in the implementation of the framework for putting away, preparing information and offering progressed types of assistance. For example, the message pop-up help of the framework is fundamentally executed in the Cloud. Like local hosts in Fog, Cloud workers have worldwide pages which can show both constant information and verifiable information in text-based and graphical structures. For getting information, end-clients can utilize the world wide web pages or a versatile application. This application is worked by PhoneGap in order to support the two IOS and Android.

13.7 Experimental Results

Gathered information at Fog-assisted entryways or gateways like angular velocity, acceleration, and ECG is prepared with 3 essential steps which include filtration of information, detecting baseline, and wander removal of baseline. As referenced, crude information is separated to take out commotion from the general climate. In the greater part of the cases, the information which is filtered has a different baseline in comparison to the reference baseline which is 1 g, 0 deg/s, and 0 voltages for increasing speed, angular speed, and ECG. Therefore, two processes i.e. detection of baseline and baseline wander removal are utilized for moving the signal's baselines into the normal ones. Two distinct techniques are applied for identifying the standard of various signals. A mean value is applied for identifying the baseline of acceleration and angular velocity.

On the other hand, Daubechies d4 wavelet transform is applied for distinguishing the standard of ECG. The information which is processed has the equivalent size and waveform as the separated information and is utilized as contributions for calculations, for example, fall discovery, pulse figuring and QT frequency extraction. The experimented parameters of the room environment are shown below in Table 13.2.

Table 13.2 Parameters of the room environment.

Parameters (experimented)	Value
Temperature	22 degrees Celsius
Humidity	31%
CO	0.6 ppm
NO2	8 ppb
S02	6 ppb

From the values given in the above table, we can see that the room environment is pretty good. Internal heat level and glucose are gathered yet it isn't utilized for the correlation since their worth only marginally changes during various exercises. For example, the gathered internal heat level and glucose of a volunteer are around 37 degrees Celsius and around 100 mg/dL for all exercises aside from preparing (e.g., running), individually. At the point when a volunteer seriously runs, the center temperature increments. The blood glucose level is different and changes with the monitoring time. For example, the glucose level toward the beginning of the day is less than in the early evening and after lunch. The glucose level of that individual vacillates around 90-98 mg/dL for all estimation cases in our experiments.

There are various waves such as P wave, Q, wave, R wave, S wave and T wave associated with ECG waveform. These waves are required for calculations (e.g., pulse estimation and QT's length extraction). On the off chance that of lying and standing, consequences of the calculations show that pulse is 59 beats per minute, the length of QT is around 390 and QTcB is 387 approximately. Some variations are expected to be encountered when the user slightly moves his body two times during lying in bed. Luckily, it is discovered that the ECG waveform in those minutes stays stable (e.g., ECG previously and during those minutes is comparative as far as the number of waves, and state of the waves.

During walking, the amplitude of the change in acceleration and angular velocity is small when compared with the already defines thresholds (i.e., 2g for acceleration and 200 deg/s for angular velocity) in the fall detection algorithm. The fluctuation however is helpful in identifying a walking status and in calculating the number of steps of a user. Activities like movement and non-movement can be distinguished by using angular velocity as a compliment parameter. The state of precise speed waveform can change contingent upon the walking or running style of the individual like swinging arms and hands during walking. ECG decently changes during walking. QT's length, QRS wave and T wave can be identified in the majority of the ECG cycles while P wave simply shows up in some ECG cycle (one for each and every 6-8 ECG cycle). In this case, QT's length is 35 ms and QTEB's is 392ms. ECG waves during walking are not as good as standing and lying in bed with respect to stability [23].

During running, there is a drastic change in data when compared with the baseline. Here, acceleration shows the number of steps of the individual (i.e., the top peaks have a lot higher amplitude as compared to the amplitude of the acceleration baseline which is about 1g). The acceleration is higher than the predefined threshold 2g in the fall detection algorithm, at the moment of 87-92nd sample. But the fall case here is not detected by the system due to two reasons. First, during the above-mentioned samples angular velocity is not more than angular velocity thresholds in the fall detection algorithm. Second, it is observed in the recorded information that none of the sensors failed. The instance of precise speed (angular velocity) at 58-64th examples is higher than the angular velocity threshold but fall event isn't identified. ECG during walking is not good as during standing and lying in bed. Some of the ECG cycles do show P, Q, R, S, and T wave (i.e., at 140-150th sample). It is not recommended to monitor ECG during intense activities like running or jumping as the value of QT's and QTeB's length varies dramatically [23].

In some experiments, users tend to fall at random moments. They can fall forward, backward, and sideways. In this chapter, fall cases are focused on because people are more prone to falling when doing some activity rather than in static cases. Fall cases during activities as well as during static statuses can be detected successfully. The ECG, acceleration, and angular velocity of fall cases during walking shows that in most cases a person tends to sit or stands after falling, so the acceleration should reach its peak values during such case.

Correspondingly it is expected that the falling peak with higher amplitude is compared with the other standing/sitting peak that occurred in both acceleration and angular velocity waveform. These two peaks appear in collected data of all experimented cases. For example, in the fall forward case, two peaks of acceleration and angular velocity appear at 58-65th sample and 110-115th sample. The highest amplitude often corresponds with the first peak which represents a fall moment while the amplitude of the second peak varies depending on different situations like sitting, standing, or crawling. Hence, the second peak can be smaller or larger than the pre-defined threshold. Depending on the situation, the distance between both peaks also varies. In fall aside, at a moment after falling, there is no dramatic change in angular velocity at 125-1130th samples while acceleration reaches to a peak value. This is because the user slowly crawls and sits up after falling. Hence, it can be concluded that ECG fluctuates during the fall moment while it remains good during other instants [24].

Power consumption of an e-health sensor node in different conditions during different experiments is observed. A sensor or a group of few sensors has been combined into a sensor node in each of the given configurations. The information is collected from the sensor and is transmitted to a gateway through nRF. Results of power consumption and detailed information on the configuration are displayed in Figures 13.5, 13.6 and Table 13.3 respectively.

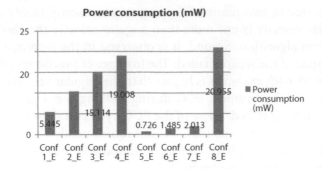

Figure 13.5 Power consumption in different configurations of e-health sensor nodes with a battery of 1000 mAh.

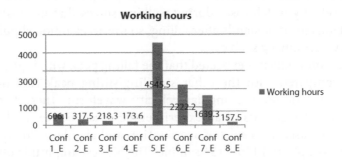

Figure 13.6 Working hours in different configurations of e-health sensor nodes with a battery of 1000 mAh.

The first four configurations from i.e. shown in Table 13.3, Conf 1_E to Conf 4_E have the configuration of high data rate e-health sensor nodes and another three configurations (i.e., from Conf 5_E to Conf 7_E) have the configuration of low data rate e-health sensor nodes. The hybrid sensor nodes having low and high data rate sensors are for the last configuration (i.e., Conf 8_E). The motion sensor and ECG sensor which are the high data rate sensors consume a higher amount of energy compared to low data rate sensors consume according to the results. The low data rate sensor node (i.e., Conf 7_E) has been utilized up to 1639 hours whereas the high data rate sensor node (i.e., Conf 4_E) has been utilized for up to 173 hours

Table 13.3 Area of gateway zones in various configurations in the event of a solitary nearby or adjacent gateway.

Configuration	Conf 1_E	Conf 2_E	Conf 3_E	Conf 4_E	Conf 5_E	Conf 6_E	Conf 7_E	Conf 8_E
BME280					X		X	X
Samples/ minute					1		1	1
Glucose sensor						X	X	X
Sample/ minute(s)						1	1	1
MPU-9250		X	X					X
Sample/ second(s)		50	50					50
AD8320	X	X	X	X				X
Sample/ second(s)	60	120	60	120				120
Voltage (V)	3.3	3.3	3.3	3.3	3.3	3.3	3.3	3.3
Current (mA)	1.65	3.15	4.58	5.76	0.22	0.45	0.61	6.35

along with 1000mAh Lithium battery (a size of 60 x 32 x 7mm). With the same battery, the hybrid sensor node can be used up to 157.5 hours [25].

In every second, data collected by contextual sensor nodes is sent to a gateway. Power consumption and configurations of the sensor nodes are shown in Figure 13.7 and Table 13.4 respectively. It is shown by results that sensors for collecting air-related parameters (i.e., Mq2, MQ7, and MQ1250) use a large amount of power. Contextual sensor nodes can be operated for up to 46 hours when applied to the 10000 mAh battery having a size of 5 x 120 x 90 mm. As mentioned, contextual sensor nodes are fixed in a room. Hence, it is suggested that wall socket power is supplied to contextual sensor nodes. Only in case of electricity cut, the battery is used.

The devices that we have used in our framework explained in this chapter i.e. the sensor node, smart gateways, and cloud server works on AES-256 encryption, AES-256 decryption & AES-256 encryption both for smart gateways and AES-256 decryption algorithms respectively. The latency of these devices is shown below in Table 13.5.

In the experiments, AES-256 is applied to sensor nodes in different configurations. The power consumption of the sensor nodes with and without is shown in Figure 13.8. The results show that when applying encrypting

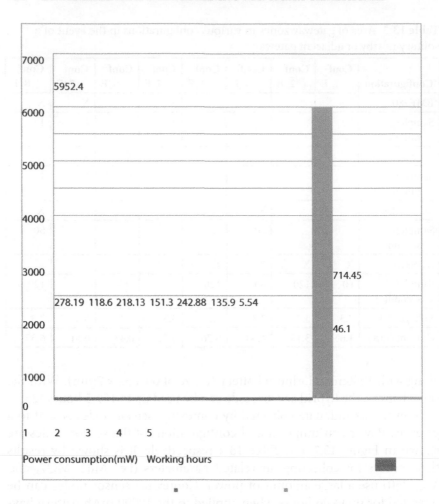

Figure 13.7 Power consumption and working hours in different configurations of context-oriented sensor nodes with a battery of 10000 mAh.

Table 13.4 Power consumption and configuration of sensor nodes.

Configuration	Conf 1_C	Conf 2_C	Conf 3_C	Conf 4_C	Conf 5_C
Voltage (in Volts)	3.3	3.3	3.3	3.3	3.3
Current (in mA)	84.3	66.1	73.6	1.68	216.5
MQ2	X				X
MQ7		X			X
MQ135			X		X
DHT22				X	X

Table 13.5 Measure of latency for different devices.

Device	Latency (in microseconds)
Sensor node (AES-256 encryption)	1358
Smart gateway (AES-256 encryption)	43
Smart gateway (AES-256 decryption)	52
Cloud server (AES-256 decryption)	10

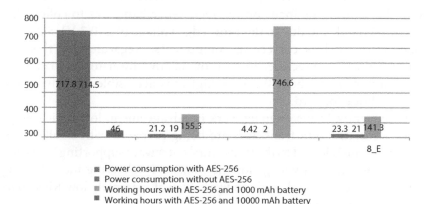

- Power consumption with AES-256
- Power consumption without AES-256
- Working hours with AES-256 and 1000 mAh battery
- Working hours with AES-256 and 10000 mAh battery

Figure 13.8 Power consumption and working hours in different configurations of sensor nodes with AES-256.

with AES-256, power utilization of the sensor node increments marginally (i.e., about 11% of the absolute power of the e-health hybrid sensor node). The hybrid sensor can operate for up to 183 hours in this case. Power utilization of nodes increments less than 0.01% in the case of context-oriented nodes. When they are supplied with the 10000 mAh battery, the contextual sensor nodes will still operate up to 46 hours [26].

13.8 Future Directions

There is a diverse field if we talk about the future directions of this work. As we have discussed in this chapter, the sensor node battery keeps going for around seven days. Replacing the battery frequently is unfortunate particularly with wearable sensors as this would lead to inconvenience and even torment in the event of embedded sensors. Energy reaping of encompassing sources can be misused for re-energizing or broadening the time between re-energizing of wearable miniature force sensor nodes. It includes changing over the surrounding energy innate in the sensor node's current circumstance into electrical energy [27].

Thusly, a sensor node will have the chance to stretch out its life to a reach dictated by the disappointment of its own parts instead of by its recently restricted force supply. A couple of sources have been explored in order to provide energy to the sensor nodes. In past works, the attainability of RF energy collecting has been researched as a hotspot for fueling to the sensor. The focus on the recurrence band was to collect 925 MHz GSM band, and due to their low edge voltage (0.2–0.3 V), Schottky diodes were used as correcting components. Regardless of this low turn-on voltage, the rectifier won't provide any power to the load aside from if a voltage of about 0.2 V or higher is accessible for driving the Schottky diode forward.

Consequently, in the ongoing work in advancement, low-limit voltage diodes associated with transistors are being prepared with smaller than usual solar panels joined to the transistors' entryways supporting in getting the necessary turn-on voltage for the transistor delivering the collecting circuit more delicate and ready to work even at extremely low RF signals accessible at its receiving wire [28].

The sensor can be directly powered right now as the RF energy harvesting is currently able to in a standard alone situation, it very well may also be misused along with a proficient force or power management unit to re-energize the battery and furthermore, expand the existence of the sensor node. Then again, the context-oriented sensor nodes and passages can be totally fueled self-sufficient when being fueled by sunlight along with a much more straightforward power management unit comprising of the following:

- lift converter
- buck converter
- voltage controller

The utilization of adaptable printed and wearable sensors is additionally being examined, other than low creation cost, better mechanical and warm properties, and lightweight contrasted with inflexible non-adaptable sensors; they prove to be more helpful and agreeable while being utilized for observing on surfaces which are bendable such as arms and thighs.

Table 13.6 Area of gateway zones in various configurations in the event of a solitary nearby or adjacent gateway.

Sensor node	Microcontroller (Mhz)	Flash (KB)	SRAM (KB)	Sensor(s)	Voltage (V)	Power consumption
O. Biros *et al.*: Implementation of wearable sensors for fall detection into smart household.	ATmega32L (8)	256	8	Motion	5	Low
S. Z. Erdogan, and T. T. Bilgin. A data mining approach for fall detection by using k-nearest neighbour algorithm on wireless sensor network data.	ATmega128L (8)	128	4	Motion	3	Medium
P. Pivato *et al.* A wearable wireless sensor node for body fall detection. In measurements and networking proceedings.	MSP430F2617 (8)	92	8	Motion	3.7	Low
Y. Li *et al.* Accelerometer-based fall detection sensor system for the elderly.	MSP430 (8)	48	10	Motion	3	Low

(Continued)

Table 13.6 Area of gateway zones in various configurations in the event of a solitary nearby or adjacent gateway. (Continued)

Sensor node	Microcontroller (Mhz)	Flash (KB)	SRAM (KB)	Sensor(s)	Voltage (V)	Power consumption
F. Wu et al. Development of a wearable-sensor-based fall detection system.	MSP430F1611 (8)	48	10	Motion	3.7	High
T. N. Gia et al. Iot-based fall detection system with energy efficient sensor nodes.	ATmega328P (8)	32	2	Motion	3	Low (36.38mW)
T. N. Gia et al. Customizing 6lowpan networks towards internet-of-things based ubiquitous healthcare systems.	Arm Cortex M3 (24)	512	32	ECG	3.3	Ultralow
R. Dilmaghani et al. Wireless sensor networks for monitoring physiological signals of multiple patients.	MSP430 (8)	48	10	ECG	3.3	Low (36mW)
S. Mahmud et al. An inexpensive and ultra-low power sensor node for wireless health monitoring system.	ATmega328 (8)	32	2	ECG	3.3	Low

(Continued)

Table 13.6 Area of gateway zones in various configurations in the event of a solitary nearby or adjacent gateway. (*Continued*)

Sensor node	Microcontroller (Mhz)	Flash (KB)	SRAM (KB)	Sensor(s)	Voltage (V)	Power consumption
T. N. Gia *et al.* Low-cost fog-assisted healthcare iot system with energy efficient sensor nodes.	MSP430 (8)	48	10	ECG	3.3	Medium (64mW)
S. Lee and W. Chung. A robust wearable u-healthcare platform in wireless sensor network.	ATmega328PPU (8)	32	2	Motion, ECG, body temperature	3	Ultralow (21.3 mW)
In our work	ATmega328PPU (1)	32	2	Motion, ECG, body temperature	3.3	Ultralow (23.4mW)

In this chapter, we have compared the power consumption of our sensor node with other nodes used in various research named in the above table. The results displayed in Table 13.6 indicate that the sensor node which we have utilized is probably the most energy-efficient despite the fact that the sensor node utilized in our framework is furnished with various types of sensors for performing various tasks such as gathering movement-related data, ECG, temperature of the body, and blood glucose level.

13.9   Conclusion

In this chapter, we have introduced a novel and savvy Fog-based framework for constant, distant observing glucose, ECG and different signals continuously. The total IoT framework comprising of sensor nodes, brilliant smart gateways with the technology called Fog Computing, and a back-end server was actualized. By concurrent checking various sorts of signals from bio-signals such as glucose, ECG, also, internal heat level to context-oriented signals (i.e., the quality of air, mugginess in the room, and temperature), the exactness of illness investigation was improved. By utilizing keen passages and Fog processing in the framework, the burden of sensor nodes was lightened while increased administrations (e.g., nearby information stockpiling, security, interoperability) were given.

Also, we proposed calculations for ascertaining the term of QT length, fall discovery, and movement status location, separately. These calculations joining with the pop-up message administration assisted with improving the nature of medical care administrations. Results from the analyses depicted that the total sensor node for collecting glucose, ECG, movement-related signals and internal heat level is perhaps the most energy-effective sensor node and it can work up to 157.5 hours with a 1000 mAh Lithium battery in a secured manner.

References

1. Robinson, R.T. *et al.*, Mechanisms of abnormal cardiac repolarization during insulin-induced hypoglycemia. *Diabetes*, 52, 6, 1469–1474, 2003.
2. Gia, T.N. *et al.*, Energy efficient fog-assisted IoT system for monitoring diabetic patients with cardiovascular disease. *Future Gener. Comput. Syst.*, 93, 198–2115, 2019.
3. Pradhan, N., Singh, A.S., Sagar, S., Singh, A., Elngar, A.A., Application of machine learning and IoT for smart cities, in: *Machine Learning Approaches for Convergence of IoT and Blockchain*, vol. 24, pp. 109–28, 2021 Aug.

4. Nguyen, H.T. *et al.*, Detection of nocturnal hypoglycemic episodes (natural occurrence) in children with Type 1 diabetes using an optimal Bayesian neural network algorithm, in: *IEEE Engineering in Medicine and Biology Society 2008*, pp. 1311–1314, IEEE, 2008.

5. Pickham, D., Flowers, E., Drew, B.J., Hyperglycemia is associated with QTC prolongation and mortality in the acutely ill. *J. Cardiovasc. Nurs.*, 29, 3, 264, 2014.

6. Kochanek, K.D. *et al.*, Deaths: preliminary data for 2009. National vital statistics reports: From the Centers for Disease Control and Prevention, National Center for Health Statistics. *Natl. Vital Stat. Rep.*, 59.4, 1–51, 2011.

7. Singh, K.K. and Singh, A., Diagnosis of COVID-19 from chest X-ray images using wavelets-based depthwise convolution network. *Big Data Min. Anal.*, 4, 2, 84–93, 2021 Feb 1.

8. Gia, T.N. *et al.*, Fog computing in healthcare Internet-of-Things a case study on ECG feature extraction. *IEEE International Conference on Computer and Information Technology (CIT'15)*, pp. 356–363, 2015.

9. Gia, T.N. *et al.*, Fog computing in body sensor networks: An energy efficient approach, in: *Proc. IEEE Int. Body Sensor Netw. Conf. (BSN)*, pp. 1–7, 2015.

10. Rahmani, A.M. *et al.*, Smart e-health gateway: Bringing intelligence to Internet-of-Things based ubiquitous healthcare systems, in: *Consumer Communications and Networking Conference (CCNC), 2015 12th Annual IEEE*, pp. 826–834, IEEE, 2015.

11. Gia, T.N. *et al.*, Customizing 6lowpan networks towards Internet-of Things based ubiquitous healthcare systems, in: *NORCHIP, 2014*, pp. 1–6, IEEE, 2014.

12. Singh, K.K., Siddhartha, M., Singh, A., Diagnosis of coronavirus disease (COVID-19) from chest X-ray images using modified XceptionNet. *Rom. J. Inf. Sci. Technol.*, 23, 657, 91–115, 2020.

13. Rahmani, A.M. *et al.*, Exploiting smart e-Health gateways at the edge of healthcare Internet-of-Things: A fog computing approach. *Future Gener. Comput. Syst.*, 78, 641–6585, 2018.

14. Negash, B. *et al.*, Leveraging fog computing for healthcare IoT, in: *Fog Computing in the Internet of Things*, pp. 145–169, Springer, Cham, 2018.

15. Mutlag, A.A. *et al.*, Enabling technologies for fog computing in healthcare IoT systems. *Future Gener. Comput. Syst.*, 90, 62–785, 2019.

16. Mehta, S., Singh, A., Singh, K.K., Resource management and allocation in Fog computing, in: *Recent Trends in Communication and Electronics*, pp. 600–603, CRC Press, 2021 Jun 29.

17. Vandenberk, B. *et al.*, Which QT correction formulae to use for QT monitoring? *J. Am. Heart Assoc.*, 5, 6, e003264, 2016.

18. Miao, F. *et al.*, A wearable context-aware ECG monitoring system integrated with built-in kinematic sensors of the smartphone. *Sensors*, 15, 5, 11465–11484, 2015.

19. Rakhra, A., Gupta, R., Singh, A., Medical imaging and diagnosis using machine learning and deep learning. *Recent Trends in Communication and Electronics*, vol. 29, pp. 390–4, 2021 Jun.

20. Singh, A. and Gupta, G., ANT_FDCSM: A novel fuzzy rule miner derived from ant colony meta-heuristic for diagnosis of diabetic patients. *J. Intell. Fuzzy Syst.*, 36, 1, 747–60, 2019 Jan 1.

21. Moosavi, S.M. *et al.*, End-to-end security scheme for mobility enabled healthcare Internet of Things. *Future Gener. Comput. Syst.*, 64, 108–124, 2016.

22. Biros, O. *et al.*, Implementation of wearable sensors for fall detection into smart household, in: *Applied Machine Intelligence and Informatics (SAMI), 2014 IEEE 12th International Symposium on*, IEEE, pp. 19–22, 2014.

23. Singh, P., Singh, N., Singh, K.K., Singh, A., Diagnosing of disease using machine learning, in: *Machine Learning and the Internet of Medical Things in Healthcare*, pp. 89–111, Academic Press, 2021 Jan 1.

24. Wu, F. *et al.*, Development of a wearable-sensor-based fall detection system. *Int. J. Telemed. Appl.*, 2015, 11, 2015.

25. Singh, M., Sachan, S., Singh, A., Singh, K.K., Internet of Things in pharma industry: Possibilities and challenges, in: *Emergence of Pharmaceutical Industry Growth with Industrial IoT Approach*, pp. 195–216, 2020.

26. Lee, S. and Chung, W., A robust wearable u-healthcare platform in wireless sensor network. *J. Commun. Networks*, 16, 4, 465–474, 2014.

27. Ali, M. *et al.*, Autonomous patient/home health monitoring powered by energy harvesting, in: *GLOBECOM 2017 - 2017 IEEE Global Communications Conference*, pp. 1–7, 2017.

28. Anzanpour, A. *et al.*, Energy-efficient and reliable wearable Internet-of-Things through fog-assisted dynamic goal management. *Proc. Comput. Sci.*, 151, 493–5005, 2019.

14

Medical Appliances Energy Consumption Prediction Using Various Machine Learning Algorithms

Kaustubh Pagar[1], Tarun Jain[1], Horesh Kumar[2], Aditya Bhardwaj[3]* and Rohit Handa[4]

[1]Manipal University Jaipur, Dehmi Kalan, India
[2]Greater Noida Institute of Technology, Greater Noida, India
[3]School of Computer Science Engineering and Technology, Bennett University, Greater Noida, India
[4]Data Analytics at Lead Technology, Synechron, Toronto, Canada

Abstract

One of the greatest inventions of the 19th century was electricity, which now has become an important part of our day-to-day life. However, many sources of electricity are exhaustible, and their production and distribution are costly, which makes it necessary to use this invention wisely and judiciously. The main focus of this chapter is the prediction of energy use of electrical appliances that are usually found in a normal household. An IOT-based wireless sensor is used to track the weather conditions of the rooms of the house that are used to estimate the electrical intake of the household devices. It is also significantly impacted by the weather conditions. In this chapter, we attempt to create a learning model using various regression analysis models like Linear Regression, Random Forest, Support Vector Regressor (SVR), K-Nearest Regressor, ExtraTree Regressor, and so on. The ExtraTree Regressor gives the best result among all models, with an R^2 score of 0.65.

Keywords: Regression, energy consumption, prediction, appliances, machine learning, temperature, humidity

Corresponding author: aditya.bhardwaj@bennett.edu.in

Akansha Singh, Anuradha Dhull and Krishna Kant Singh (eds.) Blockchain and Deep Learning for Smart Healthcare, (353–378) © 2024 Scrivener Publishing LLC

14.1   Introduction

Understanding the amount of electrical energy consumed by houses, buildings, institutes, etc. is very essential and has been the subject of various research studies. It is used to understand the supply and demand of electricity, the average energy consumed by an average household, the economic cost of production and distribution of electricity to various parts of a country, and numerous other things that eventually affect the country financially as well as deplete sources of energy faster, if not used wisely. Moreover, the demand for electricity is significantly greater than its supply, which has forced us to take measures to ensure the cautious use of electric energy.

Energy consumption from residential buildings includes household appliances like heaters, air conditioning, lights, fans, refrigerators, etc. that contribute to a major portion of the entire electricity demand of the world. Optimizing this component of energy consumption would help us reduce the waste of energy and help us create a more efficient smart energy system. Because energy consumption must be reduced, we must forecast future energy usage [10]. The energy consumption of a common household is affected by numerous factors like the size of the house, building material used, age of the building, number of residents and appliances, types and frequency of use of the appliances, and the geographic location and atmospheric conditions of the place. The type of the appliances and the frequency of their use determine a household's electricity consumption, and these appliances have a direct impact on the weather condition of the house like temperature and humidity conditions. As a result, by creating applicable models and including various environmental and electrical consumption data, it is possible to forecast the energy intake of a household [4].

Residential electricity consumption, electricity costs, gas costs, per-capita income, and weather conditions have all been studied by researchers. The relationship forecasts the growth of domestic power usage [2]. Residential electrical energy consumption forecasting gives data for further improving energy conservation methods and emission reduction efforts and can be applied for detecting irregular patterns in energy intake [3].

Predicting the energy usage patterns of residential households is also helpful for the implementation of smart grids. Electricity demand management methods are anticipated to play a critical part in smart grid infrastructures by applying a dynamic pricing scheme to lower building power use during peak hours. The main issue with this system is that it requires consumers to supply a lot of data about their household systems and appliances (for example, when they like to use each home gadget and appliance), which reduces system usability. Forecasting methods are required for this purpose to predict residents' preferences in consuming power for the following day, which can be achieved by anticipating the energy consumption patterns of a certain home [1].

In this chapter, we have taken into consideration a few features to create this prediction model. To understand this relationship between consumption and the features mentioned above, traditional analytical methods will not be of much use here, as they become computationally expensive and they are also not able to take into consideration a large number of features [5]. As a result, data-driven machine learning techniques have become crucial. Machine and deep learning models can be used to develop a model that can predict values of the target variable using feature variables using regression methods. It can also be used to figure out how many factors interact and how important they are [6, 7].

These prediction models can be used for a lot of different purposes, including detecting unexpected energy use and demand-side management, among others. All in all, it is really important for the electricity-providing companies to match the supply of electrical energy with the required energy consumption, as an overflow of energy leads to the wastage of precious resources. On the other hand, an inadequate supply of energy is also inconvenient for the consumers due to outages. It is also troubling for large companies and their factories, who have to suffer monetary as well as equipment damages due to irregular and inefficient supply of electricity.

14.2 Literature Review

A lot of research work and studies have been done regarding the energy consumption of household appliances. Many studies and prediction models have been created to estimate the energy consumption levels that help in creating better smart energy systems, reducing the wastage of energy, reducing power outages due to overload, and so on. These studies have also helped in implementing the idea of a smart grid. The data collected by the sensors and appliances also help in understating the consumption amount of the houses and help in creating better-suited grids for electricity distribution.

The dataset used in this chapter is taken from the UCI Machine Learning Repository. The dataset has been used by various authors like Luis M. Candanedo who demonstrate four models that were trained using (i) Multiple Linear Regressor, (ii) Support Vector Regressor with a radial kernel, (iii) Random Forest Regressor, and (iv) Gradient Boosting Regressor (GBM). The best model is GBM, which has an R^2 score of 0.97 in the training dataset and 0.57 in the testing dataset while using all the features [8].

The work done by R. I. Rasel, Haroon, Sultana, and Akther in their paper shows the usage of two different models: artificial neural network (ANN) and support vector machine (SVM). The researchers then used principal component analysis (PCA) to select input features. After a thorough analysis, they found the proposed BackPropagation ANN model to be very effective in forecasting energy consumption [9].

Lastly, in the research paper [11], the authors use five prediction models: random forest, extreme random forest (ERF), long short-term memory network (LSTM), support vector machine, and K Nearest Neighbor; LSTM gives the highest R^2 score of 0.97 and the lowest RMSE of 21.36 in the testing set. It is found to be the best among the models given in that research paper.

14.3 Methodology

A brief description of the dataset is given below. After analyzing and screening the data, we divide the dataset into two parts such that 80% of the data are used for training the model, while the remaining 20% are used for testing the performance of the models. We have taken appropriate steps to make the data efficient for training the models. We find correlations between various features of the data, to select the best features for training and also scale the data to prevent the outliers or varying ranges from negatively affecting the model. We have then used various techniques to maximize the accuracy of the prediction model.

14.3.1 Dataset

The residence where the data on energy use is taken is in Stambruges, Belgium. The energy (Wh) data for the appliances was recorded at a 10-min interval using an m-bus energy meter. The 10-min reporting time was chosen to better capture the fluctuating energy consumption. The data were collected for 137 days, and there was a lot of variation in appliance energy consumption. A ZigBee wireless sensor network was used to monitor and log the humidity and temperature conditions of the house. Weather features from the airport weather station near the house (Chievres Airport,

Belgium) were recorded and added to the experimental datasets. Two random variables are added to the dataset [12]. The dataset consists of 19735 data points and 26 features (Date and Light Column are not required), as shown in Table 14.1. Our target variable is Appliances, which represents the energy consumption of the household appliances.

Table 14.1 Data variables and description.

Number of features	Data variable	Variable description	Units
1	Date Time	Date and time of the data entry	dd-mm-yyyy hh:mm
2	Appliances	Appliances energy consumption	Wh
3	Lights	Lights energy consumption	Wh
4	T1	Temperature in kitchen	°C
5	RH_1	Humidity in kitchen	%
6	T2	Temperature in living room	°C
7	RH_2	Humidity in living room	%
8	T3	Temperature in laundry room	°C
9	RH_3	Humidity in laundry room	%
10	T4	Temperature in office room	°C
11	RH_4	Humidity in office room	%
12	T5	Temperature in bathroom	°C
13	RH_5	Humidity in bathroom	%
14	T6	Temperature outside the building	°C
15	RH_6	Humidity outside the building	%
16	T7	Temperature in ironing room	°C
17	RH_7	Humidity in ironing room	%
18	T8	Temperature in teenager room	°C

(Continued)

Table 14.1 Data variables and description. (*Continued*)

Number of features	Data variable	Variable description	Units
19	RH_8	Humidity in teenager room	%
20	T9	Temperature in parents room	°C
21	RH_9	Humidity in parents room	%
22	T_out	Temperature outside the airport	°C
23	Pressure	Atmospheric Pressure	mmHg
24	RH_out	Humidity outside the airport	%
25	Windspeed	Windspeed	m/s
26	Visibility	Visibility	km
27	Tdewpoint	Dew Point Temperature	°C
28	rv1	Random Variable 1	-
29	rv1	Random Variable 2	-

14.3.2   Data Analysis and Pre-Processing

The time series analysis of any database gives the comparison and graphical representation of the variables that are recorded over a period of time. This analysis gives us an idea of how the variables change with time and how a specific day, week, or month affects a certain variable. Apart from the correlation between the variables themselves, the time series adds one more variable to understand the dependencies between them. Figure 14.1 shows the appliance energy consumption for time series data. Time series is usually used in datasets containing weather attributes like temperature, humidity, rainfall, and other datasets like the stock market and so on. Since our dataset contains the weather attributes, we can know that these variables do affect the target variable Appliances [13].

14.3.3   Descriptive Statistics

Count: The number of data points of that feature attribute.
Mean: The average of the values of all data points of that feature attribute.
Std: Standard deviation

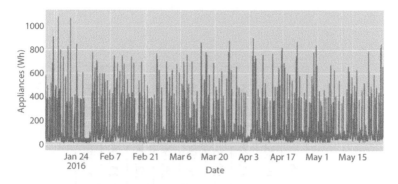

Figure 14.1 Appliance energy consumption in time series.

Min: The minimum value among all the data points of that feature attribute.
25th: The 25% percentile—25% of all data point values are lesser than this value.
50th: The 50% percentile—50% of all data point values are lesser than this value.
75th: The 75% percentile—75% of all data point values are lesser than this value.
Max: The maximum value among all the data points of that feature attribute.
   Range of Feature:

1) Temperature: −6.06 °C to 29.8 °C
2) Humidity: 1% to 100%
3) Dew Point Temperature: −6.6 °C to 15.5 °C
4) Windspeed: 0 m/s to 14 m/s
5) Atmospheric Pressure: 729.3 mm Hg to 772.3 mm Hg
6) Visibility: 1 km to 66 km
7) Appliances Energy Consumption: 10 Wh to 1080 W

We can see from the tables above that all the features have 19735 data points each, which means that there are no missing values present in our dataset. Thus, we do not need to perform any process for the missing values problem. We also see that we have varying ranges in our feature attributes that need to be dealt with to make the data feasible for training the models. Furthermore, Tables 14.2, 14.3 and 14.4 show the description of temperature, humidity and weather appliance data values.

Table 14.2 Temperature data values description.

	T1	T2	T3	T4	T5	T6	T7	T8	T9
Count	19735.0	19735.0	19735.0	19735.0	19735.0	19735.0	19735.0	19735.0	19735.0
Mean	21.687	20.341	22.268	20.855	19.592	7.911	20.267	22.029	19.486
Std	1.606	2.193	2.006	2.043	1.845	6.090	2.110	1.956	2.015
Min	16.790	16.100	17.200	15.100	15.330	-6.065	15.390	16.307	14.890
25%	20.760	18.790	20.790	19.530	18.278	3.627	18.700	20.790	18.000
50%	21.600	20.000	22.100	20.667	19.390	7.300	20.033	22.100	19.390
75%	22.600	21.500	23.290	22.100	20.620	11.256	21.600	23.390	20.600
Max	26.260	29.857	29.236	26.200	25.795	28.290	26.000	27.230	24.500

Table 14.3 Humidity data values description.

	RH_1	RH_2	RH_3	RH_4	RH_5	RH_6	RH_7	RH_8	RH_9
Count	19735.0	19735.0	19735.0	19735.0	19735.0	19735.0	19735.0	19735.0	19735.0
Mean	40.260	40.420	39.243	39.027	50.949	54.609	35.388	42.936	41.552
Std	3.979	4.070	3.255	4.341	9.022	31.150	5.114	5.224	4.151
Min	27.023	20.463	28.767	27.660	29.815	1.000	23.200	29.600	29.167
25%	37.333	37.900	36.900	35.530	45.400	30.025	31.500	39.067	38.500
50%	39.657	40.500	38.530	38.400	49.090	55.290	34.863	42.375	40.900
75%	43.067	43.260	41.760	42.157	53.663	83.227	39.000	46.536	44.338
Max	63.360	56.027	50.163	51.090	96.322	99.900	51.400	58.780	53.327

Table 14.4 Weather and appliances data values description.

	T_out	Tdewpoint	RH_out	Press_mm_hg	Wind speed	Visibility	Appliances
Count	19735.0	19735.0	19735.0	19735.0	19735.0	19735.0	19735.0
Mean	7.412	3.761	79.750	755.523	4.040	38.331	97.695
Std	5.317	4.195	14.901	7.399	2.451	11.795	102.525
Min	−5.000	−6.600	24.000	729.300	0.000	1.000	10.000
25%	3.667	0.900	70.333	750.933	2.000	29.000	50.000
50%	6.917	3.433	83.667	756.100	3.667	40.000	60.000
75%	10.408	6.567	91.667	760.933	5.500	40.000	100.000
Max	26.100	15.500	100.000	772.300	14.000	66.000	1080.000

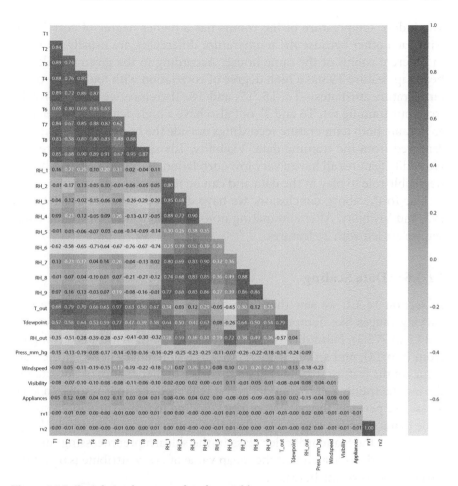

Figure 14.2 Correlation heatmap of study variables.

14.3.4   Correlation Matrix

The correlation heatmap matrix gives us a matrix representation of the correlation between all the variables using a heatmap. The values of the matrix elements lie between −1 and 1, where 1 denotes the highest correlation and −1 denotes the lowest correlation between those variables. The correlation heatmap of study variables are shown in Figure 14.2.

14.3.5   Feature Selection

As we can see from the heatmap, all the temperature attributes from T1 to T9 and also T_out have a positive correlation with the target variable.

The indoor temperature of the rooms has a higher degree of correlation with each other because the temperature differences are usually minimal in different rooms of the same house. According to the given correlation heatmap, feature T9 has a high degree of correlation with four of the other temperature attributes—T3, T5, T7, and T8. Therefore, we can remove T9 from our training set. T6 and T_out also have a high degree of correlation as they are both temperature recordings outside the house. Thus, T6 is also removed from the training data. Visibility, Tdewpoint, and Pressure and Humidity features all have a very low correlation. Random variables have a negligible role to play in the data and can be removed [14].

Due to the above conclusion, we have dropped variables T6, T9, rv1, rv2, and Visibility. After eliminating non-essential features from the dataset, we are left with 21 features.

14.3.6   Data Scaling

In section 14.3.2, we saw that the values of the various features were in varying ranges like Temperature (ranging from –6.06 to 29.8), Pressure (729.3 to 772.3), Humidity (ranging from 1 to 100), Windspeed (ranging from 0 to 14), and so on. If there are large differences between the data values of the feature attributes, then there is a higher chance of uncertainty during the training of the model and it will produce poor results. In such a case, we perform the process of Data Scaling to bring the data to such a scale that it does not negatively affect the performance of our model [15].

We used the StandardScaler class in the sklearn.preprocessing module to scale our dataset such that the mean value of every attribute is 0 and the variance of every attribute is 1.

14.4   Machine Learning Algorithms Used

The problem at our hand is called a Regression problem. In such problems, we use feature attributes to try and predict the target attribute. The regression models are trained using the training dataset with the target variable values given and the model learns to predict the target value given the feature attributes in the future [16, 21, 22].

14.4.1   Multiple Linear Regressor

This is the most basic regression technique that uses more than one feature attribute to predict the target variable. In single-variable linear regression, we use one independent variable and one dependent variable and check how they both are related to each other. On the other hand, in multiple linear regression, two or more variables are used to predict the target variable.

This is one of the simplest forms of regression technique used and is given by the following formula:

$$y = \beta 0 + \beta 1 X1 + \ldots + \beta n Xn + \varepsilon$$

Here, y = value predicted by the model of the target variable
β_0 = y-intercept
$\beta_i X_i$ = Coefficient of Regression (β_i) of the ith feature attribute (X_i)

14.4.2   Kernel Ridge Regression

Ridge regression is a method in which we try to estimate the coefficients of multiple regression models where the independent variables have a high degree of correlation between them. Kernel ridge regression is an extension to the ridge regression model as it introduces a kernel trick to improve the model performance. It combines ridge regression with classification (l2-norm regularization). This model is quite identical to a Support Vector Regressor. They only differ in the type of loss functions used. Kernel Ridge is typically faster for medium-sized datasets [17].

14.4.3   Stochastic Gradient Descent (SGD)

The SGD technique uses an iterative approach to optimize the objective function. SGD regressor is a simple SGD learning technique that fits linear regression models using multiple loss functions and penalties.

14.4.4   Support Vector Machine (Support Vector Regression)

The basic principle of an SVM is to find the best fit line also known as the hyperplane. The SVR works pretty similarly to the SVM, the only difference is that the SVR tries to find the best hyperplane with the max number of points on it.

14.4.5   K-Nearest Neighbor Regressor (KNN)

The KNN model is popularly used for non-linear regression in Machine Learning. The new data point is considered to be the same as one of the old data points using this method. The data point is then compared to the existing categories and then it is assigned to the category that best fits the data point.

14.4.6   Random Forest Regressor

Instead of using just one decision tree, Random Forest uses multiple decision trees for predicting the output, hence the name 'Forrest'. A decision tree is built by randomly selecting a few data points from the given dataset. Multiple decision trees are then created that predict the value of any new data point, where all the tree's output might vary. To get the final answer, we have to find the average of all the estimated values for the new data point [18].

14.4.7   Extremely Randomized Trees Regressor (Extra Trees Regressor)

Extra Trees is an ensemble learning algorithm. The method randomly creates extra trees in the sub-samples of the dataset to increase the predictivity capability of the model. By this approach, the method significantly reduces the variance. It then calculates the average of the outputs of the decision trees. It is very similar to a Random Forrest Regressor. Its only difference is how it constructs the decision trees for the forest.

14.4.8   Gradient Boosting Machine/Regressor (GBM)

Gradient Boosting or GBM is a very widely used ensemble machine learning algorithm. GBM uses the boosting technique, where it combines several weak learners to create a strong learner. The model uses Regression trees as the initial base learner. The errors calculated in the preceding trees are used to build the next trees in the series [19].

14.4.9   Light GBM (LGBM)

The Light Gradient Boosting Machine (LGBM) is an ensemble machine learning algorithm just like GBM. It differs from a normal GBM in its tree construction method. It grows its tree leaf-wise instead of level-wise. It chooses the leaf that it thinks will reduce the cost by the greatest amount.

14.4.10   Multilayer Perceptron Regressor (MLP)

An MLP is a deep, artificial neural network. An MLP is made up of 3 layers: input, hidden, and output layer. It uses the method of backpropagation and error correction to improve the model. The Multilayer Perceptron mainly consists of three steps:

1. Forward Pass: In this step, the initial data given to the input layer are propagated to the output layer by calculating the values at each step and applying the activation function.
2. Error Calculation: The difference between predicted and actual values is calculated. This error needs to be reduced.
3. Backward Pass: Use the values of the error to update the weight of the neural network to raise the performance of the model.

These steps are repeated for a certain number of epochs and the final values are then calculated.

The MLP uses various activation functions like bipolar sigmoid, binary sigmoid, ReLu, Leaky ReLu, etc. [20].

14.4.11   Implementation

The dataset analysis was performed as shown in section 3.2, and we reduced the number of feature attributes from 26 to 21. We removed the following attributes: rv1, rv2, Visibility, T6, and T9. After eliminating non-essential features from the dataset, we were left with 21 features for training the model. The correlation heatmap and data visualization helped us in selecting the appropriate features. After feature selection, we used StandardScaler to scale the data as required to improve the learning ability of the models and reduce any unpredictability.

For the implementation of the models, we used scikit-learn and lightGBM. The below-mentioned libraries were used to train the models:

- LinearRegression, SGDRegressor from sklearn.linear_model
- KernelRidge from sklearn.kernel_ridge
- SVR from sklearn.svm
- KNeighborsRegressor from sklearn.neighbors
- RandomForestRegressor, GradientBoostingRegressor, and ExtraTreesRegressor from sklearn.ensemble
- LGBMRegressor from lightgbm
- MLPRegressor from sklearn.neural_network

14.5   Results and Analysis

Mean Absolute Error (MAE)

MAE is an evaluation metric that calculates the average of the absolute differences between the actual values and the predicted values.

$$\text{MAE} = \frac{1}{N}\sum_{i=1}^{N}|yi - \hat{y}i|$$

where N represents the total number of data points
$\hat{y}_i$ represents the Predicted Value
y represents the Actual Value

Mean Square Error (MSE)

MSE calculates the average of the squared values of the differences between the actual values and predicted values. MSE penalizes large absolute error differences as the values get squared.

$$\text{MSE} = \frac{1}{N}\sum_{i=1}^{N}(yi - \hat{y}i)^2$$

where N represents the total number of data points
$\hat{y}_i$ represents the Predicted Value
y represents the Actual Value

Root Mean Squared Error (RMSE)

RMSE is the value obtained by calculating the square root value of the MSE.

$$\text{RMSE} = \sqrt{\frac{1}{N}\sum_{i=1}^{N}(yi - \hat{y}i)^2}$$

where N represents the total number of data points
$\hat{y}_i$ represents the Predicted Value
y represents the Actual Value

R-Squared Score (R^2)

The R^2 score is one of the most important and widely used metrics to evaluate a regression model. It calculates the amount of variance in the predictions made by the dataset.

$$R^2 = 1 - \frac{SS\ Regression}{SS\ Total} = 1 - \frac{\sum_{i=1}^{N}(yi - \hat{y}i)^2}{\sum_{i=1}^{N}(yi - \hat{y})^2}$$

where N represents the total number of data points
$\hat{y}_i$ represents the Predicted Value
y represents the Actual Value
$\bar{y}$ represents the Mean of all values

14.6 Model Analysis

Table 14.5 shows the results of our 10 energy use regression models. We know that a model having lower MAE, MSE, and RMSE values will have

Table 14.5 Performance evaluation of models on training data.

Name	Train time	Train MAE	Train MSE	Train RMSE	Train R^2 score
Multiple Linear Regressor	0.007	0.529	0.871	0.933	0.128
Kernel Ridge Regressor	42.958	0.529	0.871	0.933	0.128
Stochastic Gradient Descent (SGD)	0.078	0.442	1.011	1.005	−0.011
Support Vector Regressor (SVR)	10.552	0.355	0.770	0.877	0.229
KNeighborRegressor	0.058	0.247	0.308	0.555	0.691
Random Forest Regressor	24.334	0.112	0.059	0.243	0.940
ExtraTree Regressor	7.252	0.000	0.000	0.000	1.000
Gradient Boosting Regressor	5.488	0.453	0.682	0.826	0.317
Light GBM Regressor	0.457	0.320	0.373	0.611	0.626
MLPRegressor	22.331	0.423	0.502	0.709	0.497

relatively better performance. Furthermore, a model having a larger R^2 value has a relatively better performance. The value of the R^2 score usually lies between 0 and 1. If the R^2 score is negative, it means that the chosen model does not follow the pattern and trend of the data.

It can be observed from Table 14.5 that the ExtraTree Regressor has the highest R^2 score of 1 in the Training. Random Forest Regressor, KNeighbors Regressor, and lightGBM Regressor also show good performance with an R^2 score of 0.94, 0.69, and 0.62 respectively. The basic Linear Regression Model and Kernel Ridge Model do not perform very well, with both showing an R^2 score of just 0.12. The Stochastic Gradient Descent Regressor shows an R^2 score of −0.011, which means that the model is not able to follow the trend data.

In the testing dataset, the ExtraTree Regressor again tops the chart with an R^2 score of 0.651 and the lowest RMSE among all the models of 0.59. Random Forest Regressor, KNeighbors Regressor, and lightGBM Regressor also show good performance on the testing data with an R^2 score of 0.56, 0.49, and 0.43, respectively, and an RMSE of 0.65, 0.71, and 0.74 respectively. The worst-performing models in the testing dataset are again SGD with an R^2 score of 0.001 and Linear Regressor and Kernel Ridge Regressor

Table 14.6 Performance evaluation of models on testing data.

Name	Test MAE	Test MSE	Test RMSE	Test R^2 score
Multiple Linear Regressor	0.522	0.844	0.918	0.155
Kernel Ridge Regressor	0.522	0.844	0.918	0.155
Stochastic Gradient Descent (SGD)	0.444	0.998	0.999	0.001
Support Vector Regressor (SVR)	0.364	0.762	0.873	0.237
KNeighborRegressor	0.323	0.509	0.713	0.490
Random Forest Regressor	0.325	0.432	0.657	0.567
ExtraTree Regressor	0.282	0.348	0.590	0.651
Gradient Boosting Regressor	0.474	0.752	0.867	0.247
Light GBM Regressor	0.386	0.560	0.748	0.439
MLPRegressor	0.450	0.584	0.764	0.415

both with an R^2 score of 0.15. Table 14.6 shows the Model Evaluation Scores on the testing data.

In terms of the training time of the models, Kernel Ridge Regressor takes the number one spot with a training time of 42.9 seconds. KNeighborRegressor, MLPRegressor, and Support Vector Regressor also take a relatively long time to train the model with a training time of 24.33, 22.33, and 10.55 seconds, respectively. The best-performing model—ExtraTree Regressor—takes a time of 7.25 seconds to train the model. It is the only evaluation metric that the ExtraTree Regressor does not perform the best in.

According to the below histogram in Figure 14.3, the R^2 Score of ExtraTree Regressor is the highest (1.0 for training data and 0.65 for the testing data) followed by Random Forest Regressor (0.94 for training data and 0.56 for the testing data) and KNN with an R^2 score of 0.69 for training data and 0.49 on the testing data. We also see that the SGD Regressor gives a negative R^2 score of −0.01, which indicated that it does not follow the trends of the dataset and is not a suitable model for prediction. It also gives a low R^2 score of 0.0014 in testing data. The Multiple Linear Regressor and Kernel Ridge are also among the worst-performing models with both giving an R^2 score of 0.12 in training data and 0.15 in testing data. The LGBM

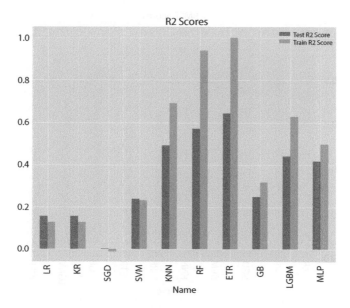

Figure 14.3 R^2 score comparison between training and testing data for different models.

and MLP also give decent R^2 scores of 0.43 and 0.41, respectively, in the testing data.

According to the below histogram in Figure 14.4, the RMSE of ExtraTree Regressor is the lowest (0 for training data and 0.59 for testing data) followed by Random Forest Regressor (0.24 for training data and 0.65 for testing data) and KNeighborRegressor (0.55 for training data and 0.71 for testing data). This means that the values predicted by these models are comparable to the actual values. The RMSE is the highest for SGD, Multiple Linear Regressor, and Kerner Ridge Regressor. SGD gives the highest RMSE of 1.0 in training data and 0.99 in testing data. The Multiple Linear Regressor and Kernel Ridge are also among the worst-performing models with both giving a very high RMSE of 0.93 in training data and 0.91 in testing data. This indicated that the worst-performing model has the greatest difference between the true values and estimated values. LGBM and MLP also give decent RMSE scores of 0.74 and 0.76 in the testing data, respectively.

In Figure 14.5, we see the histogram of the MAE scores of various models. The MAE of ExtraTree Regressor is the lowest (0 for training data and 0.28 for testing data) followed by Random Forest Regressor (0.11 for training data and 0.32 for testing data) and KNeighborRegressor (0.24 for training data and 0.32 for testing data). The low MAE represents that

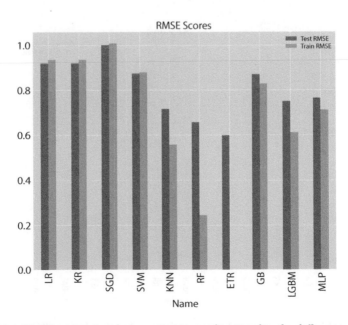

Figure 14.4 RMSE comparison between training and testing data for different models.

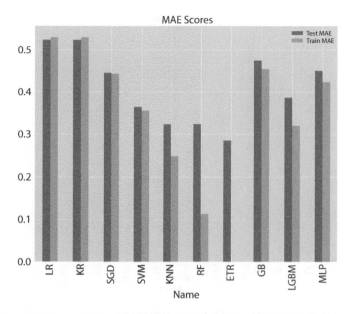

Figure 14.5 MAE score comparison between training and testing data for different models.

the model's predicted value is close to the actual values. The MAE is the highest for SGD, Multiple Linear Regressor, and Kerner Ridge Regressor, indicating the bad performance of these models. SGD gives the highest MAE of 0.44 in both the training and testing data. This indicated that the worst-performing model has the greatest difference between the true values and estimated values. The Multiple Linear Regressor and Kernel Ridge are also among the worst-performing models with both giving a very high MAE of 0.52 in both training and testing data. The LGBM regressor model gives an MAE score of 0.38 and SVR gives a score of 0.36. The MLP model gives a bit higher score of 0.45.

Lastly, we see the MSE score histogram in Figure 14.6, which indicated the mean of the squared differences of the values. The MSE of ExtraTree Regressor is the lowest (0 for training data and 0.34 for testing data) followed by Random Forest Regressor (0.05 for training data and 0.43 for testing data) and KNeighborRegressor (0.30 for training data and 0.50 for testing data). The low MSE represents that the model's predicted value is close to the actual values. The MSE is the highest for SGD, Multiple Linear Regressor, and Kerner Ridge Regressor, indicating the bad performance of these models. SGD gives the highest MSE of 0.99 in testing data and 1.0 in training data. The Multiple Linear Regressor and Kernel Ridge are also

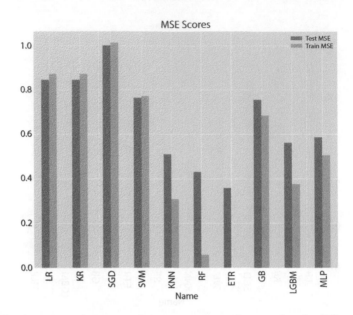

Figure 14.6 MSE score comparison between training and testing data for different models.

among the worst-performing models with both giving a very high MSE of 0.87 in training data and 0.84 in testing data. This indicated that the worst-performing model has the greatest difference between the true values and estimated values. The LGBM regressor model gives an MSE score of 0.56 and MLP gives a score of 0.58. The SVR model gives a bit higher score of 0.76.

The MAE and MSE scores work similarly to the RMSE value. They tell us the difference between the actual values of a data point and the values predicted by that model. By the analysis of the models, we can see that the ExtraTree Regressor has the lowest MAE, MSE, and RMSE value and the highest R^2 score. By this analysis, we can safely conclude that ExtraTree Regressor is the best-performing model among all.

14.7   Conclusion and Future Work

The purpose of this chapter was to apply various machine learning models to the given data to create prediction models for the appliance's energy consumption. Firstly, we were successfully able to identify the correlation between the various features and the effect that they had on the target variable. We then applied 10 machine learning models—Multiple Linear Regression, Kernel ridge, SGD, SVR, KNeighborRegressor, Random Forest, ExtraTree Regression, GBM, LightGBM, and Multiplayer Perceptron ANN to the dataset to create the best possible prediction model. Lastly, the performance metric of each model was calculated and compared with each other to obtain the best model. The result showed that among the 10 models, the ExtraTree Regressor achieved the best results on both the training and the testing dataset, with the relatively best R^2 score. Random Forest Regressor, KNeighborRegressor, and lightGBM Regressor also showed good performance on the dataset.

In the future, we plan to apply various deep learning models to the dataset to try and create even better prediction models. The results we obtained here are of significant importance and can be used for creating a model that can predict the energy consumption of a household and can help in reducing energy wastage, predicting future energy consumption, and developing smart grids and smart cities.

References

1. Barbato, A., Capone, A., Rodolfi, M., Tagliaferri, D., Forecasting the usage of household appliances through power meter sensors for demand management in the smart grid. *IEEE International Conference on Smart Grid Communications (SmartGridComm)*, IEEE, pp. 404–409, 2011.
2. Jian, H.Y., Kong, W.J., Liu, H.X., Study on influences of lighting and appliances usage behavioural patterns on household electricity consumption. *Build. Sci.*, 29, 15–19, 2013.
3. Chen, S.Q., Li, N.P., Fu, X.Z., Statistical methods of energy consumption for residential buildings. *HVAC*, 37, 44–48, 2007.
4. Zhou, J. and Song, Y.L., Study on the residential thermal environment and energy consumption-based on human occupancy. *Build. Sci.*, 34, 59–65, 2018.
5. Kavousian, A., Rajagopal, R., Fischer, M., Ranking appliance energy efficiency in households: Utilizing smart meter data and energy efficiency frontiers to estimate and identify the determinants of appliance energy efficiency in residential buildings. *Energy and Buildings*, vol. 99, pp. 220–230, 2015.
6. Zhao, H.-X. and Magoulès, F., A review on the prediction of building energy consumption. *Renew. Sustain. Energy Rev.*, 16, 6, 3586–3592, 2012.
7. Ahmed, S.T., Kumar, V.V., Singh, K.K., Singh, A., Muthukumaran, V., Gupta, D., 6G enabled federated learning for secure IoMT resource recommendation and propagation analysis. *Comput. Electrical Eng.*, 102, 108210, 2022.

8. Candanedo, L.M., Feldheim, V., Deramaix, D., Data driven prediction models of energy use of appliances in a low-energy house. *Energy Buildings*, 140, 81–97, 2017.
9. Rasel, R.I., Sultana, N., Akther, S., Haroon, A., Predicting electric energy use of a low energy house: A machine learning approach. *2019 International Conference on Electrical, Computer and Communication Engineering (ECCE)*, pp. 1–6, 2019.
10. Bharati, S., Podder, P., Mondal, M.R.H., Visualization and prediction of energy consumption in smart homes. 81–97, 1 Jan. 2020.
11. Xiang, L., Xie, T., Xie, W., Prediction model of household appliance energy consumption based on machine learning. *J. Phys. Conf. Series.*, 1453, 012064, 2020, 10.1088/1742-6596/1453/1/012064.
12. Vakharia, V., Vaishnani, S., Thakker, H., Appliances energy prediction using random forest classifier, in: *Recent Advances in Mechanical Engineering: Select Proceedings of ITME*, pp. 405-410, Springer Singapore, 2021.
13. Gupta, V., Beniwal, N.S., Singh, K.K., Sharan, S.N., Singh, A., Optimal cooperative spectrum sensing for 5G cognitive networks using evolutionary algorithms. *Peer-to-Peer Netw. Appl.*, 14, 5, 3213–3224, 2021.
14. Kim, T.Y. and Cho, S.B., Predicting residential energy consumption using CNN-LSTM neural networks. *Energy*, 182, 72–81, 2019.
15. Escobar, P., Martínez, E., Saenz-Díez, J.C., Jiménez, E., Blanco, J., Modeling and analysis of the electricity consumption profile of the residential sector in Spain. *Energy Build.*, 207, 109629, 2020.
16. Tso, G.K.F. and Yau, K.K.W., Predicting electricity energy consumption: A comparison of regression analysis, decision tree and neural networks. *Energy*, 32, 9, 1761–1768, 2007.
17. Torriti, J., Demand side management for the European supergrid: Occupancy variances of European single-person households. *Energy Policy*, 44, 199–206, 2012.
18. Torriti, J., Temporal aggregation: Time use methodologies applied to residential electricity demand. *Util. Policy*, 64, 101039, 2020.
19. Pradhan, N., Singh, A.S., Sagar, S., Singh, A., Elngar, A.A., Application of machine learning and IoT for smart cities, in: *Machine Learning Approaches for Convergence of IoT and Blockchain*, pp. 109–128, 2021.
20. Lin, J., Fernández, J.A., Rayhana, R., Zaji, A., Zhang, R., Herrera, O.E., Liu, Z., Mérida, W., Predictive analytics for building power demand: Day-ahead forecasting and anomaly prediction. *Energy Build.*, 255, 111670, 2022.
21. Soni, K.M., Gupta, A., Jain, T., Supervised machine learning approaches for breast cancer classification and a high performance recurrent neural network. *2021 Third International Conference on Inventive Research in Computing Applications (ICIRCA)*, pp. 1–7, 2021.

22. Mehta, S., Singh, A., Singh, K.K., Role of machine learning in resource allocation of fog computing, in: *2021 11th International Conference on Cloud Computing, Data Science & Engineering (Confluence)*, pp. 262–266, IEEE, 2021, January.

Part 3

FUTURE OF BLOCKCHAIN AND DEEP LEARNING

15

Deep Learning-Based Smart e-Healthcare for Critical Babies in Hospitals

Ritam Dutta

Dept. of CSE, Poornima University, Jaipur, Rajasthan, India

Abstract

With the advent of the latest technology, the healthcare system needs smart architecture. New smart technologies are compared with the conventional healthcare system in terms of results, speed, and efficiency. This work reviews several literatures and gives an insight into the demand for NICU beds in hospitals. A smart e-healthcare system that estimates the availability of NICU beds is developed. The framework consists of an application developed using Android that the users can use to interact with hospitals during crisis. Cloud storage has been used to store the data securely using the AES algorithm. Cloud storage also improves data accessibility and is reliable. The proposed framework uses machine learning algorithms to efficiently predict the availability of NICU beds in hospitals for newborn babies. The CNN model extracts the essential features from the dataset, and SVM performs the classification task. Moreover, the number of available beds in a hospital has also been reflected in the application developed so that the users can accordingly contact their respective hospitals in case of any emergency. The proposed framework has outperformed the earlier CNN and SVM models with 90.4% recall, 90.6% precision, and 95.4% accuracy.

Keywords: Cloud computing, electronic sensors, smart healthcare, machine learning, CNN, SVM, prediction analysis

Email: ritamdutta1986@gmail.com

Akansha Singh, Anuradha Dhull and Krishna Kant Singh (eds.) Blockchain and Deep Learning for Smart Healthcare, (381–398) © 2024 Scrivener Publishing LLC

15.1   Introduction

The journey from a mother's womb to the outside world is challenging for a newborn. Before birth, the baby entirely depends on the mother. For nourishment, respiration, and immunization, newborns are entirely reliant on their mother. However, after birth, babies have to perform all of these functions on their own. They need to adapt to the new environment where typical complications, viz., jaundice, skin problems, and gastric issues, may appear. Some babies experience difficulties transitioning from their mother's womb to the outside world. A complicated or premature child birth increases the chances of having health issues. These babies require intensive care and are put into neonatal intensive care units (NICUs). NICUs are specially designed to treat the little ones. They are designed with advanced technology that makes it easy for babies to cope up with new challenges. The NICU has proved to be beneficial for the treatment of babies [1]. Sometimes, babies have a lower body weight, congenital disabilities, infections, and breathing and heart problems that need special care and attention. Also, if twins or triplets are born, they may have serious health issues as they are usually premature and have a low body weight. NICUs play a pivotal role under these circumstances.

    A NICU has many components. The monitor is used to keep track of the babies' heart rate, oxygen level, body temperature, and blood pressure. Some respiratory equipment include ventilators, endotracheal tube (ET tube), continuous positive airway pressure (CPAP), and nasal cannula [2, 3]. Ventilators are used when the baby cannot breathe independently and, therefore, needs an external source to breathe. An ET tube, CPAP, and nasal cannula can be used with ventilators and help the baby breathe. Humidified air prevents the dryness of the baby's nose. The bag and mask setup can temporarily be used in the absence of ventilators or CPAP machines. Babies can effortlessly breathe using a suction setup. Medfusion and IV pumps (infusion pumps) are medical devices that inject fluids, such as nutrients and drugs, into a patient's body in controlled amounts. Phototherapy can be used to reduce the side effects of jaundice. Refrigerated breast milk can be heated up using a breast milk warmer. The kidneys of the child can be examined using the diaper scale. The stethoscope can be used to check the heart rate. The scanner scans whether the baby is receiving the correct medication and drinking breast milk on a timely basis.

    The healthcare system has to face many challenges. The patients must be treated promptly. The medical data usually have high irregularities and are high dimensional. They are sparse and not homogeneous in nature.

The healthcare system uses advanced technology to provide superior patient treatment. The collection of consistent data and analyzing them are challenging. A smart electronic healthcare, i.e., e-healthcare, system is used to maintain medical records digitally.

In this chapter, a smart e-healthcare system is developed incorporating different technologies to determine the availability of NICU beds. The patient's data are collected using the wearable sensors and stored in cloud storage in an encrypted format using the Advanced Encryption Standard (AES) algorithm [4–7]. An Android application is developed to access the patient's data securely. Patients can view, download, or forward their data to other applications. The details regarding the NICU beds are maintained in a database and are stored in the cloud. Predicting the availability of NICU beds is made using machine learning algorithms. This framework is user-friendly and cost-effective; users can ask their queries anytime using the Android application. A framework that is based on being user friendly, fast communication, and incurring lower healthcare costs is proposed.

Section 15.3 describes the proposed framework in detail:

a. How were the data collected?
b. Data processing steps administered
c. The Android application
d. Encryption algorithm used
e. How are the data handled in the cloud?
f. Workings of the proposed framework

The following sections discuss the experimental results and the future scope for the framework, along with some concluding remarks.

15.2   Literature Survey

Viegas *et al.* [8] predicted a collaborative model for readmission of ICU beds utilizing fuzzy modeling and feature selection approaches in the year 2015. A large amount Multi-Parameter Intelligent Monitoring (MIM) data for intensive care have been archived and are also publicly available. In 2019, Rayan *et al.* [9] introduced a detailed study on various machine learning and deep learning approaches, viz., Artificial Neural Network (ANN), Convolution Neural Network (CNN), and Support Vector Machine (SVM) algorithms to detect cataract detection, ICU readmission on glaucoma, and Alzheimer's disease diagnosis, to make a smart health system. Kumar *et al.* [10] have proposed a smart patient health monitoring system using

IoT in 2017. Alsamhi *et al.* [11] presented a comprehensive survey using nuclear drones with the IoT to build a smart city based on data collection, security, public safety, disaster management, and quality of life. Kharel *et al.* [12] proposed a model for a smart health monitoring system based on fog computing. The proposed architecture claims to acknowledge the fundamental problems of a clinic-centric healthcare system and change it to a smart patient-centric healthcare system. Li *et al.* [13] presented a survey on machine learning techniques applied for big data analysis in smart healthcare systems. Several strengths and weaknesses for existing approaches have also been discussed with a special focus on research challenges. Muhammad *et al.* [14] presented an elaborated review on deep learning-based methods for brain tumor classification, including preprocessing, features extraction, classifications, achievements, and limitations. The authors also investigated state-of-the-art convolutional neural network models for Biologically Targeted Coherent (BTC) by performing extensive experiments using transfer learning with and without data augmentation. The recent literature has been surveyed based on various aspects used by different researchers and has been taken into consideration in our literature study, which has helped us build a smart e-healthcare framework [15–26].

15.2.1   Methodology

In this section, the proposed work is discussed. Sections 15.2.2 to 15.2.7 explain each sub-part of the work. Section 15.2.8 describes the proposed algorithm. The performance of machine algorithms described in section 15.2.7 is compared with that of the proposed model.

15.2.2   Data Collection

In this chapter, data regarding NICU beds have been collected from a hospital and are stored in the cloud. The availability details of the equipment, viz., ventilators, ET tube, CPAP, and nasal cannula, are stored in the database. The patient's data have been collected using wearable sensors and transmitted to mobile devices. Data such as blood pressure, body weight, temperature, and oxygen level are also stored in the database. The patient's data are further transferred to the cloud with a unique identification number. The patient/family can use this unique identification number for authentication and can access the data. The patient's data are stored in a table in an encrypted format, ensuring that the data are secure.

15.2.3   Data Pre-Processing

Data preprocessing is the most crucial step in converting data into a consistent format and reducing the computational overhead. It eliminates noise, irregularities, or any other inconsistencies present in our data. Some noise will be incorporated into the data collected from the sensor nodes attached to the patient and transmitted to the mobile devices. These unwanted signals are filtered using electronic filters and are reduced to a large extent.

Feature extraction plays an essential role in this step. It reduces the computational overhead as the unwanted features are dropped, and only the useful ones are forwarded to train the model. In this chapter, the Convolutional Neural Network (CNN) model is used to extract the features.

15.2.4   Android Application

Android provides both versatility and user-friendliness for mobile users. An Android application is incorporated in the proposed work to transfer the data from sensors to the cloud. The Android application developed is similar to any other application in our mobile devices such as Facebook, Cred App, etc. Thus, the users will not face any difficulty adapting to the app, which is user-friendly.

The Android application provides a user interface so that users could interact with healthcare centers. The application initially asks the user to log in to the app. This step is for authorization purposes. Once the login is validated, the main screen views many options—Customer Support, Notifications, My Account, etc. The users can use these options on the main screen to contact their respective hospitals and get notifications through chat or email. The 'My Account' link shows the data of the patient, viz., name, age, and gender. The data entered by the users are stored in the app locally and forwarded to the cloud. The users can use the data stored in the app to download or forward to other apps. A unique identification number is provided to the user to log in to the app. This provides security to the user as nobody else can access the data without the user identification number. The data are encrypted and delivered from the app to the cloud. Figure 15.1 shows the user interface provided to the users by the Android application.

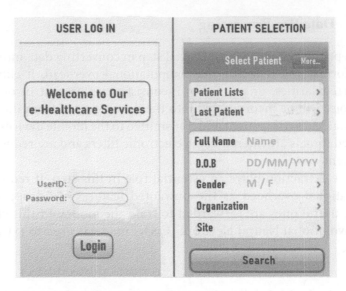

Figure 15.1 Android application user interface.

15.2.5 Data Encryption

In recent years, with the advent of trending technologies, network security has become a real challenge. Network security is a key aspect of data communication as it maintains the integrity and security of the data. The network used to transmit the data must be safe and secure. The data undergo many threats when transmitted over a network. Thus, preventive measures must be taken to safeguard the transmitted data. Encryption is a technique that converts the original data into cipher text at the transmitter end and the receiver converts the cipher text data back into its original form. The encryption techniques can use either symmetric or asymmetric keys to encrypt the data. Encryption done using symmetric keys uses the same key to encrypt and decrypt the data. Encryption done using asymmetric keys uses different keys to encrypt and decrypt the data. Asymmetric key encryption is computationally intensive, slower than symmetric key encryption techniques, and therefore unsuitable for small mobile devices [3]. In this chapter, the very well-known and extensively used encryption technique, AES, encrypts the data for transmission and storage.

The AES is a symmetrical block cipher algorithm that is fast and secure [4]. The algorithm is reliable and fast as compared to other algorithms and tested on several security applications [4]. It accepts plain text in the form of blocks of 128 bits. The number of rounds can be 10, 12, or 14 depending on the key size, i.e., it uses keys of 128, 192, or 256 bits along with the respective rounds to convert plain text to cipher text. The input is copied to a matrix named state matrix and is modified in every encryption and decryption step. The key is expanded into words so that it can be used in every encryption and decryption step. While encrypting the data using the AES algorithm, four functions are executed in each round. The 'Sub-Bytes' function represents the first transformation step in which each byte of the data is represented as two hexadecimal digits. The 'Shift-Rows' function left shifts the rows by n bytes, where n = 0, 1, 2, 3 for corresponding rows. The 'Mix-Columns' transformation works on individual columns. It transforms the columns of the state matrix. The 'Add round key' function performs matrix addition between each round key matrix and the state column matrix. Initially, the Add round key operation is performed in both encryption and decryption steps. For k rounds, the first $k-1$ rounds execute the four functions described above. The kth round will not execute the Mix-Column transformation step. Similarly, in the decryption step, the inverse of the above functions is executed in all rounds except for the last round; the inverse mix-column operation is not performed. Figure 15.2 shows the execution steps of the AES encryption–decryption algorithm.

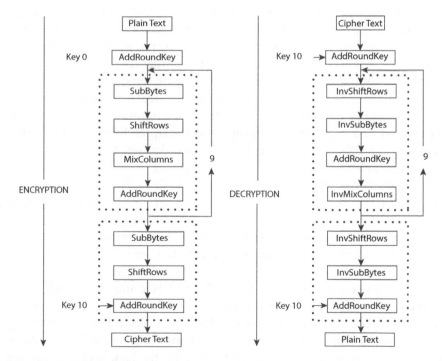

Figure 15.2 AES algorithm.

15.2.6   Cloud Storage

In this chapter, cloud storage is used to maintain the database as it is reliable, cost-effective, and efficient. If any malfunction in the hardware is encountered, the entire data are lost. In the case of cloud storage, the data can be accessed from any location using an internet connection. Also, the cloud itself provides security for data. Thus, cloud storage has been incorporated into the proposed framework. The cloud space is divided into two parts. In the first part, the data regarding the NICU beds, such as ventilators, ET tube, CPAP, nasal cannula, etc., are stored. In the second part, the patient's data such as blood pressure, body weight, temperature, oxygen level, etc., collected using wearable sensors, are stored. Each patient has a unique identification number that the patient/family can use for authenticity. The patient's data are stored in a table in an encrypted format using the algorithm described in section 15.2.7. Because the data are stored in an encrypted format, the data are highly secure.

15.2.7   Machine Learning Models

At present, machine learning is thriving in almost every field, e.g., medical settings, fraud detections, self-driving cars, and many more. It helps to close the gap between human and machine skills. Being a part of artificial intelligence, machine learning is used for predictive and regressive analysis. It requires enormous data to learn so that this knowledge can be used to analyze unseen or new data. The data are separated into two parts, namely, training and testing data. The machine learning model is trained on the training data and evaluated on the testing data. The models can be trained in a supervised or unsupervised manner. Supervised machine learning algorithms are those that use labeled datasets to train the model. Some examples of supervised machine learning algorithms are Support Vector Machines, K-Nearest Neighbor, and Naïve Bayes. Unsupervised machine learning algorithms are those that use unlabeled data to train the model. These algorithms try to find the hidden patterns in the data. In other words, data are clustered based on their similarity. Some unsupervised machine learning algorithms include K-means and hierarchical algorithms.

In our proposed work, we have combined CNN and SVM models and compared the performance with the individual CNN and SVM models. These models are widely used for classification tasks. It is a deep learning model that is widely applied with textual and image data. It consists of convolution layers that help reduce the size of the data, keep the features intact, and pool layers that help reduce the dimensionality; i.e., it can be used for extracting valuable features. To perform these tasks, the convolutional and pooling layers depend on specific parameters, viz., number of filters, filter size, strides, activation function, etc. SVM stands for Support Vector Machine. It helps generate a hyperplane, also known as the decision boundary between the classes, developed as the model learns the data to classify the unknown data in the given space. Some of the parameters of SVM include kernel function, trade-off parameter, and gamma. The parameters used in our models are described in Tables 15.1 and 15.2.

Table 15.1 Parameters used in the CNN model.

Parameters	Values
Number of convolution layers	3
Number of max-pooling layers	3
Number of fully connected layers	2
Number of filters in convolution layers	64
Kernel/filter size in convolution layers	5
Pool size in max-pooling layers	3
Activation function in convolution layers	Relu
Epochs	100

Table 15.2 Parameters used in the SVM model.

Parameters	Values
c	0.099
gamma	0.099
Kernel function	rbf
Epochs	100

15.2.8   Proposed Algorithm

Technology has progressed rapidly in the past few years. The e-healthcare system developed in this work can be used for easy access and in an emergency. If the hospital is far from the patient's location, the application comes in handy. The Android application has a feature, 'Contact Us,' that can be used by the patient/family to contact the hospital and answer their queries at any time. The novel coronavirus SARS-CoV-2 has spread worldwide. In this situation, visiting a hospital is very risky for the child. Also, the baby may require medical attention at any time. Thus, a framework is developed that uses an Android application to make this task easier.

In this chapter, a smart e-healthcare framework is developed. The data are collected using the sensors attached to the patient's body and are stored in the cloud in an encrypted format using the AES algorithm. Cloud storage is used as it provides security to the data. Also, the data are stored in an encrypted form, which make them highly secure. Unlike cloud storage, other storage options would result in a blunder if the hardware malfunctions; the data from the storage might be corrupted or lost. Also, data access from the cloud is convenient. The cloud storage is divided into two parts—one part stores the data regarding the NICU beds, and the other part stores the data regarding the patient. Each patient has a unique identification number that can be used by the patient or his or her family to log in and access the patient's data. The patient's data can be accessed by the patient/family using an Android application similar to any other application on the mobile phone. It has features, viz., Login, My Account, Notifications, and many more. These options are already familiar to the users as they are similar to other mobile applications, viz. Facebook, Cred App, etc. The application is very simple and easy to use. The users can view, manipulate, and download their data from the Android application.

The machine learning models have been incorporated to predict if the NICU beds are available in the given hospital. In the proposed work, the CNN model is combined with the SVM model. The CNN model is used for feature extraction and SVM to determine the availability of the NICU beds. The parameters used in the proposed work are described in Tables 15.1 and 15.2. The proposed framework is compared with the CNN and SVM models. The parameters used in these models are the same as that of the proposed framework. The Android application also provides the link, where the number of available NICU beds in a particular hospital can be identified. The algorithm runs every 24 h. The availability of the NICU beds is determined and updated so that the users can view the details using the app and accordingly visit the hospitals. Figures 15.3 and 15.4

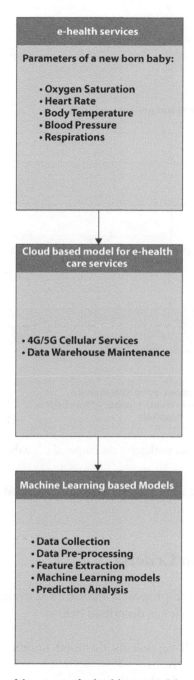

Figure 15.3 Architecture of the proposed e-healthcare model.

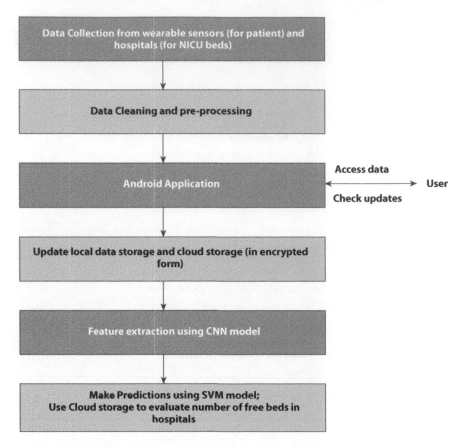

Figure 15.4 Flowchart of the working of the proposed e-healthcare model.

show the architecture and flowchart of the proposed e-healthcare model, respectively.

15.3   Evaluation Criteria

The performance of the proposed algorithm is evaluated using the well-known evaluation metrics as described below:

i.   Accuracy: It represents the total number of predictions made correctly.

ii.   Precision: It displays the percentage of all expected values for a class successfully predicted.

iii. Recall: The number of accurately predicted values for a class divided by the number of actual values for that class.

15.4   Results

The experiment was conducted on the dataset described earlier. The 5-fold cross-validation was used to evaluate the dataset; i.e., the dataset was divided into five parts, out of which four parts were considered the training data, and the fifth part was considered the testing data. The algorithm was run in five iterations such that for each iteration, one of the five parts of the dataset behaved as the testing dataset. The proposed algorithm was compared with the CNN and SVM models. The parameters used in these models are shown in Tables 15.1 and 15.2, optimized using the Grid Search technique. Figures 15.5–15.7 show the accuracy, precision, and recall bar graphs corresponding to the proposed algorithm, CNN, and SVM models. It has been observed that the proposed algorithm has outperformed the CNN and SVM models based on accuracy, precision, and recall evaluation metrics.

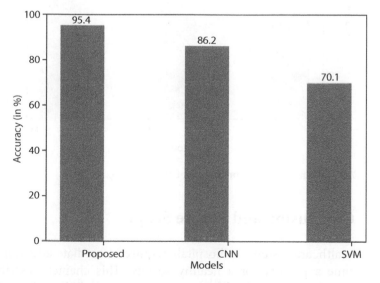

Figure 15.5 Accuracy analysis on the prediction of NICU beds.

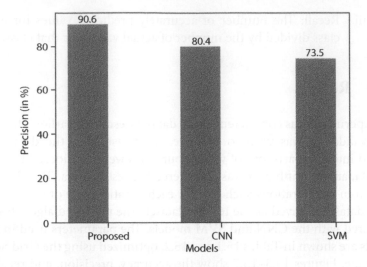

Figure 15.6 Precision analysis on the prediction of NICU beds.

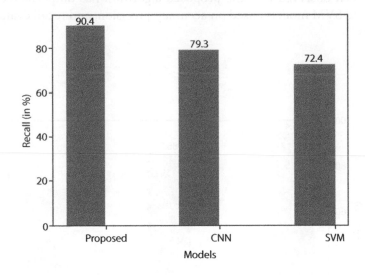

Figure 15.7 Recall analysis on the prediction of NICU beds.

15.5 Conclusion and Future Scope

Smart e-healthcare systems in hospitals require immediate attention and have become a priority for a healthy society. This chapter describes a machine learning-based e-healthcare system framework that will perform smart prediction analysis of NICU beds' availability to be easily accessed by people through their Android phones. NICUs have multiple facilities that help a newborn baby to face cognitive challenges. The demand for NICUs is increasing day by day. Thus, it is challenging to assess the availability of NICUs in hospitals in urban/suburban areas.

This chapter proposes a new framework that makes it easier to determine bed availability in hospitals. It uses an Android application that acts as a user interface. The authorized users can log in to the application, access their data, and find an option to check the availability of the NICU beds. The framework is secure and reliable as it uses cloud storage to store data in an encrypted form. Cloud storage is used to store two types of data— NICU data and patient data. The NICU data are fetched from the cloud and given to machine learning models to determine the availability of the NICU beds. The CNN model is used to extract the features, and the SVM model is used for making predictions. The cloud data are further analyzed to determine the number of NICU beds available. The proposed framework has outperformed other models in this chapter.

The framework has great importance, especially in the current COVID scenario, where the chances of reaching hospitals on time and getting assistance from the doctors are low. Also, it will be convenient for the family in that they no longer have to visit the hospital and their queries could be answered using the customer support available in the application. Such applications can be further modified to add new features that will be helpful for families during crisis. The proposed framework can also be utilized in biomedical applications for smart healthcare.

References

1. Allan, S.M., Bealey, R., Birch, J., Cushing, T., Parke, S., Sergi, G., Bloomfield, M., Meiser-Stedman, R., The prevalence of common and stress-related mental health disorders in healthcare workers based in pandemic-affected hospitals: A rapid systematic review and meta-analysis. *Eur. J. Psychotraumatol.*, *11*, 1, 1810903, 2020. https://doi.org/10.1080/20008198.2020.1810903.
2. Dias, D. and Paulo Silva Cunha, J., Wearable health devices—Vital sign monitoring, systems and technologies. *Sensors*, *18*, 8, 2414, 2018, https://doi.org/10.3390/s18082414.
3. Ugalmugle, S. and Swain, R., *Digital health market size by technology, 2021– 2027*, Global Market Insights, Inc., 2021, July 13, [Retrieved November 2, 2021] https://www.gminsights.com/industry-analysis/digital-health-market.
4. De, R., Pandey, N., Pal, A., Impact of digital surge during Covid-19 pandemic: A viewpoint on research and practice. *Int. J. Inf. Manage.*, *55*, 102171, 2020. https://doi.org/10.1016/j.ijinfomgt.2020.102171.

5. Rosenbaum, L., The untold toll — The pandemic's effects on patients without Covid-19. *New Engl. J. Med.*, *382*, 24, 2368–2371, 2020. https://doi.org/10.1056/nejmms2009984.

6. Dunn, J., Runge, R., Snyder, M., Wearables and the medical revolution. *Per. Med.*, *15*, 5, 429–448, 2018. https://doi.org/10.2217/pme-2018-0044.

7. Dutta, R., Chowdhury, S., Singh, K.K., Managing IoT and cloud-based healthcare record system using unique identification number to promote integrated healthcare delivery system: A perspective from India, in: *Emergence of Cyber Physical System and IoT in Smart Automation and Robotics. Advances in Science, Technology & Innovation (IEREK Interdisciplinary Series for Sustainable Development)*, K.K. Singh, A. Nayyar, S. Tanwar, M. Abouhawwash (Eds.), Springer, Cham, 2021, https://doi.org/10.1007/978-3-030-66222-6_8.

8. Cole, T., *Interview with Kevin Ashton-inventor of IoT*, 11th February 2018, https://www.smart-industry.net/interview-with-iot-inventor-kevin-ashton-iot-is-driven-by-the-users/ Retrieved 10.11.2021.

9. Islam, S.M.R., Kwak, D., Kabir, M.H., Hossain, M., Kwak, K., The internet of things for healthcare: A comprehensive survey. *IEEE Access*, 17, 5, Published on 2015.

10. Wang, M., Fu, F., Zheng, B., Bai, Y., Wu, Q., Wu, J., Sun, L., Liu, Q., Liu, M., Yang, Y., Shen, H., Kong, D., Ma, X., You, P., Li, X., Tian, F., Development of an AI system for accurately diagnose hepatocellular carcinoma from computed tomography imaging data. *Br. J. Cancer*, *125*, 8, 1111–1121, 2021. https://doi.org/10.1038/s41416-021-01511-w.

11. McQuee, M., *The future is at hand*, 2018, July 24, from https://www.hospital-health.com.au/content/technology/article/the-future-is-at-hand-970690498 [retrieve on 11th November, 2021].

12. Lee, G.H., Moon, H., Kim, H., Lee, G.H., Kwon, W., Yoo, S., Myung, D., Yun, S.H., Bao, Z., Hahn, S.K., Multifunctional materials for implantable and wearable photonic healthcare devices. *Nat. Rev. Mater.*, *5*, 2, 149–165, 2020, https://doi.org/10.1038/s41578-019-0167-3.

13. Park, E., Kim, K.J., Kwon, S.J., Understanding the emergence of wearable devices as next-generation tools for health communication. *Inf. Technol. People*, *29*, 4, 717–732, 2016, https://doi.org/10.1108/itp-04-2015-0096.

14. *Futurist Nikolas badminton gets implanted with a microchip*, 2014, June 28, [Video], YouTube, https://www.youtube.com/watch?v=QSWRr-Y0sLs.

15. Ha, M., Lim, S., Ko, H., Wearable and flexible sensors for user-interactive health-monitoring devices. *J. Mater. Chem. B*, 6, 24, 4043–4064, 2018. https://doi.org/10.1039/c8tb01063c.

16. Vidal, M., Turner, J., Bulling, A., Gellersen, H., Wearable eye tracking for mental health monitoring. *Comput. Commun.*, *35*, 11, 1306–1311, 2012, https://doi.org/10.1016/j.comcom.2011.11.002.

17. Rosa, B.M.G. and Yang, G.Z., A Flexible wearable device for measurement of cardiac, electrodermal, and motion parameters in mental healthcare

applications. *IEEE J. Biomed. Health Inf.*, *23*, 6, 2276–2285, 2019, https://doi.org/10.1109/jbhi.2019.2938311.

18. Lou, Z., Wang, L., Jiang, K., Wei, Z., Shen, G., Reviews of wearable healthcare systems: Materials, devices and system integration. *Mater. Sci. Eng. R. Rep.*, *140*, 100523, 2020, https://doi.org/10.1016/j.mser.2019.100523.

19. Dutte, R., Subhadip, C., Elngar, A.A., Healthcare applications of the internet of things (IoT) [E-book], in: *Deep Learning and IoT in Healthcare Systems: Paradigms and Applications*, 1st ed, K.K. Singh, A. Singh, J.W. Lin, A.A. Elngar (Eds.), pp. 215–242, Apple Academic Press, 2021, https://doi.org/10.1201/9781003055082.

20. Minoli, D. and Occhiogrosso, B., Blockchain mechanisms for IoT security. *Internet Things*, *1–2*, 1–13, 2018. https://doi.org/10.1016/j.iot.2018.05.002.

21. Petracca, F., Ciani, O., Cucciniello, M., Tarricone, R., Harnessing digital health technologies during and after the COVID-19 pandemic: Context matters. *J. Med. Internet Res.*, *22*, 12, e21815, 2020. https://doi.org/10.2196/21815.

22. Sepasgozar, S., Karimi, R., Farahzadi, L., Moezzi, F., Shirowzhan, S., M. Ebrahimzadeh, S., Hui, F., Aye, L., A systematic content review of artificial intelligence and the internet of things applications in smart home. *Appl. Sci.*, *10*, 9, 3074, 2020, https://doi.org/10.3390/app10093074.

23. Skouby, K.E. and Lynggaard, P., Smart home and smart city solutions enabled by 5G, IoT, AAI and CoT services. *2014 International Conference on Contemporary Computing and Informatics (IC3I)*, 2014, Published, https://doi.org/10.1109/ic3i.2014.7019822.

24. Roy, P.C., Abidi, S.R., Abidi, S.S., Possibilistic activity recognition with uncertain observations to support medication adherence in an assisted ambient living setting. *Knowl. Based Syst.*, *133*, 156–173, 2017, https://doi.org/10.1016/j.knosys.2017.07.008.

25. Kappiarukudil, K.J. and Ramesh, M.V., Real-time monitoring and detection of "Heart Attack" using wireless sensor networks. *2010 Fourth International Conference on Sensor Technologies and Applications*, 2010, Published, https://doi.org/10.1109/sensorcomm.2010.99.

26. Raju, G.N. and Ministry of Law and Justice (Legislative Department), *The consumer protection act, 2019 (Extraordinary, part-2, section-1, No-54.)*, pp. 1–40, The Gazette of India, Published on 9th August 2019, https://egazette.nic.in/WriteReadData/2019/210422.pdf.

16

An Improved Random Forest Feature Selection Method for Predicting the Patient's Characteristics

K. Indhumathi[1]* and K. Sathesh Kumar[2]

[1]Department of Computer Application, Kalasalingam Academy of Research and Education, Kalasalingam University, Krishnan Kovil, India
[2]Department of Computer Science and Information Technology, Kalasalingam University, Krishnan Kovil, India

Abstract

The global population has been devastated by the Coronavirus Disease 2019 (COVID-19) epidemic that started in Wuhan, China, which has overwhelmed established medical systems globally. In March of this year, there had been over 116 million infected patients along with 2.58 million deaths worldwide. Day by day, the number of confirmed COVID-19 patients grows. However, to provide efficient treatment, expert system approaches must be applied to predict the outcome of an infected patient and the increase in the number of patients. Preprocessing the patient health record and extracting the essential features from the preprocessed health record are the first steps to determine the probability of infected people. This chapter proposes a new modified algorithm for predicting the best features of a patient health dataset. It also discusses various feature selection methods and analyzes the performance of different feature extraction methods. To extract important features from health records, this chapter uses the Boruta algorithm, Rank features by importance, Recursive feature elimination, Variable importance by machine learning methods, and Random Forest feature selection process. The time complexity of Improved Random Forest, Random Forest, Boruta algorithm, Rank features, Variable importance using machine learning algorithms, and Recursive feature elimination methods are 1.12 ms, 1.5 ms, 1.78 ms, 2 ms, 2.75 ms, and 2.4 ms. As compared to the time complexity of feature selection approaches,

Corresponding author: indhu16aug@gmail.com

Akansha Singh, Anuradha Dhull and Krishna Kant Singh (eds.) Blockchain and Deep Learning for Smart Healthcare, (399–424) © 2024 Scrivener Publishing LLC

the Random Forest approach allows us to pick the most appropriate features in a fraction of the time.

Keywords: Coronavirus disease, patient health record, machine learning, feature selection, epidemics, disease prediction, time complexity, random forest

16.1   Introduction

The clinical industry is complex, necessitating the gathering and reporting of patient information in real time. This industry is also plagued by the matter of data preparation, which necessitates real-time prediction and delivery about knowledge to clinicians who will provide effective medical care. Physicians, manufacturers, clinics, and healthcare organizations have all sought to capture, retain, and resurrect data to optimize clinical outcomes and spur technical innovation.

Dealing with patient records, on the other hand, has recently become a difficult task due to the vast amount of data, security problems, wireless network device incompetence, and the rate at which it is growing. Coronavirus disease 2019 (COVID-19), which was discovered in China, has become a respiratory illness and has spread globally, causing a worldwide respiratory illness epidemic. According to studies [1–3], COVID-19 has clinical characteristics that are comparable to SARS-CoV. The most common indications are fever and cough, with gastrointestinal symptoms being uncommon.

The disappearance of temperature is more common in COVID-19-infected patients than in persons diagnosed by associating pathogens such as MERS Corona Virus (2%) and SARS Corona Virus (1%) [4]. COVID-19 infection was first linked to a major seafood and animal marketplace in Wuhan, where the virus was transmitted from animals to humans. Also, the percentages of physicians have shown no connection to animal markets, implying that the outbreak of corona from people to people [5].

The majority of medical studies have focused on understanding COVID-19 symptoms [6], categorizing them [7], and eventually predicting the incubation period [8]. COVID-19-infected patients have shown a variety of symptoms. The probability of death can be predicted depending on which signs are present. Preprocessing the unprocessed data and then utilizing feature extraction to predict the relevant features from the patient dataset would be the first steps in diagnosis.

The method of eliminating obsolete or unrelated parameters from primary data is called feature selection. As a consequence, the classifier that processes the data's execution time decreases, although accuracy increases because outliers may include noisy data, lowering prediction performance [9]. Insight could be increased, and the complexity of data management can be reduced, in respect to attribute extraction [10].

Filters, wrappers, and embedded selectors are the different categories of feature selection algorithms. Filters evaluate each feature independently including its training set, rank those attributes once they have been evaluated, and choose the best [11]. For example, entropy [12] could be utilized to perform this evaluation. A wrapper assesses the classifier's accuracy on a subsection of the core functionality before evaluating its output on a different subset.

The grouping for it is decided which classifier has the better output. Hence, wrappers are determined by the classifier chosen. Wrappers are more accurate because the classification algorithm influences accuracy, despite the fact that subset selection is an NP-hard problem [13]. As a result, it necessitates a significant amount of computing time and memory. For subset collection, heuristic algorithms such as the genetic algorithm, greedy stepwise, best first, and random search can be used.

Moreover, as a consequence, filters save time as compared to wrappers, but they ignore the fact that selecting better features might be essential to classification algorithms. Deep neural networks, for example, are embedded techniques that allow for complete selection during the learning process. Many feature extraction studies have been published, including one on why filters are favored over wrappers [14].

Our contribution includes the following:

> Preprocessing the patient healthcare data using proposed preprocessing methods.
> Deleting the irrelevant characters using proposed computation methods such as the numerical imputation method and categorical imputation method.
> Label encoding techniques are very useful to preprocess the data. They convert the label into numeric form.

   ✓ The Improved Random Forest feature selection method was found to be the outstanding method for extracting important features from patient data when compared to other feature selection techniques.

16.2   Literature Survey

Gokulnath and Shantharajah [15] provided methods from the Cleveland dataset. Four classification algorithms are discussed by the authors. To construct models for heart disease prediction, researchers used support vector machine, multilayer perceptron, J48, and KNN. Comparing the results to models depends on the primary attribute set and feature sets chosen using certain widely used attribute extraction methods, using 10-fold cross-validation. When combined with SVM Classifier (SVM), the genetic algorithm achieved the greatest precision of 88.34%, compared to 83.70% with the initial dataset.

Kavitha and Kannan [16] produced a framework for heart disease classifier that included PCA-based feature extraction. Reducing data dimensionality, as per the authors, increases the classifier's prediction accuracy while lowering the prediction's computational cost. It may be done by using the feature selection technique, which removes a new set of attributes from the original set, or attribute extraction techniques, which choose a subset of the most suitable features.

Jabbar *et al.* [17] used feature selection with a Chi-squared feature evaluator in combination with the Random Forest ML algorithm to construct a model for heart disease prediction. Chi-squared with backwards elimination was used by the authors. They rank the features according to their importance. The Chi-squared test then deletes the lowest-ranking function one by one, then builds and tests a model at each level until the model's accuracy plateaus. The most accurate model they discovered was a rate of 83.7%.

Steyerberg [18] proposed a standard variable selection approach of stepwise backward selection using p-values that have been utilized in the healthcare literature. Zou and Hastie [19] suggested the Elastic Net function selection method. It implements a Lasso extension. The L2 norm's characteristics promote a clustered impact, allowing strongly correlated variables to be held in the model or discarded together. In a similar way, the Lasso method also performs embedded variable collection.

Sanchez-Pintoa *et al.* [20] determined the variables selected, and the Lasso feature selection model with the highest AUC was used to measure the method's performance on the validation array. Hastie *et al.* [21] uses a Random Forest, which is an aggregate model made up of hundreds of decision trees that calculates a result based on the average output of all of them. Every forest is constructed using iterative partitioning of random subsets of the input variables.

The parameters are selected and the partition's specific cut-points are decided with the ultimate aim of dividing the data into subsets with the most varying proportions of the outcome or knowledge benefit. Sanchez-Pintoa *et al.* [20] used the RF Attribute selection method. It identifies different variable subsets: one for analysis, which includes all strongly correlated variables, and another for prediction, which only includes the smallest subgroup of parameters that are suitable for prediction.

Kursa and Weinberger [22] suggest a Boruta feature extraction technique. Boruta is a randomized tree method for extracting properties that are shown to be systematically less meaningful than randomized probing, which are algorithm-generated noise variables. Xu *et al.* [23] used the gradient boosting computer architecture to pick variables. By penalizing its identification of new variables, GBFS generates an aggregate of reduced regression trees for which variables are chosen irregularly.

16.3   Dataset

The "Novel Corona Virus 2019 Dataset" used in this analysis was obtained from Kaggle [24]. The information was gathered from a variety of outlets, including the World Health Organization and John Hopkins University. The dataset contains various missing and irrelevant data. Thus, before the analysis, one must preprocess the data. Table 16.1 describes the patient health data. The second column denotes the patient health attributes (such as patient id, patient location, patient country, gender, age, visit_Wuhan, and from_Wuhan) and symptoms like fever, cough, throat pain, fatigue, cold, vomiting, nausea, etc. The third column includes the description of the patients' attributes. The last column contains the data type of the patient's parameters.

Table 16.1 Patient dataset description.

Sl. no.	Column	Description	Types
1.	Id	COVID patient id	Numeric
2.	Location	The address of the patient's residence	String
3.	Country	Native nation of the patient	String

(Continued)

Table 16.1 Patient dataset description. (*Continued*)

Sl. no.	Column	Description	Types
4.	Gender	Sex of the patient	String
5.	Age	Age of the patient	Numeric
6.	symp_on	When did the patient first experience the symptoms?	Date
7.	hosp_visit	When did the patient go to the hospital?	Date
8.	visit_wuhan	Whether or not the patient travelled to Wuhan, China	Numeric/Categorical
9.	from_wuhan	If the patient was from Wuhan, China	Numeric/Categorical
10.	Fever	Illnesses that people have encountered	Numeric/Categorical
11.	Cough		
12.	Throat pain		
13.	Fatigue		
14.	Cold		
15.	Vomiting		
16.	Nausea		
17.	Difficulty breathing		
18.	Sore throat		
19.	Joint pain		
20.	Chills		
21.	Mild cough		

(*Continued*)

Table 16.1 Patient dataset description. (*Continued*)

Sl. no.	Column	Description	Types
22.	Headache		
23.	Throat discomfort		
24.	Malaise		
25.	Mild fever		
26.	High fever		
27.	Sore body		
28.	Chest discomfort		
29.	Flu		
30.	Reflux		
31.	Physical discomfort		
32	Tired		
33.	Myalgia		
34.	Runny nose		
35.	Diarrhea		
36.	Heavy head		
37.	Loss of appetite		
38.	Pneumonia		
39.	Muscle pain		
40.	Breathlessness		
41.	Sputum		
42.	Nasal discharge		
43.	Respiratory distress		
44.	Sneeze		
45.	Thirst		
46.	Aching muscles		

(*Continued*)

Table 16.1 Patient dataset description. (*Continued*)

Sl. no.	Column	Description	Types
47.	Muscle aches		
48.	Chest pain		
49.	Shortness of breath		
50.	Itchy throat		
51.	Muscle cramps		
52.	Dyspnea		
53.	Abdominal pain		
54.	Cough with sputum		
55.	Recov	If the patient was able to recover	Numeric/Categorical
56.	Death	If the patient died as a result of COVID-19	Numeric/Categorical

16.4   Data Analysis

Patients experience a wide range of symptoms. Figure 16.1 depicts the most classic symptoms observed in the patient dataset. Unlike other symptoms, fever, cough, vomiting, and shortness of breath are very common.

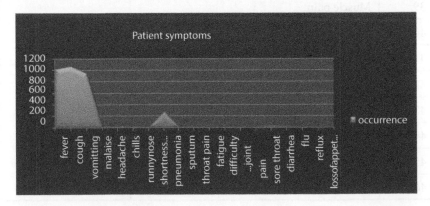

Figure 16.1 Symptoms of patients.

16.5   Data Pre-Processing

The dataset is made up of date, characters, and numbers. The information gathering also includes categorical variables. We performed label-encoding of the categorical variables because the intelligent retrieval system can only acquire the arithmetic values. This applies an integer to each and every column's special categorical values. Figure 16.2 shows the step-by-step procedure of preprocessing.

At first, the patient health dataset (raw data) is loaded. It contains missing values and repeated information. In the second step to fill the missing data, the numerical and categorical imputation methods have been used. In the third step, all the string values are converted into integer values, because the machine learning methods only accept numeric data. Finally, the process produces the preprocessed data.

When passed directly as an input, the data consist of several missing values, resulting in an error. The unknown parameters in the primary data are treated using feature engineering techniques.

The key objectives of feature extraction are as follows:

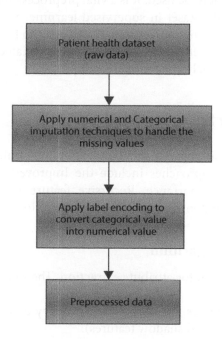

Figure 16.2 Data preprocessing.

✓ Creating a suitable input dataset that meets the specifications of the classification algorithm.
✓ The classification model's efficiency is being improved.

Two attribute extraction techniques are utilized in this study: numerical imputation and categorical imputation.

A. Numerical imputation
   Imputation is a better option than reduction since it holds the data size the same. The median imputation of the columns is used in this chapter to treat numerical missing values. Since column averages are more susceptible to outlier values, medians are a better choice.

B. Categorical imputation
   When dealing with categorical columns, replacing missing values with the highest value in the column is a good choice.

C. Label encoding
   It is the method of transforming names into integers so that they can be read by machines. Then, utilizing classification models, better decisions will be made on how those marks should be used. It is a vital preprocessing step for the structured dataset in supervised learning. String columns are position, nation, and gender, which can be found in the patient dataset. These three fields are translated to numeric form using label encoding techniques.

16.6   Feature Selection Methods

The estimation of six separate attribute extraction strategies is discussed. Machine learning approaches include the Improved Boruta algorithm, Rank features by importance, Recursive feature removal, and vector importance and Random Forest parameter extraction.

16.6.1   Boruta Algorithm

Boruta is an algorithm for attribute extraction. The steps are as follows:

✓ First, it shuffles attributes of the primary dataset randomly (which is called shadow features).

✓ It also practices a Random Forest classifier with the primary data and then uses an attribute essential to assess the significance of each element, with higher values indicating greater importance.

✓ It constantly removes attributes that are deemed unimportant and compares the consequence of a real attribute to its duplicate attributes.

✓ Eventually, when all features are verified or rejected, and a run reaches a fixed limit, the implementation comes to a halt.

The step-by-step procedure of the Boruta algorithm is given below in Algorithm 1

Algorithm 1 Boruta Pseudo Code

Input: COVID patient dataset
Output: Selected features
Repeat the below steps C times for every given attributes {A1,....., AP}

1. **Construct** a Random Forest including its given and newly created duplicate attributes.
2. **Determine** every imp (Ai) and Di
3. If imp (Ai) > Di, then increase Mi and call Ai important for execute
4. Once {Mi ...... Mp} have been determined.
5. Do the computation M0: Mi = E (M) Vs M1: Mi ≠ E(M)
6. $\overset{\approx}{Mi} \sim C\ ((0.5\ C),(\sqrt{(0.25C)}2)$
7. If Mi is greater than E(M), then the attribute is important
8. If Mi is less than E(M), then the attribute is unimportant
9. **End** the computation, if every attribute has been rejected or it is noted as unimportant. Otherwise, repeat the computation

---

Figure 16.3 depicts the feature selection output of the Boruta algorithm. In this diagram, the green symbols denote selected attributes. The yellow and blue symbols denote tentative attributes. The red symbols represent the rejected attributes. The Boruta algorithm extracts only 10 out of 52 attributes.

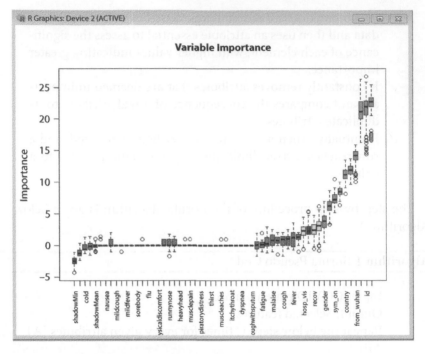

Figure 16.3 Final feature selection for Boruta.

16.6.2 Rank Features by Importance

Creating a framework can be used to estimate the value of features based on data. Decision trees have a built-in structure for specifying the variable importance. The value of other algorithms can be calculated using an ROC curve method for each and every parameter. The VarImp () function is used to determine the importance of variables.

Based on importance, the variables are ranked in descending order. Then, the top three rank attributes are selected. These three attributes are marked as important. Other attributes are considered unimportant. It is very easy to extract the important features from the original attributes, but it only takes three attributes. The procedure of Rank features by importance is given below in Algorithm 2.

Algorithm 2 Rank Feature by Importance

        Inputs:

                Patient dataset D

                Assign of m attributes

Fm = {A1, A2 .....Am}
Ranking method R (D, Fm)

Output:

Final ranking S

Code:

Iterate for j in {1: m}
Rank assigns Fm using R (D, Fm)
a* ← final ranker attribute in Fm
S (m – j+1) ← a*
Fm ← Fm – a*

Figure 16.4 shows the final result of attribute extraction. It ranks the attributes based on their importance. The rank value lies between 0.5 and 0.9.

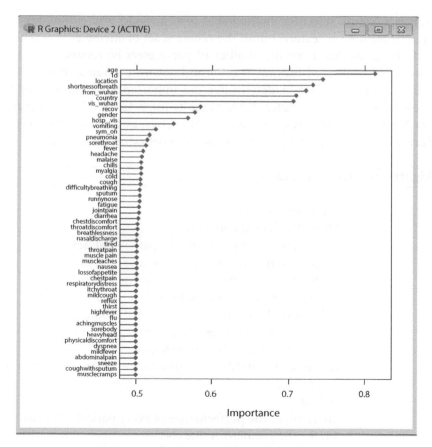

Figure 16.4 Final attribute selection of rank importance.

The rank 0.9 is assigned to the most important attribute. The rank 0.5 is assigned to the least important attribute. In this diagram, the rank 0.85 is assigned to the age attribute. The rank of patient id is 0.77. The value 0.75 is allocated to the attribute location. The shortness of breath rank value is 0.73.

The from_wuhan attribute has a rank value of 0.71. The rank value of country parameter is 0.7. Rank 0.6 is assigned to the visit_wuhan parameter. The rank 0.59 is assigned to recovery. Then, the value 0.58 is assigned to gender. The feature hosp_visit has a rank of 0.55. The rank 0.53 is set to the vomiting attribute. The Symp_on attribute has a rank value of 0.51. All other attributes are set to 0.5. Only the top three attributes (age, id, and location) are selected.

16.6.3   Recursive Feature Elimination

RFE is a feature selection method that suits a model and eliminates the poorest feature (or features) until the required set of attributes is reached. RFE demands that a certain number of parameters be retained, but the number of confirmed features is often unknown in advance. It is a very effective method. First, it determines the importance of the attributes. Then, ranking the parameter depends on its importance. Next, select the top N number of features. The value of N is given by the user. The procedure of Recursive feature elimination is given below in Algorithm 3.

Algorithm 3 Recursive Feature Elimination

Input: load patient dataset
Output: Selected Attributes
1. Train the template using the patient dataset
2. Analyze the template performance
3. Determine attribute significance or ranking
4. For every patient dataset size Pi, i = 1,2 ……..P do
5. Identify the Pi's most significant attribute
6. Again train the template using the patient dataset
7. Determine template performance
8. Calculate attribute significance for every patient attribute
9. End
10. Analyze the performance of every patient attribute
11. Set the predictor value (N)
12. Finally select N number of parameters

Figure 16.5 shows the accuracy of every attribute of patient health dataset. The accuracy range is between 0.95 and 1.00. The Id (patient id) gives an accuracy of 0.95. The attribute location provides an accuracy of 0.972. The accuracy of Country, Gender, Age, and Symp_on are 0.975, 0.985, 0.975, and 0.974, respectively.

The accuracy of hosp_visit, visit_wuhan, from_wuhan, fever, and cough is 0.975, 0.975, 0.975, 0.974, and 0.9745, respectively. The attribute throat_pain gives an accuracy of 0.975. Fatigue has an accuracy of 0.978. Similarly, it provides the accuracy of each and every parameter. The Recursive feature elimination method selects the best five parameters and marks these parameters as important. Other attributes are unimportant.

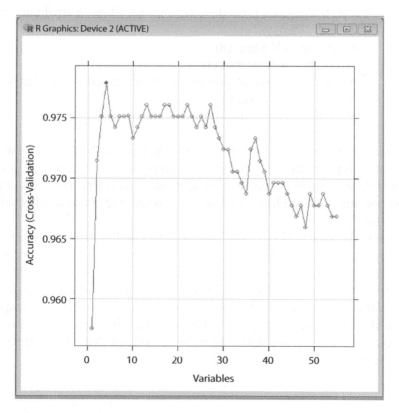

Figure 16.5 Accuracy of recursive feature elimination.

16.7   Variable Importance by Machine Learning Methods

Another important consideration when choosing features is to consider which variables are used by most machine learning algorithms. This method only selects the top five important attributes. It is a very simple and very effective method. First, it calculates the variable importance of each and every attribute and then selects the top five attributes. These five attributes are marked as important and the other attributes are marked as unimportant. The step-by-step procedure of variable importance is shown below in Algorithm 4.

Algorithm 4 Variable Importance by Machine Learning Methods

Input: Import patient dataset
Output: Selected Attributes
1. Iterate the given procedure N times for all given attributes {R1, R2..........Rm}
2. Calculate all VarImp (Rj)
3. Select the top five attributes
4. Mark the top five attributes as important. Other attributes are marked as unimportant
5. Stop the calculation if all the attributes are marked

Figure 16.6 presents the final feature selection of the COVID patient dataset. This provides the variable importance of every parameter. In this patient dataset, the importance of attribute location is 100. Thus, it is noted as important. The significance of id is 65.20 and the status of id is set as important.

The importance of the age attribute is 46.08 and it is denoted as important. The significance of from_wuhan is 34.29, and it is marked as important. The attribute shortness of breath has an importance value of 11.37. Vis_wuhan has an importance value of 11.24. This is the least significant value. The importance of all other attributes is zero. The variable importance method fetches the top five attributes. Thus, the parameters location, id, age, from_wuhan, and shortness of breath are selected. Other attributes are rejected.

	Overall
location	100.00
id	65.20
age	46.08
from_wuhan	34.29
Shortnessofbreath	11.37
vis_wuhan	11.24
reflux	0.00
nausea	0.00
respiratory distress	0.00
hosp_vis	0.00
itchy throat	0.00
sore throat	0.00
nasal discharge	0.00
difficulty breathing	0.00
Jointpain	0.00
muscle aches	0.00
Runnynose	0.00
Malaise	0.00
Country	0.00
symp_on	0.00

Figure 16.6 Feature selection of variable importance.

16.8   Random Forest Feature Selection

Random Forests are decision trees that use bagging to create a model from data. Random Forests have a correlation-based feature methodology that assigns a score and scores the attributes using the 'Gini index.' The pseudo code of Random Forest feature selection is shown in Algorithm 5. First, it splits the attribute as a node. Then, it calculates the Gini index of each and every attribute. After that, it determines the mean decrease Gini index for every attribute, compares all attributes and finds the Gini index attribute with the highest value, and sets the attribute as important.

In this patient dataset, the computed mean decrease Gini index values are denoted as both positive and negative. The Random Forest feature selection method sets the positive mean decrease Gini index value attribute as important. Other parameters (negative value features) are denoted as unimportant.

Algorithm 5 Pseudo Code for Random Forest Feature Selection

Input   : Load patient dataset
Output: Extract best features
1. Extract best Attributes:
2. For m = 1 to k do
3. Load the patient dataset in Pi
4. Generate a root node, Ri contains Pi
5. Call ConstructNode (Ri)
6. end for
7. ConstructNode (R)
8. if R consists only one node then
9. return
10. else
11. Randomly fetch V% of the probable separated attri-butes in R
12. for i = 1 to C do
13. Calculate Gini index
14. Gi = 1 - ΣC i = 1(Ri)2
15. pick the attribute S with the greatest MeanDecreaseGiniIndex and set the selected attribute as important
16. call ConstructNode (Ri)
17. end for
18. end if

Figure 16.7 depicts the final selection of attributes using the Random Forest feature extraction method. It provides the most accurate parameter extraction. It selects the best important attributes when compared to other parameter selection techniques. By comparing the value of mean decrease Gini index, the status of the attribute is set as important or not.

	MeanDecrease Gini
id	1.448858e+01
location	1.757779e+01
country	3.790483e+00
gender	9.337162e+01
age	1.241632e+01
symp_on	2.461928e+00
hosp_visit	1.124125e+00
visit_wuhan	1.670027e+00
from_wuhan	3.452200e+00
fever	9.734024e+01
cough	5.094376e+02
throat pain	6.182016e-03
fatigue	4.305009e-01
cold	4.095059e-01
vomiting	5.444868e+01
nausea	2.113025e-03
difficulty breathing	6.016126e-01
sore throat	3.471269e-02
joint pain	1.837889e-02
chills	4.600643e-02
mild cough	1.914391e-05
headache	2.249279e-02
throat discomfort	4.261178e-03
malaise	4.376392e-02
mild fever	1.000793e-03
high fever	.566710e-04
sore body	4.380852e-04
chest discomfort	5.749594e-03
flu	9.816914e-06
reflux	3.257717e-04
physical discomfort	5.606966e-04
tired	8.064232e-03
Loss of appetite	7.509945e-03
Pneumonia	1.475093e+00
muscle pain	1.015059e-02
breathlessness	6.317765e-04
sputum	3.390498e-02
nasal discharge	3.146658e-02
respiratory distress	4.043139e-04
sneeze	6.416218e-05
thirst	5.849684e-05
aching muscles	3.619702e-04
muscle aches	1.655491e-04
chest pain	6.740857e-03
shortness of breath	2.239252e+00
itchy throat	3.693587e-04
muscle cramps	8.577029e-04
dyspnea	1.696999e-03
abdominal pain	2.438491e-04
cough with sputum	6.713024e-03
recov	3.190991e+01

Figure 16.7 Final feature selection of Random Forest.

If the mean decrease Gini index value is high, the parameter is considered as an important one. Otherwise, the parameter is considered unimportant. Moreover, the positive mean decrease Gini index values are denoted as important parameters. The negative mean decrease Gini index values are marked as unimportant parameters.

In Figure 16.7, the attributes id, location, country, gender, age, symp_ on, hosp_visit, visit_wuhan, from_wuhan, fever, cough, vomiting, heavy head, pneumonia, shortness of breath, and recov are marked as important attributes, because they positive values. Other attributes are denoted as unimportant.

16.9   Proposed Methodology

The aim of the proposed methodology is to select the accurate features of the patient dataset. In this proposed methodology, the mean increase index is used. First, this method used the correction-based feature methodology that assigns a score and scores the attributes using the 'Gini index.' The pseudo code of Improved Random Forest feature selection is shown in Algorithm 6. First, it splits the attribute as a node. Then, it calculates the Gini index of each and every attribute. After that, it determines the mean increase Gini index for every attribute, compares all attributes and finds the Gini index attribute with the highest value, and sets the attribute as important.

In this patient dataset, the computed mean increase Gini index values are denoted as positive. Thus, the Improved Random Forest feature selection method selects only the attributes that contain the highest value and marked as important. It does not contain negative values.

Algorithm 6 Pseudo Code for Improved Random Forest Feature Selection

---

Input: Load patient dataset
Output: Extract best features
1. Extract best Attributes:
2. for m = 1 to k do
3. Load the patient dataset in Pi
4. Generate a root node, Ri contains Pi
5. call ConstructNode (Ri)
6. end for
7. ConstructNode (R)
8. if R consists only one node then
9. return
10. else
11. Randomly fetch V% of the probable separated attributes in R

12. for i = 1 to C do
13. Calculate Gini increase index
14. Gi = 1 + ΣC i = 1(Ri)2
15. Mi = Max(Gi,20)
16. pick the attribute S with the greatest MeanIncreaseGiniIndex and set the selected attribute as important
17. call ConstructNode (Ri)
18. end for
19. end if

Figure 16.8 shows the final attribute selection of the Improved Random Forest algorithm. It only selects the top 20 attributes in the patient health record set.

gender	9.337162e+01
age	5.241632e+0
fever	9.734024e+01
cough	5.094376e+02
throat pain	6.182016e+03
vomiting	5.444868e+01
difficulty breathing	6.016126e+01
chest discomfort	5.749594e+03
flu	9.816914e+06
physical discomfort	5.606966e+04
tired	8.064232e+03
myalgia	6.304291e+01
lossofappetite	7.509945e+03
breathlessness	6.317765e+04
sneeze	6.416218e+05
high fever	5.74655e+09
thirst	5.849684e+05
chest pain	6.740857e+03
muscle cramps	8.577029e+04
coughwithsputum	6.713024e+03

Figure 16.8 Final feature selection of the Improved Random Forest.

16.10   Results and Discussion

Using various feature extraction techniques, we extracted essential features from the COVID-19 patient health record. The following methods were used in this study: Boruta feature selection, Rank features, Recursive feature elimination, machine learning algorithms for variable importance, Random Forest, and Improved Random Forest feature selection.

Figure 16.9 shows the time complexity of various feature selection techniques. The Improved Random Forest algorithm selects the top 20 attributes in 1.12 ms, such as gender, high fever, vomiting, etc. The Random Forest method extracts the most important parameters such as id, location, country, gender, age, symp_on, hosp_visit, visit_wuhan, from_wuhan, fever, cough, vomiting, heavy head, pneumonia, shortness of breath, and recov in 1.5 ms.

Next, the variable importance method fetches the top five parameters in 2.75 ms. The Recursive feature elimination procedure gives the accuracy of each and every attribute. It selects the N (count) number of parameters. The value of N is set by the user. It takes 2.4 ms.

The Rank features by variable importance extracts the best three features. It extracts the attributes using rank-based selection. The starting and ending value of the rank lies between 0.5 and 0.9. The rank values of the selected top three attributes are 0.85, 0.77, and 0.75 in 2 ms.

Finally, the Boruta algorithm fetches the important parameters in 1.78 ms. It almost selects the most important attributes. However, it takes more

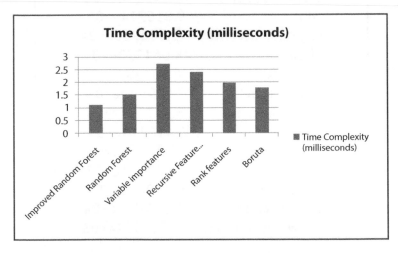

Figure 16.9 Final feature selection of the improved random forest.

time when compared to Random Forest feature selection. This is the second-best method. It extracts only the limited features when compared to Random Forest attribute selection. When compared to other feature selection methods, the Random Forest feature selection process selects the necessary features in less time.

16.11   Conclusion

Machine learning is important for analyzing medical data and designing innovative care plans. In the COVID-19 patient data collection, we introduced a feature selection approach that implements the Random Forest with a time complexity of 1.5 ms. The Random Forest feature selection method selects the most important features such as id, location, country, gender, age, symp_on, hosp_visit, visit_wuhan, from_wuhan, fever, cough, vomiting, heavy head, pneumonia, shortness of breath, and recov. Symptoms such as fever, cough, shortness of breath, and pneumonia have caused death to the COVID-19 patient. Based on the fetched attributes, predict the percentage of death caused by these symptoms. Moreover, identifying the gender-wise and age-wise death prediction depends on these symptoms.

References

1. Huang, C., Wang, Y., Li, X., Ren, L., Zhao, J., Y., Clinical features of patients infected with 2019 novel coronavirus in Wuhan, China. *Lancet*, 395, 20, 497–506, 2020.
2. Li, Q., Guan, X., Wu, P., Wang, X., Zhou, L., Tong, Y., Early transmission dynamics in Wuhan, China, of novel coronavirus–infected pneumonia. *New Engl. J. Med.*, 382, 1, 199–20, 2020.
3. Chen, N., Zhou, M., Dong, X., Qu, J., Gong, F., Han, Y., Epidemiological and clinical characteristics of 99 cases of 2019 novel coronavirus pneumonia in Wuhan, China: A descriptive study. *Lancet*, 395, 20, 7–13, 2020.
4. *Clinical management of severe acute respiratory infection when novel coronavirus (2019-nCoV). Infection is suspected: Interim guidance. IEEE Access*, 8, 130820–130839, 2020, Available online at: https://apps.who.int/iris/handle/10665/330893.
5. Pham, Q.V., Nguyen, D.C., Hwang, W.J., Pathirana, P.N., Artificial intelligence (AI) and big data for coronavirus (COVID-19) pandemic: A survey on the state-of-the-arts, 2020.

6. Wang, D., Hu, B., Hu, C., Zhu, F., Liu, X., Zhang, J., Wang, B., Xiang, H., Cheng, Z., Xiong, Y., Clinical characteristics of 138 hospitalized patients with 2019 novel coronavirus–infected pneumonia in Wuhan, China. *J. Am. Med. Assoc.*, 323, 1061–1069, 2020.

7. Shen, K., Yang, Y., Wang, T., Zhao, D., Jiang, Y., Jin, R., Zheng, Y., Xu, B., Xie, Z., Lin, L., Diagnosis, treatment, and prevention of 2019 novel coronavirus infection in children: Experts' consensus statement. *World J. Pediatr.*, 16, 223–231, 2020.

8. Lauer, S.A., Grantz, K.H., Bi, Q., Jones, F.K., Zheng, Q., Meredith, H.R., Azman, A.S., Reich, N.G., Lessler, J., The incubation period of coronavirus disease 2019 (COVID-19) from publicly reported confirmed cases: Estimation and application. *Ann. Intern. Med.*, 172, 577–582, 2020.

9. Doraisami, and Golzari, S., *A Study on feature selection and classification techniques for automatic genre classification of traditional Malay music, content-based retrieval, categorization and similarity*, pp. 14–18, *9th International Conference on Music Information Retrieval*, Drexel University, USA, 2008.

10. Arauzo-Azofra, A., Aznarte, J.L., Benítez, J.M., Empirical study of feature selection methods based on individual feature evaluation for classification problems. *Expert Syst. Appl.*, 38, 8170–8177, 2011.

11. Guyon, I. and Elisseeff, A., An introduction to variable and feature selection. *J. Mach. Learn. Res.*, 3, 1157–1182, 2003.

12. Ozkan, Y., *Veri madenciliği yöntemleri*, Papatya Publication, İstanbul, 2008.

13. Novakovic, J., The impact of feature selection on the accuracy of naive bayes classifier. *18th Telecommunications forum TELFOR*, 2010.

14. Karabulut, E.M. and Ozel, S.A., A comparative study on the effect of feature selection on classification accuracy. *Proc. Technol.*, 1, 323–327, 2012.

15. Gokulnath, C.B. and Shantharajah, S.P., An optimized feature selection based on genetic approach and support vector machine for heart disease. *Clust. Comput.*, 22, 4, 14777–14787, Springer, 2019.

16. Kavitha, R. and Kannan, E., An efficient framework for heart disease classification using feature extraction and feature selection technique in data mining, in: *2016 International Conference on Emerging Trends in Engineering, Technology and Science (ICETETS)*, 2016.

17. Jabbar, M.A., Deekshatulu, B.L., Chandra, P., Prediction of heart disease using random forest and feature subset selection, in: *Advances Intelligent System Computer Innovations BioInspired Comp App*, pp. 187–196, 2015.

18. Steyerberg, E., *Clinical prediction models: A practical approach to development, validation, and updating*, Springer Science & Business Media, Newyork, 2009.

19. Zou, H. and Hastie, T., Regularization and variable selection via the elastic net. *J. R. Stat. Soc. B*, 67, 2, 301–320, 2005.

20. Sanchez-Pintoa, L.N., Venableb, L.R., Fahrenbachc, J., Churpekd, M.M., Comparison of variable selection methods for clinical predictive modelling. *Int. J. Med. Inf.*, 116, 10–17, 2018.

21. Hastie, T., Tibshirani, R., Friedman, J., The elements of statistical learning: Data mining, inference and prediction. *Math. Intell.*, 27, 2, 83–85, 2005.
22. Kursa, M.B. and Rudnicki, W.R., Feature selection with the boruta package. *J. Stat. Softw.*, 36, 11, 1–3, 2010.
23. Xu, Z., Huang, G., Weinberger, K.Q., Gradient boosted feature selection. *Proceedings of the 20th International Conference on Knowledge Discovery and Data Mining*, pp. 522–531, 2014.
24. *Novel corona virus 2019 dataset*, 2020, Available online at: https://www.kaggle.com/sudalairajkumar/novel-corona-virus-2019-dataset/ (accessed April 23, 2020).

17

Blockchain and Deep Learning: Research Challenges, Open Problems, and Future

Akansha Singh[1]* and Krishna Kant Singh[2]

[1]SCSET, Bennett University, Greater Noida, India
[2]Delhi Technical Campus, Greater Noida, India

Abstract

Blockchain and deep learning are two disruptive technologies that have attracted considerable interest and possess transformative capabilities across diverse domains. This chapter provides a comprehensive examination of the research obstacles, unresolved issues, and forthcoming possibilities that arise at the convergence of these two disciplines. Blockchain, an immutable and decentralized ledger, has caused significant disruptions in conventional data management paradigms by offering trust, transparency, and security across diverse domains, including banking, supply chain, and healthcare. Nevertheless, the integration of blockchain technology with deep learning presents a range of complex issues. The scalability of blockchain networks is a significant barrier in terms of accommodating the processing requirements of deep learning models. It is imperative to develop efficient consensus methods and network protocols in order to guarantee the prompt execution of intricate computations. In addition, the preservation of privacy holds significant importance in deep learning tasks that include large amounts of data. This underscores the need for innovative methods to securely and selectively share data on a blockchain platform. In contrast, deep learning has revolutionized the field of machine learning by demonstrating its capacity to discern complex patterns from extensive datasets. Despite the achievements of deep learning, there exist issues pertaining to interpretability, robustness, and generalization. The integration of blockchain technology has the potential to enhance model transparency and accountability by enabling traceability and auditability of model modifications and choices. Furthermore, the integration of blockchain's data integrity with deep

Corresponding author: akanshasing@gmail.com

Akansha Singh, Anuradha Dhull and Krishna Kant Singh (eds.) Blockchain and Deep Learning for Smart Healthcare, (425–432) © 2024 Scrivener Publishing LLC

learning has the potential to bolster the resilience of models against adversarial assaults and guarantee the reliability of training data. The amalgamation of blockchain and deep learning gives rise to a multitude of unresolved issues. The task of enhancing consensus algorithms to effectively enhance the training and validation processes of deep learning models on distributed blockchains continues to pose a substantial obstacle. One area of ongoing study involves addressing the semantic disparity between on-chain and off-chain data in order to enhance the efficiency of model execution. To effectively tackle these challenges, it is imperative to foster multidisciplinary cooperation among scholars specializing in cryptography, distributed systems, and machine learning. When considering the future prospects of this synergy, it appears to hold great promise.

Keywords: Deep learning, blockchain, healthcare, research challenges

17.1   Introduction

The healthcare business stands to benefit greatly from the advent of two cutting-edge technologies—blockchain and deep learning—both of which are undergoing rapid development. With the use of blockchain technology, sensitive patient information may be safely stored and shared among medical professionals. Due to blockchain's decentralized structure, patient data may be maintained on a distributed network, which both protects the data from breaches and gives patients more say over their own medical records. However, deep learning is a form of AI that enables computers to learn from massive datasets and make inferences or judgments based on those datasets' patterns and relationships [1]. To better diagnose patients and create individualized treatment regimens, deep learning can be applied to medical picture analysis to reveal patterns that may be invisible to the naked eye. Blockchain and deep learning, when combined, can significantly improve healthcare. As an illustration, medical photos might be safely stored and shared on a blockchain-based platform, and then deep learning algorithms could be used to evaluate the images for signs of disease or harm. The combination of blockchain technology and deep learning holds great promise for the future of tailored medicine in healthcare. Doctors may tailor treatments to each patient's unique genetic composition with the help of deep learning algorithms, which analyze massive quantities of patient data to reveal patterns and correlations between genes, proteins, and diseases. Blockchain technology can protect the confidentiality of this information, giving people more say over their medical records [2]. Together, blockchain and deep learning have the potential to revolutionize healthcare by increasing precision in diagnosis, customizing therapy for each individual, and protecting sensitive patient information.

17.2   Research Challenges

While there is a lot of potential for blockchain technology and deep learning to be applied in the medical field, there are also a lot of important obstacles that need to be addressed before we can fully realize their potential. The following are some of the difficulties:

Both the quantity and the quality of the data must be taken into consideration while developing deep learning algorithms. These algorithms can only be effective when given access to vast amounts of high-quality data. Data, on the other hand, are frequently scattered, incomplete, and of variable quality in the healthcare industry [3]. In addition, there are frequent problems with the data's privacy and security, which makes it difficult to access and share data among the various companies and institutions that exist.

- Interoperability: When it comes to healthcare, data are frequently kept in several systems, each of which uses a unique format and protocol. This makes it difficult to combine and analyze data from multiple sources at the same time. Because of this, the efficacy of deep learning algorithms may be reduced, and the development of solutions based on blockchain technology may be hampered.
- Regulation: The healthcare business is highly regulated, and there are numerous rules and norms concerning the privacy and safety of patient information. Blockchain technology and deep learning solutions are required to conform to these standards, which can be difficult to understand and can range significantly between countries and regions.
- Ethical issues: Any time patient data are used in any way, there are some ethical considerations that need to be taken into mind. Patients are required to express their informed consent before their data can be used for research or treatment, and they must be fully informed about how their data will be used.
- Technical challenges: The development and implementation of blockchain and deep learning solutions in healthcare require a significant amount of technical expertise, including skills in data science, cryptography, and software

development. These are just some of the areas that are affected by these challenges.

In general, if we are going to be successful in overcoming these obstacles, we will need to work together with a wide variety of stakeholders. These stakeholders include healthcare providers, regulators, technology businesses, and patients themselves [4]. In the field of medical research, we will not be able to fully grasp the potential of blockchain technology and deep learning until we collaborate.

17.3   Open Problems

Emerging technologies such as blockchain and deep learning have the potential to revolutionize the healthcare business by providing solutions to a number of the most significant problems now confronting the field of healthcare research. The following is a list of some of the unresolved issues and difficulties that arise when combining blockchain technology and deep learning to medical research:

Protecting the confidentiality of patient information while also guaranteeing its safety is one of the most difficult aspects of conducting research in the medical field. Deep learning can be used to analyze patient data without compromising their privacy, while blockchain can provide a secure and transparent means to store and distribute patient data [5]. Together, these two technologies can revolutionize the healthcare industry. Yet, there are still many obstacles to overcome when it comes to developing blockchain systems that are secure and protect users' privacy, as well as ensuring that deep learning models do not disclose critical information.

The quality of the data and their interoperability are issues that frequently arise in the healthcare industry. The data in this industry are frequently heterogeneous and fragmented, making it difficult to combine and evaluate. A decentralized platform for sharing and exchanging data can be provided via blockchain, and deep learning can be used to glean valuable insights from the data that are shared and exchanged. Nonetheless, there are still obstacles to overcome in order to guarantee the quality of the data and standardize the data formats for interoperability.

Deep learning models are prone to bias, which can lead to unfair and discriminating outputs. This can be avoided by ensuring that the models are trained fairly. In the field of healthcare research, bias can have devastating effects on patient results as well as the general population's health. The distributed ledger technology known as blockchain has the potential to deliver a transparent and auditable record of the data and model inputs, which can assist in detecting and minimizing bias. Yet, there are still obstacles to overcome when developing deep learning models that are devoid of bias and when ensuring that blockchain systems are not influenced by prejudice.

Scalability and performance: Healthcare data are frequently huge and complicated, which can be a challenge for both blockchain and deep learning systems. Scalability and performance are two aspects of this challenge. Deep learning models need to be able to process and interpret data in real time, whereas blockchain systems need to be able to manage massive volumes of data and transactions. In the field of medical research, there are still obstacles to overcome when it comes to the development of scalable and high-performance blockchain and deep learning systems.

The use of blockchain technology and deep learning in medical research poses a variety of regulatory and ethical concerns. Some of these concerns include patient permission, data ownership, and the potential for legal liability. Designing regulatory frameworks that may address these difficulties while supporting innovation and collaboration in healthcare research is still difficult.

In general, the application of blockchain technology and deep learning in medical research is an interesting and quickly developing topic; yet, there are still a great deal of unsolved problems and challenges that need to be dealt with.

17.4   Future Possibilities

The combination of blockchain technology and deep learning has significant promise to revolutionize the healthcare sector in a number of different ways. The following are some potential applications that this technology could find in the future:

Blockchain technology enables healthcare practitioners, patients, and researchers to safely store and exchange medical data with one another while also facilitating the secure sharing of those data. These data can be examined using deep learning algorithms, which can then be utilized to enhance the results of healthcare.

Drug Development: Blockchain can be used to create a secure and transparent platform for drug development. On this platform, data from clinical trials can be stored and analyzed using deep learning algorithms to find potential drug candidates more quickly. Blockchain can be used to speed up the process of drug development.

Precision Medicine: Blockchain technology has the potential to be utilized in the development of a safe and open network for the practice of precision medicine. On this network, patient data might be evaluated by deep learning algorithms in order to devise individualized treatment strategies.

Blockchain technology can be utilized to build a platform that is both safe and open to the public, which can then be used to track medical supplies all the way from the manufacturer to the end user. This can help limit the amount of fake pharmaceuticals that are sold and guarantee that patients receive treatments that are both safe and effective.

Telemedicine: Blockchain and deep learning can be used to create secure telemedicine platforms that enable patients to receive healthcare services remotely, while at the same time ensuring the privacy and security of their data. These platforms can be used to create secure telemedicine platforms that enable patients to receive healthcare services remotely.

Ultimately, the integration of blockchain technology and deep learning has the potential to bring about a revolution in the healthcare business by elevating the standard of care provided, lowering associated costs, and broadening patients' access to medical treatment.

17.5   Conclusion

In conclusion, the combination of blockchain technology and deep learning holds significant potential to revolutionize the healthcare industry. This combination has the potential to improve data security, enhance the capabilities of data analysis, enable personalized treatment plans, and improve the medical supply chain. Blockchain technology enables the safe storage and transmission of medical records, which, in turn, reduces the likelihood of data breaches and other forms of online attack. Deep learning algorithms, on the other hand, can examine enormous volumes of medical data, recognize patterns within those data, and develop insights, which leads to more accurate diagnoses and improved treatment outcomes. When combined, the technologies of blockchain and deep learning hold a great deal of potential to revolutionize the future of healthcare.

References

1. Babu, E.S., Dadi, A.K., Singh, K.K., Nayak, S.R., Bhoi, A.K., Singh, A., A distributed identity-based authentication scheme for Internet of Things devices using permissioned blockchain system. *Expert Syst.*, *39*, 10, e12941, 2022.
2. Rakhra, A., Gupta, R., Singh, A., Blockchain and Internet of Things across industries, in: *Machine Learning Approaches for Convergence of IoT and Blockchain*, pp. 1–34, 2021.
3. Singh, K.K., Singh, A., Sharma, S.K. (Eds.), *Machine Learning Approaches for Convergence of IoT and Blockchain*, John Wiley & Sons, 2021.
4. Singh, K.K., Elhoseny, M., Singh, A., Elngar, A.A. (Eds.), *Machine Learning and the Internet of Medical Things in Healthcare*, Academic Press, 2021.
5. Singh, P., Singh, N., Singh, K.K., Singh, A., Diagnosing of disease using machine learning, in: *Machine Learning and the Internet of Medical Things in Healthcare*, pp. 89–111, Academic Press, 2021.

Index

Printed and bound by CPI Group (UK) Ltd, Croydon, CR0 4YY

27/10/2024

14580174-0004